THE MOST FAMOUS CLUB IN THE WORLD

The story of the Cavern Club

Spencer Leigh

The story of the Cavern Club

Spencer Leigh

First edition published in 2008 by SAF Publishing Ltd

SAF Publishing Ltd
149 Wakeman Road,
London. NW10 5BH
ENGLAND

www.safpublishing.co.uk
www.cavernclub.org
www.bobyoungticker.de
www.spencerleigh.demon.co.uk

ISBN 978-0-946719-90-7

Project co-ordination: Bob Young for Cavern City Tours.

Cover design: Co-ordinated by Bob Young and SAF, based on the original *Cavern: The Most Famous Club In The World* CD sleeve design by Design4music.com.

Photographic research: John Firminger.

Contents

FOREWORD
by Sir Paul McCartney

The Cavern—do I have memories of the Cavern? Do I? Oh yeah. My first memories were of us trying to get booked there, but in the early days the Cavern only booked jazz and blues artists and frowned upon upstart rock'n'rollers like ourselves. We fibbed about our repertoire and managed to get a date there, where we proceeded to announce songs like "Long Tall Sally" as being written by Blind Lemon Jefferson and "Blue Suede Shoes", the famous creation of the legendary blues artist Leadbelly! When the owners of the Cavern realised what we were doing, they sent up little notes to the stage complaining but by then it was too late and we had managed to infiltrate.

We were so persistent that we eventually managed to get some follow-up dates and soon became regulars at the sweaty little cellar below Mathew Street; and sweaty it was—sometimes the condensation on the ceiling from the people crowded in there would drip onto our equipment, causing the amps to fuse and the power to go off. We then improvised, singing *a cappella*, anything we could think of that the audience would be able to join in with. We came to know regulars like Bob Wooler, the great DJ, Paddy Delaney, the legendary bouncer and Ray McFall, the enthusiastic owner.

My second worst memory was arriving at the Cavern for one of the famous lunchtime sessions and realising I had forgotten my Hofner bass and as I was left-handed (and still am!) nobody could lend me one, so I quickly drove half an hour to my house, picked up the bass but arrived back in time for the end of the Beatles' set, having been replaced by a bass player from one of the other groups (I seem to remember it was Johnny Gustafson of the Big Three). Was I gutted? Oh yeah.

It was the breeding ground for what would become the Beatles' early repertoire, and I will always think of the place with great affection for the days spent with my pals in its sweaty, damp atmosphere with the audience chewing on cheese rolls, swigging Coca-Cola and sending up little bits of paper to the stage with requests for songs such as "Shop Around" and "Searchin'" to be played for crowd members calling themselves things like The Cement Mixers and so on.

I could go on but I won't. They were happy days, so many congratulations, Cavern, on this anniversary.

FROM ME TO YOU

Introduction

Many clubs have played a significant part in shaping popular music—Birdland and CBGB's in New York; Whisky-A-Go-Go in Los Angeles; Ronnie Scott's, the Marquee, the 100 Club in London; the Armadillo in Austin, Texas; Tipitina's in New Orleans; Tootsie's in Nashville—but none of them are as well known or as influential as the Cavern. The Cavern is the most famous club in the world and a letter simply addressed to 'The Cavern, Liverpool' will reach its destination.

The Beatles and the Merseybeat explosion would have happened without the Cavern but it would not have been the same. The Cavern was the home base for the Liverpool beat musicians and when the key players moved away, the club fell on hard times, although that was not the sole reason for its demise. In 1966, it was reopened by a Prime Minister and then demolished and now it has been lovingly reconstructed and is treated as if it were the original. And why not? We'll never have anything better. The original Cavern lasted from 1957 to 1973, but the new club has been there since 1984, already lasting seven years longer than the original.

Although its capacity is only 360, famous acts play at the Cavern, notably Paul McCartney

in 1999, and its current owners encourage new music. As they see it, the club has "a foot in the past, a hand in the future". There will always be music in Liverpool but who can say whether lightning can strike the city twice and produce another Beatles? If it does, the band will almost certainly have played the Cavern.

The Cavern: The Most Famous Club In The World may be filed alongside the Beatle books, but it is not the story of the Beatles. It is not the story of Merseybeat, which only lasted a couple of years. They are crucial components in the story, but this is the story of the Cavern with its ups and downs, its unlikely owners, its disc-jockeys, its performers, its patrons and its sanitation. I am telling the story almost as though the Cavern were a person and on the whole, I am not describing what happens outside its doors.

That the Cavern was both so small and so famous works to my advantage. A star might appear at the Liverpool Empire, do his show to rapturous applause and be rushed to the safety of his hotel room, having met few of his public. This didn't happen at the Cavern. The club attracted big-name guests and whether they liked it or not, they had to mix with the patrons because the club was so small, had a tiny band-room and for several years, only had one entrance. Hence, there are hundreds of encounters between the musicians and their public, and I hope I've found the best ones for this book.

The tale is told chronologically from its opening in January 1957 to the present day. All the numbered quotes come from my own interviews with musicians, fans and Cavern staff. I have matched the anecdotes and opinions with the dates, but sometimes this has to be on a 'best guess' basis. There are notes on the contributors at the back of the book.

When the contributors refer to contemporary payments, I have not added today's monetary equivalent. Suffice it to say, that there were 12 pence in a shilling and 20 shillings to the pound. A shilling was also known as a bob, so five bob is 25p, although five bob in 1963 would be worth about £3 today.

Both the Merseysippi Jazz Band and the beat group, the Merseybeats were known to their followers as 'the Merseys'. To avoid confusion, I have referred to the jazz band as 'the Merseysippis' throughout the text. Nowadays, Merseybeat generally is written as one word, but Bill Harry's newspaper was *Mersey Beat*.

The Swinging Blue Jeans began life as the Blue Genes Skiffle Group, then the Swinging Blue Genes and after that, the Swinging Blue Jeans. The changes are somewhat gradual but I have called them the Swinging Blue Jeans once they came back from Hamburg in October 1962 with a different sound and repertoire.

Bob Wooler often referred to Brian Epstein as "B.E." as in his notable phrase, "If B.E. had not been feeling that way, that day, it never would have happened, OK?" I write that now and I can imagine Bob, who died in 2002, stabbing me in the chest with his finger as he said it. What a fantastic guy he was: I do miss him.

However tempting it may seem, I have kept to the subject matter, that is, what happened at the Cavern. I am not telling the story of the Beatles in the wider world or, indeed, in other Merseyside clubs. This is a claustrophobic story about a particular club on its key nights. I believe that by concentrating my efforts on the Cavern, many things have come to light and I hope that there is as much to surprise and delight you as surprised and delighted me.

Spencer Leigh
February 2008

Acknowledgments

My thanks to everybody who has spoken to me for this book, and, indeed, earlier, related projects. I have tried not to plagiarise myself too much and although I have drawn on previous books, notably *Let's Go Down The Cavern* (1984), a biography of Bob Wooler, *The Best Of Fellas* (2002) and *Twist And Shout!* (2004), most of the text is new. The interviews that I have been conducting on and off since 2005 were both for this book and for a BBC Radio Merseyside series, called *Soup & Sweat & Rock & Roll*, an eight-hour series broadcast in 2007.

Phil Thompson's book, *The Best Of Cellars* (Bluecoat Press, 1994 and Tempus Publishing, 2007), has been an invaluable source, particularly as it provides day-to-day listings for the Cavern from 1957 to 1973. However, as Thompson admits, the list was comprised solely from what was advertised in the *Liverpool Echo*. This was important research but the *Echo* often omitted lunchtime sessions and some of the stated attractions were overtaken by events. At first, I anticipated publishing a complete list from 1957 to the present, but in the end, I decided that it would take up too much space and would get in the way of the story. Also, lists can be lifeless

reading, especially the heavy rock nights of the early 70s where a small group of bands appeared over and over. In the end, I have been selective in the events I have listed, although all the significant dates are there. The dates sometimes differ from Phil Thompson's book because I have also used *Mersey Beat* newspapers and other sources, sometimes a musician's diaries. I have also seen Ray McFall's diaries from 1959 to 1963. These tell you who was playing the Cavern on particular days and sometimes include the fees. It is possible that the opening night under his tenure was 2 October 1959 as that is in his diary, but he insists it was with Acker Bilk a day later.

I have believed everyone who has told me that they were there on particular nights unless I have been able to prove otherwise.

Another valuable source has been Mark Lewisohn's *The Beatles Live!* (Pavilion Books, 1986) as well as his later publications. His groundbreaking work contains brilliantly researched background on the Beatles' gigs at the Cavern, although even now in 2007, Mark admits that the listing may still not be definitive. Mark is working on the first volume of an extremely comprehensive Beatles' biography and at times, it has felt like we have established a detective agency as we sought to find some significant person or establish particular facts. There is no better way to start the day than with an email from Mark as it will always contain some witty remark.

John Firminger, who plays with Dave Berry's band, has been sifting through press cuttings to create montages between the chapters. My thanks to him, and thanks too to the various copyright owners for the cuttings from the *New Musical Express, Melody Maker, Disc, Liverpool Daily Post* and *Liverpool Echo.* I am glad to have consulted various files on the Cavern at the Liverpool Daily Post and Echo offices, Liverpool Records Office and the Cavern itself, while past issues of *Mersey Beat* are always a source of joy. Especial thanks to Bill Harry and to John Gray of the Rock and Pop Shop for permission to use some of the text and ads in *Mersey Beat.* Their website has some very tasteful memorabilia on offer, and I hope they get round to a CDR containing every issue of *Mersey Beat.* Music fans would be so grateful. Thanks also to Paul Wane at Tracks for the use of some of their 60s memorabilia. If we have omitted any copyright details, please contact the publisher and we will correct this in future editions.

My thanks to everybody at the Cavern, especially Bill Heckle, Dave Jones, George Guinness, Julia Baird and Ray Johnson, and the club's consultant for special projects, Bob Young, a man who is so perpetually up that you can't imagine him writing "Down Down". SAF Publishing are to be thanked for their faith in the project. Thanks also to Billy Butler, David Charters, Frankie Connor, James Cullinan, Geoffrey Davis, Colin Disley, Peter Grant, Jonathan Hallewell, Bill Harry, Anne Leigh, Lauren McShane, Mick Ord, Ray O'Brien (the author of *There Are Places I'll Remember*, a guide to the Beatles' early venues) and Mick O'Toole.

It is good to be able to quote from Johnny Guitar's diaries: what a shame that he never completed (maybe, never even started) his memoirs before he died. I have also seen the diaries of Ron McKay and Ritchie Galvin, which provide useful, first hand information. For five years, I have been hoping that some public body would purchase Bob Wooler's archives, which are being held privately, and that I would get to see them. It hasn't happened yet and I hope that this collection will not be broken up as I am sure it contains an astonishing array of memorabilia, press cuttings, and Bob's own written opinions. Over the years, the Cavern DJ and arch-hoarder let very few people into his various homes, and this is because he was always jotting down notes and didn't want others to see them.

Spencer Leigh

1

ANOTHER POOL OF LIFE

"There I was, digging this hole, hole in the ground."
(Bernard Cribbins' hit single produced by George Martin, 1962)

Yes, it's true: the Beatles walked on water. They also sang and played on water. When the Cavern's site was excavated in 1982, the builders stumbled upon an old shaft that led into a huge hole, a cavern underneath the Cavern, as it were. It was filled with water and bravely, the architect and the site agent investigated it in a rubber dinghy. The lake was 120 feet long and 70 feet wide and, in parts, eight foot deep. There was no other exit and because of the scrapings in the sandstone wall, they could tell it was man-made. But why was it constructed? What would anyone want with a giant underground cellar? One theory is that it was a slave hole where the unfortunates were kept before being transported, but that seems very unlikely. Liverpool was part of the triangular slave trade but there is no evidence than any of the slaves came to Liverpool. Still, whatever the reason, the site was flooded.

This is one of the mysteries of Mathew Street, but we can demolish another myth immediately. In the 1950s some national newspapers reported that an 18th century ghost known as 'Short John' had been spotted in the ladies' toilets at the Cavern. "It nearly frightened me out my nylons," said Jean McCall, "He was just like a Teddy boy,

except he wore strange clothes." When I interviewed the Cavern's founding owner, Alan Sytner, he told me that the whole story had been created for publicity—and it worked.

Despite valiant efforts by myself and others, the site retains some secrets. Why is it called Mathew Street? The unusual spelling suggests that it was named after a specific individual and that is correct. Before it was Mathew Street, it was Mathew Pluckington Street. Mr Pluckington was a merchant, and presumably a successful one if he had a street named after him, but I know nothing else about him.

Mathew Street is in the centre of Liverpool: it is a quarter of a mile long and it runs from North John Street at one end to Stanley Street and hence, Whitechapel at the other. The narrow street developed into two rows of seven-storey warehouses, being serviced by the cargoes of the ships arriving in the port. *Gore's Directory Of Liverpool* for 1857 paints a vivid picture of Liverpool life. The premises belong to fruit merchants and dealers in tea, rice and wool as well as cabinet makers. To add variety, there is a grate manufacturer and a smoke-jack cleaner and to dispense authority, a

Phoenix

Left; The excavated site of the original Cavern in 1982

Above; Going down! Builders examine the
huge hole discovered under the Cavern

Right; Exploring
the hitherto
unknown lake
underneath
The Cavern

Guitars in stock, Rushworth's music shop

Ron McKay's 1957 Skiffle set-list

STRICTLY JAZZ
RON FIGURES MERSEYSIDE'S THE RIGHT STOP...

● Bootie's wandering minstrel, 27 - year - old RON McKAY, tells me he is thinking of settling on Merseyside. He finds the local jazz scene particularly attractive after two years of freelancing in Continental clubs.

As a red-hot vocalist and a drummer, Ron will be in plenty of demand. He was heard on the river-boat shuffle and has appeared at a number of clubs in the area during the past week. Everywhere he has been welcomed like Long Lost John.

Ron has sung for his supper in recent years in—take a deep breath—England, France, Italy, Switzerland, Germany, Denmark, Norway and Sweden.

"I always sang in English," he said. "It makes no difference. They understand what it's all about."

Did he make much money on his tour?

"Sometimes I made a lot of money. But then there were times when it was difficult to get work permits and things could be difficult."

Ron has no definite ambitions. "I just want to play and sing music which makes people happy or gives them room to think. Jazz has been going on for years now. I am hoping

there will always be people willing to listen to and enjoy it."

He started in the jazz world in 1949 with a ragtime band known as the "Seven Standing Passengers." Others in the combo included Pete Danielis, Merseysippi's trumpetman, and Lonnie Donegan.

Ron stayed in London with Lonnie for some

By Derek Dodd

time. They used to play and sing together in the evenings.

He has played with Cy Laurie, Peanuts Holland, Billy Banks, Albert Nicholas and many other jazz celebrities and has helped to make a score of platters.

Ron found some good jazz clubs on the Continent, although there was rather a lackadaisical attitude about most of them. At Nice, for example, the bandsman sitting next to him fell asleep. He was the trumpeter.

When he returned to England about three weeks ago, Ron had a look round London. Then he came up to Merseyside and found jazz booming.

He will probably be a star personality at the new club to be opened in Liverpool shortly but is also expected to make countrywide appearances.

● SKIFFLE RIDDLE

WHEN is a skiffle group not a

it is run by RALPH WATMOUGH.

Ralph, who has some non-conventional views on jazz, has been experimenting recently with skiffle-type music. "We don't want to restrict ourselves with the skiffle label," says Ralph. "It will be more of a group within a group.

"We hope to play little-known tunes from original sources which have not so far been featured by many of our current favourites.

When the group played at the West Coast Jazz Club the other day they introduced "Let the Lighthouse Shine on Me." Ron McKay fronted.

BOB ALLEN, the group's guitarist, will have more feature spots in future. Bob, who did not stop playing even when he was fighting with the 8th Army, is regarded as one of the best guitarists in traditional groups.

Ralph will play guitar during inner group airings and they will use bass and drums. DAVE BLACKLEDGE, the group's Cambridge-educated clarinettist, is at present holidaying in Tangier. During his absence PETE BURKHILL, who runs the University jazz band during terms, has been deputising.

Pete has also stepped in when the Merseysippi have been short of a liquorice-stick.

impressed by the standards of behaviour on the riverboat shuffle on board the Royal Iris.

This vessel has come in for a lot of unfavourable publicity recently. Jazz fans, however, showed that they know how to behave themselves.

The cruise gave a great opportunity for followers of local bands to compare styles. Each aggregation has its own distinctive style.

For the record, the bands we heard were MERSEYSIPPI, RALPH WATMOUGH, PANAMA, MUSKRATS and GIN MILL SKIFFLE GROUP.

● DIGNIFIED

I HEAR that ...

RON McKAY

Ron McKay seen sat at left with the Cy Laurie Band 1952. With Dave Woods, John Picard, Al Fairweather, Johnny Potter, Cy Laurie and Dick Hughes (at piano)

customs officer, but strangely there is no listing for 10, Mathew Street, the site of the Cavern.

Gore's Directory for 1853 suggests that it was a private dwelling, so the most likely explanation is that, around 1857, the house was demolished and the warehouses built. Maybe the lake was cut after the house was taken down but before the warehouses were built.

The commodities changed, but from around the turn of the century to the 1950s, the building was owned by the provision merchants, the Bamford Brothers. It wouldn't have been the easiest place to work as the narrowness of the street made it difficult for trucks to deposit or collect their

goods. Still, once you had done your work, you could always pop in the Grapes, which is listed in *Kelly's Directory* for 1907 and so has been serving customers for at least 100 years.

In the Second World War, the basement of 10 Mathew Street was used as an air-raid shelter. After that, it was used for storing wines and spirits and then for eggs and Irish bacon. The basement was 58 feet by 39 feet (roughly 2,300 square feet) and was 11 feet below street level.

In 1956, the warehouse was being used to store electrical goods, but the basement was vacant. And underneath that, and unbeknown to everyone, was that lake.

2

CAVERN IN THE TOWN

Cavern owner:
Alan Sytner
1957-1959

The great thing about writing the story of the Cavern is that I know the book will be full of colourful characters, and they start with the larger than life Joe Sytner, who had been a councillor, a ship's doctor and a Liverpool GP. A fellow doctor, **Sid Hoddes**[1], knew him well: "Joe Sytner was a very pleasant bod and the senior partner of a very successful practice, Sytner, Livingstone and O'Brien, in Boundary Street. I was in general practice in the place next door and we used to meet in the local chemist. When your income got to a certain level, you paid surtax and the chemist was moaning one day, 'If I earn any more, I will have to pay surtax.' Joe said, 'If I had to give you any blessing, may you be in surtax soon and may you stay in surtax as it would be really nice for you to be earning that much money.' Other people saw the disadvantages but Joe always saw the positive side."

The hillbilly docker, **Hank Walters**[2], told me: "Joe Sytner was a superb GP who knew the name of everyone in his surgery. He circumcised me when I was 12 and he said, 'You're going to have to change your religion.' I said, 'No, no, I'm from Netherfield Road.'" That anecdote comes under the heading of too much information, but it tells

you something about Dr Sytner, religious divides in the city, and Liverpool wit.

Sid Hoddes[3] again, and try reading this in a Jackie Mason voice: "The Sytners were a Jewish family and one of the things in Jewish cooking is gefilte fish. People brag about how their mothers make better gefilte fish than their wives. Joe told his wife that she couldn't make gefilte fish like his mother. She was fed up with it. She asked Joe's mother to make gefilte fish to satisfy Joe for once. Joe said, 'And you know what? Not only can my wife not make gefilte fish like my mother but my mother can't either.'"

Joe Sytner had been the house surgeon at Wigan Infirmary and the David Lewis Northern Hospital in Liverpool. During the war, he had been a doctor to the Norwegian Government, and then he set up his own docklands practice. He and his family lived at 105 Menlove Avenue, Woolton. John Lennon and his Aunt Mimi lived at 251, and I say this to get in a gratuitous Beatles reference as early as I can. Surprisingly though, the first genuine reference is going to come earlier than you might expect.

Sid Hoddes[4]: "Joe Sytner wasn't just in general practice as he took an enormous interest in other things. He was medical officer to the local boys' club and boxing club—boxing was a fine sport in those days—and Joe gave his services free of charge. The clubs were in the Scotland Road area and the boys' clubs were wonderful. The kids were in the clubs and not creating havoc on the street."

Joe Sytner would often talk about "my boy", his son Alan, and wondering what he would be up to next. **Tony Davis**[5]: "Dr Sytner was a wonderful man. My wife worked at the British American Tobacco Company which is where we met. She knew all the girls on the factory floor and they all used to go to him, especially if they were 'in trouble' as it used to be called, and he would look after them. He was very greatly loved by the working people of the area. I am sure that Joe would have liked Alan to have been something professional but Alan had his own ideas. Doc just said, 'Well, if he is going to make his own way, he is going to make his own way', so he was a good chap."

Joe's elder son, Alan, was a bright lad. He was training to be a stock broker, but Joe's generosity worked against him. Joe had taken out an insurance policy for Alan when he was a baby and it matured when he was 21, giving him £400. In 1956 Alan, a jazz aficionado, started the 21 club at 21 Croxteth Road, close to the city centre. It was supported by a Crosby based jazz band, led by Ralph Watmough.

Tony Davis[6], founder of the Muskrat Jazz Band: "We played at the 21 Club which was Alan Sytner's way of getting the money together for the Cavern. I remember going in there one night and there was a great rhythm and blues record playing and it was Elvis Presley. I didn't know who it was, but it was a smashing record. The pianist Ron Rubin turned up wearing dark glasses and he said, 'There's nothing wrong with my eyes, I am just posing.'"

Alan Sytner[7] recalled, "I was doing okay with the 21 but I realised that if I had a better place, a more interesting place, I could open two, three or four nights a week, perhaps for different sorts of jazz including modern jazz. If I rented a property, it would work out far more economically and I would have my own say as to when I opened and what I did. I went looking for somewhere that

could be turned into a jazz club. I looked at lots of sites but nothing was of great interest."

On Friday 16 May 1947, close to Notre Dame on 5 Rue de la Huchette, a jazz club opened in Paris. It was called Le Caveau de la Huchette and it was effectively a basement club with a cave for dancing. The building was centuries old and was something of a secret place in the eighteenth century because of its underground passages. Trials were conducted on the spot and often evidence was concealed in its deep well. In 1947, after the Second World War, *la liberté* came to the area and the jazz club was opened. Many famous noted musicians have played there including Sidney Bechet, Lionel Hampton, Memphis Slim, Art Blakey and Sacha Distel. It can be seen in the films, *The Cheats* (aka *Youthful Sinners, Les Tricheurs*) (1958), *The First Time* (*Le Première Fois*) (1976) and *Rouge Baiser* (1985). On 16 May 2007, it celebrated its sixtieth birthday.

Alan Sytner[8] was impressed: "I had spent most of my school holidays in France, and most of that time in Paris, so that I could go to jazz clubs and see the bohemian life. I was only a kid, 14, when I first went, but I was dazzled by it and it was all part of the glamour of Paris after the war."

An estate agent, Glyn Evans, knew of an old, abandoned cellar with arches in Mathew Street. It was opposite one of Alan Sytner's drinking haunts, The Grapes. Sytner climbed down a rickety ladder and shone his flashlight. Glyn Evans was offering him a replica of a club he loved, Le Caveau, hence the name 'The Cavern'. Sytner thought it the perfect location as Mathew Street resembled one of those little narrow streets in the Latin Quarter. He would bring the Left Bank to Liverpool.

Sytner fought with the planning authorities over the conversion of the premises to a jazz club but it certainly helped that everybody knew, or knew of, his father. Once permission was granted, the first task was to clear the site. Sytner recruited many volunteers, including a young architect, **Keith Hemmings**[9]. "I was a very good friend of Alan's and we used to go on holiday together. He had this great idea of having a jazz club in Liverpool and I was going to be his partner. I drew up the plans and with a few friends including my future wife Angela, we knocked the walls down, worked on the toilets and built the stage."

Alan Sytner[10]: "The place had been reinforced to make an air-raid shelter and the brick reinforcements had to be removed with sledgehammers as we couldn't get in a pneumatic drill. We did it by hand and we were left with a lot of rubble. That was the ideal foundation for the stage, which was made of wood and just went over the bricks. It did a great job of balancing the acoustics, and the acoustics in the Cavern were terrific, absolutely brilliant."

However, Alan Sytner soon realised that some professional help was needed and amongst the artisans he employed were two carpenters, Harry Harris and his son, Ian. Harry Harris was Paul McCartney's uncle so two of McCartney's relations helped to build the Cavern stage—extraordinary! **Ian Harris**[11]: "My father had bought the company, Campbell and Turner, from old Mr Campbell, and I worked for him as a joiner. Alan Sytner asked him to do some work on the Cavern and we did a number of things. The staircase was in a straight line going down and we altered that so that there was a turn of 90 degrees before you got to the bottom and we had to install some regulation fire doors. There was already a Gents toilet in there and we had to create one for the Ladies, but this was not a big job as we simply extended the drainpipe from the Gents. We also put a perfume machine in the Ladies. You put in some money and it would squirt perfume at you. The stage itself was a low brick wall with timber over the top of it. This was old roofing timber and they were big, heavy pieces. They contained a lot of large iron nails that we couldn't get out. Then there was some light timbering, tongue-and-groove, that we put over the top of it."

On 12 August 1956, the White Eagle Jazz Band came from Leeds to Liverpool for £3 a man. Their leader and trumpet player, **John Cook**[12], has it recorded in his diary: "Paddy McKiernan, who ran the Manchester Jazz Club, got us gigs in Liverpool, first in the Temple Restaurant and then at the Cavern. We were playing in place of the Merseysippi Jazz Band one night at the Temple and Alan Sytner told me that he had secured a place that would make a wonderful jazz club and would I go and see it after we'd finished. I said

okay as it was only round the corner. We took our instruments with us and we walked round to Mathew Street. It was a dirty cellar down a long flight of stone steps with one light at the bottom. It was full of bricks and rubbish. Mike Paley and I were walking round it and I stuck the mouthpiece in my trumpet and blew the first few notes in the Cavern. We all agreed that it looked like a cavern and the name stuck."

So, the White Eagles blew the first notes in the Cavern and also named the place. Or did they? During 2006, *Just Jazz* magazine published claims and counterclaims as the bands slugged it out. **Gordon Vickers**[13] managed the Wall City Jazz Band, naturally from Chester: "I used to go and hear the Merseysippis at the Temple. Alan Sytner told me that he was going to open a jazz club. He had a torch so we went to have a look at it. There were three arches and there was a place like this in Chester called the Crypt. Alan couldn't call this the Crypt so we decided on the Cavern. He recruited his mates to wash and colour the bricks and concrete the floor, but they didn't anticipate the humidity of 600 people in the place. On the first night everybody had dandruff and grey flannels because the colour wash came off."

Most surprisingly, considering he was a dyed-in-the-wool jazz fan, **Alan Sytner**[14] considered starting with rock'n'roll. "I didn't like rock'n'roll but the initial plan was to launch Bill Haley and his Comets' UK tour at the Cavern. They were coming over on a liner and the *Daily Mirror* thought it would be a good idea if their first appearance was at the Cavern. It was a mad scheme that never happened. There would have been no point in putting on rock'n'roll at the Cavern. There were no local rock'n'roll bands to speak of and hardly any in London. Tony Crombie, who was a good jazz drummer, formed a rock'n'roll group in order to make some money, but I saw them at the Pavilion in Lodge Lane and they were awful."

The Merseysippi Jazz Band had been formed in 1949 and frequently appeared on national radio. They had taken part in *Traditional Jazz Scene*, 1955, a live Decca LP from the Royal Festival Hall and they recorded regularly for the Esquire label. They were semi-pro as none of them wanted to give up their day jobs and, although they travelled around, they maintained a city centre residency at the West Coast Jazz Club in the Temple bar and restaurant, about 300 yards from the Cavern in Dale Street. Cornet player **John Lawrence**[15]: "The licensee, realising that he was on to a very good thing, decided to charge us a lot of money for the room. We were rather annoyed and moved to the Cavern. The Cavern was opened by Alan Sytner, who had found this dirty old cellar in Mathew Street. I was going to say he decorated it, but that would be an overstatement. It was rough and scruffy but it had atmosphere."

Their bass player, Dick Goodwin, was a stickler for formality and he drew up an agreement transferring the ownership of their club (West Coast Jazz) to Alan Sytner with a separate agreement for the band's services. He was protecting their interests and it is a world away from the casual beat club bookings that were to follow.

On 18 August 1956, the *Evening Express* carried a story in its *Strictly Jazz* column about the Cavern, although it did not have a name as yet. Under the heading "You Shift Umpteen Tons…", a reference to 'Tennessee' Ernie Ford's hit, "Sixteen Tons", Derek Dodd described how Sytner had recruited musicians as unpaid navvies. They would chant the chain gang song, "Take This Hammer" as they toiled. They were rewarded with beer at the end of the session, but Sytner soon found that he needed professional help as well. The *Strictly Jazz* column also referred to the drummer Ron McKay returning from a continental tour to London, and this was not lost on Alan Sytner.

27-year-old Ron McKay had been making his way in the jazz world as a good-looking, effervescent vocalist and drummer. He was described as "the boy who explodes when he sings" and having spent some time with Cy Laurie's Jazz Band and other noted musicians, he returned home to Bootle in August 1956 and formed a skiffle group. **Ron McKay**[16]: "I had been playing in Scandinavia with Albert Nicholas and Peanuts Holland. I was sitting in a musicians' restaurant, the Star, in Old Compton Street and this chap came up to me. He asked me if I was from Liverpool and he knew that I played the drums, and he wanted to know if I would like to open a jazz club for him in Liverpool. I was out of work, so I said, 'Okay, that sounds good.' I had my drums downstairs and he just said, 'Put them in the car and let's go.' We left for Liverpool, and we pulled up in Mathew Street. It didn't look like very much. His name was Alan Sytner and he said, 'It isn't fixed yet but you can form a band and we'll be opening soon.' Alan and I had a lot of Chinese meals together and we would repair to the Slaughterhouse, which had hooks in the ceiling and gigantic barrels of bass which didn't do you any favours the next day, that's for sure."

Prior to its opening, the Cavern was mentioned in the music press in the *Melody Maker* on 8 September 1956. Although there were half a dozen flourishing jazz clubs on Merseyside, this would be the first to have its own premises.

At this juncture, a rock'n'roll club would never have been feasible as there was very little of it on Merseyside. The first ad for this new music in the *Liverpool Echo* was for the Bobby Whittle Rock Group at Wavertree Town Hall on 30 June 1956, and this was followed by Bobby Brown's Coloured Band at the same venue on 15 September 1956.

The doorway was lit by a single bulb. Eighteen stone steps led down to the cellar which was divided by archways into three long, dimly-lit barrel vaults, each a hundred foot long and ten foot wide. The arched ceiling gave a catacomb effect. The walls were painted plainly with emulsion and there were no curtains or decorations. The entrance to the first vault was used to collect admission money and there was also a cloakroom. The central and largest area contained the stage and a few rows of wooden chairs, which had been discarded by a church and Sytner paid £5 for the lot, hymn-book holders and all. The performers would have to bend to go through the arch into the dressing-room. All the lighting (no coloured filters or bulbs) was concentrated on the stage. There was only dancing—the Cavern stomp—when there was room to move. Given the circumstances, it was an excellent arrangement, but the lavatories were appalling, the band room tiny, and the air rancid. Most people smoked and within minutes of opening, the Cavern could contain hundreds of sweaty bodies. Condensation would cover the walls and drip off the ceilings. There was no ventilation. So much for the Clean Air Act of 1956.

Tony Davis[17]: "The great thing about it was that we discovered speckled paint. There was a colloidal solution of paint with bits of colour in it. It is quite common today but it was unbelievable as up to then, you had to put the wash down first and put the dibs on afterwards. The lavatories in the Cavern had this spotted paint and that was the most exciting thing about it. When you went into the Gents at the Cavern you could see people walking overhead through the thick glass roof."

In a move that would have far-reaching effects, **Alan Sytner**[18] decided against a liquor licence: "I wasn't anti-booze but my heart wasn't in it and I didn't think that I could meet the requirements for a licence. I was going to get a lot of young people in the place and so it wasn't a good idea to have booze there. They could always get a pass-out and go to the White Star or the Grapes, where incidentally they might find me."

Although many commentators remark on the Cavern having no liquor licence, that was hardly significant as it applied to many other venues at the time: consider the 2 I's in London or the Jacaranda in Liverpool. Serving alcohol wasn't an essential requirement for a music club back then, although it would be now.

John Parkes[19] recalls his audition for the Merseysippis in January 1957: "Dick Goodwin was the manager of the Merseysippis and somebody had recommended me. I was playing every night in Artie Williams' 18-piece band in Ellesmere Port, and Dick asked me if I would like to join. I had been teaching a trombone player from the band to read music, so I knew they were busy and I wanted to play with them. Dick asked me to do an audition at the Cavern, which was on the point of opening. I was very nervous as I hadn't played jazz before except for an occasional solo with the big band. They put all these numbers in front of me and I floundered through them. Dick said, 'I'll take you to the Grapes' and I thought, 'This is it, it'll be "No thanks".' He said, 'I've never heard anything like that—you've never played jazz before and yet you were marvellous.' So I was in."

Wednesday 16 January 1957

Missing the Christmas and New Year trade, the Cavern opened on Wednesday 16 January 1957. The opening bill featured the Merseysippi Jazz Band, the Wall City Jazzmen (from Chester), the Ralph Watmough Jazz Band and the Coney Island Skiffle Group (despite the name, from the Wirral). The main attraction was to be the 21-year-old drummer, the Earl of Wharncliffe.

And who was this mysterious Earl of Wharncliffe? **Alan Sytner**[20]: "The Earl of Wharncliffe had nothing whatever to do with jazz or blues: he had a very iffy rock'n'roll band which only got PR because he was an earl. However, I was keen to make an impact and there was a jazz promoter in Liverpool who had a monopoly on the main jazz bands so I couldn't hire any of them. I couldn't get Chris Barber, Ken Colyer or Humphrey Lyttelton for the opening and I had to do something to make an impact."

The journalist and jazz fan **Bob Azurdia**[21] was standing in line: "The queue stretched all the way down Mathew Street and into Whitechapel. Prior to the Cavern, the Temple was the only evening venue for jazz in the city and it only opened on Sundays. The only other places you could go to were a cinema, a palais for strict-tempo dancing and a coffee bar. Young people tended not to go to pubs, which in any case closed at ten without any drinking-up time. The Cavern was therefore very welcome."

Ralph Watmough[22]: "We played on the opening night of the Cavern. The Cavern was an old bonded warehouse and someone had lime washed the walls. The unexpected din from the musicians caused the lime wash to flake off. The Wall City Jazz Band from Chester played the first set and they came off looking like snowmen. They were covered from head to foot and Alan Sytner had to do something to stop it happening again. The Cavern must have been a fire officer's nightmare. There was one entrance and exit combined and it was down a very narrow steep flight of steps. There were no toilets to speak of and conditions like that could never exist these days."

The opening notes that evening at the Cavern were played by the Wall City Jazzmen, but what an unlikely choice for the first tune on the premises. Trumpeter **Tom Jones**[23]: "We were playing at a luxurious gig on Mondays at Quaintways in Chester and a lot of places outside of town were very nice too. We also played the massive King George's Hall in Blackburn, which was one of

Melody Maker 8/9/56

LIVERPOOL JAZZ FANS CONVERT CELLAR HQ

A NEW Liverpool jazz club is soon to be opened in a former basement air-raid shelter in Mathew Street. Musicians and fans are voluntarily undertaking the work of conversion and decoration.

The club will hold about 700 and will open three or four nights a week, with the Ralph Watmough Band in residence.

Promoter is 21-year-old Alan Sytner, who already runs the 21 Jazz Club at Croxteth, Liverpool.

There are some half-dozen flourishing jazz clubs on Merseyside, but this will be the first to have premises of its own.

Liverpool's New Jazzy Club Opened

JAZZ fans get " in tre groove " as Ron McKay plays the guitar at Liverpool's new jazz club headquarters, The Cavern, Mathew Street, which opened last night.

Nearly 2,000 people were queueing outside when the premises copied from the famous Parisiene Jazz Club, Caveau, opened. Quite a few able to get inside and they sat or stood in the dimly-lit chamber to hear various jazz bands.

Dressed in jeans, skirts and sweaters, they filled every corner of the club, standing packed between the bricked arches.

Right;
The Ralph
Wattmough Jazz Band

JAZZ

THE CAVERN

FABULOUS OPENING TO-NIGHT!
WITH THE **MERSEYSIPPI** JAZZ BAND
WALL CITY JAZZMEN
RALPH WATMOUGH JAZZ BAND
Coney Island Skiffle Group and Guests :
West Coast, Muskrat and 21 memberships
valid.

NOTE THE ADDRESS:
THE BASEMENT, 10 MATHEW STREET
(between North John St. & Stanley St.)
Doors open 7 p.m. Remember your cards !
AND COME EARLY !

MUSKRAT JAZZ CLUB!
EVERY FRIDAY AT THE CAVERN.

Above; The Dolpins Jazz Band who played the Cavern's first Saturday session at the Cavern on 120th. January, 1957

Liverpool Daily Post, Thursday, January 17, 1957 **7**

Eighteen-year-old Colin Rimmer, of Hoylake, singing with the Coney Island Skiffle Group in The Cavern, which was opened in Mathew Street, Liverpool, last night.

Albert Kinder's shows. We got to the Cavern and it was so grotty and smelly, although the sound was good. In those days we opened with an old folk song, 'The Miller Of The Dee', which we would jazz up and use as our signature tune. (Sings)

"There was a jolly miller who lived on the river Dee,
He worked and sang from morn til night,
No lark more blithe than he.
And this burden of his song as ever used to be,
I care for nobody, no, not I,
If nobody cares for me."

We would also do 'Tiger Rag', 'At The Jazz Band Ball', 'Muskrat Ramble', 'St Louis Blues' and 'Tin Roof Blues'. We didn't have a vocalist then so I would have been singing the odd vocals."

Paul Blake[24]: "The place had been painted and with the heat, everything started to fall down. I came off wanting a cigarette and I couldn't even tell that I was smoking. The atmosphere was that bad."

The Wall City Jazzmen didn't play the Cavern for another two months. **Tom Jones**[25]: "Too busy, I would guess. There were six of us, seven of us with Gordon's cut, and we got 25 bob per man for that first night."

Skiffle was a homemade music incorporating cheap makeshift instruments, which were as likely to come from a chandler as a music shop. The King of Skiffle was Lonnie Donegan, although he and his band played conventional instruments. **Roger Planche**[26] of the Coney Island Skiffle Group: "We met at about 5pm in Liverpool and decided to have a Chinese before going to the Cavern. The doors did not open until 7pm and we thought we had plenty of time. We went into Mathew Street at 6.45pm and there was a queue from the Cavern entrance down to Whitechapel. We managed to get in with our instruments and we made our way to the band room at the side of the stage. It was already full of musical instruments which belonged to the other bands. At one stage I thought that there must be a leak in the premises above as water was pouring down the walls but it was caused by 600 bodies in close confinement. Roger Baskerfield passed out at one stage and he had to be carried over heads to the door to recover. We performed pretty well and we received £4 between us for our efforts. As it was

impossible to get out before the last train to the Wirral, it was all blown on a taxi."

And **Roger Baskerfield**[27] has the best memories of all: "It was so hot on the opening night that I fainted in the dressing room. When I opened my eyes, I found four girls undoing my shirt, so I quickly closed them again."

Alan Sytner[28]: "I was a member of Liverpool Press Club and one of the boys suggested the Earl of Wharncliffe and said they would write about it. In the end, he didn't show up because he was at Cirencester Agricultural College and he'd had an ultimatum—'Stop doing gigs and get back to college or be expelled.' He was hauled back but he didn't bother to inform me. Eventually I got a call when everybody was in the club. I had to announce that he wasn't coming, but nobody was the least bit bothered because everybody was thrilled to be in the Cavern on its opening night. We had good bands on and everybody had a great time. The fact that the Earl never showed was a much better story than if he had. He did gigs all over the place and so his not showing was a national story."

Many Beatle books have the Fabs entertaining over 1,000 fans at the Cavern but that is impossible. **Alan Sytner**[29]: "The maximum ticket sale that we had was 652, and that was on the opening night where we turned more away than we let in. Only a third of the people got in. We had mounted police to control the queue which stretched for half a mile, but, unlike today, there was no trouble when they told people to go home. We got very close to 652 on several other occasions, but it got very heavy when it got to 600. It's good to say 'Sorry, we're full' when you're in the entertainment business. We didn't get to 600 that often, but when we did, we would say, 'That's enough'."

John Lawrence[30], cornet player with the Merseysippis: "I don't know what triggered the Cavern's instant success as I can't remember Alan doing a lot of advertising. I thought that we were taking a bit of a chance by moving from a moderately comfortable pub to a damp cellar, but it was the best thing that ever happened to us. The audience came flooding in every time we played there. The stage was just about big enough for an eight-piece band, but the piano was hanging over the edge. Acoustically it was very good as there were three long tunnels—the outside tunnels were full of benches and chairs and the centre tunnel with the stage at the end was acoustically just right. It was a long room with hard surfaces, brick and a stone floor, which is always good. If you play in a room full of curtains and thick carpets, you can blow your teeth out trying to make the sound right."

Pianist **Frank Robinson**[31]: "Quite surprisingly, the piano at the Cavern wasn't all that bad and it was kept in tune. It didn't have a brilliant tone and it was a bit muddy, but it did the job."

Stan Roberts[32]: "The acoustics in the Cavern were very good but I often had sore fingers through notes which didn't play right or were sticking on the piano."

Don Lydiatt[33]: "We only had one microphone and the amplification wasn't very good anyway. We just blew and hoped for the best. We got used to it."

Jazz critic **Steve Voce**[34]: "Acoustically, the Cavern wasn't brilliant but we were all much younger and our hearing was much more acute. I can't remember any problems in hearing bands there. If you'd had a few pints, it was a good place to hear jazz but then I don't think I ever tried to hear it without having a few pints."

Speaking at the fortieth anniversary of the Cavern, **Keith Hemmings**[35] informed me: "Right from the first night, I knew the Cavern was going to be a tremendous success. There was such a spirit in the place—it was so vibrant and exciting. I was going to be Alan's partner, but we fell out and I disappeared from the scene about a fortnight after it opened. I went into the family business and I had forgotten about my involvement with the Cavern until now."

Unknowingly, Alan Sytner had one of the great components for success. **Bill Heckle**[36]: "People like crowds. People may say it is jammed solid but they go away and tell people how great the atmosphere was. If a concert had been a quarter full, people wouldn't go away with feelings of being somewhere special. The Cavern was special because it was a relatively small place and it was packed out."

Friday 18 January 1957

Nothing on Thursday, so the second night on Friday featured two jazz bands (Muskrat Jazz Band and Liverpool University Jazz Band) plus the Gin Mill Skiffle Group. The Gin Mills featured both Tony Davis and Mick Groves, and Tony had left the Muskrat Jazz Band. **Mick Groves**[37] says, "I was the first washboard player to join the Musicians' Union. I had a nice letter to thank me for joining, but they didn't think that they would be able to place a lot of work my way."

Ray Ennis[38] of the Blue Genes: "Nobody had any money so the tea chests came out and the washboards too. All this was a damn sight cheaper than a drum-kit. If you got three or four guitars strumming away it was quite loud and almost amplified. You then started putting a pick-up on your acoustic guitar and after that, you would save up for an electric guitar and an amplifier. We couldn't afford anything better at first."

Brendan McCormack[39]: "Skiffle started us all off. I remember the excitement of being able to do this (Sings and plays 'Freight Train'), no chord changes and it was wonderful. Bert Weedon was on TV and he offered us a three chord sheet. About six weeks later, it arrived and during a school lunchtime, I was 10 or 11, I tried it. The first chord was an E chord and it was the secret of the universe to me."

Saturday 19 January 1957

Four jazz bands were on offer: the Panama, the Dolphins and Ralph Watmough's and Pete Galvin's. Author **Brian Jacques**[40]: "I went to my doctor, who was Dr Sytner in Boundary Street, and he asked me what I was doing that night. I said, 'Nothing really.' He said, 'Want to go to a night club?' He said that his son had opened the Cavern and he gave me two tickets for the Saturday. I said to my bird, who lived in Norris Green, 'Guess where we're going.' She said, 'To the Cavern.' I said, 'How do you know?' She said, 'My uncle is a commissionaire and he's on the door.' (Laughs) It stunk like a toilet; the water was pouring down the walls, you couldn't move and it was shoulder to shoulder. I was hit over the head by some girl's feet as a beatnik with a check shirt and a red beard had thrown her over his shoulder. She wore those flat shoes with the laces that went up the leg and smack! I got a bang on the head." No wonder the less active Cavern Stomp was devised.

Wednesday 30 January 1957

The drummer Ron McKay, who was with Ralph Watmough's band, was asked to be the Cavern's compère and to form a resident skiffle group. He recruited Brian Curtis from the Coney Island Skiffle Group and they played together for a year. Ron McKay's Skiffle Group and the Architects Jazz Band launched Alan Sytner's innovation of lunchtime sessions, which was visited by members of Chris Barber's Jazz Band, who happened to be in town. It was a shrewd move: the Cavern was close to the business quarter so office staff could come along in their lunch breaks. These people would be smartly dressed and the publicity stated "Persons in dungarees not admitted".

Many of the acts weren't advertised because it was scratch bands made up from whoever was around. Sometimes Don Lowes' Dixielanders represented an *ad hoc* band of whoever was available including Paul Simpson, Ron Rubin, Tommy Smith and Ron McKay. These were gifted musicians—Paul Simpson played with Mick Mulligan and Tommy Smith with Vic Lewis—but they were notably eccentric, if not mad. Simpson and Smith had a double act on the streets in which they would lie on the tramlines doing a Pearl White as the trams came towards them.

The lunchtime sessions had to be rough and ready as most of the musicians had day jobs. "We didn't do many lunchtime sessions," says **John Lawrence**[41] of the Merseysippis, "but we were lucky as I was my own boss and Ken Baldwin had a flexible job at the docks. We could all get there and we could get set up very quickly. We could arrive at 12.45 and be ready to play at one."

John McCormick[42]: "I first heard about the Cavern when I was 16 and I had a day job in Stanley Street. Someone who worked round the corner said to me, 'You like jazz so why don't you come to the lunchtime session at this new place?' There was a lunchtime session every day from 12 til 2 and they were fantastic. The sessions were fairly loose: the bands had been put together for the occasion but they were musicians who knew each other and knew each other's styles. Alan Branscombe stands out as he went on to become one of the leading lights of the British jazz scene,

in fact, the world jazz scene, and on several instruments too. He played all kinds of styles, especially in the early days, but he became associated with modern jazz after John Dankworth discovered him."

The lunchtime session could be followed by another one. **John McCormick**[43]: "Red Carter used to play in the lunchtime sessions and I would go and see him. He would play 'til two and I would go back to work. The guys would put their instruments down and go across the road to the Grapes and sit down for a breather and a pint. After about 40 minutes, the door would open and Alan would come in and say, 'Fancy coming back and playing for me?': it would be perhaps him and a couple of pals and he would pay them. He couldn't keep on going like that."

The club had only been going for a fortnight but already they had used 17 acts with the Merseysippis and Ralph Watmough leading the field with five appearances apiece. The Merseysippis played that night with the Tony Brown Quartet. The drummer Tony Brown liked a few jars and was jokingly known as 'Incapability Brown'.

Alan Sytner decided to have skiffle nights, and Ron MacKay and the Gin Mill Skiffle Group would alternate as hosts. **Tony Davis**[44]: "When I was in the Muskrats, the brass men would need a chance to wet their whistle, and so we had a blues session. My wife's sister, Muriel, was on piano, and our drummer went to washboard. The banjo player stayed and I sang and we did 'Midnight Special' and 'I Ain't Gonna Give Nobody None Of This Jelly Roll'. We didn't call it skiffle because that wasn't a well-known word then. When the skiffle bands came in, they were playing the Lonnie Donegan repertoire. We didn't, as we were doing jazz songs with a skiffle line-up and that is what we did in the Gin Mills too. There was a photo in *Blighty* of Mick and me with our beards and our guitars and there was also a banjo, tuba, bass, drums and clarinet at the time. The Gin Mill Skiffle Group was rather different."

Saturday 2 February 1957

The evening featured Ralph Watmough Jazz Band, the Panama Jazz Band and Ron McKay's Skiffle Group. **Mick O'Toole**[45]: "The Cavern was a jazz club but skiffle was just kicking off and we were the first on our block to put a skiffle band together. Someone told us that they had skiffle bands on at the Cavern. I was 14 and a half and I went with a good mate, Vinnie Murphy. I was the youngest there but they looked after us. We could go in as it wasn't licensed, an orange juice or a tea for us, and we went for the skiffle bands. I liked Ron McKay's skiffle group most of all. He had a cracking, good-looking singer called Brian Newman and we were convinced that he was going to be a star but I've never heard of him since. Brian thought we were far too young to get in but he would sing our requests. He would sing the Josh White song, 'If you're white, you're all right. If you're brown, stick around. If you're black, get back.' He would get enormous applause for this and I always wondered if it was because of his performance or because he was a half caste?"

John McCormick[46]: "Ron McKay was a larger than life character and I became aware of his charisma in the band when I was in a skiffle group myself and we had a half hour spot at the Cavern. Ron was amazing behind those drums and he blew us away. We were gobsmacked that he had found a black American singer who looked and sounded great, and that seemed to be the real deal for us. He might have come from Burtonwood, but you never knew with Ron as he did use poetic licence. Ron McKay reminded me of Gene Krupa or perhaps I should now say, Animal in the Muppets. His arms were everywhere and he sang big and he announced big and he was a monster drinker and once he'd had a few pints, he was really going for it. He was pretty shy until he had had his first taste. His announcements were big and don't forget we were teenagers and we would say timidly, 'And now we would like to play,' and Ron would shout "AND NEXT WE'RE GOING TO HIT YOU WITH LEADBELLY'S SO AND SO." We went wow!"

Sunday 3 February 1957

The American jazz guitarist Eddie Condon was with his All-Stars at the Empire, supported by Humphrey Lyttelton and his Band. Alan Sytner invited them to the Cavern after the concert. **Peter Morris**[47] of the Dolphin Jazz Band: "Eddie Condon was the worse for wear, which was state usual, and he hadn't appeared in the second half of the show, and it was the two bands minus leaders who came to the Cavern. George Wettling was

playing drums watched by all the jazz drummers on Merseyside. One girl threw a bottle at Johnny Parker, who ducked and it hit Jim Bray's bass. I don't know what he'd done to upset her."

Saturday 9 February 1957

The White Eagle Jazz Band in their blue jackets and red bow-ties arrived from Leeds for their Cavern debut and became regulars. They were also their own interval band as the Martin Boland Skiffle Group. **John Cook**[48]: "I have walked on the Salford Road in thick fog, carrying a torch so that the driver could see where he was going, just to play at the Cavern. One evening I decided to go for a Chinese meal in Lime Street and as I was walking over, I heard someone about to fire a gun. Being an ex-marine, I knew what to do. I ducked and the bullet hit the wall near my head. Maybe it was somebody who thought the band was rotten."

Bob Frettlohr[49]: "I was in civil engineering but somehow I managed to burn the candle at both ends. I was also doing up my bungalow. I would get four or five hours' sleep a night. I'd have a good breakfast and I'd be all right."

Thursday 21 February 1957

The first modern jazz session took place with the West Indian trumpeter Dizzy Reece, saxophonist Harry Klein and the Trond Svennevig Quartet. Alan Sytner knew he would lose money with modern jazz, but he was determined to present the best he could afford. Twenty-five year old Trond was a Swedish musician based at Manchester University. In later years, the beat groups could play comfortably alongside the trad bands, but the mix of trad and modern jazz never worked and Trond was booed off a jazz festival in Manchester.

Within a month, the Cavern had established itself as the hippest place on Merseyside, not that there was much competition. **Alan Sytner**[50]: "There were very marked demographics according to the night of the week and what was being put on. On Thursdays I put on modern jazz to please myself and I got a very hip, very cool audience—crew-cuts, button-down collars and little skinny ties. They thought they were massively superior and cleverer than everybody else. These were people who had their own cars and so we could stay open a little later. Sunday was the Merseysippis' night and they attracted a very middle class audience with lots of people from the Wirral and Crosby. These people didn't cause any trouble at all, obviously, and as they formed the majority, nobody else did either. Friday night was completely different. We used to get kids from the top end of London Road. There were quite a few gangs and they used to love making trouble, similar to football hooligans today and the same sort of people. If I'd had any sense, I would have closed on Fridays. On Saturdays you got a cross-section. If there was a band with a strong appeal, you would get a nice audience. If it was a so-so band, you would just get whoever was out on Saturday night and going to the Cavern for want of somewhere to go."

Saturday 23 February 1957

First appearance by Manchester's Eric Batty's Jazz Aces. **John Cook**[51]: "Eric Batty, sadly, was no double bass player. He had a three string bass and they were all tuned the same. The star of that band was Roy Williams, who is a tremendous trombone player. They were once on stage at the end of a concert with Sidney Bechet and Sidney asked Eric to take a solo. Eric was so embarrassed that he never played again." That's a bit heavy duty, isn't it? Poor bloke.

Thursday 28 February 1957

Modern jazz night with a leading light, saxophonist Don Rendell, who had just formed his own sextet. **Owen Clayton**[52]: "I have been at modern jazz evenings at the Cavern where there were only five other people in the audience, but they still played their hearts out. I prefer to call it progressive jazz and I've always thought it was great for the people who are playing it, but not so great for those who are not technically into it."

In March 1957 the public health inspector blew up some football bladders at the Cavern to obtain air samples. Outside it was 52 degrees Fahrenheit and inside 82 degrees, a remarkable difference as there were no radiators in the club. The public health inspector lacked the powers available to environmental health officers today and had to rely on persuasion. Nevertheless, a ventilation shaft was installed, but as it extended only 30 feet up in a narrow passage between two high buildings, the air coming into the building was stagnant. Electric fans were installed to circulate the air but, being warm, it was already fetid.

What did **Alan Sytner**[53] think? Should he have improved conditions at the Cavern? "I didn't have the finances to do that and anyway the places in Paris were pretty stark. I knew that if I fancied it, they would fancy it, simple as that. I was 21, a little more sophisticated than the average Scouse 21-year-old, but nonetheless, I was a 21-year-old Scouser and I knew that they would like it. The Cavern was bigger than the places I'd seen in Paris, which were also licensed and charged more for admission. Their clubs had an ambience and I knew how to get that at the Cavern."

Wednesday 6 March 1957

The Merseysippi Jazz Band and Ron McKay's Skiffle Group. **Mick O'Toole**[54]: "The singer Brian Newman broke a string on his guitar one night and said he would have to go to the car for a replacement. Ron McKay picked up a bucket, turned it upside down and drummed on it until he came back. I'd never seen anything like that—it was fabulous."

Thursday 7 March 1957

The Jamaican saxophonist Joe Harriott fronts a modern jazz night with his quartet. His son, Aynsley, is now a TV chef.

Saturday 9 March 1957

The South Side Stompers, the Ron McKay Skiffle Group and the Paul Beattie Skiffle Group. Paul Beattie came from Manchester: he switched to rock'n'roll and recorded as Paul Beattie and the Beats for Parlophone ("I'm Comin' Home", 1957: "A House A Car And A Wedding Ring", 1958). Paul Beattie is therefore the first *bona fide* rock'n'roller to play the Cavern.

Ron McKay's diary reveals just how much work there was around for a decent skiffle group. Not only was he playing at the Cavern, he also had dates at the 21 Club, Bedford Club and Wilson Hall as well as clubs in Wallasey, Ellesmere Port and Prescot.

Wednesday 13 March 1957

American blues singer, Big Bill Broonzy, making his only Cavern appearance, with the Merseysippi Jazz Band. Although George Harrison would have been too young to attend, he is often cited as one of George's favourite musicians. Broonzy arrived at Lime Street Station but fell off the train, causing him to be introduced as "Big Bill Bruised

```
AT    THE    CAVERN    NEXT    WEEK
          NEW ORLEANS UNLIMITED !
- - - - - - - - - - - - - - - - - - - -
     FRIDAY!    FRIDAY!    FRIDAY!

          SPECIAL FEATURE

          MR ACKER BILK'S
        PARAMOUNT JAZZ BAND
         WITH RON MCKAY
   Plus -    THE NEW CLIMAX JAZZMEN
- - - - - - - - - - - - - - - - - - - -

          SATURDAY -

         MICKY ASHMAN'S
        NEW ORLEANS SIX
   And - THE "SWINGING BLUEGENES"
- - - - - - - - - - - - - - - - - - - -

          SUNDAY -

          SONNY MORRIS
        NEW ORLEANS JAZZMEN
   Plus - THE "SWINGING BLUEGENES"
- - - - - - - - - - - - - - - - - - - -

   IN FUTURE ALL SESSIONS START AT 7.45 PROMPT

          SO COME EARLY
- - - - - - - - - - - - - - - - - - - -

   WATCH THE "ECHO" FOR FURTHER NEWS FROM THE CAVERN
```

Clinton Ford singing with the Merseysippi Jazz Band

```
          JAZZ
    CAVERN   TO-NIGHT
           SKIFFLE SESSION
DIRECT  FROM TRIUMPHANT TOUR
RON  MCKAY
Plus Dark Town, Deltones, Quarry Men
      and the Demon Five.
RIVERBOAT SHUFFLE !
     FRIDAY AUGUST 16
     THE MERSEYSIPPI
   WALL CITY JAZZ BAND &c.
GIN MILL SKIFFLE GROUP
MISS  CAVERN  BATHING BEAUTY
          FINAL
      Licensed Bars Till 11 p.m
TICKETS 1/-  Lewis's and Rushworth's
   GET  YOURS  NOW !
CLUB PERDIDO   THURSDAY
ALAN BRANSCOMBE
        QUINTETTE
  & THE DARRYL DUGDALE TRIO
   The Cavern 10 Mathew Street.
NEW CLUBMOOR HALL
Back Broadway, Friday, Saxon Skiffle,
Saturdays, Resident Rockers & Skiffle.
```

Hot and sweaty; Jazz'n'skiffle nights at the Cavern as shown above & left

Hank Walters

Champion Jack Dupree (right)

Right; The Gin Mill Skiffle Group who included Tony Davis and Mick Groves who later went on to form The Spinners

Barrelhouse sound

Knees". When Broonzy was introduced to Tony Davis, who was six foot seven, he said, "From now on they'd better call me Little Bill Broonzy." Broonzy was given a bottle of whisky which he finished in the half-hour before going on stage. He went into a transport café and asked if everything was with chips. On being told it was, he said, "In that case I'll have a double Scotch with chips."

Tony Davis[55]: "I was in a taxi with Bill and another local musician, Ron Rubin, and Big Bill said, 'I could do with some whiskey. If when I was born, anybody had told me that there weren't no whiskey, I would have said, "I'll go right back where I came from."' Ron said, 'Bill, you've been trying to get back to where you came from ever since you were a boy.' Bill was a remarkable man, beautiful voice and great guitar playing. I got a lovely letter in which he said that he wouldn't be coming over anymore to sing with us but he would come and play his guitar. This was when he had cancer of the throat, but he never returned. We really loved him and he was a good friend." Big Bill Broonzy died in 1958.

Ron McKay[56]: "Big Bill Broonzy's voice would fill the Cavern on its own. He didn't need anything else but his own guitar. The girl I married was a non-drinker and she was the only person he would trust with his bottle of whisky when he went on stage. He didn't want to share it with anybody else."

Thursday 14 March 1957
First appearance by the Tubby Hayes All Star Quartet, supported by the Trond Svennevig Quartet. **Steve Voce**[57]: "Jazz was still being polarised between modern fans and traditional fans, and Ronnie Scott and Tubby Hayes would never have had a platform in Liverpool if it weren't for Alan Sytner. Alan Sytner deserves a lot of credit for what he did."

Alan Sytner[58]: "Some of the modern jazz musicians were really laid-back and terribly unpunctual. They took playing seriously but they didn't take making a living seriously. They were all pros, but they were very hard to deal with. Tubby Hayes, the little giant, was the worst. Once he came to Liverpool on the train and he drank 28 bottles of Worthington Green Shield between Euston and Lime Street. He was all right, he was an amazing bloke, but he wasn't *that* all right. He still played. Another night he turned up at 10 o'clock for an 8 o'clock gig. He was full of apologies and said he would play until one in the morning, knowing full well that we had to close at 11.30."

Saturday 16 March 1957
Hello to the Dickie Bishop Skiffle Group. Bishop had replaced Lonnie Donegan in Chris Barber's Jazz Band and, in 1999, his song, 'No Other Baby', was performed by Paul McCartney at the Cavern. **Dickie Bishop**[59]: "I have very fond memories of the Cavern as I spent my wedding night there. When we went back to the hotel, everything was laid on for us, so they are lovely people and lovely memories. When Paul McCartney recorded 'No Other Baby', he didn't know how he knew the song, but I know. I would include it in my set, so quite possibly he heard me sing it."

The West Coast Skiffle Group (who became the Deltones) was a skiffle group with an electric guitar. **Alan Willey**[60]: "It was only electric because I'd made my own amplifier. I had enough technical knowledge to build my own amplifier, but it was only a single-ended thing, probably between 6 and 10 watts. It wasn't very loud initially and my friend, Bernard Whitty said that I needed a decent speaker. He told me to get a Goodman's Audium 50, which was a 12-inch speaker. It was on a Saturday and we installed it in the amplifier and I used it on the Cavern that night. We put it right at the front of the stage, and I wound it up full and hit an E chord and the first four or five rows went 'Oooh!' I knew then that it was loud enough."

Sunday 31 March 1957
First appearance by Johnny Duncan and the Blue Grass Boys, supported by the Merseysippi boys. Duncan still had to take the last train to San Fernando.

Wednesday 3 April 1957
A top UK band, Alex Welsh Dixielanders played both a lunchtime and an evening session.

Not quite the Beatles in Hamburg, but from 13 to 27 April 1957, Ron McKay took his skiffle group on a tour of Denmark.

Thursday 9 May 1957
Modern jazz with Alan Branscombe, Bobby Orr and Stuart Hammer. 21-year-old Branscombe

from Wallasey played modern jazz at the Cavern before moving to London. He toured Europe with Stan Getz in 1970.

Friday 24 May 1957

The Muskrat Jazz Band with the Gin Mill and Texans skiffle groups. Rory Storm made his Cavern debut as leader of the Texans, sometimes billed as the Ravin' Texans. He became the first of the key Liverpool beat figures to play there.

The Gin Mill Skiffle Group with Tony Davis and Mick Groves added English folk songs to the mix such as "D'ye ken John Peel" and "The Lincolnshire Poacher", arranged for banjo and whistle. They supported Michael Holliday at the Liverpool Empire and played a fête for the Conservatives at Aigburth cricket ground in 1958. Shortly after this, they became the Spinners, not a cricket reference but a reflection of working traditions of Lancashire. In September 1958, they opened their own club in the basement of Sampson and Barlow's in London Road, which held about 40.

Tony Davis[61]: "The show with Michael Holliday was lovely. He had a bright red shirt and he said, 'You like the shirt, I got it from the skiffle group.' (Laughs) My dad was in the balcony and he was never particularly keen on me doing these things. When I got a clarinet in the early jazz days, he wanted me to have lessons and I said, 'They didn't have lessons in New Orleans.' That was very silly of me because they did have lessons in New Orleans, very much so. I might have been a decent clarinet player, who knows, but I insisted on teaching myself. But my dad was on the front row of the balcony saying, 'That's my son', and my mother was saying, 'Shut up, Jack'."

Sunday 26 May 1957

An excellent week for skifflers: Dickie Bishop (Sunday), Ron McKay (Wednesday and Friday), the Smokey River Skiffle Group (Friday) and the Gin Mill Skiffle Group (Saturday), all at the Cavern. Over at the Empire, there was a week of Lonnie Donegan and he came to the Cavern on the Saturday morning for a meeting with his fan club. The national *Hit Parade* magazine reported that "more than 100 fans in Liverpool enjoyed buns and Coca-Cola with Lonnie in the Cavern Jazz Club". Ron McKay told Pete Morris of the

Dolphins that he had seen Lonnie's car, "an American job which stretches all the way to Bootle".

Ron McKay[62]: "I compèred Lonnie Donegan's fan club meeting and I think Des O'Connor played the piano and Lonnie played the banjo and I sang. It was a lunchtime thing. I lived with Lonnie for a time in a flat that was run by a gangster. I was with Cy Laurie at the time and he was with Chris Barber and he was, as always, very opinionated." Ron's diary reveals that he played 14 sessions at the Cavern during May 1957 and received £39.10s for the month. He had another nine nights playing Wilson Hall, the 21 and Bedford Clubs and two other venues for £17.10s. Ron was working long hours but £57 for the month was good money in 1957.

Alan Willey[63]: "One night the buzz had gone round that the film star John Gregson was coming to the Cavern. Then the word came in that he was outside. We were about to go on and Ron McKay engineered things so that he would be playing and I stood at the back and saw John Gregson with a large cigar and a light camel-haired overcoat and he looked at the place with disdain."

But not for long. **Arthur Johnson**[64]: "John Gregson, my uncle, was a man who liked to enjoy himself. He discovered the Cavern just after it opened and he was absolutely raving about it. He took his uncle, my great uncle Paddy Gregson, who was a musician and they went with George Melly. John Gregson felt as though he was in Paris, and he went there quite a bit, and he really did like the place."

Sunday 2 June 1957

Bruce Turner, who had just left Humphrey Lyttelton's band, freelanced with the Merseysippis, plus Ralph Watmough's Jazz Band

Wednesday 5 June 1957

Skiffle session with five different bands including the Gin Mills. **Alan Sytner**[65]: "There were hundreds of skiffle and blues groups in the country, the Lonnie Donegan factor was mega, so on Wednesdays I put on a competition for local talent. It encouraged kids who were learning to play, and I would have a couple of more accomplished groups who could play. These kids did the Lonnie Donegan, Dickie Bishop and Johnny Duncan repertoires and they were all pretty awful. Talent night was no talent night as far as I was concerned but I wasn't being altruistic as skiffle was very commercial."

Jazz fan **Steve Voce**[66]: "We disliked skiffle with almost the same contempt that we disliked rock'n'roll. I didn't like Lonnie Donegan in the least, but he saw an opening and seized it. The only reason that skiffle was tolerated at the Cavern was because it made some money for some jazz musicians with whom we were sympathetic. The genuine skiffle music—Big Bill Broonzy, Blind Lemon Jefferson, the people from the 20s—was marvellous, but the later thing was a fraud."

Around this time, Alan Sytner had a further idea. **Ian Harris**[67]: "The warehouse originally had a brick floor but this was very unsuitable for dancing, so Alan Sytner thought about concreting the middle section and having tables and chairs in the other aisles. In the end, he wanted to concrete the lot and the place was closed for a few days around June or July 1957 and we got the concrete in through a trapdoor in the street. I used to play trumpet in a jazz band but we were never good enough to play the Cavern. My friend Bob Parr and I used to take our instruments to work with us and we would practice in the lunch hour. We were doing some work at the Cavern one day around June 1957—I can date it because my future wife and her friend were off school on exam leave—and both Acker Bilk and Chris Barber came down to see the place. There was no one else in but they saw us playing and as they had their instruments with them, they joined in on 'The Saints'."

Wednesday 3 July 1957
Skiffle contest with the Gin Mill, Black Cat and Mathew Street skifflers. **Alan Stratton**[68]: "Alan Sytner said that he would only have jazz bands, rhythm bands or skiffle bands at the Cavern and if you were playing in a rhythm band, you were something like a steel band. The Black Cats played rock'n'roll but they called themselves the Black Cats Rhythm Group so that they could play there. They did what they considered blues, 'St. Louis Blues', 'Guitar Boogie' and 'Frankie And Johnny', and I saw them and was made up."

Saturday 6 July 1957
The Merseysippi and Ralph Watmough jazz bands were at the Cavern, but just a few miles away, John Lennon met Paul McCartney for the

first time at the garden fête in the grounds of the Woolton Parish Church. On that same day, there was also a summer fête at Quarry Bank school, although the Quarry Men were at the church event. That's not all the entertainment you could choose from on that warm summer day. **Sam Leach**[69]: "On the night that John and Paul met in Woolton, I rented a garage with a band called the Black Diamonds and we called it The Attic as opposed to The Cavern. The Cavern was exciting but I didn't like going there because they weren't my kind of girls—they were beatniks. The beatniks wanted to be different and yet they all dressed and acted the same. I did go there to see the Ken Colyer jazz band, who were my favourites and I also liked Dick Charlesworth and the City Gents, but I got a bit bored with evenings that were all jazz. I bought a brand new pair of Hush Puppies for this date with a girl in the Cavern and she was gorgeous. She wasn't a beatnik. My shoes got ruined because of the broken glass and cigarette ends on the floor. The sweat came down the walls and I came out looking like a tramp."

John McCormick[70] of the Black Diamonds: "We would do anything that any of us fancied. The guitar player loved Hank Williams and Django Reinhardt and we had some instrumentals that were guitar led. They were very fast and technical, and we had a good strong rhythm guitarist too. Playing the tea chest bass wasn't bad. I could get a scale out of it as I would move the pole forward and back and different pitches of notes. I tried corrugated bins, upside down and right way up, all kinds of things, and then I found a bass advertised very cheap in a corner shop and bought it. I was once there with the Black Diamonds supporting a band from London who had had one hit record and the bass player picked on me and said, 'Give it up now, son, you're not going to make it. Bass players are born and you're not one. Go and find a nice steady day job.' I thought, 'Thank you very much!' I never heard of them again."

Wednesday 24 July 1957
Skiffle session with country from Hank Walters and his Dusty Road Ramblers. **Hank Walters**[71]: "We got a lot of bookings and we didn't do the Cavern too often as it was only £7.50 for five people. Still, that was reasonable as a lot of them were doing it for nothing. It was also a hot gig as I

wore a buckskin coat and had an accordion. The sweat must have been squirting out of me."

Sunday 28 July 1957

The Merseysippi and Panama jazz bands. The Panama's drummer, Bill Williams, was a regimental drum major. **John Cochrane**[72]: "I went to the Cavern when it was a jazz club and I saw the Panama and Merseysippi jazz bands. They were good, but the place was awful. It is very difficult to get an eight-piece band with piano and drumkit on stage and the facilities were dreadful too. However, the atmosphere was tremendous."

Wednesday 31 July 1957

Eddie Clayton had just formed his skiffle group with a certain Richard Starkey on drums and hence, Ringo, by a week, was the first Beatle to play the Cavern. On the same night, Ray Ennis and Norman Kuhlke made their Cavern debut with a band that mixed skiffle with trad, the Blue Genes. Alan Sytner said that they swung, hence the Swinging Blue Genes but the spelling wasn't anything clever: Spud Ward wrote 'Blue Genes' on the drums (moving up in the world!), thinking he was spelling 'Blue Jeans'. "I wish we'd worn jeans from the outset," says **Ralph Ellis**[73], "but wearing a suit on stage was a sign of success." Those Martini shirts perhaps, but certainly not the fluorescent socks that Spud wore when he was cycling there and back.

Ray Ennis[74]: "We had been to the Cavern before we played there and we had watched the jazz bands. We knew Rikki Ashen, who was employed by Alan Sytner as the day-to-day manager. When the bands took a break, nothing much happened and Bruce McCaskill said that that we were a skiffle group and we could keep everything going. After a few weeks of humming and hawing, Rikki gave us a try. We would fill in for nearly all the jazz bands, just doing half an hour here and there."

Wednesday 7 August 1957

The Quarry Men with lead vocalist John Lennon made their Cavern debut. Paul McCartney was a Quarryman but he was at scout camp in the Lake District. **Alan Sytner**[75]: "Skiffle was a breeding ground for musicians—one or two of them became jazz musicians, but more ended up doing rock'n'roll. I knew John Lennon quite well as we lived in the same area: he lived 400 yards up the road from me. He was 16 and arrogant and hadn't got a clue, but that was John Lennon."

Len Garry[76] played tea-chest bass with the Quarry Men: "I knew John wanted to do some Elvis numbers but I hoped he wouldn't as we might get turfed out."

Their drummer was **Colin Hanton**[77]: "We did some skiffle numbers to start off with at the Cavern but we also did rock'n'roll. John Lennon was passed a note and he said to the audience, 'We've had a request'. He opened it up and it was Alan Sytner saying, 'Cut out the bloody rock'n'roll.'"

Len Garry[78]: "I got TB soon after this and I did wonder if I had picked it up in the Cavern. There was no ventilation in there."

Dave Jamieson[79]: "I used to like the Gin Mill who always started with 'Down By The Riverside', the Smokey River, the Atlantics, and Ron McKay, who was a very good drummer. The Darktown Skiffle Group was my favourite as they had been put together to back a very good girl singer, Jill Martin. I went down in August 1957 because the Deltones and the Darktown were on. The Quarry Men were on too and that was the first time I met John Lennon. He wasn't interested in talking about football. John would see something happening and he would make a joke about it." That girl singer, Jill Martin, was to join the Merseysippis, while Ringo Starr sometimes sat in with the Darktown group.

This evening showed the division within the different skiffle groups. The first ones had emerged from the jazz bands and were there to provide entertainment while the brass players had a rest. Now younger bands like the Quarry Men were coming along. They did not know of the jazz tradition, taking their cue from Lonnie Donegan's records, and they were more interested in the new rock'n'roll records than jazz.

Ron McKay, although he didn't know it, would have been the first person to introduce John Lennon at the Cavern. Ron received £4 for his work that evening, mostly for playing with his own skiffle group. Their repertoire included "My Bonnie Lies Over The Ocean", a folk song that the Beatles recorded with Tony Sheridan in Hamburg in 1961.

Ron McKay[80]: "When I finished at the Cavern, it would be about 11 o'clock and I used to walk home to Bootle. I would go along Scotland Road and past the Rotunda at one or two in the morning. It was a hell of a walk but it used to keep me fit and I would sing all these songs as I was going along. I would try and remember the words of 'Frankie And Johnnie'."

Friday 16 August 1957

The Cavern's first riverboat shuffle on the Royal Iris with the Merseysippi Jazz Band, the Gin Mill Skiffle Group, the Wall City Jazzmen and a bathing beauty competition, all for five shillings. Anne Thirlwell was voted Miss Cavern 1957—a good choice as, two years later, she was fourth in the Miss World competition. The intention was to emulate the riverboats in New Orleans. The boat would take audiences up and down the Mersey, a genuine case of the music going round and round.

Sunday 1 September 1957

Should the legendary New Orleans clarinet player Johnny Dodds have a Cavern brick? True, he never played the Cavern, but Cy Laurie believed that he was the reincarnation of Dodds, conveniently ignoring the fact that their time on earth overlapped by 14 years. **Ron McKay**[81]: "Cy Laurie certainly played in the style of Johnny Dodds, but to me he always chose the worst parts of Dodds and ignored his beautiful, lyrical phrasing. He had a very good band with musicians like Al Fairweather on trumpet."

Sunday 15 September 1957

An unusual lunchtime mix—the Merseysippis with the Royal Caribbean Calypso Steel Band. **Alan Sytner**[82]: "I was forced into booking a steel band for the Cavern and people thought they were awful: they were asking me not to book them again. They left their tins behind and I went up to Toxteth to ask them to collect them, but they stayed in the dressing room for weeks."

Sunday 29 September 1957

As the overhead railway was being dismantled, something was coming together underground. This session was Clinton Ford's first performance with the Merseysippi Jazz Band. **Ken Baldwin**[83]: "We didn't know Clinton Ford and his face was hidden by a pair of sunglasses. I thought he was a poser—you don't wear sunglasses in a cellar—but there was a reason for this as he had two black eyes. He had finished a season at Butlin's in Pwllheli. He sang in the bar every night and had become friendly with one of the girls who worked there. He had taken her to his chalet but she happened to be the chef's young lady who sussed out where she was. The chef duffed him up and he still had the shiners when we saw him. He knew a few jazz numbers and he had a good voice and we loved playing with him."

Clinton Ford[84]: "I had family in Bebington but I had never really come to Liverpool until I went to the Cavern. I sang 'Ace In The Hole' with Ralph Watmough and then someone asked if I could sing with the Merseysippis. Frank Robinson said, 'Not another one', and I've been singing with them on and off ever since. I liked playing the Cavern with them but it's hard to convey how squalid it was. When it was packed, the moisture would rise and settle on the ceiling. It would condense and drip down your neck. It was an awful place but we loved it."

Not having a better offer, Clinton Ford secured a bedsit in Canning Street for 15 shillings a week. The pianist Ron Rubin lived opposite. During the winter, Clinton would sing with the Merseysippis and return to Butlin's in the summer.

Wednesday 2 October 1957

Ron McKay and Lise West Hansen were married at Bootle Registry Office in the morning and the *Daily Mail* reported that as McKay didn't possess a suit, he wore a green sports coat and blue flannels. Two hours later, he was wearing a multi-coloured shirt and jeans and playing at a lunchtime session. Lise, a jazz singer, also performed. In one of the press reports, Ron is quoted as saying, "I may only be a skiffle singer but I'm sure that given the breaks we can forget that Lise's father is wealthy and make a go of it."

Ron McKay[85]: "I married a Danish girl whom I had met when I was touring with Cy Laurie in 1954. She came to London and stayed with me and Lonnie and then she came up to Liverpool with me. We got married at Bootle Registry Officer. It was front page news—'Skiffle Singer Weds Heiress'. Her father was said to be a Danish millionaire but he only owned a fish factory and a restaurant."

As a result there was no evening session as such, but Alan Sytner went to the Philharmonic Hall to see the Jack Teagarden and Earl Hines All Stars. **John McCormick**[86]: "Alan Sytner used to look out for the big names that were on like Duke Ellington or Woody Herman or Gerry Mulligan. He would go to the shows and then he would invite them to the Cavern for an after hours session. More often than not, the bandleaders would go to the hotel, but the musicians would come down and jam. They could jam all night. I was there when Earl Hines did that and on other occasions, there was Bob Brookmeyer, the trombone player with Gerry Mulligan, and Johnny Hodges and other musicians from the Duke Ellington band. Alan was really good at PR for the Cavern and it was helped by having his own private bar. It was the only time that there was alcohol and he sometimes served champagne. When the Merseybeat thing took it over, the place calmed down in a way as the late night parties stopped when Alan left."

Sunday 13 October 1957

Johnny Parker and his Band were booked for the Cavern but their transport, a 1931 Rolls-Royce ambulance, broke down three times. They took out the instruments to get the spare wheel and left a trombone by the roadside. Clinton Ford with the Joe Shannon Skiffle Group kept the crowd entertained for 90 minutes until they arrived at 9.15pm.

On 14 October, Ron McKay left Liverpool to join Acker Bilk's Paramount Jazz Band and his vocalist, Brian Newman, took over his skiffle group. Acker promised him £25 a week and his invitation to join the group said, "Think quick man, as there is a hell of a lot of paperwork to be dealt with." Lise had no qualms about going as she told the local press that Liverpool was too damp. Liverpool, the Cavern, or both?

Wednesday 23 October 1957

(lunchtime) Merseysippi Jazz Band
(evening) The Brian Newman and Red Valley skiffle groups and Ralph Watmough's Jazz Band. Ralph Watmough took a Wednesday night residency in the absence of Ron McKay while Alan Sytner had decided to include skiffle groups on most nights.

Saturday 26 October 1957

The Alex Welsh Dixielanders returned to the Cavern, much to the delight of local journalist, Keith Bradley: "The band has no gimmicks. There will be no beards or weird individuals or strange clothing. Instead a bunch of conventional individuals will play jazz."

Thursday 21 November 1957

Modern jazz night with the Jazz Couriers featuring Tubby Hayes and Ronnie Scott. **Ronnie Scott**[87]: "The Jazz Couriers was two tenor saxophones with a rhythm section and we lasted a couple of years. We played the Cavern fairly regularly and I thought it was a nice little place."

Colin Middlebrough[88]: "When the Jazz Couriers came to the Cavern, it was unusual as they were a famous band and it was great to see these guys that I idolised on record. Phil Seaman was my absolute idol on drums, of course he had problems and drugs played a big part in it. One night we got there early because they were on, but there were only about 40 people to hear them anyway. Tubby Hayes and Ronnie Scott came in wearing black duffle coats and they disappeared to the White Star and had eight or nine pints each. Phil Seaman was in the dressing room for two hours with a practice pad and all you could hear was 'da-da-da-da-da-da'. That was absolute dedication and it was great to hear him do that. It was punctuated by a few pauses and I can now imagine what he was doing. The needle was his substitute for drinking."

John Gorman[89]: "I used to go down for the modern jazz and we saw great musicians like Tubby Hayes. My friend Terry Moscrop and myself used to sit in the front row and we would be very cool and dig the jazz, man. We would click our fingers to the music. Rock'n'roll started to come in and we turned our noses up at that because we liked 'proper' music. I wouldn't have dreamed of going to the trad nights either as that too wasn't 'proper' jazz. It was just people swinging and stamping their feet and enjoying themselves. You didn't do that with modern jazz. You sat there and listened and got tuned in: cool, calm and collected. You didn't applaud wildly: you just nodded appreciatively."

Jazz critic **Steve Voce**[90]: "The jazz that the Cavern put on covered all the extremes. We had

Ronnie Scott and Tubby Hayes where you needed to use your intelligence a bit more and the rewards were substantially greater, while the Merseysippi Jazz Band was at the banjo end of jazz, the boozing end where you don't have to use your brain. The fact that they stuck together demonstrates either great loyalty or restricted imagination."

Saturday 23 November 1957

The Saints Jazz Band from Ashton-under-Lyne, which was formed in 1950 and had recorded for Parlophone, were supported by the Blue Genes. **Ray Ennis**[91]: "We watched the jazz bands closely and tried to do with guitars what they were doing with brass, using lots of harmony guitar. We did the jazz songs that we liked and we didn't do Elvis songs as we felt that we were being different. I did like rock'n'roll though and I was singing 'Blueberry Hill' and 'Hound Dog' with Frank Wibberley's Rhythm Rockers at Wilson Hall. We would not have got the Cavern gig if we were rock'n'roll because Alan Sytner hated it and the audiences would boo anyone who attempted it."

Sunday 24 November 1957

The Merseysippi Jazz Band was at the Cavern but Michael Holliday was starring at the Empire in a benefit show for Harold House youth club with Lita Roza, the Kaye Sisters and the Gin Mill Skiffle Group.

Monday 25 November 1957

How did Vic Lewis's Big Band fit on the stage? Vic Lewis had supported Bill Haley and his Comets on their UK tour and he would become a director of NEMS Enterprises.

Wednesday 30 November 1957

The *Evening Express* wrote a feature on the lunchtime session with the Merseysippi Jazz Band. Christine Alkins, a 17-year-old typist from a shipping office, said, "Dad hates the stuff but he doesn't mind me coming here. I find that jiving is good for my figure."

Thursday 5 December 1957

Modern jazz with the Tony Kinsey Quartet

Tuesday 24 December 1957

Ralph Watmough Jazz Band and the Deltones Skiffle Group. The Cavern held a sweepstake with a £60 prize to entertain a needy child at Christmas. The winner, the gorgeous Anne Mitchell, with the help of the Liverpool Child Welfare Association chose 8-year-old Cecilia Traynor, one of a family of six orphaned children from Garston. The rest of the family also received gifts as well as a huge hamper of Christmas goodies.

Tuesday 31 December 1957

Seeing in the New Year with the Merseysippi Jazz Band, Clinton Ford, the Blue Genes and the Los Toros Skiffle Group. **Ken Baldwin**[92]: "We would go over to the Beaconsfield in the interval and Mr Cosgrove with his steel grey hair was immaculately dressed with a flower in his lapel. The doors would burst open and the whole band would clatter down the steps and Mr Cosgrove would say, 'Jim, the boys', and Jim would start pulling the pints. Mr Cosgrove was in charge and he never pulled a pint himself. Mr Cosgrove knew we played at the Cavern, and every Christmas he would send us a bottle of Scotch, a bottle of gin and a bottle of rum. That was because we used to bring custom into the Beaconsfield."

Friday 3 January 1958

The Merseysippi Jazz Band with Clinton Ford and the Texans Skiffle Group. Johnny Guitar of the Texans records in his diary: "Playing at Cavern. Didn't do too well."

Sunday 12 January 1958

TV contest winners, the Second City Jazzmen. How dare they come here and tell us that Birmingham is the second city. It also marks the Deltones' final appearance. **Alan Willey**[93]: "One night for devilment we thought we would do 'Wake Up Little Susie' and I maintain that we were the first band to play rock'n'roll on the Cavern. Alan Sytner got hold of Charlie's guitar lead and tugged him over to the side of the stage and told him that if we played any more of that rubbish, we were finished. We looked at each other and thought, 'Do we really want to play here anymore?' and we went into 'Giddy-Up-A Ding Dong' and 'Shake, Rattle And Roll'. Alan Sytner said, 'I am never booking you again' and we said, 'Well, that suits us.'"

Wednesday 15 January 1958

The Cavern's first birthday party with the Merseysippis, Ralph Watmough, Brian Newman, Cooke's Dixielanders and the Katz Skiffle Group. Jazzman (that is, Steve Voce) of the *Liverpool Echo* profiles Alan 'Napoleon' Sytner: "A short,

BUNS AND 'COKE' for LONNIE'S FANS

is for permission to meet Tommy in person. As Tommy can't possibly meet every one of his 2,000 members, the club issues passes to a few lucky ones each week.

How are they selected? "Well, it's difficult to say," said the secretary. "But we look at the letters, and try to decide which are Tommy's keenest fans."

Membership, by the way, costs 5s. a year, and brings fans a photo every time a new picture is taken, a newsletter from Tommy, and a quarterly magazine.

LONNIE DONEGAN

★

A Year In The Cellar

IT is Napoleon's birthday on Wednesday. Before the historically minded write to us angrily on the subject of accuracy we may add that we mean Alan "Napoleon" Sytner, the local emperor of Liverpool jazz.

He ascended to his title just 12 months ago on Wednesday when he opened the Cavern, the underground Liverpool fruit warehouse, which he converted into a replica of a Paris left bank jazz cellar. The cellar had stayed a vision in his mind since as a schoolboy in Paris in 1950, he had sneaked out of his parents' hotel and gone into a smoky cellar to spend the night listening to the great SIDNEY BECHET.

A short, tubby young man with a close resemblance to the French emperor, Alan paces up and down in the approved tycoon fashion

often deliberately loses money to bring the best modern groups in Britain to Liverpool. Knocked out by the Modern Jazz Quartet he took in two of their London concerts and two in Manchester as well as the Liverpool Philharmonic one.

"My chief aim with the Cavern now is to build a bigger public for modern and mainstream jazz" he says. For next week's anniversary celebrations there will be more important groups at the Cavern than ever before in one week. The MERSEY-SIPPI head the birthday bill on Wednesday, the DILL JONES TRIO with JOE

Fan Club Page
conducted by TONY BROMLEY

Lonnie Donegan's fan club is run by Manchester girl Sheila Richardson, who came to London seven months ago to work for Lonnie, and the club has its own office at Faraday House, 8-10, Charing Cross Road, London, W.C.2.

In the seven months since it was formed, the club has enrolled something like 3,000 members. Membership costs 5s. a year, for which members receive a guitar brooch, an autographed picture, and four glossy magazines a year.

Other facilities include tickets for Lonnie's TV shows, and plenty of opportunities to meet Lonnie in person.

When Lonnie returned from the States earlier this year, the club ran coaches out to London Airport (free, too !). And during the past few months the singer has been holding regular "Get Togethers" with his fans in various parts of the country.

In May, more than 100 fans in Liverpool enjoyed buns and Coca-Cola with Lonnie in the Cavern Jazz Club. There were similar meetings in Manchester in June, and in London in July.

One special feature of the club is that a great many members are amateur guitar and skiffle enthusiasts, and frequently write to Lonnie for advice.

Lonnie takes these queries very seriously, and a large part of the club magazine is devoted to articles by Lonnie about guitar-playing, the origins of skiffle, etc.

Romantic footnote : Sheila, the club secretary, herself receives a lot of fan mail from club members, asking her for dates. But already ha...

(partial column cut off)

By Jazzman

when he talks and, invariably has plenty to talk about. His other approach in business is to take someone aside and whisper in their ear with the air of imparting next year's Grand National Winner.

Son of a well-known Liverpool doctor, 22-years-old Alan travelled to jazz promotion via way of a broker's office and furniture salesmanship. He opened the 21 Club in Croxteth Road, then started cellar hunting. "I worried the life out of every estate agent in Liverpool about cellars and they thought I was mad," says Alan. "Then having found my place, I had fight after fight with the planning authorities about the conversion. But now we've won our battle and I challenge anyone to come to the Cavern and find anything that gives jazz a bad name."

Napoleon Sytner has toured Europe — France, Italy, Germany, Switzerland, Holland — to widen his knowledge of the jazz scene. His ten-year collection of records is one of the best on Merseyside.

His great passion is modern jazz. On Thursday nights, he

(Left) Queen of the washboard
Beryl Bryden

AT THE CAVERN NEXT WEEK

NEW ORLEANS UNLIMITED !

FRIDAY! FRIDAY! FRIDAY!

SPECIAL FEATURE

MR ACKER BILK'S
PARAMOUNT JAZZ BAND
WITH RON McKAY

Plus - THE NEW CLIMAX JAZZMEN

SATURDAY -

MICKY ASHMAN'S
NEW ORLEANS SIX

And - THE "SWINGING" BLUEGENES

SUNDAY -

SONNY MORRIS
NEW ORLEANS JAZZMEN

Plus - THE "SWINGING" BLUEGENES

IN FUTURE ALL SESSIONS START AT 7.45 PROMPT

SO COME EARLY

WATCH THE "ECHO" FOR FURTHER NEWS FROM THE CAVERN

tubby young man with a close resemblance to the French emperor, Alan paces up and down in typical tycoon fashion when he talks, and invariably has plenty to talk about."

Thursday 16 January 1958

Modern jazz session with "TV and radio stars": welcome the Bill Jones Trio and Joe Harriott.

Sunday 19 January 1958

First Cavern appearance by the popular Terry Lightfoot Jazzmen.

Friday 24 January 1958

The Merseysippis top the bill, but the Quarry Men are back, this time with Paul McCartney. **Alan Sytner**[94]: "McCartney was as arrogant as Lennon, no doubt he caught it from him. They'd only been playing for a short while so you wouldn't expect them to be any good but they became world class, the best. At the time, they couldn't play to save their lives and all I can remember is their cheek and their chat."

Wednesday 29 January 1958

Ralph Watmough Jazz Band and Eddie Clayton Skiffle Group. Ringo was with Eddie Clayton so John, Paul and Ringo all play the Cavern within a week.

Friday 14/ Saturday 15 February 1958

Acker Bilk and his Paramount Jazz Band, so Ron McKay returned. Acker had moved from Bristol to London and his office, the Bilk Marketing Board, was run by his brother David.

Saturday 1/ Sunday 2 March 1958

Clarinettist Sandy Brown left his architectural job in London for a weekend at the Cavern

The northern heats of Stanley Dale's Skiffle Contest were at the Liverpool Empire, hosted by *6.5 Special* star, Jim Dale. The Darktown Skiffle Group won and was given a TV spot on *6.5 Special*.

Sunday 16 March 1958

Vocalist and washboard player ("Rock Island Line"), Beryl Bryden was the guest of the Merseysippis. The washboard was obligatory: you couldn't have Beryl without it.

Thursday 27 March 1958

A female saxophonist from Leicestershire—welcome the Betty Smith Quintet

Tuesday 1 April 1958

Johnny Guitar of the Texans records in his diary: "Playing at Cavern. Took Pat. Police trouble." What happened?

Wednesday 2 April 1958

Coming from a jazz rather than pop background, Lonnie Donegan was uneasy with screaming fans and did not want a Fan Club *per se*. He hit upon the Lonnie Donegan Skiffle And Folk Music Clubs and so he was encouraging amateurs to form their own groups. They opened in many major cities—Birmingham, Bristol, Cardiff, Leeds, Liverpool and Manchester—with headquarters in London. A special branch was set up at a college for the blind in Sheffield. The members would pay a shilling a week, which was largely to cover expenses such as the hire of halls. When Lonnie went to a city for a week's variety, he would go to the club on a Saturday morning, signing autographs and listening to local talent, but not playing because his contract with Moss Empires would not permit it.

Mick Groves[95], who became a Spinner, was the Merseyside president. "Lonnie's secretary was a girl I'd known in Salford and she said, 'You're singing and playing a bit and Lonnie's looking for people to run this club for him.' I said, 'Lonnie's great but I can't be bothered sending out signed photos.' She said, 'No, he just wants somewhere in each of the main cities that will be a focus, like a local skiffle club.'"

Thursday 3 April 1958

The first of several performances from Manchester's modern jazz unit, the Joe Palin Quintet

Friday 4/ Saturday 5 April 1958

Acker Bilk and his Paramount Jazz Band, but this time Acker's drummer Ron McKay also performed with his old skiffle group. The poor bloke never left the stage. **Alan Sytner**[96]: "I opened the club on Good Friday for an appearance by Acker Bilk and I was heavily criticized. The club was full as nowhere else was open."

Sunday 6 April 1958

Ah, the jet set life: Beryl Bryden had been appearing at Le Caveau in Paris with *6.5 Special* the night before, but here she was with the Merseysippi Jazz Band at both the Cavern and the New

Shakespeare Theatre. Mick Mulligan made a guest appearance at the Cavern.

Imagine a club owner today saying that he did not permit snogging on his premises, but Alan Sytner did. **Maureen Hayden**[97]: "Alan Sytner was a friend of my boyfriend and I was at the beginning of a modelling career, which sank without trace. He asked me to be the anti- smooch girl. I was supposed to stop the smooching in the dark corners of the Cavern. In those days, there wasn't that much as the club was pretty innocent with everyone dancing and chatting. It was just a publicity thing for the Cavern as it meant that a pretty 17-year-old girl was on the front page of the *Liverpool Echo*. Alan gave me an honorary membership of the Cavern so that I could go there whenever I wanted, but I didn't stop many people smooching."

Wednesday 9 April 1958

The Lonnie Donegan Skiffle Contest begins at the Cavern and goes through on Wednesday nights in April. The prize was an appearance on *6.5 Special*. The Atlantics in their cowboy shirts crossed to Liverpool on the ferry and practised on the top deck. The captain appeared and told them, "If you don't stop this racket, I'll have you thrown overboard."

Saturday 12 April 1958

The gospel singer Sister Rosetta Tharpe was backed by the Merseysippi Jazz Band in Manchester and by the Wall City Jazzmen at the Cavern. No rehearsals were necessary as she sang familiar material such as 'When The Saints Go Marching In'. She voiced her doubts about appearing at the Cavern by saying, "You might wonder what a woman of God like me is doing in a place like this. Well, our Lord Jesus went down into the highways and the byways and if it's good enough for Him, it's good enough for me."

Alan Stratton[98]: "I went to the jazz nights with the bigger bands—Acker Bilk, Cy Laurie, Tubby Hayes. They had a Thursday night modern jazz which I loved, but they also had the Merseysippis with Sister Rosetta Tharpe. She was wonderful and she had this gold-top single coil Les Paul guitar."

From time to time, the visiting musicians would ask if anyone had a bed for the night, but it was no problem if Alan Sytner's parents weren't home. **John McCormick**[99]: "Alan said, 'Right, let's go', and he invited everyone back to his place in Menlove Avenue because his parents were away. Everybody crashed out at five o'clock—and this is what Red Carter was telling me, I was too young for this scene—and at 11, they were woken up by waitresses serving breakfast on silver trays."

Thursday 17 April 1958

The American trombonist Ray Premru had come to the UK in 1956. He liked it and found a regular job with the London Philharmonic Orchestra. On days off, he would play modern jazz.

Thursday 24 April 1958

Benny Green with the Joe Palin Quintet. At the time, Green reported on jazz for *New Musical Express*. He became a leading journalist and Radio 2 presenter. He was also part of Lord Rockingham's XI, although, in later years, he did not want to admit it.

Friday 25 April 1958

Acker Bilk can't stay away. He is the first man to appear at the Cavern in a bowler: another one is coming up soon.

Saturday 3 May 1958

Summer is a-comin' so how about a riverboat shuffle with the Cy Laurie Jazz Band, the Merseysippis, the final of the Lonnie Donegan Skiffle Contest and another 'Miss Cavern' competition.

Thursday 15 May 1958

The *Jazz At The Philharmonic* tour with Oscar Peterson, Ella Fitzgerald and Dizzy Gillespie plays at the Odeon. Some say that the musicians came to the Cavern when it had finished, but I have my doubts.

Friday 16 May 1958

The gospel singer, Sister Marie Knight and the first appearance by Humphrey Lyttelton, with support from the ever-present Merseysippis. Marie Knight recorded the original version of "Come Tomorrow", a Top 10 hit for Manfred Mann in 1965. **John Lawrence**[100]: "Marie Knight was a charming lady and she sang spirituals with Humphrey Lyttelton's band. She had recorded with Sister Rosetta Tharpe, but when I mentioned her to Rosetta, she was scathing and said that Marie hadn't lived a blameless life like herself. We now know that Rosetta was something of a hypocrite."

Steve Voce[101]: "The Merseysippi Jazz Band would stay behind after all the music had finished officially in the Cavern and we would hold jam sessions or parties there. It was Dick Goodwin's responsibility to make sure that the place was locked up and there was a big roll-down door, a massively heavy thing which you had to reach up and pull down. This particular night we were coming out in the small hours of the morning and the two tallest guys were Ken Baldwin and John Lawrence. These two fellows with Dick in the middle were reaching up to pull it down, but Dick couldn't reach. The door came flying down and Dick, who was still trying to reach it, didn't get out of the way in time and it hit him fully on the bridge of the nose. It seemed so funny to us at the time, although it must have been excruciatingly painful. Dick clapped his hand to his nose and was running round Mathew Street in small circles shouting, 'I hate you all, I hate you all.'"

After the Cavern there could be after hours drinking at the Press Club in Lime Street. I once asked Stan Reynolds if the club was for journalists and he said, "No, drunks." Ken Baldwin[102]: "The Press Club was for members of the press but they accepted associate members. Alan Sytner was an associate member. Dick Goodwin joined and then I joined, and it was a marvellous place. It was a way of drinking late, and Cecil the barman would stay there as long as you did. When the London bands came up to play, we would take the drinking members—they didn't all drink—to the Press Club and we might drink there all night. No ladies were allowed but there were card games. We would get jolly and hilarious and dawn would break at six o'clock. People would say, 'It can't be very late, the buses are still running', but we'd been there all night. Usually we would break up around two or three and Dick's mother would get extremely annoyed. One night he couldn't get in 'cause he couldn't find his key so he sat in the porch and nodded off. In the morning his mother found him in the porch and she said, 'Dick, what are on earth are you doing?' and he replied, 'I'm waiting to pay the milkman.'"

Thursday 5 June 1958

Modern jazz with the saxophonists Ronnie Ross and Red Price. Rockin' Red Price came from the Wirral. At the time, he was with Ted Heath's Orchestra but he would soon be honking in Lord Rockingham's XI.

Sunday 8 June 1958

Beryl Bryden with the Merseysippi Jazz Band. On the same night, Chris Barber's Jazz Band was playing the Empire with Sonny Terry and Brownie McGhee. By now, Alan Sytner had a very successful club and was no longer restrained by other promoters as to whom he could book. Chris Barber, however, eluded him and, indeed, other Cavern owners, as he has never played the Cavern.

Tuesday 10 June 1958

With skiffle losing its popularity, Lonnie's club became the Lonnie Donegan Folk Club, offering ballads, blues and spirituals as well as skiffle.

Saturday 14 June 1958

Alex Welsh Dixielanders with the Blue Genes Skiffle Group. Ray Ennis[103] of the Blue Genes: "What we tried to do was combine good quality music with a bit of fun. We even rehearsed comedy scenes, which we don't do now: it just comes naturally. I was always impressed by the Gin Mill Skiffle Group. Big Tony Davis had great repartee with the audience, some of the best I've seen."

Colin Middlebrough[104]: "The Gin Mills were like the Blue Genes really, neither one thing nor the other. I think the Gin Mills already had folk in mind when they were doing skiffle. It wasn't skiffle as I knew it."

Sunday 6 July 1958

Debut of the Mick Mulligan Band with George Melly. Trombonist Frank Parr[105] had been with the Merseysippis but left in 1956 and joined Mick Mulligan: "We played a lot of dance halls in Mick Mulligan's band but I always preferred jazz clubs and I liked the Cavern very much. It reminded me of the Students' Club in Bradford, which was another boiling hot, underground place. We were a little more disciplined than we're given credit for. We did have a set list although we wouldn't necessarily stick to it."

Frank Parr[106] also kept wicket for Lancashire and was considered for the England team. Unfortunately for him, his captain, Cyril Washbrook, was bowling him bouncers. "We were of different generations and he never approved of me playing jazz. I was considered for the West Indies tour of 1953 but Washy didn't like me and I was out. I was very upset at the time but it's all buried deep in the past now." Well, maybe not, there is a picture of Washbrook in Frank's apartment with the caption, "Washbrook is a wanker."

Tony Davis[107]: "We knew George Melly from Mick Mulligan's band and I liked him a lot. He would throw himself into the audience when he got shot in 'Frankie And Johnny'. The first time I saw him do it, I thought it was an accident. It was terrific. He even fell off the Philharmonic stage."

Friday 11 July 1958
A 'Miss Cavern' heat with the Merseysippi Jazz Band. As the girls showed what they'd got, Frank Robinson accompanied the girls on piano with an instrumental version of "Ugly Woman". Fortunately for him, no boyfriends recognised the tune.

Thursday 24 July 1958
Jazz trumpeter Kenny Baker, noted for his radio series, *Baker's Dozen*.

Friday 25 July 1958
A lunchtime session spelt trouble for the Texans Skiffle Group. According to Johnny Guitar's diaries, the Texans played well, but Rikki Ashen was unimpressed and cancelled future bookings. Annoyed by this, Alan Caldwell (later Rory Storm) sacked the bass player, Spud Ward. Maybe this spurred Johnny Guitar to think about his own future as he went to the Employment Exchange. Some good news—his girlfriend, Pat, has almost finished his pullover. A week later, it's finished and Johnny gives her some bath salts.

Friday 1 August 1958
The Merseysippis, the Wall City Jazzmen and skiffle groups. **Kingsize Taylor**[108]: "We were on with the Merseysippis and they assumed we would be playing skiffle. They weren't amused when they found we had changed to rock'n'roll. We only did one spot as the manager didn't want us back. I can't remember if we got paid or not, but it would only have been peanuts anyway."

Thursday 28 August 1958
Don Rendell's trumpet player, Bert Courtney, with his own group. On the same day, Jim Ireland tells of his plans for a luxury jazz club, the Mardi Gras. It will open six days a week, three of them

offering local groups the chance of playing (that is, playing for free).

Sunday 14 September 1958
A touring package, *Jazz From Carnegie Hall*, was at the Empire, featuring the twin trombones of J.J. Johnson and Kai Winding. **John Parkes**[109] of the Merseysippi Jazz Band recalls, "J.J. Johnson came down the Cavern and I said, 'Are you going to play for us, J.J?' and he said, 'That's a thing I never do. I've come to hear you play.' Here's J.J. Johnson, the most famous trombone player in the world, sitting there and nodding approvingly while my nerves are going." On the other hand, professional musicians working at the Grafton or Reece's Grill Room would jam at the Cavern when they had finished.

Friday 26 September 1958
American blues shouter from the Count Basie band, Jimmy Rushing, known as Mr Five-by-Five because of his height and girth, with the Merseysippis and Ralph Watmough jazz bands

Saturday 4/ Sunday 5 October 1958
The Cy Laurie Jazz Band. Ken Colyer, as eccentric as Laurie, considered that only he and Laurie were flying the flag for authentic New Orleans music in the UK, and he called Laurie a traitor when he moved to India to study comparative religions.

Saturday 11 October 1958
Lonnie Donegan played the Empire the week commencing 6 October 1958, and at Saturday lunchtime, he visited his club at the Cavern. He came with his compère, Des O'Connor. The Liverpool solicitor **David Deacon**[110] recalls, "The meetings were wonderful and I got an invitation to meet Lonnie at 1.30pm at the Cavern and when I got there, he was at the bottom of the steps, shaking hands with everybody as they came in. It made me think, 'If I can meet a star like this when I am 15, I can meet anyone'—and indeed it has worked out that way." Lonnie was convinced that he saw the Beatles as the Quarry Men play that afternoon but that is unlikely. Even if he had, why would he remember? The club kept going, with a move to Sampson and Barlow's until the end of 1959.

In the wake of Alan Sytner's initial success, many new clubs had opened on Merseyside. Jimmy Ireland had tried jazz at the Minorca Coffee Bar in Tarleton Street and then he opened the Mardi Gras, which had been the Crompton Club, on 30 October 1958. It was in Mount Pleasant and near the Adelphi Hotel. The advertisements stressed that the club was very different from the Cavern: "Come and enjoy genuine jazz in luxurious surroundings." It had carpets and furniture, was licensed and could admit the same number as the Cavern. The Mardi had top-line guests including John Dankworth, Kenny Ball and, most significantly, Muddy Waters.

Brian Linford[111], who managed the Mardi Gras, recalls, "Kenny Ball was on the first week that the Mardi opened. Unfortunately, he felt that his loyalty was to the Iron Door. There was a difference between the Mardi Gras and the Cavern as they had their jazz bands and we had ours. When the Cavern decided to abandon jazz, we took on most of the jazz bands that were playing in the Cavern."

Ralph Watmough[112]: "The Mardi Gras was far superior to the Cavern. It was a much superior set-up as it was a genuine night club and we used to have some very good sessions there."

Music fan **Valerie Dicks**[113]: "There was rivalry between the Cavern and the Mardi Gras, but the Cavern was definitely the place to see someone. It had atmosphere whereas the Mardi was up-market and didn't quite make it. I associate jazz with dark, dank, seedy places."

Friday 31 October/ Saturday 1 November 1958

Mickey Ashman and his Ragtime Band with the Merseysippi Jazz Band. Ashman had played double bass with Lonnie Donegan's skiffle group and now had his own band. Ragtime though was out of date and *The Sting* wouldn't be around until 1973.

Sunday 2 November 1958

A strong bill with Dickie Bishop, Mickey Ashman and the Merseysippis. It needed to be strong to compete with Muddy Waters at the Mardi Gras.

Sunday 30 November 1958

Beryl Bryden with the Alex Welsh Dixielanders and the Merseysippi Jazz Band with vocalists, Clinton Ford and Jill Martin

Sunday 7 December 1958

One night "Festival of Jazz" with Acker Bilk, Cy Laurie, Bruce Turner and Ron McKay

Ron McKay[114]: "We came down here to do a Sunday job but we had nothing to do all day Sunday and so I said I would take them to a shebeen I knew in Upper Parliament Street. There were two big lads who were trying to cut each other to pieces with razors, and I had to push the band under the stairs. Acker said, 'Don't ever take us to a place like that again.'"

Thursday 11 December 1958

London modern jazz saxophonist Harry Klein

Sunday 21 December 1958

George Melly and Mick Mulligan's Jazz Band.

Thursday 25 December 1958

The Cavern opened on Christmas Day, but was modern jazz the right fare? The Cavern probably had 30 to 40 grumpy young men who hated Christmas. It was the last of the regular Thursday nights devoted to modern jazz. Cavern regular **Dave Williams**[115]: "As I was working in North John Street, I used to go to the Cavern at lunchtime and I would often see Clinton Ford with the Merseysippi Jazz Band. More frequently I went on Thursdays to the modern jazz nights to see the likes of Tubby Hayes, Ronnie Scott and Don Rendell. I was miffed when Merseybeat took over and modern jazz nights were discontinued. I felt I was being robbed of one of the few venues in Liverpool that had modern jazz."

Wednesday 31 December 1958

Ah, this is more like it. Seeing in the New Year with Mick Mulligan, George Melly and, yes, you've guessed it, the Merseysippis.

Sunday 11 January 1959

Mick Mulligan's Jazz Band with George Melly and Beryl Bryden

Friday 23/ Saturday 24/ Sunday 25 January 1959

Three nights on the run for the Merseysippi Jazz Band with Clinton Ford. They are joined by Acker Bilk's Paramount Jazz Band on the Sunday, who were paid £50. **Clinton Ford**[116]: "I know I was down there a lot but the Cavern was a really grotty place. I liked singing with the Merseysippis and Bags Watmough and sometimes I sang with one of the country bands. I have no particular preference for either, although I have a lifelong aversion to my hit record, 'Old Shep'. That has stuck to me like chewing gum."

Sunday 1 February 1959
Terry Lightfoot's New Orleans Jazz Band with the Merseysippis and Clinton Ford and Beryl Bryden. A great night out—well, maybe not. Johnny Guitar's diary says, "Al and I went to Cavern. Not much good."

Friday 27 March/ Saturday 28 March 1959
Come along please: it's the Cavern debut of Bob Wallis and his Storyville Jazzmen

Sunday 29 March 1959
Mick Mulligan's Jazz Band with George Melly, supported by the Texans and Blue Genes skiffle group. So, three noted front men of the 60s (George Melly, Rory Storm and Ray Ennis) share the stage. **Johnny Guitar**[117]: "I liked George Melly very much although I preferred it when he sang with the Merseysippis, and I also liked Acker Bilk. Ron McKay's skiffle group with Brian Newman was excellent. I used to sit on the wooden chairs and I liked to sit in the middle so that I had a clear view of the stage. I liked jazz but I knew rock'n'roll was coming in and that was more my type."

Ralph Ellis[118] of the Blue Genes: "The front line of a normal trad jazz band would be clarinet, trombone and trumpet, but we had three guitars, and Ray and I used to play harmony on our guitars. That was the sound we had—a rock'n'roll front line with a trad jazz rhythm section. We had double bass, drums and Tommy Hughes and then Pete Moss playing driving banjo, which you can hear on our demo of 'Yes Sir That's My Baby'." Many private recordings of the Bluegenes exist, which reveal that they were magpies, putting several influences into one song. In the course of a single track, you can hear trad, rock'n'roll, pop and music hall as well as their own lively personalities.

Ron Jones[119]: "I lived round the corner from the Pivvy, the Pavilion in Lodge Lane, and I saw Ken Colyer and Lonnie Donegan there. I found out that they had jazz at the Cavern and so myself and a mate started going down there. I saw the gradual introduction of rock'n'roll, particularly in the early days with the Blue Genes. They were like a tame rock'n'roll band at that stage: they were

palatable to the jazz crowd but they also appealed to teenagers like me who were just discovering rock'n'roll. My favourite performer was George Melly because he was such a showman. He was so entertaining and so theatrical singing those old Bessie Smith songs."

Monday 30 March 1959
Mickey Ashman plays jazz while Dickie Bishop, the Blue Genes and the Texans offer skiffle. From Johnny Guitar's diaries: "Cavern. Valerie never turned up. Our amplifier never worked. Borrowed Blue Genes' amplifier. Played lousy."

Saturday 4 April 1959
Birmingham's Zenith Six Jazz Band with the Blue Genes
On 6 April 1959 Bruce McCaskill writes to the BBC, requesting an audition for the Blue Genes and saying that they played 'rhythm and blues'. This is a curious description but it is possibly because Robin Boyle had hosted a BBC jazz series, *Rhythm And Blues*, which had been similarly misnamed.

Sunday 12 April 1959
The Merseysippi Jazz Band with three guest vocalists—Clinton Ford, Jill Martin and Beryl Bryden—and the Blue Genes as support.

Saturday 18 April 1959
Syd Lawrence Dixielanders with vocalist Peggy Karvelle: Syd Lawrence was a trumpeter with the BBC Northern Variety Orchestra, who played jazz on the side. In 1967, he formed a Glenn Miller tribute orchestra and secured his future.
On April 30, the Texans were on Radio Luxembourg's *Amateur Skiffle Club* programme playing 'Midnight Special'.

Saturday 2 May 1959
Blues singer, The Angel, plus the London-based Mike Daniels Jazz Band and the Swinging Blue Genes: note their new name.

Sunday 3 May 1959
Alex Welsh Dixielanders with Beryl Bryden, supported by the Swinging Blue Genes.

Sunday 10 May 1959
Dr Jazz, trumpeter Sonny Morris and the Swinging Blue Genes

Friday 15 May 1959
Climax Jazz Band and the Swinging Blue Genes

Friday 29 May 1959

Squire Richard Colbreck's Jazz Band with the Climax Jazz Band, the Swinging Blue Genes and the Connaughts and the Metronomes skiffle groups

Sunday 31 May 1959

Cy Laurie Jazz Band. The Swinging Blue Genes couldn't make it at the last minute and asked the Texans to step in.

Despite being dry (even if the patrons smuggled in drink), the Cavern's membership reached 25,000 in two years, and the figures are surprisingly high in view of the dinginess of the Cavern and the fact that it concentrated on jazz. Alan Sytner's lunchtime sessions had been a brilliant innovation but he was losing the plot with bingo afternoons.

Although the club was thriving, there were flies in the ointment. Sytner was easily bored and, recently married, he was spending most of his time in London. He had a lavish lifestyle, confusing personal and company expenditure and buying expensive sports cars he could ill afford. Although the club had started successfully, it was running into trouble. Skiffle had lost its novelty appeal: modern jazz had only an élitist following: and trad fans were moving to the newer and plusher Mardi Gras, not to mention the Merseysippis themselves.

Beat music was threatening jazz's popularity, and **Alan Sytner**[120] had no interest in that. "Whatever they played, it was all crap. Not just the Beatles, all of them, but it was very popular and people wanted it to happen. Wednesday night was talent night, but I didn't want to turn the club into no talent nights." To make matters worse, the commissionaires were ineffective and from to time, fights between rival gangs could break out.

By June 1959 it looked as though the Cavern might have to close in view of Alan Sytner's debts. **Gordon Vickers**[121]: "I got a call from Dr Sytner, Alan's father, and he said that he had some words with his son, and his son had left Liverpool. He asked me if I wanted to buy the Cavern and I said, 'No thanks, I am too busy with other promotions.'"

John Parkes[122]: "I can remember Alan Sytner putting the Cavern up for sale. He wanted £2,000 and he said that anyone who had £2,000 could have it. After one lunchtime jazz session, I went to see my nan, my mother's mother, to see if she'd lend me £2,000. She had £2,000 but she wouldn't let me have it because it sounded too precarious."

Saturday 6 June 1959

All-nighter with the Graham Stewart Jazz Band, the Climax Jazz Band and the Blue Genes Skiffle Group. Finished at 6am.

Sunday 7 June 1959

Cut rate summer prices to see Mickey Ashman with the Swinging Blue Genes

Friday 12 June 1959

The Climax Jazz Band, supported by the Swinging Blue Genes and the Texans. According to Johnny Guitar's diaries: "Played at Cavern, played lousy. Took girl to Pier Head. She'd been engaged, so I ditched her."

An indication that Alan Sytner was past caring. The *Echo* ad says, "Britain's Greatest Jazz Club. We are not naming the bands. Everyone knows they're always the best." Alan Sytner had moved to London to work for the National Jazz Federation. His accountants were the same as his father's and Joe asked one of the company's clerks, Ray McFall, to take over the running of the club.

Sunday 21 June 1959

Dick Charlesworth City Gents Jazz Band and the Swinging Blue Genes. **Ray Ennis**[123]: "Dick Charlesworth looked like a bank manager with his bowler hat, black jacket and pinstripe trousers. They were a very good band. I don't remember any of the visiting jazz bands being bad: they were all good players."

Saturday 27 June/ Sunday 28 June 1959

Acker Bilk's Paramount Jazz Band. The Saturday session is an all-nighter. Johnny Guitar took a girl to the Pier Head at two in the morning. His diary records that it was a 'good night'.

On Saturday evening, 25 July 1959 the Blue Genes recorded two songs for *The Carroll Levis Talent Show*, which was broadcast on the BBC Light Programme on 9 September. They performed 'Guitar Boogie Shuffle' and 'Streamline Train' and were paid 24 guineas plus £32 for hotel and train fares. This was, hopefully, split between the six of them, although with Bruce McCaskill signing the contract, one never knows.

Tommy Hughes[124]: "Bruce McCaskill's dad was an electrician and he had a job in Cleethorpes. He said, 'Why don't you come here and play?' Bruce told the audience, 'We're going to do a tour of the east coast.' People didn't travel much then and most of the audience wouldn't even know where the east coast was. We got to Cleethopes and there were no bookings but we spoke to the fella who ran the bar where his dad was staying. We got one booking but Bruce told the *West Derby Reporter* about it and our tour was in the papers. We had a good time though: the trawler men looked after us."

Sunday 9 August 1959

Ken Colyer's Jazz Band with the Swinging Blue Genes. **Ray Ennis**[125] of the Blue Genes: "We didn't look forward to supporting Ken Colyer because his fans despised anything outside his music. We were totally outside his music and we would get a lot of heckles. People would shout 'Get off' and they were very bigoted. They turned the seats round and faced the back until Ken came back on. I said, 'It's lovely to be playing to all these smiling chair-backs.'"

Tom Jones[126] of the Wall City Jazzmen: "That rings true because those New Orleans fans were like that, bloody crazy. Most of those New Orleans band were awful anyway and Ken Colyer is one of the worst trumpet players I have ever heard. Still, he had a cult following and he used to fill the clubs. I've got a photograph of myself shaking hands with him, but that must be before I'd heard him. Alex Welsh, Kenny Ball and Mike Cotton were far better players."

Saturday 22 August 1959

Al Storm and the Hurricanes and Mathew Street Skiffle Group. The Texans Skiffle Group has progressed and Alan Caldwell is halfway to becoming Rory Storm.

Friday 4 September 1959

The Southern Stompers, Johnny Goode and the Country Kinfolk, and Hank Walters and the Dusty Road Ramblers. **Hank Walters**[127]: "Johnny Goode was a big strapping blond lad with curly hair, a handsome fella and a good entertainer. A few years later, he said, 'You're looking old, Hank.' A few years went by and I sat looking at Johnny Goode and realised that he wore a toupee. Eddie

Miles said, 'Tell him to take off his toupee and put his false teeth on the counter and ask him who looks the oldest now.'"

Saturday 5 September 1959

Johnny Guitar's diary shows how he had to juggle playing times, transport and personal relationships: "Cavern jazz club, all nighter. Went to Cavern, played good. Pat came to take photos. Got back in van and went to St Luke's Hall in Crosby. Played okay. Pat took photos. Drove back to Cavern and played again. Joan was there, but very cool, so I left her and went with Pat and Lil. Stayed 'til end." A further note says, "Joan's a nice kid. I'll see her in the Cavern next Saturday."

Friday 11 September 1959

Ken Colyer Jazzmen and the Red River Jazzmen. Not a Blue Gene in sight.

Saturday 12 September 1959

The Saints and Kenny Baker play jazz and the Texans add skiffle. Johnny Guitar records, "Cavern. Ritchie (Ringo Starr) could only play first stand. Charlie and I spent hours in town trying to get bass E guitar string. Got one for £2.17.6d, put down 30 shillings, pay next week. Played okay first stand. Alan Hardy played second, not bad. Joan from Martin's didn't turn up. Joan Rimmer was there but we never spoke. Picked up nice girl from Kirkby. We went to Pier Head, good time."

Sunday 27 September 1959

Dick Charlesworth's Jazz Band and the Swinging Blue Genes. That same night, the Weavers, Sonny Terry and Brownie McGhee, and Johnny Duncan and his Bluegrass Boys were whooping it up at the Empire.

Although the Beatles found success at the Cavern in Ray McFall's tenure, **Alan Sytner**[128] is sure of his place in history: "Without me, no Cavern: without me, no Beatles: without me, none of those bloody things really. If there had not been a Cavern, none of this would have happened. The talent came out at the Cavern, there was nowhere else and there wouldn't have been anywhere else because the Cavern created a precedent. People opened the Mardi Gras and the Iron Door and all the others, but they didn't think of it for themselves: they looked at the Cavern and created an alternative. None of the owners had any interest in music or knew anything about music. They thought it was a good business and jumped on the bandwagon. I don't think any of this would have happened without me. Obviously, Lennon and McCartney were geniuses, but would they have flourished without the Cavern? If they had been playing in church halls in Maghull, would anyone have taken any notice?"

Friday 2 October 1959

The Jazz Hatters and the Dark Town Skiffle Group were playing at the Cavern, but Johnny Guitar gave them a miss: "Walked to West Derby to see new club, the Casbah. Quite good. Tried to get a booking but the Quarry Men are playing there."

3

NEED A SHOT OF RHYTHM AND BLUES

Cavern owner:
Ray McFall,
First years, 1959-1961

Ray McFall[129] was a 32-year-old accounts clerk who worked for the company which dealt with the Cavern's finances. "The Cavern concentrated on traditional jazz but it also featured modern jazz. Skiffle came in, mushroomed enormously and went out equally quickly. Alan Sytner promoted modern jazz, which he liked, but it was foreign to me and an acquired taste and, more importantly, loss making. Of the five days he was open, two were taken up with skiffle and modern jazz and the other three were traditional jazz, so he retained Friday, Saturday and Sunday for traditional jazz. Attendances declined and Alan went to London where he went to see if somebody wanted to acquire an interest, and his father looked after the place. Dr Sytner had enough to do and he wanted to dispose of it quickly, so we came to an agreement. The deal was done and the club reopened, if you could ever say it closed, on 3 October 1959."

McFall bought the Cavern for £2,750 and stated that he wanted to "put Liverpool on the map as the leading jazz centre in the country outside London". He added, "I have long felt that something needs to be done to draw off the excess heat when the club is full." Fine words, but, as it turned out, the first objective was ditched and the second proved impossible.

A trump card was employing the powerfully built but friendly, 29-year-old, former Guardsman **Paddy Delaney**[130] to head his security. "I said I'd do it for £1 a night. I wore an evening suit with the full regalia. It was too formal for the Cavern, but I had brought it with me from the Locarno where I was a trainee manager. I thought it was a club with soft lights and carpet but it was a dank, dark cellar. The dress of the day was then a big fluffy pullover with corduroy trousers and rope sandals. Teddy Boys were taking over the club and I had read about the trouble with Teddy Boys in the *Echo* and I knew I had to sort it out. I did get a broken jaw because one of them came at me from behind, but I did put five of them that night in hospital. My main rule was that when people were banned, they were banned for life. Too many clubs let them back after a week or so and then the trouble started again. I told Ray McFall that I could clean the place up, but it would take three months and I'd need more men. That's the story and I never looked back. I was there fifteen years." Delaney did his job very effectively: he knew how to resolve problems and how to escort trouble-makers off the premises peacefully.

Saturday 3 October 1959

This was the opening night under Ray McFall's regime. A strong bill with Acker Bilk and his Paramount Jazz Band and the American blues duo, Sonny Terry and Brownie McGhee.

Ron McKay[131]: "Sonny Terry, who was blind, would say, 'Where are you going?', and Brownie would come with us. We would get back in the bandwagon, and Sonny would say, 'Where you been?' Brownie would say, 'Oh, I just been a little walk.' 'But you had cream cakes.' 'No, I ain't, I ain't had no cream cakes.' 'Yes, you have. Why didn't you get me a cream cake? I wanted a cream cake.' This absurd conversation could go on for hours. Sonny did something like a fox hunt with his mouth organ, which was very clever."

Alan Stratton[132]: "I loved having the Americans at the Cavern. People like Brownie McGhee were playing guitars like you never heard. In Liverpool, guitarists would play little solos for maybe fifteen seconds but these guys were going for a minute or a minute and a half with wonderful chords. I used to think, 'How can a guy play all those notes and know what's coming next?'"

Ray Ennis[133]: "Sonny Terry and Brownie McGhee were out of this world. They were great showmen who managed to sound like their records, which were also great. They were natural entertainers and it didn't seem to bother them whether they were in a small club or on a big stage. They had no egos at all. I stood in awe and watched them."

Mike McCartney[134]: "I saw Sonny Terry and Brownie McGhee too, who were fantastic. At first we didn't like the Cavern because it was jazz, George Melly stuff, and I never liked trad. It was like a failed version of American music. I loved Art Blakey and Thelonius Monk who came to the Phil, but the Cavern as a jazz venue left me cold. Then slowly it went to rock'n'roll, starting with the lunchtime sessions. That was more like it, and I saw rock'n'roll take over."

Saturday 10 October 1959

Kenny Baker, the Zenith Six Jazz Band and the Dark Town Skiffle Group. Meanwhile, the Merseysippis are at the Mardi Gras in Mount Pleasant (Friday October 9) followed by the Blue Genes

with the Chris Hamilton Jazz Man (10) and the Fairweather Brown All Stars with the Bags Watmough Band (11).

Saturday 17 October 1959

The Yorkshire Jazz Band topped the bill, but the support, Al Storm and the Hurricanes, held the attention. The Hurricanes with Ringo Starr wore telephone-box red suits, but according to Johnny Guitar's diaries, there were "some complaints about us." Maybe the colour didn't go with the décor. **Ray McFall**[135]: "The club's fortunes were going down and there was a tremendous interest for beat music. Skiffle had come and gone and I felt that I had to introduce beat music steadily, which worked very well. It took two or three years for jazz to be phased out and some bands like Acker Bilk's retained their popularity. He opened the club for me and maintained regular appearances throughout."

Sunday 18 October 1959

Mick Mulligan Band with George Melly, supported by Swinging Blue Genes. In a wonderful phrase, Ray McFall says that George Melly was always looking for "the available femininity."

Thursday 22 October 1959

Eric Ferguson and Syd Levin came from Manchester to play modern jazz. Syd Levin couldn't be too anti-rock'n'roll as he proposed Al Storm and the Hurricanes for the Musicians' Union.

Friday 23 October 1959

Al Storm and the Hurricanes get £3.10.0d for their efforts. Johnny Guitar's amp packed up in the first set and he had to pay 8/6d for a taxi to borrow one from the Blue Genes.

Thursday 29 October 1959

Modern jazz with saxophonist Joe Harriott and pianist Eric Ferguson. After this gig, Harriott joined the Modern Jazz Quartet for a UK tour.

Friday 30 October 1959

Country meets skiffle with Johnny Duncan and his Blue Grass Boys, Johnny Goode and the Country Kinfolk and Hank Walters with his Dusty Road Ramblers.

Sunday 1 November 1959

Acker Bilk's Paramount Jazz Band with the Blue Genes and the Hurricanes. From Johnny Guitar's diaries: "Just going home when a chap in a taxi wanted a trio for the Boomerang Club. Went in taxi with our stuff. Played okay and got £2 each."

Monday 2 November 1959

Now called the Lonnie Donegan Club, the Monday night residency only lasts until the end of the year.

Ray McFall was also very lucky in having exceptionally loyal catering staff, led by **Thelma Hargrove**[136]. "It was mainly jazz at first. You would kick off an evening with jazz, then have a group, then jazz, and a group to finish. We got mixed audiences for a time: those who liked jazz and those who liked the groups. You got the two types in there and that filled the place up. When we first went, we did Monday, Thursday, Friday, Saturday and Sunday. It was closed on Tuesday and Wednesday, and Monday wasn't much. It was the Lonnie Donegan Club and there weren't a lot of them. Thursday was modern jazz which I hated and the other days were jazz at first: then Ray McFall brought in the groups."

I was on a roll as I did this interview and asked **Thelma Hargrove**[137] what she served: "Salmon rolls, hot dogs, cheese rolls, coffee and tea. No spirits and no cigarettes, but we did have Coca-Cola and Fanta. At lunchtime we did hot dogs with onions. On an all-night session, we would do Scouse. They got a good variety."

She was assisted by her sister **Betty Fegan**[138]: "They used to say that nobody made coffee like the Cavern. We would do it half milk and half water."

Thelma Hargrove[139]: "Quite right. We would put the coffee in the cups and put the milk on top of it. It was nice, wasn't it? We had a big teapot too, but the biggest sale was with coffee and soft drinks."

Saturday 7 November 1959

All nighter with Cy Laurie, Bob Wallis, the Wall City Jazzmen and Al Storm and the Hurricanes. Johnny Guitar wrote, "Played good, went down well, got rise. Al and I stayed until 3.30pm. Got taxi home with two girls."

Thursday 12 November 1959

Humphrey Lyttelton Jazz Band

Friday 20 November 1959

It took a month but Al was now Rory, hence arriving at Rory Storm and the Hurricanes. They supported the Red River Jazzmen. Johnny Guitar writes, "Played good and went down well. Took girl to bus stop. May see her next Friday." **Dave Jamieson**[140]: "Ringo would bang both cymbals for 'Johnny B Goode' and Johnny Guitar would lean right back and put his head under the ride cymbal as Ringo was banging away. Rory didn't have a good voice but that band had a lot of charisma."

Mike Byrne[141]: "Rory would make use of anything and the others would have to get out of the way. One of his tricks was kicking his leg over the mike and the mike would be full height, about five foot six."

Saturday 21 November 1959

Dizzy Burton's Aces plus Johnny Goode and the Country Kinfolk

Sunday 22 November 1959

Mick Mulligan's Jazz Band with George Melly and the Swinging Blue Genes

Friday 27 November 1959

The Southern Stompers with Rory Storm and the Hurricanes. From Johnny Guitar's diaries: "Cavern, played lousy due to Ritchie not playing (John B stepped in but it went down awful). Maureen was there but she got sick of waiting for me as I was with two other girls."

Sunday 29 November 1959

New Orleans pianist, Champion Jack Dupree enjoyed his UK tour so much that he settled in Yorkshire. He is supported by the Cy Laurie Jazz Band.

Saturday 5 December 1959

The Saints Jazz Band, Eddie and the Cadillacs and Rory Storm and the Hurricanes. Storm was a last minute substitute for the Darktown Skiffle Group. Johnny Guitar writes, "Jive Hive, Crosby, 8.15 to 8.45, 10.45 to 11.15 and Cavern, 9.15 to 10. Al James took us in van. Went down well at Cavern, played okay at Crosby."

Sunday 6 December 1959

George Melly[142] with Mick Mulligan's Jazz Band: "We used to play the Bodega in Manchester on Saturday and the Cavern on Sunday. The Beatles used to play in our interval. We ran over the road to the Grapes when they were on, and Lennon always resented British jazz. He used to say that these old men had got in their way and they would have been more successful earlier. My father much preferred it when we moved from the Cavern to the Mardi Gras as it was a much more commodious place."

Saturday 12 December 1959

All night session with Terry Lightfoot's New Orleans Jazz Band (actually from Potters Bar), the Yorkshire Jazz Band, the Red River Jazzmen, the Swinging Blue Genes and Rory Storm and the Hurricanes. From Johnny Guitar's diaries: "We bought new amp. We played Crosby, went to the Cavern, then to Crosby, and back to the Cavern for all nighter. Played excellent, but bad reception. Stayed with Lesley and Carol. My Crosby girl was there."

Thursday 17 December 1959

Modern jazz saxophonist Kathy Stobart

Thursday 31 December 1959

Seeing in the New Year with Mickey Ashman's Jazz Band, Yorkshire Jazz Band, Dallas Jazz Band, the Swinging Blue Genes, Hank Walters with his Dusty Road Ramblers—and all for 4/6d.

Friday 1/ Saturday 2/ Sunday 3 January 1960

You want to see the Cy Laurie Jazz Band? Okay, take your pick. Friday, they're with the Swinging Blue Genes: Saturday, Johnny Goode and the Country Kinfolk, and Sunday, Rory Storm and the Hurricanes

Friday 8 January 1960

The Red River Jazzmen, the Southside Jazzmen and Little Bernie and the Drifting Cowboys

First Ever Liverpool Jazz Festival— January 1960 (8 consecutive days)

It's unclear what constitutes a jazz festival as these nights look like any other and are not exclusively jazz, with country, skiffle and (Lord have Mersey) rock'n'roll groups in support. No jazz at all on Friday! The admission fee ranged from five shillings for Acker Bilk to 3/6d for Alex Welsh. The Cavern printed an impressive programme, cost two shillings, with an advert for draught Coca-Cola at 8d a glass. How big was the glass? There was also a special Souvenir Programme, cost £1, which guaranteed admission every night, a saving of 14/6d.

Around this time, it was rare to have a jazz festival outside the south of England, due to the problems in securing the leading groups. In pro-

moting the festival, the *Liverpool Daily Post* said, "Jazz is what you make it. Magistrates denounce it. Local authorities ban it. Educationalists think it is halfway to juvenile delinquency." Er no, that's rock'n'roll, mate.

Sunday 10 January 1960

Mr Acker Bilk's Paramount Jazz Band and Swinging Blue Genes. **Ray Ennis**[143] recalls, "Acker Bilk played with us that night. We did 'My Bucket's Got A Hole In It' and Acker sang and played clarinet with us. That was good fun but he thought that we were too loud."

The noted music critic, Derek Jewell, wrote about the audience in the *Liverpool Daily Post*, "They absorbed the music, with its catchy melodies, its powerful rhythms and its tremendous air of joyousness as if it were the breath of life itself." He added, "This is British jazz, adding elements of its own to the original American forms of several decades ago, not a pale, lifeless replica of the music produced in Basin Street."

Jewell praised Cavern favourite and now Bilk's drummer, Ron McKay, "McKay is as good a traditional-style drummer as I have heard on either side of the Atlantic, thrashing out a tremendous, thunderous beat that lifts the band on its shoulders and he also has a neat line in scat-singing." On the other hand, "The Swinging Blue Genes are, unhappily, more in line with contemporary mass-produced and mass-reflected taste—all whining words and jangling guitars. For all that, their skiffle had a certain verve and freshness which was plainly to many tastes, but not to mine."

Monday 11 January 1960

Terry Lightfoot's New Orleans Jazzmen and Hank Walters and the Dusty Road Ramblers. **Terry Lightfoot**[144]: "Memory blurs with time, but I can't remember any nastiness or aggravation about the Cavern, you know, the kind of niggling things that arise when people are packed together in an uncomfortable way."

Tuesday 12 January 1960

Alex Welsh Dixielanders and Johnny Goode and his Country Kinfolk. "Fans were thin on the ground," said the *Liverpool Daily Post*, but added that the Welsh band was impeccable: "It lifted 'Everybody Loves My Baby' a couple of feet off the ground and kept the music there for the rest of

JAZZ AT THE CAVERN

* TONIGHT
  THE NEW:—
  BASIL KIRCHIN BAND.
* FRIDAY
  THE MERSEYSIPPI!
  QUARRYMEN SKIFFLE
* SATURDAY
  THE ZENITH SIX!
  CAVENDISH SKIFFLE
* SUNDAY
  THE MERSEYSIPPI!
  DRUIDS JAZZ BAND
  BLUE GENES SKIFFLE

(LUNCHTIME JAZZ FRIDAY)

Cavern Doorman
Paddy Delaney

Mersey jazz by Don Smith

They dance all night and sleep all day

I TRIED to find out last night how teenagers can listen to jazz for 12 solid hours — and even dance to it for about ten of them.

These all-night jazz sessions are becoming regular features of Merseyside jazz life.

Tonight the Cavern Club puts on another one starting at 8 p.m. and finishing—with a bit of luck—about 8 a.m.

"We usually dance or listen until about 10 a.m.," said attractive 18-year-old Beryl Johnson, of Queens-drive, Liverpool. And she starts that sort of session after a full day at the office.

"I am not the only one. And perhaps we do get into trouble

with our parents. But we don't do anything we didn't oughter and we just get sent by the music to such an extent that we don't realise the passing of time," she said.

The same thing applies to the hepcats among the boys. Said 27-year-old builder's contractor Arthur Robins: "Once you get started it is difficult to finish with a good jazz group.

"I usually spend the following day flat on my back in bed. That's why the jazz clubs put on these all-night sessions on Saturday."

Rocking

The Graham Stewart Seven are the main attraction at tonight's all-night do at the Cavern—but they can't take it all themselves. The Bluegenes, Climax, and other jazz guests will fill in the night.

Tomorrow Mickey Ashman's Band, with the Bluegenes again, will keep the Cellar Club rocking.

The Unicorn offers the Hot Spots tonight, plus the Delicadoes. And tomorrow night what is probably Merseyside's favourite jazz outfit—the Wall

DISC of the DAY

Father of British post-war revivalist jazz George Webb (below) playing the piano at an after hours party at the Cavern in 1958

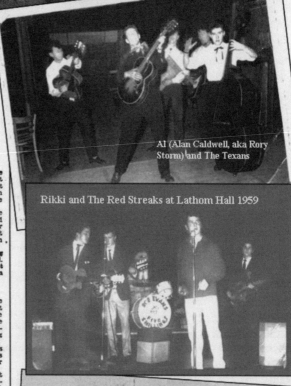

Al (Alan Caldwell, aka Rory Storm) and The Texans

Rikki and The Red Streaks at Lathom Hall 1959

Lance Fortune, the first pop star to appear at the Cavern, seen here in 1960 backed by the Jaywalkers

the evening." Three of the Merseysippi Jazz Band plus Frank Parr increased the front line of Welsh's band to six for "Blues My Naughty Sweetie Gave To Me".

Wednesday 13 January 1960

The Saints Jazz Band, Pete Haslam's Collegians, both from Manchester, with the Swinging Blue Genes. Wallis stayed over for a Sunday session: total fee for his band, £180. The Saints didn't claim to be brilliant musicians and trumpeter Bob Connell said, "I'd rather be a slow handwriter with something to say than a high-speed typist with nothing to say."

The *Liverpool Daily Post* reviewer, George Elgin, called the Swinging Blue Genes a skiffle group and remarked that "the tottering fort of skiffle has collapsed almost everywhere except in Liverpool." The reviewer commented that "many of the jiving teenagers apparently aim to be sex-kitten copies of Bardot", adding "The girl from Aigburth hitched up her black tights." Hey, Elgin, we sent you to review the music.

Mick O'Toole[145]: "As long as skiffle lasted, the Cavern lasted for me. By then I was into rock'n'roll and I couldn't see the point of spotty-faced, local lads doing third rate versions of songs that I loved. I was a purist and I never saw the Beatles."

Thursday 14 January 1960

Modern jazz session with Ronnie Scott, Bert Courtley and Pete King, with the Eddie Thompson Trio. According to the programme, "Pete King has yet to prove the wild statements about him." Did he succeed?

"Terrible," noted Johnny Guitar in his diary. The *Liverpool Daily Post* sent a grouchy reporter who complained, "I wish that one and all would not blow quite so hard into the microphone because then the hollering in my ears would stop and I would hear the music better."

Friday 15 January 1960

Johnny Duncan and his Blue Grass Boys with Hank Walters and the Dusty Road Ramblers

Saturday 16 January 1960

Third birthday night—Ken Colyer's Jazzmen and Johnny Goode and his Country Kinfolk. A country group playing to partisan Colyerites—I feel for them.

Sunday 17 January 1960

On paper, a normal night—Mickey Ashman and his Band, supported by Rory Storm and the Hurricanes—in actuality, a legendary one. Rory and his mates had been working towards rock'n'roll, but this was the night that they presented flat out, full steam ahead, raucous rock'n'roll. The audience hated them. **Johnny Guitar**[146]: "The jazz brigade was all duffle-coats and they were into trad jazz and would just about accept the Blue Genes, who did a lot of jazz numbers. We did skiffle, which was okay for a while, but we saw the way things were going with rock'n'roll. Our set list included 'Maggie May' and 'Hi-Lili, Hi-Lo' but we said, 'To hell with it, let's do some rock'n'roll.' We didn't know many numbers but we knew 'Great Balls Of Fire' and 'Whole Lotta Shakin' Goin' On', and Rory said we would throw them in. We did 'Whole Lotta Shakin'' first and I don't think we reached the second one because the atmosphere was deadly. People were whistling at us and shouting disapproval. Then came a barrage of pennies and I was ducking as those old pennies used to hurt you. The stage was covered in copper coins, and I went round later and picked them up and it came to more than our fee. When we went to get paid, Ray McFall said he was fining us 10 shillings for playing rock'n'roll and he said, 'We are not going to tolerate that music down here,' and he came to regret those words. I liked jazz but I knew that rock'n'roll was coming in and that was more my style."

Friday 22 January 1960

The Dallas Jazz Band with Little Bernie and the Drifting Cowboys

Sunday 24 January 1960

The Sonny Morris Jazz Band, the Swinging Blue Genes and Rory Storm and the Hurricanes. Rory played first at the Casbah and then here. The Cavern set was taped but where is it now?

Thursday 28 January 1960

The Betty Smith Quintet from Leicestershire

Saturday 30 January 1960

All nighter with Bob Wallis, the Saints, Johnny Goode, Hank Walters and the Blue Genes. Bob Wallis stayed over for a session on Sunday.

Saturday 6/ Sunday 7 February 1960

A blast from the past: pre-war jazz trumpeter, Nat Gonella, with the Georgia Jazzmen. In 1960 he was featured in *This Is Your Life*.

Sunday 14 February 1960

Ian Menzies and the Clyde Valley Stompers with the Swinging Blue Genes. The Scottish band made a popular album, *Have Tartan, Will Trad*.

Thursday 18 February 1960

High-powered modern jazz from the Jazzmakers (Ronnie Ross, Alan Ganley, Art Ellefson and Keith Christie)

Saturday 20 February 1960

Birmingham's Zenith Six Jazz Band with Rory Storm and the Hurricanes. Microphone trouble meant a late start.

Sunday 21 February 1960

Alex Welsh Jazz Band with the Swinging Blue Genes. **Tommy Hughes**[147]: "The first rows of seats emptied and these guys sat there with their legs up and then one of them pulled our plug out. It was a load of wires that we used to stick in a plug with matchsticks. Ralph Ellis said, 'Don't do that, you'll electrocute yourself.' This yobbo replied, 'We'll have you afterwards.' When we finished two girls came in and said, 'Those fellas are going to get you. That's Fat Harry's gang and they've got axes and they'll chop your arms off.' We stayed in the band room long after the club closed and then went out in the fog expecting to get attacked but nothing happened. Don't know why they didn't like us. Perhaps it was one of their girls fancying one of us: that could do it." (This would be the infamous Fat Harry who approached Liverpool police in the 50s offering to sort out the Teddy Boys if they paid him enough.)

Friday 26 February 1960

The Southside Jazzmen with Dale Roberts and the Jaywalkers. **Gordon Vickers**[148]: "The fans abandoned jazz at my club in Chester and I started putting guitar groups on during the interval. I would give them £2 or £3 and they would come with a side drum from Ellesmere Port on the bus. I said to Ray McFall, 'Why don't you do that?' He said, 'No, I run a jazz club.' I said, 'So do I, but skiffle has gone by the wayside'. I sent him Dale Roberts and the Jaywalkers."

Jaywalker **Dave Williams**[149]: "Dale Roberts and the Jaywalkers came from Ellesmere Port. I worked in Bowater's and I had the furthest distance to travel to get to the Cavern. I bought a scooter and I would ride with the guitar between my legs. I spent two years with the band and we did 270 gigs and I was still working in Bowater's five or six days a week."

Sunday 6 March 1960

Time for 'San Francisco Bay Blues' with the one man band, Jesse Fuller, supported by Terry Lightfoot's New Orleans Jazzmen. "Jesse Fuller had a weird machine rather like a harpsichord," says **David Deacon**[150], "but I can't tell you anymore as I am only five foot six and I wasn't at the front."

Hughie Jones[151] of the Spinners: "It was a real do-it-yourself job and it took him a long time to set up. He had a pick-up on the guitar and a microphone on the rig and as soon as he had sorted himself out, they threw the switch and the whole thing went up in sparks and it took another half-hour to get him going again. He gave us an acoustic set and it was marvellous."

Tony Davis[152]: "Jesse Fuller played a fodella which he worked with his foot and it was like a miniature double bass. He had a guitar and he had a rig round his neck with a harmonica and a kazoo. He wasn't unique as on every street corner in the south and mid-west, you would have found similar one-man bands and in London too, but he was fantastic and he did a little dance as well."

Saturday 19 March 1960

Woody Guthrie's sidekick, Cisco Houston, on an all-night session with Dick Charlesworth's City Gents, the Zenith Six, Hank Walters and Johnny Goode

Sunday 3 April 1960

Humphrey Lyttelton and his Jazz Band with Hank Walters and the Dusty Road Ramblers

Sunday 10 April 1960

Mickey Ashman's Ragtime Jazz Band with the Swinging Blue Genes

Friday 15 April 1960

The blues performer who conquered Broadway, Josh White, with Pete Haslam's Collegians Jazz Band and the Yorkshire Jazz Band. White was paid £100. The entry in John Cook's diary reads, "£2.10s—bloody hell, Barclay". **John Cook**[153]:

"That's Bob Barclay, who paid us a pittance. He was a robber. One night he gave us all £2 and Mike Paley said, 'Is it £2, Bob?' and he, quick as a flash, said, 'No, it's 30 bob. You owe me 10 shillings.' Bob Barclay once took us to the Cavern in the band bus and I went into Leeds to meet him. I said, 'Where's the band?', and he said, 'We'll pick somebody up on the way over.' We got to Manchester and we picked up Pete Appleby, who was the drummer with Mick Mulligan. We saw Brian Goldsborough walking along the street and he was an itinerant banjo player plus a frequent visitor to the jails. Good player though. We went to the Cavern—tuba, trumpet, banjo and drums. What a funny combination: the four of us as the Yorkshire Jazz Band. We started off and it was horrendous. Josh White and his sidekick Brother John Sellers were playing there that night, and so Brother John joined our band."

Steve Voce[154]: "Josh White played the Cavern and we then went to the Press Club and I took him back to my home in Crosby at about 3am. I put Josh to sleep in the spare room. Sometime later, my first wife, who didn't know he was there, was awakened by coughing. She got up, went onto the landing and turned on the light. There stood a large, naked black man who was looking for the lavatory. When he left, he wrote on the wallpaper of my jazz room, 'Steve, I'll never forget you, Your true friend, Josh White' and I never had the room re-papered."

Tony Davis[155]: "Josh White was a professional to his fingertips and we did a Pete Seeger fundraiser with him in London and Josh had Jack Fallon on bass. He did 'Evil Hearted Woman Blues' and on the last chord, he snapped a string. 'Aaah,' he said, 'I am going to have to change it.' While he was doing it, Jack was playing away and Josh started to sing 'Summertime' gently, and then he put the string on and he tuned it up while he was singing 'Summertime'. Then we went to see him at the Cavern and the fifth song in was 'Evil Hearted Woman Blues' and on the last note, ping!, the string goes again. He said, 'Gonna have to change the string', and Jack started playing and it was exactly the same thing. The first time it was breathtaking and the second time it was breathtaking for a different reason."

Sunday 17 April 1960

Mike Daniels' Delta Jazz Band with Hank Walters and the Dusty Road Ramblers. On the same day, Sister Rosetta Tharpe returned to Liverpool for a concert at the Empire with Chris Barber's Jazz Band. **Tony Davis**[156]: "We loved Rosetta dearly and I remember my wife hauling her into her corset when she was at the Empire. She said, 'C'mon, honey, heave!' We sat in her dressing room at the Empire and one of her fans asked to see her. She said he could come in and he was a colossal black guy who said, 'Hello der sister, how are you?' in a broad Liverpool accent. She could have held her position as a guitar-player in almost any band. She wasn't a great picker, it is the same phrases on all her records, but the rhythm was terrific. She and Ottilie Patterson did a duet of 'The Saints' (Sings) and it made the band jump. She could lift a whole band. She came down to the Cavern after she had played the Empire and we had a party for her. She was imbibing considerably and her husband was a lovely man who was a minister. She was sitting on everyone's knee and cuddling everybody."

Friday 22 April 1960

Skiffle had moved on: the Chas McDevitt Four with Shirley Douglas, plus the Southside Jazzmen. "The Cavern was known as a jazz club so I felt we were on the periphery of the scene when we played there," says **Chas McDevitt**[157], "It was an okay night, but nothing special."

Sunday 1 May 1960

Only a fortnight after her appearance at the Empire, Sister Rosetta Tharpe made another visit to the city, backed in the Cavern by Mickey Ashman's Ragtime Jazz Band and supported by the Swinging Blue Genes. **Ray Ennis**[158] of the Blue Genes: "Sister Rosetta Tharpe was wonderful— when she sang. She was preaching to the audience like they were in chapel which didn't go down well with Scousers who wanted to hear her sing."

John Cochrane[159]: "Sister Rosetta Tharpe had an amazing voice and a guitar that might have been a metal dobro. It certainly looked good and I had never seen anything like it before."

David Deacon[160]: "The Cavern was a safe place to be, not having the stress of other places in the heart of town. Not having a liquor licence was part of that, but I also think it was for people who wanted to hear the music. I felt that we were privileged to see people like John Lee Hooker, Sister Rosetta Tharpe, Jesse Fuller and Memphis Slim. I loved Sister Rosetta Tharpe and I saw her as a big star, although she wasn't making hit records."

Denny Seyton[161]: "I was in the dressing room with Memphis Slim and he drank half a bottle of whisky before he went on stage. I had never seen anybody drink that much whisky before, but he still played well."

Saturday 21 May 1960

The Saints Jazz Band, the Vintage Jazz Band (with Ken Sims and Ian Wheeler), the Swinging Blue Genes and Johnny Goode and the Country Kinfolk

Wednesday 25 May 1960

Come back, Rory Storm, all is forgiven. The jazz festival was not a financial success, and already, Ray McFall had lost several hundred pounds. Rock'n'roll nights were popular in the suburbs but there was no outlet in the city centre. Ray McFall bit the bullet and on 25 May 1960 the Cavern held its first Rock Night, featuring Cass and the Cassanovas (who later became the Big Three) and Rory Storm and the Hurricanes. The jazz fans stayed away but it attracted a new, younger audience—paying 2/6d admission—and Ray McFall expected that he would have mid-week rock'n'roll, Thursday modern jazz and weekend trad. The Rock Nights were such a success that the rest would be elbowed away. And dig Jonny Guitar, dressing for the occasion in black shirt and white tie. Well, the band was getting more than a £3.10.0d support fee.

Wednesday 1 June 1960

'Direct from the Cliff Richard Show, Billy Woods Five'. Er, yes. Bet most people went for Rory Storm and the Hurricanes.

Sunday 12 June 1960

The US blues and folk musicians may not have been money-spinners but Ray McFall is to be applauded for his bookings: this time, the albino barrelhouse pianist, Speckled Red. Support from Alex Welsh's jazz band.

Wednesday 15 June 1960

Rock night with Cass and the Cassanovas as well as Eddie Storm and the Clubmen

Wednesday 22 June 1960

Dale Roberts and the Jaywalkers, with Danny Leroy and the Tornados, but not *the* Tornados.

Wednesday 6 July 1960

Fantastic! Local rock'n'roll acts: Dale Roberts and the Jaywalkers and, wait for it, Wump and his Werbles. **John Cochrane**[162]**,** drummer with Wump and His Werbles, recalls, "One of the band members rang Ray McFall and said, 'This brilliant new band is available for one night only.' We had played about three gigs. He said he would fit us in and we were totally out of our depth. We were terrified because the Cavern had a reputation that if the audience didn't like you, you got pulled apart. There was no back exit so the groups had to leave through the front. If you hadn't gone down very well, you would have to hide in the back until everyone had gone. To make it worse, one of the band members had a father-in-law in the fruit business in Mathew Street and he said, 'If you go in there, you won't come out alive', which did nothing for our confidence."

Dave Williams[163]: "What a bunch of characters Wump and his Werbles were. The drummer didn't have the little screw that kept the top of the cymbal on. He was crashing away on this and it came off the stand and flew into the audience. It could have taken someone's head off."

John Cochrane[164]:"Dale Roberts and the Jaywalkers, who were also from the Wirral, had the full Cliff Richard gear, shiny suits and matching hankies, and the right equipment. We were playing Little Richard songs with two guitars and a snare drum. The Jaywalkers sensed that there could be a riot so they packed up and left. We felt embarrassed when we saw the amount of equipment they were taking away. Our performance was a complete disaster, but the audience left as well. We must be the only band to have emptied the Cavern. I was in a group that I hoped people would forget. Unfortunately, because of the ridiculous name, it keeps coming up all the time." Wump and his Werbles were given £5 to share between them. And Dale Roberts and the Jaywalkers were to sell them their suits.

Sunday 10 July 1960

Humphrey Lyttelton's Jazz Band with the Swinging Blue Genes

Wednesday 13 July 1960

The Black Cat Rhythm Group with the Delacardoes. The Delacardoes incurred Ray McFall's wrath by going over their allotted time. Their saxophonist, Neil Foster, wrote a semi-fictional account of being in a Liverpool beat group, *Cradle Of Rock* (Top F Books, 2004).

Wednesday 27 July 1960

Another significant debut—rock'n'roll instrumentals from the Remo Four.

Wednesday 30 August 1960

Sweet dreams with Dave Sampson and the Hunters, Remo Four, Royal Brothers, and Dale Roberts and the Jaywalkers. **Dave Williams**[165]: "Dave Sampson and the Hunters was a great group. The lead guitarist even changed all his strings before they went on. He had a Fender Jazzmaster with a tremolo arm and they were very good."

Thursday 1 September 1960

Jazz saxophonist and flautist Harold McNair.

Saturday 17 September 1960

The Cavern promoted a Riverboat Shuffle on the Royal Iris with Acker Bilk and his Paramount Jazz Band, Terry Lightfoot's New Orleans Jazzmen and the Swinging Blue Genes. Perfect: with their bowler hats and striped waistcoats, the Bilk band resembled riverboat gamblers. Their summer set included their Top 10 single, "Summer Set". Terry Lightfoot's brother, the banjo-playing Paddy, sat in with the Blue Genes.

Colin Middlebrough[166]: "I remember a Riverboat Shuffle with Terry Lightfoot and they had set them up on the top deck on a rough day. I went up to get some fresh air just at the point where the boat listed to starboard, and the whole drum-kit went over the side and into the Mersey. They had put a dais up, which wouldn't be allowed now with Health and Safety regulations, and whoosh! The drummer Lennie Hastings was all right, but his drums were bobbing up and down on the waves."

Wednesday 5 October 1960

Duke Duval, the Del-Renas, and the Cavern debut of Gerry and the Pacemakers. **Alan Stratton**[167] of the Black Cats: "Gerry and the Pacemakers were introduced as being directly from Blair Hall and they wore grey suits. Gerry played a Futurama guitar and I liked the way they did 'Mona Lisa' and 'Pretend'. I thought they were very professional."

Dale Roberts[168]: "Gerry and the Pacemakers was the first group on Merseyside to have its own PA system. They had a Watkins Copicat for an echo effect and I remember being knocked out the first time I heard it."

Freddie Marsden[169]: "The hardest thing was taking the bass drum into the Cavern as it was difficult to negotiate round the little tight bend at the bottom of the stairs. If there were a lot of people there, you had to lift the case above your head and work your way through the dancers. I don't think it would have worked if they had one drum-kit permanently there as everybody had their own adjustments, especially with the snare drum and cymbals. I never liked playing with anybody else's drums, but the Cavern was brilliant for sound as there was no echo and it was a dead sound so you could hear exactly what you were playing. I enjoyed every minute that I played at the Cavern, every dinner-hour, every evening, because it was always packed and we always got a good reception. The worst place to play was the Tower Ballroom in New Brighton because they never had a piano that was decently tuned. If you have a piano that's out of tune, there's nothing you can do about it."

Sunday 9 October 1960

Nat Gonella and the New Georgians Jazz Band with the Swinging Blue Genes. **Geoff Davies**[170]: "Nat Gonella was advertised as Britain's Louis Armstrong and my dad told me he had been going 30 years. I was very impressed by him and it was still a young audience. I don't recall people of my dad's age being there at all." Gonella, an Italian Cockney, had difficulty saying his r's and many people were fascinated by the way he sang 'The Isle Of Capri' (Cap-wi).

Wednesday 12 October 1960

Dale Roberts and the Jaywalkers with the Remo Four. **Dale Roberts**[171]: "We were the first group on Merseyside to wear suits. We took the sleeve of the Buddy Holly and the Crickets LP to a tailor and told him that we wanted five suits like that. Cliff Richard had just released "Nine Times Out Of Ten", which had a great bass drum part. We got the record and we played it that same day."

Tuesday 18 October 1960

Luncheon beat—the first lunchtime beat session, from noon to 2pm. **Ray McFall**[172]: "It seemed to me that working people would come into the club in the middle of the day if the supply of snacks was adequate and the supply of music was appealing." There were no guests for the session: just records, hot dogs, soup and sandwiches. A further indication, if any were needed, that beat music was taking over.

Wednesday 19 October 1960

Rock night with Cass and the Cassanovas and the Del-Renas

Friday 21 October 1960

(lunchtime) Tommy Lowe and the Metronomes again

(evening) The Noel Walker Stompers. **Noel Walker**[173]: "We had seen the Merseysippis and we wanted to form our own band. Derek Vaux had been playing tea-chest bass with a skiffle group and we formed the band shortly after I left school. Mike McCombe was the drummer and he also played with the Merseysippis for a long time. I was the leader because my parents were the only ones who let us use the telephone to get gigs and arrange things. I was a bandleader even though I had never picked up an instrument, and it became clear that I would have to be a trombone player if I wanted to play in my own band. The person who owned the Iron Door offered us six gigs if we would help him build his bar, which we did. We became a viable attraction, playing at the Iron Door, the Mardi Gras and the Cavern, and also Fort Perch Rock at New Brighton." And what did they wear? "Striped shirts and white cardboard collars. The collars went to pieces in the intense heat."

The first specifically created beat club in the city centre, the Top Ten, burnt down in mysterious circumstances. Some think its owner **Allan Williams**[174] torched the place, but he had no reason to do that. He says, admittedly with hindsight, "History would have been altered if the Top Ten had not caught fire. That would have been my Cavern club. The Cavern was only doing jazz at the time and there wasn't a venue in the centre doing rock'n'roll. Still, I opened the Blue Angel and that was a luxurious night club." A railway clerk, Bob Wooler, had gone off the rails to become the Top Ten's compère and booking manager but soon he was out of a job. He organized a few shows for the impresario, Brian Kelly, and then headed for the Cavern.

Wednesday 26 October 1960

Bob Wooler[175] sets foot in the Cavern: "The Remo Four told me about the Cavern and I went there one lunchtime. At the end of his set, Johnny Hutch of the Big Three thrust a Reslo mike at me and said, 'Make an announcement'. I'd had a little wine and I said, 'Remember all you cave-dwellers, the Cavern is the best of cellars.' The owner of the Cavern, Ray McFall, heard me—and that's how I got the job of introducing the Cavern's lunchtime sessions."

So, the most famous Woolerism came into being that first day at the Cavern. **Bob Wooler**[176]: "I didn't top 'the best of cellars' but I used to run newspaper ads for the Cavern which said, 'The venue with the menu with the mostest' or, even worse, 'Meet the beat that's reet for the feet.' I did try and put some humour into my ads. I remember, 'What is geological music?' and the answer was 'Rock, rock, rock.' One of the ads for Hambleton Hall announced 'Bob Wooler's married' and added 'to the best rock sessions in Liverpool', but that was inserted by Vic Anton and not by me. I thought it ridiculous to give me prominence in this way and besides, it wasn't even a good joke." Occasionally, Bob would amend 'the best of cellars' to 'the best of smellers', but only when Ray McFall wasn't listening.

Saturday 29 October 1960

All nighter with the Yorkshire Jazz Band, the Sonny Morris Jazz Band, the Red River Jazzmen, and Hank Walters and the Dusty Road Ramblers. Did **Hank Walters**[177] feel out of place on a jazz bill? "Not at all as I had a good blues voice and could do some Jimmie Rodgers' songs. I would go on with the Red River Jazzmen from Wigan and sing a blues with them, and they would sit in with us. They were a good band, but all the trad bands were very good. Ron McKay wanted to join our band but we didn't want a drummer at the time. He said he was short of cash."

Wednesday 2 November 1960

The first *bona fide* pop star plays the Cavern. Birkenhead's Lance Fortune had a Top 10 in

February 1960 with "Be Mine", but not much had happened since. He was backed by the Jaywalkers and supported by Cass and the Cassanovas and Nick Olsen and the Aces. Bob Dylan biographer, **Michael Gray**[178], recalls, "I went to Birkenhead School with Chris Morris and at our school concert, he was the first person I heard doing rock'n'roll. He wowed us with 'That'll Be The Day' and then he dropped out of school altogether—unforgivable at the time—and he went full-time into the music business and became Lance Fortune. He made a terrific impression on me and his performance made me realise which side of the barricades I was on."

Dave Williams[179]: "I had been in a group with Chris Morris, who became Lance Fortune, and we did make a private recording of 'That'll Be The Day' in 1957. He was a very clever lad but he opted out of going to university and went to the 2 I's and his parents were very annoyed. He had a hit with 'Be Mine' and we backed him in Northwich and in the Cavern. He was a nice singer and a good entertainer and had a good way about him. When he sang with the Jaywalkers, he did quite a bit of our act. He did 'Stuck On You' and we had to do 'Be Mine', which is just like a Buddy Holly song."

Wednesday 16 November 1960

Emile Ford and the Checkmates was the first Number One artist to play the Cavern, having topped the charts with "What Do You Want To Make Those Eyes At Me For" a year earlier. He was still a big name and 'Counting Teardrops' was a Christmas hit. Strong support from Gerry and the Pacemakers and Cass and the Cassanovas. **Ray Ennis**[180]: "Emile Ford had speakers all round the place to spread the sound around and as a result, he sounded tremendous. I was very impressed."

Saturday 26 November 1960

Act like nothing's happened: a jazz all-nighter with the Yorkshire Jazz Band, the Zenith Six and Pete Haslam's Collegians.

Wednesday 30 November 1960

Gerry and the Pacemakers with Cass and the Cassanovas. **Geoff Davies**[181]: "I'd heard about the Cavern as a jazz club and I'd been told that they were beatniks there. I liked jazz and the beatnik atmosphere intrigued me. I was seventeen and I went on the wrong night and saw Cass and the Cassanovas. I had got fed up with American rock'n'roll as it had passed its heights but I liked the night and the atmosphere."

Friday 2 December 1960

Welcome to Papa Blue's Viking Jazzmen from Denmark—Viking helmets too but no raping and pillaging is reported.

Sunday 11 December 1960

Ray Ellington with Carol Simpson, supported by the Swinging Blue Genes. **Ray Ennis**[182]: "The Ray Ellington night was a cracking one. He had Judd Proctor playing guitar who was phenomenal. I was very impressed by his car registration RE 1 on a Ford Consul. He parked in Mathew Street right outside the Cavern: you could park anywhere then."

Wednesday 14 December 1960

John Barry Seven, supported by Duke Duval and Cass and the Cassanovas. **Hank Walters**[183]: "Duke Duval was a great drummer who was very boisterous in everything he did. I hated rock'n'roll and didn't think it would last and thought the country bands had more taste and panache, but Duke Duval impressed me."

Ray McFall was looking for change. **Bob Wooler**[184]: "The country and western brigade regarded rock'n'roll groups as a novelty, while the jazz bands poured contempt on them. I got a hell of a bad name for encouraging rock'n'roll to be played at the Cavern. The Cavern was a jazz cellar and the followers didn't want rock'n'roll groups coming in."

Ken Baldwin[185] from the Merseysippis: "I can't really criticise the groups because they were pinching American songs just like us, but at the time we never bothered listening to them. It was electric noise and we were very much against that. We were so anti-beat music that we never stopped to speak to them and ask them how they were doing."

Saturday 17 December 1960

All nighter with the Clyde Valley Stompers, Terry Lightfoot's New Orleans Jazzmen, the Zenith Six Jazz Band, the Swinging Blue Genes, Hank Walters and Johnny Goode.

Saturday 24 December 1960

The Yorkshire Jazz Band with the Hillbilly Bandits

Tuesday 27 December 1960

John Tippett Jazz Band with the Swinging Blue Genes

Don Lydiatt[186] from the Merseysippis: "Amplifiers had just come in and you could pick up a guitar and get a great sound. However, you couldn't pick up a trombone or clarinet or trumpet and get a great sound—it takes hours of learning. It's remarkable when you think about it. These people had no real desire to play their instruments or undertake any proper learning, but they could get a good sound, and the Swinging Blue Genes were very good."

The Swinging Blue Genes was a hybrid in both repertoire and instrumentation, being not quite a jazz group and not quite a rock'n'roll band. **Ray Ennis**[187]: "Bob Wooler was very important. He came in when jazz was on the wane. Bob brought polish and continuity to the shows. He called us the Swinging Blue Geniuses and so we were highly flattered."

Returning from Germany, the Beatles looked and sounded very different. Their gig at Litherland Town Hall on 27 December 1960 when they were billed as "Direct from Hamburg" is legendary. Brian Kelly had booked them sight unseen and he was amazed by the reaction. Compere **Bob Wooler**[188]: "Brian Kelly then wanted to sign up the Beatles before I could get to them as he knew I promoted some dances and I might also tell Ray McFall at the Cavern about them. He got his diary out and immediately signed them for a string of dates at £7.10s, or 30 bob a man. I was talking with Dave Forshaw in the coffee-bar upstairs and he was equally impressed. He gave them some bookings at St John's Hall in Bootle."

Alex McKechnie[189]: "On the very first time they played Litherland Town Hall, everybody thought they were from Germany. Beverly Kelly had announced that they were from Germany and would be here next week. Me and my friend were so excited by the Beatles that we stood at the front of the stage. You went to a dance to show off your suit and your haircut, like me and my friend who tried to look as much like the Everly Brothers as we possibly could. We wanted to get girls

and the band was a bit of an interruption really. My friend and I stood by the front at Litherland Town Hall because the Beatles were so charismatic. They were in black leather and banging their feet on the wooden stage and we were standing at the front and getting a closer look. Two girls had black sweaters which had 'The Beatles' embroidered across the front in bright red letters. They danced right in front of the band. I never saw any merchandise for Elvis, and this is the first time I'd seen anything for a performer."

Saturday 31 December 1960

All nighter with the Yorkshire Jazz Band, the Clayton Jones Jazz Band and the usual suspects—the Blue Genes, Hank Walters and Johnny Goode. Did they really see the New Year in without a drink?

Friday 6 January 1961

The Sunset Seven Jazz Band is playing at the Cavern, but whisk me over to St John's Hall in Bootle. **John McNally**[190]: "Early in 1961, I came home from work and bought the *Liverpool Echo* to see who would be on with us that night at St John's Hall in Bootle. It said, 'The Silver Beatles, Direct from Hamburg.' and I wondered who the hell they were. I had my tea, picked up my guitar and amp, and got the bus with my amplifier underneath the stairs. The Beatles were in black leather jackets and black T-shirts, a real motley crew, and wearing boots too. They put their amplifiers on chairs, which I had never seen before. We put ours on the floor and so did everybody else. They did Chuck Berry stuff with lots of solos and they ran amok on stage. They were fantastic and it was definitely something new."

Wednesday 18 January 1961

Harry Prytherch[191], drummer with the Remo Four: "We were doing the lunchtime session and the dressing room was a hole in the wall. You could feel when someone is watching, and when we were playing one of the Shadow's numbers, I saw Tony Meehan, Hank Marvin and Bruce Welch looking at me. We finished our set and we had to move our stuff out quickly so they could rehearse."

Ray Ennis[192]: "I was there for the lunchtime session and then we got kicked out so that the Shadows could rehearse and we stood outside and listened. We went down in the evening and the Remo Four were on. The Remo blew them off the stage but then Jet Harris was drunk. It was a pity because they would have been exceptionally good. They had had a rehearsal and they had brought in extra PA speakers to spread the sound around a bit."

John Booker[193]: "When I was queuing to go in, Hank Marvin walked down Mathew Street as cool as can be. He had his guitar with him and he looked great. This is before there was cool."

Colin Manley[194], as part of "Liverpool's Fender Men" the Remo Four was on the same bill as the Shadows. "They set up their gear, brand new amplifiers and all that. They had a sound check, which was unheard of at the Cavern. The club was packed that evening and their sound balance was completely wrong. It's totally different when the place is full. The crowd thinned out when we went on, but we were loud and could be heard. People were coming up and saying, 'Oh, you're much better than them.'"

John Cochrane[195]: "It seemed to me that all the groups in Liverpool had come to see the Shadows and the place was packed. Jet Harris did fall off the stage, but the Remo Four were so much better, anyway, as Colin Manley was a brilliant guitarist. The Shadows hadn't got their sound right. I couldn't hear Hank's guitar properly from where I was, and the Remos knew how the Cavern worked."

Ian Edwards[196] of Ian and the Zodiacs bursts with Scouse pride: "I don't think it mattered whether Jet Harris was drunk or not. I don't think that there was anyone to touch Colin Manley, not even Hank Marvin in the Shadows. Colin was absolutely fantastic."

Karl Terry[197] of the Cruisers: "We auditioned at the Cavern that night and when I turned up, a lot of people thought I was Cliff Richard. We did okay, doing some Gene Vincent stuff. Jet Harris was out of it and my brother-in-law had to get him out of the dressing room and prop him against the piano before they started. I didn't expect that from one of my idols. I didn't see him fall off the stage because I was in the band room."

Colin Middlebrough[198]: "I was there that night but we went for a pint while the Shadows were on. We didn't want to see southern softies in their posh suits. Also, you never knew who was going to be on at lunchtimes and if it was Freddie and the Dreamers, we'd go straight out again."

It was the Shadows' walk during 'Shadoogie' that let them down. **Hank Marvin**[199] steps from the Shadows: "It was one of our first gigs independent of Cliff and it was a very difficult stage to perform on. Since we'd been with Cliff, we'd been used to concert halls and theatres where we'd had room to move and perform. Going to the Cavern was like going back to the 2 I's with the audience looking up our nostrils. Jet Harris had consumed vast quantities of alcohol and could barely stand up, let alone play. He fell forward at one point, stiff as a board and the front row caught him and pushed him back up again. I made an excuse about Jet not being well and some Scouser shouted, 'He's pissed.' We were a four-piece band, and the bass and the drums was our anchor. When the bass player is out of time and playing wrong notes, it doesn't make things easy. I've no doubt that the Remo Four were a better proposition than us that night. They were very good, excellent, but we'd have beaten them any other night."

Jet Harris[200]: "It was getting too much for me: four blokes together, sleeping, eating and drinking together and working all the time. I think everybody in Liverpool knows about my appearance at the Cavern. It was a disaster and I was shattered, tired and drunk. I fell off the stage and though I can laugh about it now, it mattered back then. People have done far more outrageous things on stage since then. "

Bill Buck was proud of his Premier kit with a Ludwig snaredrum. **Dave Williams**[201] of the Jaywalkers: "The Shadows were our heroes and it was upsetting to see Jet Harris the way he was. While they were doing their set, Tony Meehan damaged his snare drum and without any hesitation, he snatched the nearest snare drum, which belonged to our drummer Bill Buck and he popped it on the stand and away he went. As soon as Bill got wind of this, he was furious and I was trying to cool him down in the dressing room. I was saying, 'But it's Tony Meehan' and he was saying, 'I don't care who he is, he's got my snare drum', which was quite right, on reflection."

THE CAVERN PRESENTS THE FIRST EVER LIVERPOOL JAZZ FESTIVAL

AT THE CAVERN
TO-NIGHT
THE GREAT
TUBBY HAYES QUARTET
FRIDAY AND SATURDAY:
BOB WALLIS'S
STORYVILLE JAZZ BAND
RIVERBOAT SHUFFLE
Aboard M.V. ROYAL IRIS
Friday, August 25.   7.45 p.m.
With MR. ACKER BILK'S
PARAMOUNT JAZZ BAND
AND THE BEATLES
Tickets (8 6) Now on Sale at
Lewis's, Cranes, Rushworth's and
AT THE CAVERN
CENTRAL 1591.

The Cavern
PRESENTS
SATURDAY, 5th AUGUST
FABULOUS
ALL-NIGHT SESSION
WITH
PANAMA JAZZMEN
PLUS—AFTER MIDNIGHT
• KENNY BALL'S JAZZMEN
• MIKE COTTON'S JAZZMEN

The Swingin' Bluegenes who often performed at the Cavern's jazz and rock sessions during the interval and were later given their own weekly guest night

Johnny
Duncan

READERS' LETTERS

I've tried everywhere else and you seem to be my last resort. PLEASE could you give me some gen on George Harrison guitarist with "The Beatles". I saw "The Beatles" at the Cavern on July 21st at the lunch-time session and I think George is the utmost, ginchiest, skizziest, craziest cool cat I've ever seen. Why don't "The Beatles" record "The Hully Gully Song"? I'm sure it would be a hit.

Audrey McDowall,

112 Coronation Road,
Lydiate, nr. Maghull,
Lancs.

Cass & the Cassanovas were the first band to play at the Cavern's Wednesday night beat session

Photo by Bob Dean

THE BEATLES AGAIN ! SEEN HERE DURING THE
RECENT ALL-NIGHT SESSION AT THE CAVERN

Courtesy of Mersey Beat/Bill Harry

Bill Buck[202]: "Tony Meehan could have asked me first and I would have said yes. It was just his arrogance that I didn't like. I told him what I thought when they'd finished."

Wednesday 25 January 1961

Kingsize Taylor and the Dominoes, supported by the Pressmen. Their former pianist, **Sam Hardie**[203]: "The first time I went to the Cavern, the Dominoes were playing on stage. I left the band for two years to go in the police and at the time, they were still an amateurish group. I went into the Cavern to see them after seeing an ad in *Liverpool Echo* and I was amazed by their sound. I walked into the back of the Cavern and the Dominoes were on stage playing 'Slow Down', the Larry Williams' number, and I thought it was absolutely fantastic. I couldn't believe that they could sound like that. John Kennedy was doing harmonies with Bobby Thomson and it didn't sound like kids having a go. Part of it was down to the Cavern itself which had a very intimate, closed-in sound. Wherever you were standing, you felt part of the sound."

Tom Earley[204]: "I always regarded Kingsize Taylor as the founding father of what was happening. Kingsize Taylor and the Dominoes were a really class bunch of musicians. Bobby Thomson, their bass player and vocalist, was a joy to watch."

Thursday 9 February 1961

The Beatles made their first Cavern appearance, starting the lunchtime beat sessions as it happened. It marks George Harrison's debut on the Cavern stage as well as Stu Sutcliffe's: five musicians sharing £5. **Ray Ennis**[205]: "When the Beatles first came to the Cavern, I thought they were absolutely dreadful and musically awful. Stuart was on bass and he was making an horrendous noise. They were smoking on stage, and Stu was sitting at the piano, facing Pete Best on the drums and not even looking at the audience. Paul was just strumming a Rosetti guitar. By way of contrast, we rehearsed a lot and I suppose we were perfectionists."

Bob Wooler[206]: "The first time the Beatles came back from Hamburg they wore leather jackets and jeans, not leather pants. They got those in Hamburg on their second visit and then they performed in full leather. Ray McFall didn't like the Beatles playing in jeans. Jeans spelled trouble

in his book and he said to me, 'You know the policy at the Cavern, I don't allow people in with jeans, so they can't play in them.' I groaned as I didn't want to tell them. The Beatles were terrible when they ganged up on you—all of them, Pete Best as well. Their tongues could be savage if you criticised them for arriving late or messing around on stage. I knew that John would say, 'Who the fuck is he to tell us what to wear?' I went back to Ray and asked him to tell them himself. He put on his pained expression, which meant 'Aren't you capable of doing it yourself?' He went into the dressing-room to see them and I waited for him to come out. There were no four-letter words then as he was the guy with the pay packet."

Ray McFall[207]: "Bob Wooler would say to me, 'That's the way they are. Listen to their music.' They were different and they were very well rehearsed because they had come back from three months of torture in Hamburg. The other groups were like Cliff Richard and the Shadows, but the Beatles' music was so vibrant. As Bob said, 'They had ear and eye appeal.' However, I didn't like them wearing jeans which were taboo in the Cavern. Our doormen would stop anyone wearing jeans. I felt that if people were wearing good, clean clothes they would be more likely to behave themselves as they wouldn't want them getting dirty and damaged."

Owen Clayton[208] of Steve Bell and the Syndicate: "The Syndicate was very highly rated at the time and we had a big following, lot of girls and young lads. When the Beatles played, we could feel our following going away. They were all handsome and we weren't. When I first saw Stu, he wasn't wearing dark glasses but he was later on."

Dale Roberts[209]: "Stu Sutcliffe was as the back of the stage and I remember George Harrison bringing him forward for 'Love Me Tender' and the place went wild. They loved it."

At one Cavern gig, Stu Sutcliffe tried out what can be seen as the prototype of the Beatle jacket. The audience chuckled about the jacket, but the rest of the Beatles saw something there.

Friday 10 February 1961

Usually at the Mardi Gras or the Liverpool Jazz Society, Kenny Ball and his Jazzmen played the Cavern. Clinton Ford was singing with them and they were supported by the Blue Mountain Boys. They stopped over for an all-nighter the next day with the Yorkshire Jazz Band, Johnny Goode and the Swinging Blue Genes.

Sunday 12 February 1961

Bob Wallis and the Storyville Jazzmen with the Swinging Blue Genes and Dale Roberts and the Jaywalkers. Cliff Richard and the Shadows were playing at the Liverpool Empire. **Dave Williams**[210]: "Jet Harris was back in Liverpool. He looked in at the Cavern in a white mac and apologised for being drunk with the Shadows. He asked if he could sit in with us. Phil Rogers had just bought a new Burns bass and Jet Harris made it talk, he was absolutely brilliant."

Tuesday 21 February 1961

It was a busy day for the Beatles as they played the Cavern at lunchtime and the Cassanova Club and Litherland Town Hall in the evening. At the Cavern, Ray McFall booked the Swinging Blue Genes for a weekly guest night, a skilful move as they had a foot in both camps. Their first guests were the Remo Four. **Ralph Ellis**[211]: "We had a jazz flavour but we had a front line-up of three guitars rather than sax, trombone and trumpet. We had a trad jazz feel but with a Merseybeat sound about it. In the end the people wanted rock'n'roll. Bob Wooler has never got over the fact that we changed to rock'n'roll as he thought we had a unique sound, but we wanted to make records that would sell."

Geoff Nugent[212]: "The Beatles came on at the Cavern and it was a great sound. Not many groups had an electric bass then: we didn't have one with Bob Evans and the Five Shillings, and Rory Storm had the first bass. The Beatles were raw and vivid and I knew that they would do something. It does all seem to have started at the Cavern. To us as kids, fire regulations meant nothing and it didn't matter that it was a dirty, stinky, sweaty place.

Thursday 23 February 1961

(lunchtime) Gerry and the Pacemakers. **Lee Curtis** 213: "My first memory of the Cavern is going down there with my brother Joe when Gerry and the Pacemakers were on. I didn't think about getting up on stage but my brother asked Gerry if I could do a song or two with him, and Gerry said, 'Why not?' I went on and blew into the micro-

phone which had little ribbons in it. Gerry went white and told me not to do that. Just say, 'One, two' or tap, tap, but no blowing as you could shatter it. I did 'Rip It Up' or 'Blue Suede Shoes' and it went down fine."

Friday 24 February 1961

Cass has gone and the Cassanovas have become the Big Three. Check them out at lunchtime. **Alan Stratton**[214]: "Only four people had the coffin-type amplifiers that Adrian Barber of the Big Three used to make and I was one of them. He used to get the circuits from Goodman's and then he would build the cabinets. The first thing that you heard as you walked into the Cavern was that deep bass sound. The bass drum thumping away that was the essence of Merseybeat. Everybody tried to get the bass as deep as the Big Three could get it. They wanted big cabinets and 18 inch speakers, just like reggae musicians later on."

Prem Willis-Pitts[215]: "Adrian Barber had made these huge coffin-like amps, and I got hold of Johnny Gustafson's bass one night and struck a chord and the vibration nearly knocked me over. It was Johnny Gus's thumping great bass sound which made Merseybeat, in my opinion."

Karl Terry[216]: "I thought that the Big Three sounded the best of all the bands at the Cavern. They had those speakers but they were also excellent musicians. Johnny Hutch could play both right and left handed drums and he was a great vocalist as well."

Colin Middlebrough[217]: "Usually, you are playing rhythm on your top cymbal with your right hand and your left hand is playing the snare drum. Johnny Hutch could do it the other way round as well. He could play on the top cymbal with his left hand and hit the snare drum with his right. He also played with the drum sticks reversed and you could get more volume doing it that way."

Tuesday 28 February 1961

The Blue Genes guest night with Derry and the Seniors. **Bob Wooler**[218]: "The Blue Genes played a mixture of pop and traditional jazz tunes then, and they were very popular. Indeed, I was most impressed with the Swinging Blue Genes as a jazz band. They had an upright, string bass and they played at a lower volume than they did later. There was none of the stridency of 'Good Golly

Miss Molly' when they performed 'Down By The Riverside'."

Mike Brocken[219]: "Howie Casey and the Seniors were more like an Irish showband with their horns. The Beatles put the Cavern on the map even though it was known regionally. It was the German experience which made their sound very different."

Wednesday 1 March 1961

The Four Jays, later the Fourmost, support Dale Roberts and the Jaywalkers. **Dale Roberts**[220]: "My wife at the time was in the dressing room and Billy Hatton said, 'Would you turn round please while I take off my shoes as I've got holes in my socks?' He was always a comedian."

Billy Hatton[221]: "Well, you need holes to get your feet inside. We had been doing Holyoake Hall and it was a status symbol to do the Cavern. We could say we were a 'Cavern band'. I'm not claustrophobic but I thought that if something happens down here, the group has had it. We were the furthest away from the stairway. We could have tunnelled our way out through the toilets but that would have been death anyway."

John McCormick[222]: "The toilets wouldn't be tolerated now but we didn't mind them at all. It was part of the atmosphere. It was grime and smoke and sweat and even the fact that there was no bar was good as you went out and got some fresh air when you went to the Grapes."

Thursday 2 March 1961

Johnny Dankworth was booked to appear with his orchestra, and so a carpenter was hired to expand the stage, just for the night. The orchestra was currently in the charts with 'African Waltz'. **Colin Middlebrough**[223]: "They had the full Johnny Dankworth Orchestra at the Cavern one night and they did 'Doodletown Pipers' by the Sauter-Finnegan Orchestra and they couldn't put the flutes in their mouths as they were against the wall. It was hilarious as they had no room at all. It was nice to be so close to these people as normally they would be remote. I was six foot away which was incredible."

John McCormick[224]: "I was expecting the Johnny Dankworth Seven but he brought the big band and he even had a tuba player. They filled the stage and spilled into the dance area too. He even had Frank Holder with him who played the bongos and sang. Dankworth's big band in full cry was something to marvel about, really exciting."

John Dankworth[225]: "I only have a vague memory of what the Cavern was like. It was well known as a traditional jazz venue and we were on the modern side in the days when trads didn't talk to mods, so they probably only booked us when they were running out of trad names. It was 1961 so probably Dudley Moore was with us. He was with us for a year until he asked to have three weeks off to go to the Edinburgh Festival to do some silly show that he and his fellow undergrads had got together. That was *Beyond The Fringe*. I thought he would be back, but of course, he never came back because he became a star."

Colin Middlebrough[226] of the Kansas City Five: "Count Basie has a group called the Kansas City Seven and so obviously some people thought we were a jazz band. They put us on with the Johnny Dankworth Seven and the audience was totally bemused. It was a stony silence when we performed. They came round a bit but it was out of politeness."

Monday 6 March 1961

The Beatles kick off a week of lunchtime sessions. They do Monday, Wednesday and Friday: the Big Three, Tuesday and Derry and the Seniors, Thursday. **Frieda Kelly**[227]: "I heard of the Cavern when I was at college and then at Princes Food in Stanley Street. It was Simpson, Roberts and Co back then, just round the corner from the Cavern and a lot of the staff there, especially the male staff, used to go to the Cavern and I started going with them. That was in 1961, but I did go once before and I saw the Blue Genes and they were playing a type of jazz, and I liked them. I didn't like it when they changed: they should have left well alone. Once I got the job in Stanley Street I went in my dinner hour, not every dinner hour, but the majority of them. I liked the dinner hour sessions far better. You could communicate with the groups and shout up what you wanted them to play. It was a good laugh. It was very relaxed. I would try and stretch my lunch hour to an hour and a quarter as I liked the second part best. Then the Cavern closed. Sometimes I would leave late, about 10 past 1 to do that."

Wednesday 8 March 1961

An awkward name but an evening treat: Faron's Tempest Tornados, supported by Gerry and the Pacemakers and Johnny Rocco and the Jets.

Saturday 11 March 1961

An okay night at the Cavern with jazz from the Saints and country from Johnny Goode. A few roads away at the Liverpool Jazz Society (soon to be the Iron Door), promoter Sam Leach had organised the first all night beat marathon on Merseyside with 12 groups in 12 hours for just 7/6d. The Beatles were featured and Sam Leach was to use them for many more of his promotions.

Tuesday 14 March 1961

(lunchtime) **John Booker**[228]: "I was walking around in the lunch-hour and I heard this fantastic music coming from a doorway in Mathew Street. I walked in and paid my ninepence and it was the Cavern. I started going about three times a week and I saw the Beatles and Gerry and the Pacemakers a lot. The Beatles were so good and they stood out. They had a repertoire that was different from anybody else's like 'Your Feet's Too Big' and 'Besame Mucho'. They were not rock'n'roll songs. I had forgotten until I saw Gerry a couple of months ago how good a rock'n'roller he was and he can still rock it up as well as anybody, and with that piano, they could do Little Richard and Jerry Lee Lewis numbers very well."

Wednesday 15 March 1961

If I had use of the Tardis, this day would suit me fine. A lunchtime session with the Beatles, after which they take their gear to Liverpool Jazz Society for a five hour afternoon session with Gerry and the Pacemakers and Rory Storm. Not all of Rory's mates could get off work so he sang with a makeshift band, the Wild Ones. Then it's back to the Cavern for Dale Roberts and the Jaywalkers and some more of Gerry and the Pacemakers.

John Frankland[229]: "Rory would pull out an old telegram wishing him good luck and pretend it was something he had just received." That sentence completely and utterly sums Rory Storm up.

Monday 20 March 1961

(lunchtime) **John Booker**[230]: "I worked at Coastlines in Water Street and I was an accounts executive

there. The company had a staff canteen in Princes Dock and with judicious timing, I could wolf my lunch down in 10 minutes and dash up Water Street, go through India Building and get into Mathew Street and down the steps. I didn't want to sacrifice my lunch for the Cavern's hot dogs. Bob Wooler was always announcing the time because he knew that people would have to get back to work. He would say, "It's 10 to 2" and then "It's 5 to 2" and people would be scurrying out. I'd go in at about 1.15pm, so I saw half an hour. Usually I would catch one band. When I got back, people would say, 'You haven't been to that awful place again, have you?' but I thought it was great."

Ray O'Brien[231]: "I would get to school at 9am and we would have lunch at noon. The doors opened at 12.15pm at the Cavern. It would take about fifteen minutes to walk from Mount Street, which is up by the Cathedral and we were usually among the first to be there. If we went back to school, we would have to leave after 40 minutes and run back up past Lewis's back to school. A little bit of the excitement was not getting caught and getting back in time. I've not only gone past Lewis's: I've been in the Cavern. (Laughs) When we got a bit older, about sixteen, we went into the Grapes too. My first drink was in Ye Cracke and that was the devilment too: just half a pint. If we stayed off for the afternoon, then we would stay at the Cavern until half-past two. We didn't let the teachers know we had been to the Cavern. We would have got the cane for that. It would be worth getting the cane to see the Beatles but I don't know about some of the other groups."

Rogan Taylor[232]: "I consider myself very lucky as I was born in 1945. I was fifteen in 1960, so how perfectly timed is that? My brother was in Paul McCartney's class, going up through the years, at the Institute and I a couple of years behind. He told me about the Beatles, and the lunchtime sessions were great. I would sag off from the last Geography period and go down town. I used to love them doing 'Some Other Guy' and 'Roll Over Beethoven' and 'Mr. Moonlight', which was a great song, I remember the girls throwing toilet rolls at Pete Best to attract his attention as he was so handsome and apart. The others looked okay in a kind of knockabout way, but it was Pete they went for. I had an absolute ball at the Cavern and I loved doing that swaying dance, the Cavern Stomp. I would come back to school pretty moist and my eardrums would be so battered that I could hardly hear the teachers anyway."

Frieda Kelly[233]: "You could never deny that you had been at the Cavern because of the smell on your clothes. I might be sitting upstairs on the bus and I hadn't been to the Cavern and I could recognise the Cavern smell from someone sitting in front of me. Some people say it was offensive but it wasn't. It was a unique smell, it was a mixture I know of all different horrible things, but it was unique. No other club had that."

Mike McCartney[234]: "They should have bottled the smell of the Cavern. Those lads from Cains Brewery could do it, so listen to this, lads. You have to have the smell of slippy steps going down into the Cavern, a smell of something like those thick ropes at the ferries, and Paddy Delaney would let you in if you were good boys or related to one of the bands. We would go down the steps and get into the Cavern and then it was the smell of sweat, the smell of rotten fruit as outside in Mathew Street were these warehouses. And the bogs would leak too. Put all this into a nice little bottle and you would make a fortune."

Ray O'Brien[235]: "You took your tie off and if it was summer, you put your blazer in a bag. Edwina Currie went to Blackburne House and she was doing a similar thing at the girls' school. She used to take off her school jersey and put it in a bag. You would put your collar up to look a little bit tough and you had your white or grey shirt on and went in. George Harrison hardly ever had a school badge on. His mother hadn't sewn it on, and he would hold it in place with a paperclip and a pen and take it off immediately he got out of school. That is in keeping with his character. He stood out at school because of his appearance."

Tuesday 21 March 1961

The visiting guest group for the Blue Genes' Guest Night was the Beatles: their first evening appearance at the Cavern. **Ray McFall**[236]: "Bob Wooler had told me about the Beatles and I had become aware of the Beatles earlier when Pete Best's mother, Mo, phoned me to say, 'My son is

in a wonderful group, they do very well, so why don't you book them?' My response was, 'I'll let you know.' When it came to beat music, Bob was the expert and I relied on him to select the groups. He told me that the Beatles had come from Hamburg and he was at Litherland Town Hall and saw their return, and he said, 'You've got to have them.' Brian Kelly, who ran Litherland Town Hall, booked them for all his shows, which were all on a Wednesday. I couldn't have them on Wednesday, I wasn't open on Thursday or there would be modern jazz, and the weekend was traditional jazz, and so I decided to book them on a Tuesday. This was the Blue Genes guest night, and they wanted good, well-organised, clean beat groups, ones that weren't too loud and wild, and they would suggest groups to me."

Ray Ennis[237]: "Ray McFall had booked the Beatles for our Guest Night without telling us and we were very annoyed about it. They played so badly then. The Beatle fans had annoyed our fans by getting there early and sitting in the front rows. They watched us and it was like, 'What's all that?' they wanted the Beatles."

Ralph Ellis[238]: "Their singing was very rough and their guitars were out of tune. We rehearsed a lot to get our sound right and we weren't too happy to see the Beatles going down so well with something they'd only rehearsed five minutes before."

Joey Bower[239] from the Four Jays: "This was the first time I had seen the Beatles and they were in black leather and dripping with sweat. They were doing songs that I'd never heard before and I wondered where they had got them from. They did an absolutely fabulous version of 'Besame Mucho', one of the best things I've ever heard on stage."

Bob Wooler[240]: "I'd been talking to Paul McCartney about American records in my collection and he'd borrowed Chan Romero's 'Hippy Hippy Shake'. To my surprise, he featured the number of their first evening appearance."

Ray McFall[241]: "Afterwards, three of the Blue Genes tackled me in Mathew Street and they were most upset. As far as they were concerned the Beatles didn't have the musical talent and they weren't clean, fresh and well-organised. I said that if the place is full, there are a lot more people watching the Blue Genes."

John Cochrane, drummer with Wump and the Werbles, kept a list of what other groups were performing in order that his own band would not duplicate numbers. It's an invaluable document. The list dates from early in 1961 and, taking the groups together, the Shadows' material appears 44 times and Cliff Richard's 31. Elvis Presley heads the American rock 'n' rollers with 21 appearances, while Gene Vincent and Buddy Holly both have 11. **John Cochrane**[242] comments, "The groups did a lot of Gene Vincent's songs and this was because they were easier to play than Chuck Berry's. The Shadows' tunes were dead easy to play. They must have been. They'd release a record on Friday and every group would be playing it by Saturday night."

The Beatles' repertoire is the most distinctive and it drew on a wide range of sources. John Cochrane listed 19 of their songs—the Beatles were ultimately to record only one of them, 'Boys', for Parlophone. Rock'n'roll is represented by "C'mon Everybody" (Eddie Cochran), "Twenty Flight Rock" (Eddie Cochran), "Mean Woman Blues" (Jerry Lee Lewis), "Lucille" (Little Richard) and "New Orleans" (Gary U.S. Bonds). Buddy Holly is featured with two of his lesser known songs, "Crying, Waiting, Hoping" and "Mailman, Bring Me No More Blues". Rhythm and blues is there with two Ray Charles songs, "Hallelujah, I Love Her So" and "What'd I Say". Turning to country music, there's Hank Williams' "Hey Good Lookin'" and Bill Monroe's "Blue Moon Of Kentucky", which had been rocked up by Elvis.

The Beatles' ballads are "Love Me Tender" (Elvis Presley), "Red Sails In The Sunset" (already an oldie, and the Beatles' version predates Fats Domino's rock'n'roll treatment), "Over The Rainbow" (presumably taken from Gene Vincent), "Corrina, Corrina" (an early Phil Spector production and a US hit for Ray Peterson) and "Don't Forbid Me" (a ballad hit for Pat Boone). Also on the list are the Shirelles' "Will You Love Me Tomorrow?" and Elvis Presley's "Wooden Heart". This included a passage in German and no doubt the Beatles primarily did it to amuse Hamburg audiences.

John Cochrane[243]: "After Paul sang 'Til There Was You', John used to say, 'Now I'm going to do my Peggy Lee song' and he would start yelling 'Peanut Butter'. I thought, 'That doesn't sound like a Peggy Lee song to me' and it took me a little while to realise that he was winding us up."

Owen Clayton[244]: "I was very impressed with George Harrison from the start as he could do those Carl Perkins riffs and get them right. Lennon could play lead as well and he could do Chuck Berry riffs. John and Paul's harmonies were better then than when they made it big. Paul would do 'Over The Rainbow' and it was brilliant. It was much better than Gene Vincent's version and it was done more like Judy Garland. He would go very high on 'Somewhere'. Absolutely superb. The girls would always be asking for it. They were all following that—Gerry with 'You'll Never Walk Alone' and Rory with 'Beautiful Dreamer'. I wish the Beatles had recorded 'Over The Rainbow': it would have gone down great."

Dave Williams[245]: "We wanted to sound exactly the same as the original records and we thought we were quite clever when we did that, but we weren't as clever as the Beatles. They never did the songs just like the records because they wanted to put their own mark on them, and that was brilliant. 'Over The Rainbow' went down so well that they could have done it as a single."

Bob Packham[246]: "I loved the Beatles doing 'Over The Rainbow', they should have recorded that. They did it brilliantly and it was a bit more up-tempo than Judy Garland's version."

Geoff Davies[247]: "The one I used to really love was Barrett Strong's 'Money'. They used to vary that twangy guitar intro quite a lot. The first time I saw them do it, it was a really really long intro and then when Lennon came in, it was like the dirtiest voice you had ever heard in your life. 'The best things in life are free'—he would sing it with this disgusting sneer. I certainly heard them do it with lots of different lengths to that intro, and I had never seen bands doing this sort of thing before. The interplay between them was great, they would turn their backs on the audience or give irrelevant introductions. McCartney used to say, 'This one's by Fatty Waller' and that was 'Your Feet's Too Big'. I had never heard that song before they did it."

Frieda Kelly[248]: "I loved the way the Beatles were larking about on stage. I didn't know of anyone who wore black leathers then and I went straight out and got a black leather coat made. Then I saw Gerry and the Pacemakers and they were all wearing red V-neck sweaters. I saw Pete Maclaine with the Dakotas and the Big Three. There were a lot of songs that I knew already but then they started doing their own songs like 'Love Me Do'. I loved John doing 'Anna' and I used to shout up for that one, and Paul doing 'Besame Mucho'. I don't know if they went out on stage with a running order but even if they did, they never stayed with it as people would shout out for things and they would do them."

Overall, John Cochrane's list suggests that the Beatles repertoire wasn't as rough and tough as some have imagined, although, to a certain degree, it ain't what you do, it's the way that you do it. **Ian Edwards**[249]: "The Beatles knew that they were the best in Liverpool so they didn't care what they did on stage, like smoking or swearing, but only John did the swearing. They had the audience in the palms of their hands."

Mike Brocken[250]: "The sound was very interesting at the Cavern. John Lee Hooker said that R&B was like a sonic boom. Well, it certainly was in the Cavern, so even if you didn't see the Beatles because you were in one of the side arches, you would have still been able to appreciate their sound. Their sound would have been different from anybody else's sound. The Big Three had a really big sound but the Beatles had an amazing sound. Also, the choice of the material was so interesting. They were a covers band in their early days but it was a very sensible selection of covers. Instead of playing the A-side of something that they might have found in the deletion bin at Rushworth's, they would turn it over and look at the B-side. It appealed to the audience. They were all record collectors and it was just that some of them also played. You could imagine Lennon saying, 'We are going to play this Arthur Alexander song now, I wonder if anybody knows it out there.' If they do, they're cool and they think 'I'm cool', so we're all cool together: 'I know this and they don't.' There is an implied arrogance about this, but you do need a bit. The Hamburg experience would have given them a lot of confidence.

They stole a march on most groups by going over there early on."

Here are a few unlikely examples from the other bands:

Gerry and the Pacemakers: "Ginchy" (a Bert Weedon instrumental), "Skinny Minnie" (Bill Haley), "You'll Never Know" (Shirley Bassey) and two songs shared with the Beatles, "What'd I Say" and "Will You Love Me Tomorrow?" Johnny Gus called Gerry "the human jukebox" because he knew so many songs. **Neil Foster**[251]: "Gerry also did 'Nature Boy', which is a very hard song to sing, and Bobby Darin's instrumental, 'Beachcomber'."

Frieda Kelly[252]: "Although Gerry was good at larking about, the other Pacemakers wanted to get on with it, so they would have a more structured show. Once George or Paul didn't turn up and Gerry went on with the Beatles. They got an orange box from the Fruit Exchange so he could sing into the same mike."

Gerry Marsden[253]: "The Cavern had a good atmosphere but then Liverpool had a good atmosphere. I loved it at the Cavern where they would shout out songs to sing. It was a dirty horrible cellar but it was wonderful. It is a privilege to have played at the greatest club in the world."

Continuing with John Cochrane's list, we have for the Swinging Blue Genes: "Easter Bonnet" (Irving Berlin standard), "Calendar Girl" (Neil Sedaka), "I Love You" (Cliff Richard), "Wheels" (String-A-Longs), "Samantha" (Kenny Ball) and, like the Beatles, "Wooden Heart". The Blue Jeans also did "Sucu Sucu" wearing large Mexican hats.

Because Les Braid had a domestic tape recorder, the Swinging Blue Genes made private recordings of much of their repertoire. There may be as many as 60 or 70 songs that they recorded and I asked **Ray Ennis**[254] to talk me through a couple of tape boxes. "Lonnie Donegan did 'Over In Gloryland' originally and 'Yip I Addy I Ay' was done by the jazz bands on a Sunday night at the Cavern. I am sure 'Bigamy Liz' was one of these obscure records we found and changed it about. 'Once In A While' is a standard and 'That Ole Dixie Line' was picked up off the jazz bands. Les Paul and Mary Ford used to do 'Bye Bye Blues'. 'I've Got A Feeling I'm Fallin'' is an old country and western song and we got it from a Dean Martin

LP. 'Hanchen Klein' was done by the Alan Elsdon Band which was just a bit of fun. We sang it in German and we had no idea what we were singing—this is long before we went to Germany. We didn't do it when we were there as we might have been saying something awful. 'It Ain't What We Do' is an old jazz song. 'What A Crazy World' is Joe Brown and 'Bonaparte's Retreat' is another country song, which we changed to a jazz feel. 'Ain't She Sweet' is another classic. 'Georgia Grind' was done by Ottilie Patterson and 'Lawd, You've Been Good To Me' is another jazz song. 'April Showers' is a standard. 'It Ain't No Secret' is a bluesy, religious song and 'I'm Satisfied With My Girl' is an old blues. We used to rehearse in the Cavern and we had a Dansette and we would play these records. We would rehearse there on Sunday mornings and then we would go to the White Star for a pint and go home, and then do the song on the Tuesday which was our Guest Night. We would bed them in on those nights. We all loved rock'n'roll but everybody was playing it and we all loved Trad too. We had the Trad backline of string bass, banjo and drums, and then the front line of three guitars, which were taking the place of trumpet, trombone and clarinet. It gave us a distinctive sound."

Wednesday 22 March 1961

(lunchtime) The Beatles
(evening) Derry and the Seniors, the Four Jays and Cliff Roberts and the Rockers

Friday 24 March 1961

After their lunchtime session, the Beatles went to Lime Street Station to travel by train to Germany. They hit the stage at the Top Ten on 27 March.

Tuesday 28 March 1961

Blue Genes' guest night with the Pressmen and Kingsize Taylor and the Dominoes.

John Booker[255]: "When I was 12, I lived with my grandmother in Liverpool and she insisted that I went to a church. It didn't matter which one, I looked around Penny Lane and I noticed that Elm Hall Drive Methodist had a youth club attached. There would be girls there and that was my spiritual conversion to Methodism. I had some records, but not many, and I would play the records for the dances there. I would start with 'Rockin' Goose'. I was in youth clubs until

I was sixteen and then I was working in town and I went to the Cavern. It was a stepping stone between youth clubs and licensed night clubs as the Cavern wasn't licensed. No one there was over 20. It was a good musical education. I thought Bob Wooler was very stylish as a DJ, saying, 'Hey there, cats and kittens' and the like."

Wednesday 5 April 1961

The Searchers make their Cavern debut with Johnny Sandon as their lead vocalist.

Friday 7 April 1961

Bob Wallis and the Storyville Jazzmen with Dale Roberts and the Jaywalkers

Sunday 9 April 1961

Humphrey Lyttelton Jazz Band with the Swinging Blue Genes

Tuesday 11 April 1961

Blue Genes' guest night with Kingsize Taylor and the Dominoes

Tuesday 18 April 1961

Blue Genes' Guest Night with Johnny Sandon and the Searchers and the Remo Four

Wednesday 19 April 1961

The Pressmen with Faron's Tempest Tornados

Friday 21 April 1961

The Yorkshire Jazz Band with Kingsize Taylor and the Dominoes. **John Frankland**[256]: "We did several shows with jazz bands. We would play for an hour and then it was over to the Grapes and back again. I did think that the trad bands sounded great though."

Sam Hardie[257]: "The piano at the Cavern was a rickety thing, but it had notes on it. When we played at Samson and Barlow's, I couldn't play at all as the piano only had about two notes. You could get a tune out of the Cavern's piano. It had to be because the jazz bands all had pianists."

Tuesday 25 April 1961

Blue Genes' Guest Night with Gerry and the Pacemakers and Robin and the Ravens

Trouble is looming for the Cavern. Following an inferno at Henderson's store in the city centre, there has been legislation for compulsory fire sprinklers. Another disaster at a club in Bolton caused Liverpool Corporation to look at the Cavern and it received a summons on May 4. There was no fire exit and the only means of escape would be through a doorway, along a passage three foot wide, through another door and up the steps. The Corporation commented, "In the light of recent events, there is not one authority in the country which has not said to itself, 'Is there anything further we can do to stop the same thing happening within our own boundary?'" The basement had been approved for occupation by 20 people, but what did 'occupation' mean? Could it apply to 600 Cavernites who were not sleeping or working there? The legal arguments might be considerable, but no one would deny the advantage of a second exit. The question really was: who should pay for it?

Saturday 6 May 1961

The White Eagles Jazz Band with Ian and the Zodiacs. **Ian Edwards**[258]: "Playing in Liverpool was the biggest decision we ever made. We were resident at St Luke's Hall in Crosby every Wednesday and Saturday and the money was paying the HP on our amps and guitars. We got invited to the Cavern and we talked about it for hours and hours before deciding to go. We thought that we might get the sack from St Luke's. We were apprehensive because every group that played at the Cavern was too loud as the sound bounced off the back wall. It was the first time we had played in the city centre and we loved it and we wanted to get back as often as possible."

Tuesday 9 May 1961

Blue Genes guest night with Gerry and the Pacemakers and Kingsize Taylor and the Dominoes. **John Cochrane**[259]: "Kingsize Taylor and the Dominoes impressed me far more at first than the Beatles. The Beatles were incredibly exciting and raw but musically they were absolutely awful. Kingsize wasn't quite that raw and the band's music was much better."

Sam Hardie[260]: "We did a lot of songs before anybody else. The Isley Brothers' 'Respectable' and 'Twist And Shout', 'The Twist', 'Do You Love Me' and the Dovells' 'Bristol Stomp' and 'Bristol Twistin' Annie'. We heard 'Fortune Teller' on a jukebox in Germany and did that first and Johnny Kidd copied our version of 'I Can Tell'."

John Frankland[261]: "Some groups didn't have enough songs in their repertoire and far too many of them did 'Johnny B Goode' and 'Matchbox'.

If you go to Merseycats tonight, chances are you will hear those songs."

Tuesday 16 May 1961

(lunchtime) Cliff Roberts and the Rockers
(evening) Blue Genes' Guest Night with the Remo Four and Ian and the Zodiacs. **Ian Edwards**[262]: "The Swinging Blue Genes weren't a beat group and I found them very funny. Where else would you hear someone doing 'When Father Papered The Parlour'? They did some very strange songs, half jazz and half popular music, and they were nothing like the group they became. It was their night and we were their guests, we certainly didn't regard them as competition. It wasn't like being on the same bill as the Beatles or Gerry where we would have to work hard."

Gerry Marsden[263]: "We certainly regarded the Beatles as our biggest threat and although we were all good friends, we did want to bury them musically."

Monday 22 May 1961

Acker Bilk and his Paramount Jazz Band

Sunday 28 May 1961

The Clyde Valley Stompers with the Swinging Blue Genes

Saturday 3 June 1961

Kenny Ball and his Jazzmen supported by Gerry and the Pacemakers. Cilla Black sang with Gerry, and Kenny Ball offered her a job with the band, which has become a chart act with "Samantha" and "I Still Love You All". Cilla said, "No". Later she was offered a trip to Hamburg with Kingsize Taylor and the Dominoes, but again, it's a no. **John Frankland**[264]: "Cilla had a cracking voice and a feel for R&B. She did 'Unchain My Heart' with great vocal backings from us. She sounded nasal, but what's wrong with that?"

Thelma Hargrove[265]: "I used to do the cloakroom lists in the back kitchen at home, and I'd be thinking, 'Better give that Priscilla White something or she'll be crying.' She used to pester the groups and ask if she could sing with them. She was very theatrical when she did 'Fever' with Gerry and the Pacemakers. She would screech it and you'd want to drown your bloody self. She had a voice, yes, but not one we liked. She went for lessons once Brian Epstein signed her."

THE CAVERN

LUNCHTIMES

Tomorrow. Friday 15th—THE BEATLES

Next Monday 18th. }
Wednesday 20th. } **Gerry and the Pacemakers.**
Friday 22nd.

Tuesday 19th.. }
Thursday 21st. } **The Beatles.**

EVENINGS

Tomorrow. Friday—
   Collegians, Remo 4.
Saturday—
   White Eagles Jazzband, Gerry and the Pacemakers.
Sunday—
   Doug Richford's London Jazzmen, The Bluegenes.
Next Tuesday 19th—
   The Bluegenes, Remo 4, Gerry and the Pacemakers.
Wednesday 20th—
   The Beatles, Ian and the Zodiacs, Karl Terry and Cruisers.
Thursday 21st—
   DANKWORTH ALL STARS Featuring Alan Ganley (drums), Art Ellefson (tenor), Eddie Harvey (trombone, piano) Ken Wheeler (trumpet, piano), Spike Heatley (Bass).
Friday 22nd—
   Red River Jazzmen, Johnny Sandon and Searchers.
Saturday 23rd—
   Gerry and the Pacemakers, The Saints Jazzband.
Sunday 24th—
   ......men The Bluegenes.

George Pete, John
& Paul pose with
their van outside
Cavern

THE CAVERN

presents

CAVERN KALENDER

OCTOBER

EVENING SESSIONS

Wednesday, 4th—
   King Size Taylor and the Dominoes. Johnny Sandon and the Searchers. The Strangers.
Friday, 6th—
   The Yorkshire Jazz Band Ian and the Zodiacs.
Saturday, 7th—
   The Saints Jazzband.
Sunday, 8th—
   Humphrey Lyttelton, The Blue Genes.
Tuesday, 10th—
   King Size Taylor and the Dominoes. Gerry and the Pacemakers. The Blue Genes.
Wednesday, 11th—
   Mark Peters and the Cyclones. The Remo Four. Clay Ellis and the Raiders.
Friday, 13th—
   The Red River Jazz Men. Gerry and the Pacemakers.
Saturday, 14th—
   Terry Lightfoot's New Orleans Jazz Band with Sonnie Terry and Brownie McGhee.
Sunday, 15th—
   The Melbourne New Orleans Jazzband. The Blue Genes.
Tuesday, 17th—
   The Blue Genes. The Remo Four. Gerry and the Pacemakers.
Wednesday, 18th—
   The Beatles. The Four Jays. Ian and the Zodiacs

The Searchers

THE BEATLES FAN CLUB
PRESENTS

"THE BEATLES FOR THEIR FANS"

OR AN EVENING WITH GEORGE, JOHN, PAUL & PETE

GUEST ARTISTS WILL INCLUDE

THE FOUR JAYS

AND THE BEATLES' FAVOURITE COMPERE

BOB WOOLER

7-30 p.m. THURSDAY, APRIL 5th, 1962

AT THE CAVERN

TICKETS 6/6d.

Ticket holders will receive a FREE PHOTOGRAPH and may apply for
FREE Membership of the Fan Club. (See over.)

(Above) The Four Jays

GREAT PACKAGE SHOW AT THE CAVERN

On Saturday, 14th of October, The Cavern presented a great package show in which folk artistes Sonny Terry and Brownie McGhee and Terry Lightfoot's New Orleans Jazzmen featured. Terry has enjoyed enormous success recently with his recording of 'True Love' and Sonny Terry and Brownie McGhee are of course, well loved in Britain and frequently appear with Chris Barber's Band.

George, Paul, Pete and John backing American
singer Davy Jones

Tuesday 13 June 1961

(lunchtime) The Big Three

(evening) Blue Genes Guest Night with the Remo Four and Gerry and the Pacemakers

Valerie Dicks[266]: "I was a student nurse at Sefton General and I used to wear my uniform on the bus because the bus conductor wouldn't take the fare and I never had enough money to pay it anyway. Everybody has somebody who is sick sometime and maybe a nurse looked after your mother or sister, so we didn't get charged. It was a shilling to get in at the Cavern and I would get in for half price because of my uniform. I would go into the toilets and change into my clothes and put my uniform in a bag. The water ran down the walls: you went in with straight hair and you ended up with curls. One side was for those who hadn't done much educationally and the other side was for the ones who went to grammar school, and we kept to our sides. Thelma ran a coffee bar at the top end and would dish out Cokes and hot dogs. When the pop groups came on, who were the fill-ins for the jazz groups, we would go to the White Star or the Grapes with a bottle of Coke from Thelma. We would empty the Coke down the grid and come back with Cherry B and cider in the Coke bottle, drinking it through a straw. Thelma often wondered why we were so happy at the end of the night. I would put my uniform back on and go back home on the bus."

Wednesday 14 June 1961

(lunchtime) Johnny Sandon and the Searchers

(evening) Kingsize Taylor and the Dominoes, Johnny Sandon and the Searchers and the Decker Rhythm Group

Saturday 17 June 1961

The Saints Jazz Band and, making their fifth appearance of the week, Gerry and the Pacemakers

Sunday 18 June 1961

Cy Laurie Jazz Band supported by the Swinging Blue Genes

Wednesday 21 June 1961

(lunchtime) The Remo Four

(evening) The Remo Four, the Four Jays and the Rockin' Blackcats

Sunday 25 June 1961

Humphrey Lyttelton and his Jazz Band, plus the Swinging Blue Genes

Wednesday 28 June 1961

(lunchtime) Gerry and the Pacemakers

(evening) Kingsize Taylor and the Dominoes, Robin and the Ravens and the Galvinisers. **Bob Packham**[267]: "I was in the Galvinisers with some lads from school and we were all about fifteen. We didn't know much about instruments. I bought my guitar, a big white one from Frank Hessy's. I got the money as I was working as a butcher's boy, riding a bike and delivering meat. We were very nervous before we went to the Cavern for the first time but it was fantastic. We did Gene Vincent, Little Richard and the Shadows' songs and we did the Shadows' steps too. We did the instrumentals better as none of us were good singers, but Ringo used to follow us round and he would join us for 'Be Bop A Lula'."

Edwina Currie[268]: "My father's friend Mr Hesselberg, 'Hessy' we called him, had a shop close to NEMS and I remember him saying to my dad one night, 'I don't know what all this rock'n'roll is about, but everybody wants electric guitars. I try to sell them other instruments and they don't want them.' My dad said, 'But it's making you a fortune, Hessy' and he said, 'Yes, I suppose it is.'" Intriguing, isn't it: Liverpool's Jewry was not large and yet it played a very significant role in the Mersey explosion: Alan Sytner, Brian Epstein and Frank Hessy.

Thursday 29 June 1961

(lunchtime) Mark Peters and the Cyclones

On 6 July 1961, **Bill Harry**[269], another student from the Liverpool College of Art, launched a fortnightly newspaper, *Mersey Beat*: "I was trying to get backers for a jazz magazine I'd designed, but I'd got so involved with the Beatles that I decided to do a rock'n'roll mag instead. I borrowed £50 to start the paper and thought of the name *Mersey Beat* and that was when the Mersey beat scene officially began. The music didn't have a name before. When I started *Mersey Beat*, I got together with Bob Wooler and we came out with a list of over 400 bands covering the area from Liverpool to Southport and over the water. I knew that there was no other scene like this in the entire country, probably not in the whole world, and it was very like New Orleans at the turn of the century when jazz began."

Friday 30 June 1961

(lunchtime) Gerry and the Pacemakers
(evening) Yorkshire Jazz Band with the Strangers

Saturday 8 July 1961

George Martin produced the Temperance Seven's Number One "You're Driving Me Crazy", and their second hit, "Pasadena", was climbing the charts when they played the Cavern, supported by the Saints Jazz Band. One of the Cavern's fullest houses, and on 2 February 1962, they star at the Philharmonic Hall. **Geoff Davies**[270]: "That was a thoroughly enjoyable and very crowded night. The Temperance Seven were playing real old-fashioned jazz and they dressed up like funeral directors, so it was a very visual act."

Owen Clayton[271]: "I saw the Temperance Seven play the Cavern and they were brilliant. The drummer had a 22 inch bass drum, it had a small cymbal, coconuts and a wooden bar on the top. The vocalist had a megaphone and he had an echo through that, and it went perfectly with the music."

Thursday 13 July 1961

A lunchtime set from Karl Terry and the Cruisers. The Cruisers had two drummers but they didn't play together. One had a weak bladder and the other was epileptic, and neither could be certain of completing a set. The jazz standard, "Buddy's Habits", which dates from 1923, was so-called because the saxophonist Buddy Gross would rush off the stand at the end of each set to relieve himself.

Owen Clayton[272]: "Karl Terry did lots of Bill Haley and Gene Vincent songs, but not the obvious ones. He did 'Wedding Bells Are Breaking Up That Old Gang Of Mine' which Gene Vincent did. I bet you've never heard anybody else doing that. He was just as wild as he is today. He would climb anywhere, climb all walls and always doing the splits, even at the Cavern. If there was a prop for him to use, he would use it."

Jimmy Campbell[273]: "Bob Wooler showed Karl Terry how to use a mike, to hold it about four inches from your mouth. Of course, John Lennon took no notice of this advice as he would practically swallow it. I've always loved Karl Terry.

Even now when you see him, he makes you feel good."

Karl Terry[274]: "The Reslo microphones were not much good for harmonies as one side was louder than the other, so you would always try and get the louder side for yourself. You didn't get any foldback as there were two 12 inch speakers and they were in the archways. The sound would be going forward and the vocals would be round the corners!"

Billy Hatton[275]: "They had Reslo mikes at the Cavern and there was always a dominant side on those mikes and if you are the lead singer, you would want that dominant side. You can see that with the Beatles as one is closer than the other to get the balance right. There was no one in the back doing the balance for you, but I don't remember working it out much. It was instinctive. There was no foldback or monitor speakers either. The best you could hope for was a mate who went to the back of the room and told you it was all right."

Dave Jamieson[276]: "I went to the lunchtime sessions. I was an apprentice panel-beater at Garlick's in Bootle. I would be on the bus in my boiler suit and I would get about 20 minutes in the Cavern. I would be clean again because I was sweating so much. I met up with people I knew, some friends were in the same trade from Watson's who were nearer. Liverpool was a great place for one's teenage days. Bob Wooler said it was no different from any other city, but it was."

Friday 14 July 1961

Shortly after their appearance on the Blue Genes guest night, the Beatles returned to Hamburg. This was their "Welcome Home" appearance, really as conquering heroes, and it was followed by residencies on Wednesday nights. The Beatles, totally in leather, were supported by the White Eagle Jazz Band and Ian and the Zodiacs. **Ian Edwards**[277]: "The Beatles didn't make an impression until I saw them that night. The long hours had knitted them together. I loved to hear Paul singing 'Besame Mucho'. That was very different and it suited his voice. You can't really imagine a beat group doing 'Besame Mucho', but they did it very well."

David Backhouse[278]: "I always think that the Beatles or anybody else sounded best at the

Cavern because of the reverberation and the compactness of it. The Beatles were tremendous and had the *je ne sais quoi* which set them apart from the other bands."

Monday 17 July 1961

The format for lunchtimes was taking shape—the Beatles on Mondays, Wednesdays and Fridays and Gerry and the Pacemakers on Tuesdays and Thursdays. This week the Beatles also played Wednesday evening, while Gerry was with the Blue Genes on Tuesday and with the Yorkshire Jazz Band on Friday. **John Cook**[279]: "We got on with the beat groups okay, but I never warmed to Gerry Marsden. I asked him once, 'What are you doing after you've finished here?' and he said, 'Going to bed with a bird.'" I think this is failing to appreciate Liverpool wit. **Gerry Marsden**[280]: "I met my wife in the Cavern so it has got a lot to answer for."

Wednesday 19 July 1961

Effectively the start of the Beatles' Wednesday guest nights, though with the Beatles, who needs guests? The Remo Four and the Pressmen are their first ones.

Tuesday 25 July 1961

(lunchtime) The Beatles

(evening) The Blue Genes accept the Beatles on their Guest Night, plus Gerry and the Pacemakers and the Remo Four.

Terry McCusker[281]: "I left school in the summer of 1961 and I got a job in the same block as the Cavern. I worked for the Liverpool Trade Protection Society which sounded ominous. A friend of mine, Brian Harney, had been going to the Cavern and he told me that I had to see this band, who were the business. I was put off going to the Cavern because the girls in the office would come in from the lunchtime sessions and they had this terrible smell which permeated their coats. It was a smell of disinfectant, newly turned grave and a soupcon of sewage, a strange mix. If anybody walked past you in the street, you would know that they had been to the Cavern. Still, Brian persuaded me and I went to my first lunchtime session. We got to the Cavern and they were very deep steps: the pitch on the steps would not be allowed now. I stumbled on the stairs as it was dark. There was a red glow at the bottom

and we turned left, and there were two or three more stairs and there was a table with this little red light. The noise was immense and I thought my chest was going to cave in with the bass drum sound. The band was playing 'Memphis Tennessee', a song I'd never heard before, and the band was the Beatles. I fought my way up through the arches and saw the band and all my senses were assailed by this fabulous band. John Lennon had his back against an upright piano and in-between numbers he was picking his nose. I thought, 'Wow, this guy is being paid for picking his nose and the girls are screaming at him!' Actually, the girls were screaming for Pete Best who was at the back and he didn't seem perturbed at all, a very assured person, and he was knocking seven bells out of his white pearl Premier drum-kit. Paul McCartney was exactly as he is now and they had a fabulous sound. I consider the period from July 1961 and December 1961 to be the golden age for the Cavern. Things changed when Brian Epstein took over the Beatles. There was no alcohol, certainly no drugs, and yet you would come out flushed and hot and exhilarated."

Wednesday 26 July 1961

(lunchtime) Gerry and the Pacemakers

(evening) The Beatles guest night with Johnny Sandon and the Searchers and the Four Jays. **Joey Shields**[282]: "I was lined up for an apprenticeship in BICC in Frodsham and I was just sixteen and my sister Franny came in the living room and I was ironing a shirt. I said it was for an interview tomorrow and I was going to be an electrical engineer. She said, 'The Beatles are playing tonight at the Cavern and they are fabulous.' I went down there and it changed my life. I didn't bother with the interview. The Beatles walked on in leather jackets and opened with 'Rockin' Robin'. They were knockout, they appealed to boys as much as girls because of their rebellious attitude. I met a clique in there and soon I was going to see a never ending list of bands. Most of them had the same repertoire. I loved Kingsize Taylor and I went to see him more than the Beatles. He had a brass section at one stage, they had a trumpet player as well as Howie Casey. It was like an American big roll band with backing singers"

Tuesday 1 August 1961

(lunchtime) That's livin' alright—Joe Fagin fronts the Strangers, but this group had no sartorial style. They look like sewage workers, which of course might be appropriate at the Cavern. **Hank Walters**[283]: "I remember somebody taking his shoes off and walking through the pee in his bare feet. It could go up to your ankles so you got used to rolling your kecks up."

Wednesday 2 August 1961

(lunchtime) The Beatles

(evening) The Beatles, Karl Terry and the Cruisers and Dale Roberts and the Jaywalkers.

From a 2006 conversation with the Jaywalkers:

Dale Roberts[284]: "We had never seen the Beatles before and we saw these black leather trousers and black jackets and long hair. They got on stage and they blew me away. They were louder than anyone else, but they had the equipment."

Dave Williams[285]: "Oh, we had the equipment too, but they turned it up louder. They had to because Pete Best was a very loud drummer. Everything was four to the bar on that bass drum."

Bill Buck[286]: "Exactly. He was a very basic drummer but very very effective. That is what drove the Beatles forward."

Dale Roberts[287]: "Johnny Hutch was even louder. He tied his bass drum to the drum stool to stop it moving away from him as he would whack it so hard."

Billy Hatton[288]: "One time Johnny Hutch glued a piece of wood onto his bass drum and he had the short shaft of a hammer tied to the pedal, and he would whack that bit of wood with the hammer and he put a hole in the front skin to channel the bass drum sound out. That was going some. The three of them were louder than the four Beatles. Adrian designed some amazing speakers and then there was Brian Griffiths. Griff was a fantastic guitar player, and he was bending and breaking strings. He used to use a first string, then a first string as a second string and a second string as a third string. He could get that bendy sound: he must have worked out through some drunken haze. The Beatles had a lot more going for them with their repertoire than the Big Three, but the Big Three were a better rock band than the Beatles."

Saturday 5 August 1961

A handbill for Kenny Ball and his Jazzmen with the Beatles fetched over £1,000 at the Beatles Auction in Liverpool in August 1996. **Kenny Ball**[289]: "I remember the Beatles doing the interval for us at the Cavern and I had never seen guys in all-leather suits before. It can't have been much fun for them as it was very damp down there. The fellers liked us and the girls liked them and I thought there must be something wrong with us."

Geoff Davies[290]: "This was an all-nighter with Kenny Ball and various jazz bands, but the Beatles and the Remo Four were also on the bill. At about one o'clock in the morning, the Mike Cotton jazz band finished and we heard a rock band tune up. It sounded horrible, loud guitars and heavy drums, and so we left quickly. We got a pass-out and went to the Pier Head for a pie and a cup of tea. We thought we would wait until this bloody lot had finished. When we went back, we found that they had gone and Kenny Ball was about to go on, and he was great."

Did the Cavern make the Beatles or did the Beatles make the Cavern? **Mike Brocken**[291]: "Both statements are accurate. The Cavern was existing for many years before the Beatles arrived and there were various mutations of the Beatles that played at the Cavern. They were late to pick up on rock'n'roll. The Beatles put the Cavern on the map as a venue, somewhere to go, somewhere in town as well, as a lot of the venues were suburban, in and around Queens Drive. There were very few places in town and even before the Beatles, Alan Sytner was determined to get people in from the suburbs but ultimately it was Hamburg that made the Beatles, as the performance regime they had had to adopt was forceful and long. Their tenure on the stage was hours and hours and hours. The experiences in Hamburg over a period of time together with their ability to relate to people in the Cavern contributed to it. But if you take the Hamburg experience away from the Beatles, they may not have been the same band."

Johnny Rogan[292]: "That's like an exam question. Why not both? It is not a fair question as there has to be give and take. The Cavern is such an important part of the Beatles' mythology and it put the Cavern on the map as far as Liverpool was concerned. I was brought up in London and yet I knew of the Cavern. It was a small club with a great glamour and it was great that you could see them at lunchtime. You go for your lunch and see the Beatles and get back to work half an hour late. It was so cheap to get in and you could socialise with them. That was amazing."

Bill Heckle[293]: "The Cavern didn't make the Beatles because you could have the same argument for Hamburg. There are a lot of different factors but the fifth Beatle was always Liverpool, and it is more pertinent to say that Liverpool made the Beatles. There were so many elements to the Beatles that are typically Liverpool, and if they had been, say, 20 miles away in Wigan or Widnes, they would not have been the Beatles. The Cavern was a venue where they learnt their trade, but if there hadn't been a Cavern, they would have played somewhere else. "

Dave Jones[294]: "The Beatles didn't make the Cavern as it had been a successful venue since 1957. It was a marriage of convenience for both, and both benefited considerably from each other."

Bill Heckle[295]: "With one caveat. There would be no interest in the Cavern today if the Beatles hadn't been discovered there or played there that many times. It would be like the Sink or the Mardi, just a place that is talked about."

Saturday 12 August 1961
The Zenith Six Jazz Band with Ian and the Zodiacs. **Ian Edwards**[296]: "At first I couldn't see why anyone would want to play the Cavern as it was a dirty smelly place but I soon changed my mind. I remember that evening as the Zenith Six didn't want to have anything to do with beat music. They dashed to the Grapes before we got started."

Wednesday 23 August 1961
(lunchtime) The Beatles
(evening) The Beatles, the Rockin' Blackcats and Carl Vincent and the Counts
  Geoff Davies[297]: "I worked in a tailor's, Hepworth's, in London Road. It was a five and a half day week with a half-day off on Wednesday so I went down with a mate and the Beatles were on and I stood close to the stage and I watched them and I was sold. That was it: I dropped all my prejudices about pop, and it was one of the finest things that I have ever seen in my life. It wasn't just the music: it was the whole attitude

they created, the style, the couldn't-care-less attitude, the jokes between the songs. I knew most of the songs as they were from Chuck Berry, Fats Domino and Little Richard but they gave them such life. In some cases, they sounded better than the originals. Of course, they could care and I went to see them as often as I could. Sometimes I saw the lunchtime sessions where they played two sets and later on I would see them doing two sets in the evening as well. That was very convenient for them as they could leave their gear in the Cavern. I have lost count of the number of times I saw the Beatles but it was dozens and dozens and it was always in the Cavern. I saw a lot of the other bands, but there was a massive drop in quality down to the others."

Friday 25 August 1961
The Cavern promotes a riverboat shuffle aboard the Royal Iris with Acker Bilk's Paramount Jazz Band, currently enjoying their third Top 10 hit with "That's My Home", and the Beatles. **Acker Bilk**[298]: "The boat used to go down the Mersey a bit and out in the channel and the Beatles did our interval spots. They wore black leathers and I liked the tunes they played. I was quite impressed with them but I was more impressed to be steering the boat as the Captain gave me the wheel whilst the Beatles were playing."

  Pete Best[299]: "Acker's drummer was Ron McKay, who came from Liverpool, and he said that I could use his drums. I thought nothing of it but when we got on stage, I found that it was set up wrong for me as he was a left-handed drummer. I frantically rearranged them and we played all right. It was a great night as the cabin at the back of the stage was crammed with beer and we had a great drinking session with Acker and his band."

Wednesday 30 August 1961
(lunchtime) The Ravens
(evening) The Beatles and the Strangers
  Al Peters[300]: "The Beatles liked the intensity of rhythm and blues and put it into their own music. 'What'd I Say' is a cliché now but at the time, it was part of the fight against what was going on before. It had a rhumba beat but it had a very menacing bass intro. Ray Charles played it on the piano, but the Beatles played it with bass and guitar."

Bob Wooler writes an extraordinary article about the Beatles in *Mersey Beat*. An outsider reading it would think that this was the biggest and most original group in the country. He ends his eulogy with "Such are the fantastic Beatles. I don't think anything like them will happen again."

Ray Ennis[301]: "Bob Wooler announced everyone from the band room. I don't ever remember him on stage. Compères were for theatres and nightclubs and so it was unusual to have someone in a small club. Bob would play records to start the evening off and that gave the evening a bit more atmosphere. He told the audience who was coming on soon and things like that. He would do it from the bandroom and even if you were in the front row, you wouldn't see him at all. The arch on the left went into the bandroom and he was round the corner sitting by the Vortex amplifier with a small mike. Bob would have been a brilliant radio DJ."

Monday 4 September 1961
A lunchtime date for Gerry and the Pacemakers back from their first stint in Hamburg.

Wednesday 6 September 1961
(lunchtime) Gerry and the Pacemakers
(evening) The Beatles, Johnny Sandon and the Searchers, and Ian and the Zodiacs

Bob Wooler[302]: "I didn't know Brian Epstein at the time, but I bought my records from NEMS because they gave me a 10% discount as I told them I was a disc-jockey. In return for the discount, I told them that I would mention that I was playing a record that I had bought from NEMS in Whitechapel. He was getting an advertisement for less than one shilling! They were my own records because if they had belonged to the Cavern, I couldn't play them at Aintree Institute or Litherland Town Hall. Ray McFall bought some too, mostly jazz like Kenny Ball's 'Midnight In Moscow', and he also liked Anthony Newley's 'Why', which I would dutifully play."

Willy Russell[303]: "Bob Wooler was fantastic. Everyone forgets that for the first 40 minutes you were in there, you were treated to one of the best DJ sessions imaginable, all kinds of records, and lots that I had never heard. He used to play Chan Romero's 'Hippy Hippy Shake', usually to start the evening, and it was a stunning version. Bob had worn a copy out as he had played it so often

and someone had brought him a second copy. There were records by the Coasters and lots of obscure cuts, all made fantastically accessible by this brilliant showman, but when I heard him at the Cavern, I couldn't put a face or a body to the voice. The voice came out from the back of the band room and created its own very special magic. He was never patronising like Pete Murray, those DJs who were from a different generation. They were like hip adults talking down to the kids and Bob didn't do any of that. He injected everything with a sense of showmanship but there was always a bit of wry, self-parody in it. He wasn't trying to con us."

Tuesday 19 September 1961
The Remo Four advertises for a drummer in the *Liverpool Echo*. **Colin Middlebrough**[304]: "I saw the ad and I went to the Cavern for an audition and met Don Andrew. They did 'Peter Gunn' and I played it in totally the wrong style and Billy Buck got the job, quite rightly."

Thursday 21 September 1961
(lunchtime) The Beatles
(evening) Return of modern jazz with Art Ellefson and Johnny Dankworth. **John Dankworth**[305]: "Art Ellefson was a Canadian tenor saxophone player who played with our big band and quite often we worked as a splinter group. It is most likely to have been a quintet with him on tenor and me on alto with the rhythm section. The pianist would have been Alan Branscombe who came from Liverpool and had a slight Scouse accent. He was a great pianist, a wonderful vibraphone player and a really good alto player and I made sure that he didn't outshine me on the alto by leaving that until the end of the evening and hoping for the best. He could blow me off the stage whenever he wanted to."

Wednesday 27 September 1961
(lunchtime) The Beatles
(evening) The Beatles, Gerry and the Pacemakers, and Mark Peters and the Cyclones

Friday 29 September 1961
(lunchtime) The Beatles. After this show, John and Paul take a fortnight's holiday in Paris.
(evening) Alan Elsdon's Jazz Band, the Remo Four, Gerry and the Pacemakers and Pete Haslam's Collegians Jazz Band

Friday 6 October 1961

Lunchtime session with Ian and the Zodiacs. "If you say I did a lunchtime session, then I did, but I'm surprised," says **Ian Edwards**[306], "I worked with people who were long in the tooth and I can't imagine taking a couple of hours off."

Geoff Davies[307]: "The Cavern was part of my early courting days. The first time I put my hand down a girl's blouse was at the Cavern and the first time I put my hand up a girl's skirt was at the Cavern too. A whole new world was opening up to me."

Wednesday 11 October 1961

The Remo Four, Mark Peters and the Cyclones, and Clay Ellis and the Raiders

Saturday 14 October 1961

A big night—Bob Wallis and his Storyville Jazzmen, Terry Lightfoot's New Orleans Jazzmen and Sonny Terry and Brownie McGhee. **Geoff Davies**[308]: "There was a full house and Sonny Terry and Brownie McGhee were great. I saw them about a year later on the Philharmonic and it wasn't the same. It was similar material but it didn't have the atmosphere of the Cavern. And all of this was achieved without alcohol, which is amazing."

Sunday 15 October 1961

The Melbourne New Orleans Jazz—for once, the name matched from where they came.

Thursday 19 October 1961

After the lunchtime session, the Pacemakers met up with the Beatles at the Mandolin and decided over a few beers to form a supergroup for one night only, so they combined forces as the Beatmakers at Litherland Town Hall. Meanwhile, Tubby Hayes entertained at the Cavern.

Saturday 21 October 1961

All nighter with the Beatles, Gerry and the Pacemakers, the Remo Four and three jazz bands—Yorkshire, Panama and Pete Haslam's Collegians **John McCormick**[309]: "I thought the Beatles were amazing and I thought their stamina was amazing. It reminded me of when I went to a night club in Zurich and I played jazz for five or six hours every night and I realised where the Beatles had got their stamina from as they had the same experience in Hamburg. I knew that when I went home every gig that I did was going to seem

so easy and short, and it did for a while. That's how they felt too, they were flying through the gigs in England as they were almost over before they started.

Wednesday 1 November 1961

(lunchtime) Around this time, **Terry McCusker**[310] saw the Beatles at a lunchtime session: "I remember that Ringo played with the Beatles at a lunchtime session: I suppose Pete Best was ill. When I got down there, the guitars and the amps were there, but there was no drum-kit, just a hi-hat and some cymbals. We were waiting and waiting and people were shouting, "Come on, it's our lunch-hour." The Beatles came on stage but Ringo didn't have a kit and he was just stamping on the stage and tapping cymbals as they were playing. After 20 minutes, somebody came down with a drum-kit and they set them up and off they went again."

(evening) The Beatles, the Strangers and Gerry and the Pacemakers. **Alex Young**[311]: "Gerry Marsden was always my favourite. You could ask him, 'What's the second chord in 'Dream Lover'?' and he would show you. That meant a lot to me. His mob also learnt songs very fast. I can recall 'Take Five' being big in the charts and Gerry went on the piano for it. It was very well played too, so different from the other numbers."

Joey Shields[312]: "I was working at Cooper's in Church Street for £6.10 a week. It was a food emporium. There was a fantastic smell of coffee at the front. I worked in the warehouse at the back. I encouraged most of the staff to come along to the Cavern. Every week our crowd was bigger. We had 20 people in the end. Our lunch break was for half an hour. If George Harrison was late, I would miss the Beatles as they wouldn't be on before 12.30pm. I wanted Cooper's to extend our lunch hour and they said we could have an hour. We always kept to the time. Sometimes they would come on at 12.15pm and we would see 45 minutes."

Wednesday 8 November 1961

The Beatles, the Remo Four and Ian and the Zodiacs. **Ian Edwards**[313]: "The Beatles were always going through songs in the band room and didn't mix with the other bands too much. On reflection, we might have been bigger if we'd spent more time writing songs and not gone to the pub."

Thursday 9 November 1961

How did **Raymond Jones**[314] come to be talking to Brian Epstein? "I used to go to NEMS every Saturday and I would be buying records by Carl Perkins and Fats Domino because I heard the Beatles playing their songs. My sister's ex-husband, who played with Mark Peters and the Cyclones, told me that the Beatles had made a record and so I went to NEMS to get it. Brian Epstein said to me, 'Who are they?' and I said, 'They are the most fantastic group you will ever hear.' No one will take away from me that it was me who spoke to Brian Epstein and then he went to the Cavern to see for himself. I didn't make them famous, Brian Epstein made them famous, but things might have been different without me."

Bob Wooler[315]: "Brian Epstein learnt that the Beatles were playing close to his shop in Whitechapel. He was intrigued to see what they were like and he phoned Bill Harry at *Mersey Beat* and asked him to smooth his entrance into the Cavern. Bill arranged this with Ray McFall and with Paddy Delaney on the door. On 9 November 1961, Brian took his PA, Alistair Taylor, along for support and they stood at the back of the crowd and heard John, Paul, George and Pete on stage, although they can't have seen much. Nevertheless, Brian was bowled over by them. It was fortunate that Brian saw a good performance when he came down to the Cavern that lunchtime. He also liked how they behaved, and he found them very animalistic. They were unkempt, they didn't comb their hair—and, most importantly, they were lithe and physically attractive." And Bob summed it up thus, "If B.E. hadn't been feeling that way that day, it never would have happened, OK?"

Brian Epstein's personal assistant at NEMS, **Alistair Taylor**[316], remembers: "One day Brian asked me to join him for lunch but he wanted to look in at the Cavern first to catch one of the Beatles' lunchtime sessions. I recognised the Beatles from their visits to NEMS, though I don't remember them buying many records, and we looked out of place in white shirts and dark, business suits. The Beatles were playing 'A Taste Of Honey' and 'Twist And Shout' but we were particularly impressed that they included original

songs. The one that sticks in my mind is 'Hello Little Girl'."

John Booker[317]: "Wearing a suit was not unusual at the Cavern. I worked in Water Street and I would see people walking out of the station with bowler hats and striped suits and furled umbrellas. Our auditor used to wear a morning suit so it looked as though he had come from the Bank of England. When I went to NEMS, I would see Brian Epstein dressed like a city businessman but he was in a record shop and this didn't quite fit with that. He had an air of a prosperous stockbroker and it was like he was doing you a favour by condescending to do business with you. About half the audience in the Cavern would be wearing suits and the girls would be typists who were handbag dancing and I certainly wore a suit and tie."

David Backhouse[318]: "I first went to the Cavern in the lunchtime sessions in 1959. I was an office boy in an architect's office in Tower Buildings and the bosses didn't like us going down there. We would be drenched and we come back wringing our shirts out and putting our ties back on. We would dance and jive and watch the Beatles and it was pretty exhilarating."

Mike Byrne[319]: "I was working round the corner at my dad's shop, who had a tailor and outfitters in Century Buildings. I had a very smart, single-breasted two piece suit, and I had to wear starched collars as my dad had come from an even posher tailors, Geeves and Hawkes, the tailors to the military. He was a dapper gentlemen. The starched collars were terrible to wear and I must have looked overdressed at the Cavern."

David Backhouse[320]: "I would go and see the Big Three and the Beatles when I could as they had both got good drummers and were very beaty. I was there when Brian Epstein came to the Cavern. He was a beautifully-suited, elegant man and he looked totally incongruous. I knew who he was, although I had never spoken to him."

Ray Ennis[321]: "I'd met Brian Epstein before and I asked him what he was doing in the Cavern. He said, 'I've come to watch the Beatles. I believe they are very good.' He didn't say anything about signing them."

Paddy Delaney[322]: "Brian Epstein was well-groomed in a smart, dark blue suit and looked out of place. When it was all over, he was still hanging about, so I approached him and said, 'It's all over now, sir.' He said, 'It's all right, I'm going to meet the Beatles.'"

An American jazz legend, Zoot Sims, headlined the evening session, while the Beatles played for what was to be their last time at Litherland Town Hall. **Geoff Davies**[323]: "The modern jazz nights were always poorly attended and there were only about 30 people for Zoot Sims. He was one of those people whom I should have loved but I was not crazy about him that night." So, all in all, a great day for the Beatles but a dreadful one for Ray McFall's finances.

Tuesday 14 November 1961

What a night. The Blue Genes played host to the Beatles, Gerry and the Pacemakers, and the Remo Four

Wednesday 22 November 1961

The Beatles, Gerry and the Pacemakers, and Earl Preston and the TTs. **Earl Preston**[324]: "I had started to write songs in the TTs. They weren't much good but it was something I wanted to do. We did one called 'Sweet Love' on stage. Paul McCartney used to call me Wee George as I was smaller than George Harrison and he said, 'That was good, Wee George, I didn't realise you wrote songs.' I said that I'd only written a couple and he said, 'We've written a few but we don't think that they're good enough to do on stage.'"

Alan Stratton[325]: "The Beatles were the first band to have harmonies and they would switch lead vocalists, so that made it interesting as a lot of the bands only had one lead singer. I also loved hearing the deep throbbing bass with Pete Best's drums. The exciting thing was watching Pete Best set up his drums and the atmosphere was electric as we knew what was coming."

Alex Young[326]: "When the Beatles came on stage, the front men would come on first and they would plug in and tune up. When they were in tune, Pete Best would walk on and the Cavern would erupt—waaah! All the girls would be screaming as he was such a handsome and good-looking lad. He was like a film star."

Friday 24 November 1961

Cavernites would sing "There is a Cavern in the town" when Terry Lightfoot's New Orleans Jazz-men played 'Tavern In The Town'. They were now hit-makers with their version of "True Love".

Sunday 26 November 1961

And so were Bob Wallis and the Storyville Jazz-men with 'I'm Shy, Mary Ellen, I'm Shy'.

Thursday 30 November 1961

Don Rendell was a London-based modern jazz saxophonist. He played "You Stepped Out Of A Dream" as "You Loomed Out Of Loch Ness". **Geoff Davies**[327]: "The modern jazz evening that stands out for me was the one with Don Rendell. I remember Brian Epstein ordering an LP for me, *Roarin'*, which I still have. I always looked for Brian at NEMS as he was so efficient and knew what he was doing."

Jean Catharell[328]: "You would hear bands doing numbers that I had never heard before and I would get some of the original versions from NEMS. We had a record shop at the bottom of the street where I lived but it was nothing compared to NEMS. They would even get the catalogues out if you weren't sure what you wanted."

Tuesday 5 December 1961

Bob Wooler[329]: "After one lunchtime session, the Beatles and I repaired to the Grapes—it was three o'clock closing then—and they told me that Brian Epstein wanted to see them with a view to securing a recording contract and even managing them, but they were very dubious. They asked me to go with them to NEMS to suss him out. It was very embarrassing because we were late and it was half-day closing. They knocked on the glass door and it looked as though he had gone, but he came up from the basement and unlocked the door. The introductions were made at the classical counter on the ground floor. I should have done the intros but I didn't because I felt I was only there as an advisor. John came to the rescue and said, 'This is me dad', which I resented, by the way. I was older than him, but surely I didn't look that much older. Epstein was bewildered by all this and he didn't want to say anything about management whilst this outsider was there. He was very nice and very polite, but he arranged another meeting when 'Dad' wouldn't be there. At that first meeting, he asked about 'My Bonnie', and said he was in a position to import copies if he was sure it would sell enough to be worthwhile."

Thursday 7 December 1961

Enough's enough. Ray McFall dropped modern jazz after this evening with the Tony Kinsey Quintet.

Friday 8 December 1961

Bob Wooler[330]: "We didn't have a strong drug scene by any means. Originally, it was just purple hearts, amphetamines, speed or whatever you want to call it. When the Beatles went down south, they sometimes brought back cannabis and gradually the drug scene developed in Liverpool. There was a rare instance of cocaine when Davy Jones, a black rock'n'roll singer who'd been with the Beatles in Hamburg, appeared at the Cavern. He was a Little Richard/Derry Wilkie type, very outgoing and bouncy. His big record was an oldie, 'Amapola', and its lyric about the 'pretty little poppy' must have appealed to him."

Karl Terry[331]: "I saw Davy Jones at the Cavern and he was a real showman. I thought he worked with the cramped conditions better than I did."

Back to **Bob Wooler**[332]: "Alan Ross, who was a local compère, brought Davy down to the Cavern, and that was when I had cocaine for the first and only time in my life. I told Davy Jones about my sinuses, and he said, 'This'll clear it.' Alan Ross gave me a smile of approval, I tried it…and nearly hit the roof. There was laughter galore, and I rushed out into Mathew Street, trying to breathe the effects out. I remember Pat Delaney saying, 'What's wrong, Robert?' and I said, 'Nothing, I'm just a bit giddy.' The Beatles welcomed Davy Jones with open arms, so I'm sure the drug-taking didn't stop with me. That is the common factor with the Beatles—whatever was going, they wanted to be part of it." Davy Jones was with the Beatles that night for promoter Sam Leach's marathon at the Tower Ballroom.

Sunday 10 December 1961

Humphrey Lyttelton and his Jazz Band, with Johnny Sandon and the Searchers. **Geoff Davies**[333]: "I liked Humphrey Lyttelton very much as he was more mainstream and he didn't have a banjo. That made it cooler without being modern jazz."

Meanwhile, the Beatles gave a lackluster performance at Hambleton Hall, Huyton. They had been at a disastrous gig at Aldershot for Sam Leach the night before and they were fed up.

Bob Wooler gave them a piece of his mind. **Sam Leach**[334]: "They got back late from Aldershot, not through my fault, but they were shattered. That was the night they decided to go with Epstein. I wanted to manage them too but it had been a terrible night and they felt it wouldn't have happened with Epstein."

Wednesday 13 December 1961

(lunchtime) The Beatles
(evening) The Beatles, Gerry and the Pacemakers, and the Four Jays

Friday 15 December 1961

(lunchtime) The Beatles
(evening) Yorkshire Jazz Band with Gerry and the Pacemakers

Saturday 23 December 1961

All nighter with Beatles, Searchers, Gerry, Remo and the Saints and Mickey Ashman's jazz bands. **Arthur Johnson**[335]: "I started coming here when I was fourteen or fifteen. I know I went to an all night session when I was sixteen. I got on a bus at Crosby and went to Skelhorne Street and then walked down here and spent the entire night enjoying myself, but it was only coffee and Coke. There were no parental problems for me and there were no worries about me being there. The band I liked most was the Big Three—they were very loud and very big- and I enjoyed the Undertakers very much as well. I almost felt as though I was in a youth club because it wasn't licensed and it was halfway between a youth club and the adult world. It was good to stay up all night. You felt slightly naughty without doing anything naughty."

Sunday 24 December 1961

Eric Allandale's New Orleans Knights, Johnny Sandon and the Searchers and the Swinging Blue Genes

Tuesday 26 December 1961

The Swinging Blue Genes' Christmas Party with the Remo Four and the Four Jays. **Ray Ennis**[336]: "We would do 'Easter Bonnet' at Easter and 'Jingle Bells' at Christmas. Funnily enough, not many of the bands did those holiday hits." "Not quite," says **John Cochrane**[337], "I can remember the Blue Genes doing 'Easter Bonnet' at Christmas."

The Christmas party was an ideal time for the Four Jays, later the Fourmost, to do their impersonations. **Dave Lovelady**[338]: "So far as I know, we were the first group to do impressions. We did them long before the Barron Knights and the Rockin' Berries. Brian O'Hara was doing impressions of Gracie Fields and Chic Murray."

Don Andrew[339] of the Remo Four: "We could hardly cope with our daytime jobs as we were playing six or seven nights a week and maybe doing lunchtime sessions too. Apart from the Beatles, I'd say we were the highest paid and the busiest group on Merseyside. We wanted to turn professional and when we saw an advert in a national paper for groups to go to France and play on the American bases, we thought we'd have a go. We auditioned in Soho on Boxing Day 1961 and we went over there in February 1962."

Wednesday 27 December 1961
The Beatles' Christmas Party with Gerry and the Pacemakers and Kingsize Taylor and the Dominoes.

Friday 29 December 1961
The Beatles with the Yorkshire Jazz Band. **John Cook**[340], who was also with the White Eagle Jazz Band: "They weren't playing our type of music and we weren't playing theirs. I know John Lennon later said that jazz was shit, but he wouldn't have dared say it to our faces. I'm an ex-Commando, Bob is ex-para and Martin Boland is an ex-rugby league professional with a very short fuse."

Another White Eagle, **Bob Frettlohr**[341]: "Nobody ever made jokes about me being German. They called me 'Bert Trautmann' which was fine by me. It wouldn't have bothered me anyway. My wife was very helpful and through her I got to speak English properly, admittedly with a York-shire accent. You can ask me to spell anything and I can, and that's down to her. Maybe it came easy because I was a musician and so I was working with sound all the time."

Saturday 30 December 1961
The Beatles with the White Eagle Jazz Band

Sunday 31 December 1961
Seeing in the New Year with Terry Pitt's Jazzmen, Swinging Blue Genes, and Johnny Sandon and the Searchers.

During December 1961, Brian Epstein got in touch with "Disker", a *Liverpool Echo* pseudonym for **Tony Barrow**[342], a Crosby boy who had moved to London to work for Decca: "Brian played me an acetate of the Beatles recorded at the Cavern. The sound quality was abominable, although it did convey the atmosphere of the place. It wasn't for me to say, 'Don't call us, we'll call you.' I spoke on the telephone to the marketing department and said that I had one of their customers here, a record dealer from Liverpool, and they might want to put pressure on the A&R department for an audition. As soon as I mentioned NEMS they said, 'NEMS, oh yes. Brian Epstein's group must have an audition.'"

Hence, the Beatles weren't performing on New Year's Eve: they were on their way to London for an audition at Decca Records. For whatever reason, they gave a decent but lacklustre performance and were rejected in favour of Brian Poole and the Tremeloes. On any other occasion, signing Brian Poole and the Tremeloes would have been regarded as a good day's work.

4

SOUP & SWEAT & ROCK & ROLL

Cavern owner:
Ray McFall,
the key year, 1962

This was a fantastic year: a superb year for the Cavern, a superb year for the Beatles, a superb year for anyone who was in a Liverpool beat group really. I was eight miles from the city centre doing my A-levels and even though I bought records in NEMS and read the occasional *Mersey Beat*, it never occurred to me to go the Cavern: how sad is that? Occasionally, I went to a dance at the local St Luke's Hall in Crosby and my most vivid memory is of irate dancers turning on the organiser because one of his friends had won the raffle.

The *Mersey Beat Popularity Poll* was published on 4 January 1962 and the top three bands were the Beatles, Gerry and the Pacemakers and the Remo Four. The Swinging Blue Genes don't make the Top 20, but they are still regarded as a jazz band and *Mersey Beat* concentrates on beat music.

Ozzie Yue[343]: "Before I saw Gerry and the Pacemakers, I was a Shadows man. Gerry did a lot of Buddy Holly things. The groups didn't do the run of the mill Top 20 numbers and so they were educating you musically. Chuck Berry more than anyone else. It made me want to find out more about Chuck Berry which is what I did: straight from the Cavern and into NEMS."

Tommy Steele was in pantomime at the Royal Court. During his stay, he went to the Cavern to hear the songs for a new musical, *Half A Sixpence*. He was to star in the West End show, which also became an enduring film.

Wednesday 3 January 1962
(lunchtime) Beatles
(evening) Beatles, Johnny Sandon and the Searchers, Kingsize Taylor and the Dominoes

Friday 5 January 1962
(lunchtime) Beatles
(evening) Tony Smith Jazzmen with Kingsize Taylor and the Dominoes. **Sam Hardie**[344]: "I think that traditional jazz was artificially promoted for a long time by the likes of the BBC and *Saturday Club*. Nobody would tune into *Saturday Club* for the jazz bands, but they got them. With jazz being the original thing at the Cavern, the bands carried on for a while, past the time they should have done really. I love jazz but it was promoted artificially after its time."

Chris Barber[345]: "We never played the Cavern but we did concerts every six months in Liverpool, usually at the Phil. We did meet the Beatles a couple of times and bought them drinks and were friendly. The Beatles were quite surprised because I don't think they'd met any jazz musicians who'd been friendly before. It didn't stop John making his famous pronouncement that he didn't like jazz."

John Lawrence[346] of the Merseysippis: "I remember with some embarrassment that when we came off stage to go to the pub and the Beatles came on stage, we never spoke to each other. We had a barely concealed contempt for each other. We were older than they were and later on John Lennon described us as the old buggers who didn't want them on stage, which was correct. We lived in different worlds." In 2007, over 40 years later, those old buggers still have a weekly residency in Liverpool.

Saturday 6 January 1962

Pete Haslam's Collegians with the Beatles. **Bob Wooler**[347]: "There was a short period at the Cavern where beat groups would be billed alongside jazz bands. It was a strange combination and it wasn't clear for whom Ray McFall was catering. Ray would book the jazz bands, who would say it was no use to be on such a bill. The jazz element became disenchanted with the Cavern and so the club turned completely to rock. Most of the jazzmen now say, 'Oh, I knew right away that the Beatles were going to be stars.' Absolute rubbish. I have heard the country singer Hank Walters talking on Radio Merseyside about how he enjoyed playing alongside the Beatles—more rubbish. His attitude was, 'Do we have to suffer this lot?' Fair-weather friends, or what?"

Tuesday 9 January 1962

(lunchtime) Beatles
(evening) Blue Genes Guest Night with the Remo Four and Johnny Sandon and the Searchers

Ann Upton[348]: "There were so many places to go to—the Iron Door, the Cavern, Aintree Institute and Litherland Town Hall and all the Co-op halls too. The Cavern was handy as it was in town and I worked in Dale Street. Everybody would know somebody in a band. I lived in the Dingle and Gerry Marsden was two streets away from me and up the road lived Billy Fury and my grandma lived by Brian O'Hara from the Fourmost. I would go and see the bands at lunchtime and then go back to what was like a church atmosphere with Lloyd's underwriters with bowler hats.

We would be dripping with sweat and smelling of the Cavern and disinfectant. We wouldn't have had any lunch. Then we would go home and go and see somebody else. It was absolutely wonderful."

Wednesday 10 January 1962

Beatles and Gerry and the Pacemakers

Friday 12 January 1962

Mike Cotton Jazzmen with the Beatles. The Beatles also appeared at the Tower Ballroom, New Brighton and found themselves headlining as Screaming Lord Sutch and his Savages didn't turn up.

Saturday 13 January 1962

The Saints Jazz Band with Gerry and the Pacemakers

Sunday 14 January 1962

Mickey Ashman's Ragtime Jazz Band with Gerry and the Pacemakers

Sunday 21 January 1962

Visiting from Australia, the Melbourne New Orleans Jazz Band with the Blue Genes

Monday 22 January 1962

The start of one-hour lunch sessions instead of two with one shilling admission. First artists—the Beatles.

Tuesday 23 January 1962

(lunchtime) Gerry and the Pacemakers
(evening) Blue Genes Guest Night with Remo Four and Strangers

Wednesday 24 January 1962

(lunchtime) Beatles
(evening) Beatles, Gerry and the Pacemakers and Four Jays

Earl Preston[349]: "I used to love Paul McCartney singing Little Richard and Ray Charles songs. One lunchtime the electricity went off and they had no mikes and no instruments. Paul went on the piano and did some Ray Charles songs—'Hallelujah I Love Her So' and 'What'd I Say'—and he was brilliant. He could do that scream in 'What'd I Say' perfectly."

Saturday 27 January 1962

Pete Haslam's Collegians with Johnny Sandon and the Searchers and Gerry and the Pacemakers

Sunday 28 January 1962

Ken Colyer Jazz Band

Tuesday 30 January 1962

(lunchtime) Beatles

(evening) Blue Genes Guest Night with Johnny Sandon and the Searchers and Ian and the Zodiacs. **Ian Edwards**[350]: "Trying to get your amps down those stairs was bad enough but getting them through the crowd was terrible. You couldn't move and we were passing amplifiers over the top of them."

John Cochrane[351]: "Sometimes I would take the drums out through the audience, up the stairs, do another gig and then come back to the Cavern and do the same thing. I wish I played the flute on a number of occasions."

Wednesday 31 January 1962

(lunchtime) Gerry and the Pacemakers

(evening) Beatles, Remo Four and Kingsize Taylor and the Dominoes

Ron Jones[352]: "I worked with Don Andrew and he was the bass player in the Remo Four. Their guitarist was probably the best guitarist in Liverpool and he could play all the Chet Atkins numbers and I was one of their camp followers. Even if the Remo Four were on with the Beatles, the Beatles were like second billing to me."

Friday 2 February 1962

(lunchtime) Gerry and the Pacemakers

(evening) Red River Jazzmen with the debut of Pete Maclaine and the Dakotas. **Mike Maxfield**[353]: "We were the first Manchester band to play in Liverpool. It was somewhere in West Derby and these girls told us about the Cavern. We went down there and we nagged Ray McFall into giving us a gig. He was reticent at first because he said there were already too many groups in Liverpool."

Ray McFall[354]: "The excellent reaction to Pete Maclaine and the Dakotas convinced me that I should broaden the horizons and book some beat groups from outside Liverpool."

Ray Ennis[355]: "The audience loved the Dakotas, so there wasn't any Liverpool/ Manchester rivalry there, not even between the bands. It was a little different when the Hollies came as they were all wearing leather and copying the Beatles."

Ian Edwards[356]: "The Hollies were the guests when they held the *Mersey Beat* awards night at the Majestic. Everybody clapped when they came on stage but when they saw their leather suits, they booed them for copying the Beatles. Their

harmonies were fantastic but we thought that they had a bloody cheek to be doing that."

Ann Upton[357]: "There was some Liverpool and Manchester rivalry but it was all very friendly: they were gently ribbing each other. Cy Tucker always wanted a certain guitar, but obviously, they were all playing cheap ones and wanted better ones. One time, the Hollies came in and they tried to be like the Beatles with their leather gear. Graham Nash said, 'You'll never guess what I've got here', and Tucker saw it was the guitar he wanted. Tucker said, 'It's got no strings' and Graham Nash said, 'I haven't learnt to play it yet, but I don't want to stand up there doing nothing.'"

Dave Boyce[358]: "The fans loved it when the Hollies came on in leathers as they looked like the Beatles used to look, pre-Epstein. The Beatles were being perceived as drifting away from Liverpool and the Hollies were really a Beatles tribute band, who were filling the gap."

Billy Hatton[359]: "The Manchester band which really impressed me was Pete Maclaine and the Dakotas. Tony was the first guy I'd seen who played bass drum patterns as opposed to thump-thumping. He was like a modern jazz drummer but he was in a rock band—and he had a Ludwig kit as well. They were very very impressive. Mike Maxfield was equally good—he was very meticulous and a great player. He'd written a great instrumental, 'The Cruel Sea', which they often performed at the Cavern."

Pete Maclaine[360]: "We played in a talent contest at the Plaza in Manchester and the manager said, 'Why don't you all dress up as Indians and call yourselves the Dakotas?' We liked the idea of the Dakotas, but we didn't like the idea of dressing up. Most Indians don't drink pints of bitter. We used to do standards like 'Lover Come Back To Me' and we also did impressions. My impression of Gene Vincent went down very well at the Cavern. I did it once singing 'Baby Blue', which calls for 16 bars of very heavy drumming. Tony Mansfield collapsed and fainted over his kit because it was so hot in the Cavern."

Colin Middlebrough[361]: "My favourite drummer was Tony Mansfield from the Dakotas as he had an American kit, a Ludwig. They did instrumentals like 'The Cruel Sea' and Tony did this

George singing onstage at the Cavern

Delbert McClinton & Bruce Channel

Pete MaClaine & The Dakotas

Kingsioze Taylor

Gene Vincent and Dave Williams

AT THE CAVERN CLUB
10 Mathew St., off North John St.
TO-NIGHT: THE COLLEGIANS
KINGSIZE TAYLOR & THE DOMINOES
TO-MORROW (SATURDAY):
RED RIVER JAZZMEN
THE FOUR JAYS
SUNDAY: KEN SIMS
VINTAGE JAZZ BAND
Plus THE SWINGING BLUEGENES
LUNCHTIME SESSIONS
NEXT WEEK:
MONDAY, WEDNESDAY, & FRIDAY
GERRY & THE PACEMAKERS
TUESDAY AND THURSDAY
PETE McLAINE & THE DAKOTAS
DON'T MISS MAY 14 TO 18:
JOHNNY KIDD & THE PIRATES
MAY 21 TO 25:
MIKE BERRY & THE OUTLAWS
APPEARING IN PERSON
LUNCHTIME AND EVENING
AT THE CAVERN
Central 1591.

Remo Four

ten minute drum solo much to my delight on Gene Vincent's 'Baby Blue'. He built it up and up and he collapsed one day with the heat over the drums. Only Roy Dyke or Aynsley Dunbar could have competed with that."

Monday 5 February 1962

It's back to two hour lunchtime sessions and again, it's the Beatles.

Tuesday 6 February 1962

(lunchtime) Gerry and the Pacemakers

(evening) Blue Genes' Guest Night with the Four Jays and the Strangers

Wednesday 7 February 1962

(lunchtime) Beatles

(evening) Beatles, Gerry and the Pacemakers, and Dale Roberts and the Jaywalkers

Friday 9 February 1962

(lunchtime) Beatles

(evening) Pete Haslam's Collegians, Beatles and Gerry and the Pacemakers

Tuesday 13 February 1962

(lunchtime) Beatles

(evening) Blue Genes Guest Night with Gerry and the Pacemakers and Kingsize Taylor and the Dominoes

Saturday 17 February 1962

The Beatles, Cyril Preston's Excelsior Jazz Band and the Zenith Six Jazz Band. **Geoff Davies**[362]: "One of my favourite bands, and nobody has ever heard of them, was a jazz band from Manchester called the Zenith Six, who were absolutely great and quite funny as well: they had some good chat between the numbers. They did old favourites like 'Tiger Rag' and 'Savoy Blues', but there was something different and cheeky about them."

Monday 19 February 1962

(lunchtime) Beatles

(evening) Blue Genes Guest Night with the Four Jays and Johnny Sandon and the Searchers

Wednesday 21 February 1962

(lunchtime) Beatles

(evening) Beatles with Ken Dallas and the Silhouettes. Also, Steve Day and the Drifters, who were Wump and his Werbles with a new name: wonder why they changed.

Friday 23 February 1962

(lunchtime) Beatles

(evening) Saints Jazz Band with Johnny Sandon and the Searchers. **Joey Shields**[363]: "People were queuing just after midnight for the show the next day. George Harrison came in his Consul and asked them how long they had been waiting. He knew that they would be out in the elements all night and he went to the Pier Head and brought back 25 steak-and-kidney pies."

Saturday 24 February 1962

All nighter with Beatles, Red River Jazzmen, Tony Smith's Jazz Band, Ken Sims' Vintage Jazz Band, Gerry and the Pacemakers, and Ken Dallas and the Silhouettes. The Beatles had a gig earlier in the evening at the YMCA in Hoylake, where, astonishingly, they were booed for their long introductions and pauses between songs.

Lawrence Swerdlow[364]: "As soon as you entered the cellar stairs, you could feel the dampness and smell the place. It had a very distinct edge to it. It gave you a lift, it was exciting, like walking into a party. It was a friendly atmosphere with the dinner lady doing sandwiches and cakes."

A catering conversation:

Thelma Hargrove[366]: "Even on an ordinary Saturday night I would get home at one o'clock in the morning. Paddy Delaney used to drive us in his Jazzmobile—there was me, Paddy, Alan Graham and Bob McGrae and we would have supper at a Chinese on Prescot Road. They would be expecting us."

Sandra Hargrove[365]: "I'd be up waiting for you and I'd look out through the curtains for the Jazzmobile. It would head out to Page Moss and Paddy would be the last one home."

Thelma: "When we had an all night session, I would get up on a Saturday morning and I wouldn't see my bed until Sunday night and I had four children. I had to do the shopping lists and I had to do the cloakroom rota. I would be sitting in the back kitchen and my fella would be cursing and swearing at me. I had a horrible marriage and the Cavern helped me get over it. I don't think I would have survived had it not been for the Cavern. It got me out of it and it gave me money which I wasn't getting from my husband. The Cavern had a lovely atmosphere."

Sandra: "My mum would give me a big list for Waterworth's—potatoes, herbs, carrots, onions, what have you—and she would make Scouse. I had two cloth shopping bags and it killed me to carry them home. Also, I had to go to the butcher's shop for the meat. We never made enough. They could have sold twice the amount. It was all fresh food: nothing was frozen. The bread rolls would be delivered…"

Betty Fegan[367]: "…and they had to be put in bins in case the rats got at them. (Laughs) If I came down into the Cavern and rattled, I would hear the rats scatter."

Thelma: "Rats the size of cats and they would be running on the wires above you."

Sandra: "Mum was screaming that there was a rat behind the bar where the dishes were. I was about 13 and I reached in and caught it. It was a whopper. I held it by its tail and she was battering me, telling me to put it down in case it bit me. The rat catchers used to come but they were warehouses and they couldn't keep them down."

Betty: "The young ones used to queue overnight sometimes and they would take turns at watching out for the rats coming down the street. They would be standing guard in case the rats got in amongst them."

Thelma: "That's why they had to have a new stage. They had been chewing it away."

Sandra: "The toilets could be a foot deep in water and you would have to paddle through it the next day. It would depend on what had been thrown down the toilet the night before. If anybody stole a purse, they would put it down the toilet or in the cistern. It would be used hundreds of times during the night and I remember going down a couple of times of a morning with my mum and it was out with the brushes and mops, trying to get rid of the water. They had cleaners but when they were that bad, everyone would get stuck in to do a bit. They always used the black San Izal disinfectant and they got through gallons of it."

Thelma: "The girls would keep their purses with them so they could come to the snack bar. If they had left them in the cloakroom, they wouldn't have been pinched. After an all-night session, I would have a tray full of stolen purses from the toilets." I thought it better not to ask what else the tray was used for.

Sandra: "Considering the hundreds of people who used the Cavern of a night, the cleaners did

a fantastic job as the Cavern was spotless. Mrs Judge was excellent. By the time it was due for the next session, the place was gleaming, even the tables and the benches were clean. There was no such thing as, 'We're not doing that: we're going on strike.'"

Thelma: "Amy Judge did an excellent job, but she had to watch her language. She would call them all the dirty b's under the sun." Did you know it was a health hazard? "Of course I did but I kept my mouth shut. It was my money, wasn't it? (Much laughter)"

Wednesday 28 February 1962

(lunchtime) Gerry and the Pacemakers
(evening) Beatles, Johnny Sandon and the Searchers, and Gerry and the Pacemakers. This was Johnny Sandon's last appearance with the Searchers as he was joining the Remo Four for bookings on US military bases in France. Following the Cuban missile crisis, US personnel had been sent to France to combat potential Russian aggression.

Thelma Hargrove[368]: "Bob Wooler was a smashing bloke. When I was having my youngest daughter, he got on the mike and he said, 'Well, we all know Thelma off the snack bar. She is leaving us for a short while' and the tune he played was Karl Denver's 'Never Goodbye'."

Betty Fegan[369]: "Bob Wooler was professional when other shows were being done on a very amateurish basis. Nobody could present *The Generation Game* like Bruce Forsyth, and in the same way Bob Wooler was the only one who could run those beat sessions."

Thursday 1 March 1962

(lunchtime) **Beryl Marsden**[370] saw the Beatles: "The Beatles' lunchtime sessions were a lot more informal than the evening ones. You could shout up numbers and you could talk to them. They knew the names of most of the people who went to the lunchtime sessions."

Did **Thelma Hargrove**[371] take food to the Beatles? "Certainly not. They'd have to come and get it like everybody else. They had to pay for it, but they might say on the mike, 'Thelma, send us up a coffee and we'll pay you after.' Cilla Black would do the same and she'd drink Coke."

Terry McCusker[372]: "You'd walk down the stairs and tread in pools of unmentionable liquids and we bought the hot dogs and we didn't get food poisoning. Cilla Black used to work in the cloakroom and I remember her getting up with the Big Three and singing 'Fever'. The same girl had given the coat of my oppo, Roddy Kelly, to somebody else by mistake and he never got it back. We thought she was a bit of a dumb cluck, but there she was with the Big Three."

Saturday 3 March 1962

Jim McHarg's Jazzmen with the Beatles. McHarg, who played double bass, led the Clyde Valley Stompers in the early 50s and after moving to Canada, returned to form his own band.

Sunday 4 March 1962

Mike Cotton's Jazzmen with the Blue Genes

Tuesday 6 March 1962

(lunchtime) Gerry and the Pacemakers
(evening) Blue Genes Guest Night with the Beatles and Gerry and the Pacemakers

Wednesday 7 March 1962

Johnny Sandon and the Remo Four, Kingsize Taylor and the Dominoes, and the Moroccans. **Mike Byrne**[373]: "I loved the Remo Four. Colin Manley would sit at the front of the stage with his Fender and do Chet Atkins' 'Trambone', which was always something I wanted to hear. They were the group's group and George Harrison admired him. It's often forgotten that the Remos also did vocals and Keith's version of the standard, 'Once In A While', was outstanding."

Wednesday 14 March 1962

The Beatles, Gerry and the Pacemakers, and Clay Ellis and the Raiders

Friday 16 March 1962

Pete Haslam's Collegians with the Beatles

Saturday 17 March 1962

The Saints Jazz Band with the Four Jays

Sunday 18 March 1962

Papa Bue's Viking Jazz Band with the Blue Genes

Tuesday 20 March 1962

(lunchtime) Gerry and the Pacemakers
(evening) Blue Genes Guest Night with Beatles and Ian and the Zodiacs

Tuesday 22 March 1962

(lunchtime) Peppy and the New York Twisters
(evening) Peppy and the New York Twisters with the Beatles

Earl Preston[374]: "When the twist came out, there was an Italian/American from New York called Peppy who came to the Cavern to demonstrate how to do the dance. He was on for half an hour and he was very good as I'd never seen anyone demonstrate a dance before. The twist was unheard of in Liverpool as everybody was jiving. The Beatles wrote a song called 'Pinwheel Twist' and it was brilliant. It was a twist song with a great arrangement."

Dave Dover[375]: "Shortly after Peppy and the New York Twisters did their set, the Beatles came on and said that they had written a song in the band room called 'The Pinwheel Twist'. It was a one four five, C-F-G song, not much more than 'Come on, do the pinwheel twist'. It wasn't a brilliant song but it showed that they had kept their ear to what was going on and I'd never heard anybody say before that they had written a song during the break. I liked the spontaneity of it all and it was another first for the Beatles."

Billy Kinsley[376] saw the Beatles "who drank soup on stage and wore leather jackets and old jeans. They came on singing 'Memphis Tennessee' and changed my life forever. They were playing rock'n'roll, raw and alive, just as it should be played. Paul jumped into the audience screaming 'Long Tall Sally' while Lennon laid on the floor and played guitar solos."

Sunday 25 March 1962

Terry Pitts Jazz Band with Blue Genes. Pitts played trombone for Cy Laurie's Jazz Band and he took over the unit when Laurie went to India.

Sunday 1 April 1962

Melbourne New Orleans Jazz Band with Blue Genes

On the same day, the Cavern promoted a concert by Kenny Ball and his Jazzmen at the Liverpool Empire. This was recorded for a live LP, *The Kenny Ball Show*, and McCartney later told Ball that he was in the audience. He couldn't have seen the whole show as the Beatles were playing at the Casbah that night.

Tuesday 3 April 1962

Blue Genes guest night with Gerry and the Pacemakers and the Cavern debut of the Merseybeats. **Bob Wooler**[377]: "I discovered the Merseybeats rehearsing in a church hall behind the Jacaranda.

They were only sixteen-year-old lads and I asked them if they played elsewhere, and they didn't. I brought them into Aintree Institute and then into the Cavern. They were influenced by the Beatles, and I told them, 'This is what I am going to do, and don't tell the other groups. You're going to get a good spot. I will put you on right before the Beatles and it is up to you to win the crowd round by your performance and your communication.' I did a similar thing with the Escorts and the Dennisons, and it worked each time.

I didn't like the group's name at the time: they were called the Mavericks, which suggested country and western. I accept now that the Mavericks is a wonderful name! I told Bill Harry that if we changed their name to the Merseybeats, it could be good reciprocal publicity for his paper, and he agreed."

Tony Crane[378] of the Merseybeats recalls how the name change came about: "We were happy with our name, the Mavericks. We dressed in long jackets and boots like the actors on the *Maverick* TV show. Bob wanted us to do some sessions at the Cavern but he didn't like our name. He asked us to be the Megatons instead and he would guarantee that we would go down a bomb. We didn't like that. He booked us for the Aintree Institute and when we looked in the *Echo*, we saw that this band, the Merseybeats, was topping the bill. We had no idea it was us and we went to the Cavern and complained to Bob that we weren't on the bill. He said, 'That's your new name. Don't you like it?'"

Thursday 5 April 1962

(lunchtime) Gerry and the Pacemakers

(evening) A Beatles fan club night with the Four Jays. This was the first Thursday night opening since the demise of the modern jazz session. **Bob Wooler**[379]: "Brian Epstein hired the Cavern on a Thursday night in April 1962 and it was for the Beatles to thank their fans and they had the Four Jays as their guests. Because it was a special night, they asked me to sing with them and I said no. On the other hand, Ray McFall did two songs with them—the Elvis song, 'Can't Help Falling In Love', and the title song of the film *Tender Is The Night*, which had been recorded by Vic Damone. The Beatles played a few chords behind him and the audience dutifully applauded. He had a good

voice and he did well." I asked **Ray McFall**[380] about this, "It was good fun but I should have stuck to the one song that they knew. The second song was an unwise choice, but how could they refuse me? I owned the club."

Again, the Beatles played their 'Pinwheel Twist'. While Paul McCartney played drums, Pete Best went on the floor and twisted with his girlfriend, Kathy, later his wife. **Billy Hatton**[381]: "This was one of the most fulfilling nights we did at the Cavern. We were chuffed about it: it was the Beatles fan club night and the only bands were the Beatles and the Four Jays. Frieda Kelly had asked the Beatles who they wanted and they settled for us. I remember doing 'Mama Don't Allow' with the Beatles. Paul was on piano, John stayed on guitar, I played guitar, we had two drummers with Ringo and Dave Lovelady, and Brian O'Hara brought out an old violin. George Harrison found an old trumpet and he was blowing that. It sounds good but it was ten minutes worth of crap."

Saturday 7 April 1962

Last show before Hamburg for the Beatles, supported by the Saints Jazz Band, but no George Harrison, who was unwell.

Wednesday 11 April 1962

Gerry and the Pacemakers, Ian and the Zodiacs, and Johnny Peters and the Crestas

Sunday 15 April 1962

Coming from London, Doug Richford's Jazzmen with the Blue Genes. Clarinet player Doug Richford had left Bob Wallis's band to form his own group.

Wednesday 18 April 1962

(lunchtime) Pete Maclaine and the Dakotas

(evening) Pete Maclaine and the Dakotas with the Searchers, and Ken Dallas and the Silhouettes.

Robin McDonald[382]: "We'd do gigs in Doncaster or Sheffield, but there was nothing like coming to Liverpool for the Cavern. I loved the lunchtime sessions with a bowl of Campbell's Vegetable Soup. The atmosphere was great. It seemed that everybody who worked in Liverpool was a character."

Monday 23 April 1962

Dave Williams[383]: "We did a show on Easter Monday and we were the first group on at four in the afternoon. As soon as we began to play, there was a massive surge towards the stage to get the front seats. I thought, 'This lot is keen to hear us play.' They got out their sandwiches and their flasks of coffee and began to eat and drink. When they had finished eating, they took out their rollers and got ready for the Beatles, who were on later on."

Thursday 1 May 1962

(lunchtime) Pete Maclaine and the Dakotas
(evening) Blue Genes Guest Night with the Searchers, Group One and the youngest of the Liverpool bands, the Dennisons. Take two Remo Four and add a Jaywalker and a Flamingo and you have Group One.

Wednesday 2 May 1962

(lunchtime) Gerry and the Pacemakers
(evening) Gerry and the Pacemakers, Ken Dallas and the Silhouettes, and rockabilly from Sonny Webb and the Cascades. Louis Armstrong was playing the Philharmonic Hall that night and some say he came to the Cavern after the show and sat in with the musicians. This is surely apocryphal.

Saturday 5 May 1962

Gerry and the Pacemakers (farewell before Hamburg) with the Red River Jazzmen. **Lee Curtis**[384]: "The first time I heard Gerry do 'You'll Never Walk Alone', I was standing at the back at the Cavern. I was singing along with him but I didn't know he was going to stop and I continued straight on. I'd gone for the big note and was giving it the biftahs."

Sunday 13 May 1962

Mike Daniels Delta Jazz Band with the Blue Genes. **John Cook**[385]: "Mike Daniels had a very accomplished band. They came from London. They had a tenor player, Frank Brooker, who would go on drums after the interval, and somebody else would play the trumpet, and so on."

Monday 14 May 1962

(lunchtime and evening) Johnny Kidd and the Pirates. **Mick Green**[386] of the Pirates: "We had been playing in Hull the night before and we had to get to Liverpool for a lunchtime session, which was unheard of. It was a drab cellar with a weenie stage and we thought, 'We drove all night to get to this rotten place.' We got the gear in and got set up and once the punters started to come in, it

was an unbelievable atmosphere. It was an incredible week."

Not everything went as planned. **Mick Green**[387]: "Johnny would take out his cutlass and throw it at my feet while I was doing a blues solo. However, I could see that the lino on the stage had worn away and it was concrete underneath. I tried to indicate that he shouldn't throw the sword but he took no notice. It landed inches from my foot and bounced into the audience. Some Scouser grabbed it and ran out of the club as fast as he could. Our road manager, Johnny Irving chased him and managed to get the sword back."

John Frankland[388]: "Kidd would do 'My Babe' and when it built up to a crescendo, he would lift the sword in the air and stick it into the stage. Everybody would clap, but sometimes it would bounce into the audience and everyone would scatter. That sword could do somersaults."

Sam Hardie[389]: "See that scar on my hand. That was Johnny Kidd's sword. He had two real swords and Bobby Thomson and I picked them up and had a sword fight. Next thing, whoosh! I fainted too at the sight of the sword going up my hand. I'm proud of that scar now."

Tuesday 15 May 1962

(lunchtime) Johnny Kidd and the Pirates
(evening) Blue Genes Guest Night with the Searchers and, would you believe, Johnny Kidd and the Pirates. **Ray Ennis**[390]: "Johnny Kidd and the Pirates were dressed from head to toe in pirate outfits, big heavy stuff, and yet the Cavern was the sweatiest place in the world. Johnny Kidd pulled his sword out and threw it and it stuck in the floor of the stage—there were people about two feet away and it went boinnnng! If he had missed, it could have killed someone. He was excellent and a great singer. I thought the Big Three were louder but when you heard the Pirates, you thought the place was going to crumble."

John Cochrane[391]: "As a British rock'n'roll band, Johnny Kidd and the Pirates were amazing. I hadn't seen anything this good from Britain. They could sound like their records."

Billy Butler[392]: "Johnny Kidd and the Pirates were the nearest to what we imagined American rock'n'roll groups sounded like. Kidd had such assurance when he was on stage and he could pull birds with no trouble at all. He wore his eyepatch the whole time, on and off stage, and there was a lot of discussion as to whether it was just for show. I've seen lots of bands live, but they were definitely one of the best."

David Backhouse[393]: "I'd got tunnel vision once I'd seen the Beatles and everyone else seemed second tier. However, the Pirates were excellent and I had a good, rocking evening."

Mick Green[394]: "All the Liverpool kids were telling us about the Beatles but of course we had never heard of them. Then we went to Hamburg and again, everybody was talking about the Beatles. They were very good and we nicked 'A Shot Of Rhythm And Blues' from them, but I thought it was the Big Three that was going to be the really big band."

John McNally[395]: "They died on their backsides when they were on with us. I thought they were great but the audience didn't like them one bit. They were all dressed as pirates and it just wasn't the thing for Liverpool, was it? The audience thought it was a strange thing to do."

Steve Lister[396]: "Mick Green was the outstanding person in the band. He played a nice Gibson, a Les Paul Junior, which had only one pick-up but he got the most amazing sound out of it. The thing I remember about Johnny Kidd and also Joe Brown is that they were used to touring theatres and had a half hour show prepared. When it was time for the next spot, they did the same show again, and so on. That was all they had: it was a very tight, worked-out show but they did not have a large repertoire like the Beatles."

Willy Russell[397]: "I had a purist, fundamentalist take on Johnny Kidd and the Pirates. This was an act that had lost it in the mainstream and was slumming it at the Cavern. I saw Johnny Kidd and the Pirates as coming from that Tin Pan Alley, very manufactured, Larry Parnes-styled world, which was odious to me, although I know that they weren't managed by Parnes.

The Beatles, on the other hand, embodied the black essence that I was hearing on Forces radio, it was not English pop, and that is why it hit Tom Evans and me like a sledgehammer. Six miles from where we lived was music that contained the same DNA as this stuff that made you want to jump up and down as though you had snakes in your pants. I hate the bullshit that the Stones

were the great rock and roll band and the Beatles were a great pop band: come on, do me a favour. Anyone who heard the Beatles at the Cavern will tell you, they were the greatest kickass band ever. That raw Southern state, fighting, joyously angry black vein ran through it all."

Wednesday 16 May 1962

(lunchtime) Johnny Kidd and the Pirates

(evening) Johnny Kidd and the Pirates with Pete Maclaine and the Dakotas, and Ken Dallas and the Silhouettes. **Lee Curtis**[398]: "The Pirates did a couple of numbers before Kidd came on and he was talking to me in the dressing room. Bob Wooler rushed up to him and said, 'Johnny, Johnny, you're on'. 'Great,' said Johnny, 'and how am I doing?' Johnny Kidd would send the band out first to do a couple of numbers and I thought that was a great idea and I picked up on it. If anything is wrong with the PA, you find out during those songs."

Thursday 17 May 1962

(lunchtime) Johnny Kidd and the Pirates

Friday 18 May 1962

(lunchtime and evening) Johnny Kidd and the Pirates. While at the Cavern, thieves stole some suits from Kidd's van.

Saturday 19 May 1962

Pete Haslam's Collegians with the Merseybeats

Sunday 20 May 1962

Clyde Valley Stompers with the Blue Genes

Monday 21 May 1962

(lunchtime and evening) Joe Meek recording artists, Mike Berry and the Outlaws, are featured for the week. At the time, Mike had only had one Top 30 hit, 'Tribute To Buddy Holly'. **Chas Hodges**[399]: "I was the bass player with the Outlaws. We played the Cavern with Mike Berry and at the time, we were making a name for ourselves as a band and we weren't sure if we could take time off to back Mike Berry. But it seemed that we could. 'Thank Christ for that!' said Mike, 'I was going to have to be backed by this band called the Beatles and I didn't fancy that. I heard they were backing a girl singer at the Cavern and ended up putting a sack over her head!' Could that have been Cilla Black? When we arrived in Liverpool, I remember seeing posters around advertising bands and in brackets saying 'Beatles style group'. I thought what are these Beatles like if these bands are using the Beatles' name to sell themselves? Not long after the Beatles started making records and I found out."

Mike Berry[400]: "It was difficult to get a good sound down there but the atmosphere was so good. We did a Roy Orbison song, 'Dream Baby' and a load of girls started singing the vocal backing. Everyone was clapping on the off-beat which is most unusual. Usually audiences clap on the on-beat which is jarring to anyone who knows anything about music. I was really impressed and that week gave me a great buzz."

Tuesday 22 May 1962

(lunchtime) Mike Berry and the Outlaws
(evening) Blue Genes Guest Night with Mike Berry and the Outlaws, and Mark Peters and the Cyclones

Wednesday 23 May 1962

(lunchtime) Mike Berry and the Outlaws
(evening) Mike Berry and the Outlaws with the Searchers, and Johnny Peters and the Crestas.
Mike Berry[401]: "We didn't see the Beatles when we were at the Cavern but Brian Epstein took me and a couple of the Outlaws to his place and played us a tape of the Beatles. The quality of it must have been pretty bad as I can't remember anything about it, but maybe I wasn't interested. It is very easy to be smug when you're from London and you think that only bands who are recording can be any good. I do, however, remember thinking that Johnny Gustafson from the Big Three had a great voice."

Thursday 24 May 1962

(lunchtime) Mike Berry and the Outlaws

Friday 25 May 1962

(lunchtime) Mike Berry and the Outlaws
(evening) Mike Berry and the Outlaws, and the Dennisons

Saturday 26 May 1962

Zenith Six Jazz Band with Vic and the Spidermen

Tuesday 29 May 1962

Blue Genes Guest Night with the Dennisons, and Johnny Peters and the Crestas

Friday 1 June 1962

Red River Jazzmen, Searchers and Group One

Tuesday 5 June 1962

Blue Genes Guest Night with the Merseybeats and the Sorrals

Wednesday 6 June 1962

Big Three, Mark Peters and the Cyclones, and Clay Ellis and the Raiders

This was going to be the Beatles' 'Welcome home' session but instead they had to audition for Parlophone, so the Big Three stood in at short notice.

Friday 8 June 1962

Johnny Templar's Hi Cats with Barbara, Pete Haslam's Collegians and the Dennisons

Saturday 9 June 1962

An astonishing crowd gathers for the Beatles' return from Hamburg, and they are supported by the Red River Jazzmen, Vic and the Spidermen, the Four Jays and Ken Dallas and the Silhouettes.

Bob Wooler[402]: "I thought they might have been tired after the travelling and their strenuous sessions in Hamburg, but not a bit of it. This was one of their finest performances."

Ray Ennis[403]: "John Lennon didn't mix very easily and very often he would read a book in the dressing-room. Cynthia was with him a lot of the time. I remember John and George asking me what we felt like playing our own songs on stage as they were scared about playing them. I said, 'The only way you'll find out whether people like them or not is to play them. We write something, we play it and if it goes down well, we keep it in. If it doesn't, we don't do it anymore.' I didn't know what they had written until they started playing them and it was good stuff."

Geoff Davies[404]: "I remember the first time they did one of their own songs and it was 'P.S. I Love You'. We didn't like that at all. It was pop and not like the raucous Little Richard covers or the R&B stuff. I was prejudiced against those sloppy songs coming in as they were not suited to the Cavern. I preferred the harder end of the Beatles but, again, those songs won me over."

Frank Townsend[405]: "I was about 13 when I first went to the Cavern and my mother had given me 2/6d. My dad was a jazz musician and so my parents were very much on my side. I saw

(Left) Memphis Three (Right) The Chants

At The Cavern
To-night — FRIDAY — To-night.
A Really Fabulous Night Out with
The Kirkbys
The Toggery 5
The Pilgrims

TO-MORROW AFTERNOON (Saturday)
JUNIOR CAVERN CLUB
Presents for 13 to 16 year olds
Chick Graham
The Coasters
The Chancellors
1 p.m. start. Members 2/-. Visitors 3/-.
PLEASE COME ALONG EARLY!

TO-MORROW NIGHT (SATURDAY)
7.15 p.m. to 11.15 p.m. 4 Groups
The Notions
The Riot Squad.
The Chessmen
The Chancellors

SUNDAY 8-Hour Show!
This SUNDAY — This SUNDAY
Fabulous 8 Hour R & B Marathon
Starring America's Greatest Blues singer
Jimmy Witherspoon!
Jimmy Witherspoon!
Plus The Cordes Also
The Bluesounds
The Abstracts
The Excerts
The Faces
The Mark Four
MARK ANTHONY AND THE AVENGERS
THIS SHOW YOU
Must Not Miss!
This Sunday starting at 3.30 p.m.
TELL YOUR FRIENDS!
LUNCHTIME SESSION

Above youngsters queuing up for the Cavern's Junior sessions

Above Cavern Comic Jimmy Tarbuck chats to fans (Left) Billy J. Kramer entertains the kids

Faron's Flamingos

the Merseybeats at a lunchtime session and I thought the sound of their Gibson Jumbos was absolutely amazing. I couldn't go in the evening as they wouldn't have let me in then, but I would go about once a month at lunchtime and I would stay for the whole session and not go back to school. I saw the Beatles one lunchtime but John's Rickenbacker sounded awful as it sounded like a Hofner Club 40. I told John about this a couple of years later and he said it was always very chunky, but the overall sound of the band was amazing. People have written that the Beatles' talent was in their writing but I disagree. The sound they produced was totally different from any other band I'd heard. They became much tighter with Ringo but whenever they did 'Some Other Guy', I was mesmerised."

On 11 June 1962, the Cavern hired a coach and took a party of members to see the Beatles record a show for the BBC Light Programme in Manchester. **Ray McFall**[406]: "I was waiting to see what the Manchester audience would make of the Beatles and it was the same as the 'Welcome home' reception, but on a smaller scale. Brian Epstein was delighted."

Tuesday 12 June 1962

The Blues Genes no longer objected to the Beatles on their guest night.

Wednesday 13 June 1962

(lunchtime) Beatles

(evening) Beatles, Pete Maclaine and the Dakotas, and the Dennisons

Colin Middlebrough[407]: "I always thought McCartney was a born leader. Lennon stood there leaning on the piano, looking arrogant, and we would be waiting with great anticipation for him singing 'Please Mr Postman' with bent knees and looking down his nose as he sang. Lennon didn't have much time for people and he totally ignored me most of the time. Paul was very much in your face. I remember Mike Millward bringing a cake down for Paul's birthday one lunchtime and he was so pleased. He was jumping about because he had been given this cake."

Friday 15 June 1962

Beatles, Group One, and Vic and the Spidermen

Tuesday 19 June 1962

Blue Genes Guest Night with Beatles and Merseybeats. **Billy Butler**[408]: "George Harrison offered me 10 bob if I could slip their name into the *Spin-A-Disc* section of *Thank Your Lucky Stars*. I told him I couldn't do that and anyway, the Merseybeats were my favourite group."

Wednesday 20 June 1962

(lunchtime) Beatles

(evening) Beatles, Kingsize Taylor and the Dominoes, and the Sorrals

Thursday 21 June 1962

Terry McCusker[409]: "There were three records that were played all the time at the Cavern— 'Hey! Baby' by Bruce Channel, 'This Time' by Troy Shondell and 'I'll Be There' by Bobby Darin. Seeing Bruce Channel was brilliant. We couldn't believe he was here in this scruffy dump as even Liverpool was a backwater then. But when we saw some of these Americans, we realised that the Beatles could blow them off the stage so we knew just how good they were."

Following the success of 'Hey! Baby', the American Bruce Channel did club dates in the UK with his harmonica player, Delbert McClinton. They played the Cavern at lunchtime and also the Tower Ballroom in New Brighton with the Beatles in support, this being one of Brian Epstein's promotions. **Delbert McClinton**[410]: "We were touring in an old ambulance from the war. I had to find somewhere to shave as I was looking dishevelled. I couldn't get my electric razor to work and I didn't know that you needed a special adaptor to make it work. I remember going in early to the Cavern and having to shave in cold water."

David Deacon[411]: "I was struck with the way Bruce Channel looked with his cropped hair and his tab-collared shirt. Nobody in Liverpool looked like that."

Bruce Channel[412]: "There were lots of kids there, a whole sea of people, and I said to Delbert, 'They can't all have come to see us', and we soon found out that the Beatles were very popular. Delbert was in the dressing-room with John Lennon who was very interested in his harp. Delbert played something for him and evidently John kept the idea and used it for the sound on 'Love Me Do'. We had heard the harmonica on blues records by Jimmy Reed and people like that, and that influenced 'Hey! Baby'. It's a great thrill to know that our record influenced the Beatles and that our music was appreciated by a group of that stature."

Delbert McClinton[413]: "Nearly everyone of the Liverpool bands asked me to show them something, so John Lennon was doing nothing unusual. We hung about a couple of days and I did show him some things. I never saw him again and I've never thought too much about it, but everybody sees a similarity between 'Hey! Baby' and 'Love Me Do'."

Friday 29 June 1962

Returning from Hamburg, Gerry and the Pacemakers, supported by Ian and the Zodiacs, and Clay Ellis and the Raiders. The main action, however, was with the Beatles and nine other groups on Sam Leach's *Operation Big Beat III* at the Tower Ballroom.

Saturday 30 June 1962

Red River Jazzmen, Searchers and Group One

Sunday 1 July 1962

The first Sunday without any jazz content—Gene Vincent backed by Sounds Incorporated and supported by the Beatles and the Kansas City Five. A recording of Vincent's set has come to light and some have said it is Vincent with the Beatles. It isn't. You can hear the saxophones: it is Sounds Inc.

John Duff Lowe[414] of the Quarry Men: "I only used to go the lunchtime sessions with one exception when I went to see Gene Vincent. It was a really good show and I remember thinking, 'Wow, this is Gene Vincent at the Cavern', while he was performing."

Billy Butler[415]: "Gene Vincent asked me where he could get a drink and when I told him, we didn't sell alcohol, he was horrified. I had a bottle of beer with me and he asked if he could buy it off me. I was so overawed with Gene Vincent that I gave him my beer for free and he said, 'Thank you, sir.'"

Maybe he bought everybody's beer. **Ritchie Galvin**[416]: "I was a great fan of Gene Vincent and I was disappointed by his performance. He was totally boozed. I saw him about three years later in London and he was okay that night."

Colin Middlebrough[417]: "I was with Rory Storm in the audience and we were eagerly awaiting Gene Vincent. Rory pulled out a match and lit one and it immediately went out. There was no oxygen in the air at all. My wife collapsed, fainted, and it was just as Gene Vincent was starting and rather selfishly, Rory and I passed her over the top of the heads. We saw Paddy and he got the message and sat her outside. Gene was excellent. He was confined on that little stage but he was backed by Sounds Incorporated, who had a good drummer with dyed blond hair."

Mike McCartney[418]: "Gene Vincent was top of the bill and he knew Our Kid was important. That is why he had his picture taken. He had full leathers and Our Kid had his full leathers, wow, and there is Gene the master, like Marlon Brando in *The Wild One*, he is on the Cavern stage and he is going (sings) 'Be Bop A Lula, echo, echo, echo' and you can see the fans bored out of their heads. 'Gene Vincent? Excuse me. We're waiting for the Beatles.' The picture tells the story. One of them has a David Frost shirt. Our Kid was going down to London and he had a couple of bob, doing well and he would buy David Frost shirts, very thick striped shirts. I got one and the fans got them. The photo is on my website and you will see the girl with the David Frost shirt."

Tuesday 3 July 1962

Blue Genes Guest Night with the Searchers and Cavern debut for Manchester's Freddie and the Dreamers. **Betty Fegan**[419]: "The snack bar was at the back of the first aisle and so I couldn't see the stage. When Freddie and the Dreamers came on, one of us went to have a look and she was killing herself with laughter when she came back. We took turns to go and see Freddie and he was absolutely mad. He was dancing all over the place."

Here's a surprising admission from **Sam Hardie**[420]: "I loved seeing Freddie and the Dreamers on the Cavern as he gave people their money's worth. One day Freddie had a top hat and he turned his back on the audience and pretended to pee into it. Then he turned round and threw the contents over the front row. It was just bits of paper that he had in the hat."

Friday 6 July 1962

A Riverboat Shuffle, promoted by the Cavern, with Acker Bilk's Paramount Jazz Band and the Beatles

Sunday 8 July 1962

Willy Russell[421]: "I was by some lock-up garages where a couple of mates and I were riding round on our bikes—the way you do at 14, you are neither boy nor man, nor fish nor fowl, and you don't know what to do in life. An older kid of 15, who had left school and was working in an office, came over and was talking to us. He was showing off but he was talking about his work and how he would go to 'the Cave'. He told me that he went to hear the groups. I had seen the Shadows at the Empire but the thought of hearing live music at lunchtime in Liverpool was fantastic.

Tommy Evans and I must have lied to our parents as to where we were going as we were only 14. We couldn't go to a lunchtime session because of school but we went on a Sunday night and we were supposed to be home by 9.30pm. When we got into the Cavern, we were hit by that fabulous, intoxicating smell of cheap perfume, disinfectant and rotting fruit, which was very heady for 14-year-olds. It wasn't packed when we went in and we saw the first groups who had alliterative names like Shane Fenton and the Fentones, but not them of course. We had seen Fender Strats in big theatres but to see them in a tiny club was amazing.

We were blown away with the warm-up acts. It got to 9.15pm and we had to think about heading home when these guys dressed in black walked onto the stage, and we were seeing the Beatles for the first time. We had to stay for the first number. By then the club had filled up massively and we were being pushed forward as more and more people came in. They were laughing with the audience and the girls were taking out their rollers and had gone from wearing scarves to looking really glam. The Beatles kicked into 'Some Other Guy' and that was like the end of life for me, and a whole new life began from that very moment. Neither of us got home until after 11pm and both of us got a bollocking for being out late, but I was gone then and I would try and get to any lunchtime session when the Beatles were on."

Monday 9 July 1962

Jimmy Justice had had a Top 10 hit with 'When My Little Girl Is Smiling' and was back in the charts with 'Ain't That Funny'. He was booked to appear at the Cavern in July 1962 on the same session as Billy Kramer and the Coasters, Gus Travis and the Midnighters and Mark Peters and the Cyclones. **Tony Sanders**[422], drummer with the Coasters, recalls: "Jimmy had a record in the charts and so the Cavern was packed. The changing room was tiny and Jimmy Justice was standing talking to Billy J. Kramer. I was setting my drums up and I stopped for a second and looked at the two of them. Kramer looked every inch a star, but Jimmy Justice didn't, although he was then the big event and Kramer was a nobody."

Billy was being managed by **Ted Knibbs**[423]. "Billy had pride in his appearance. He was an apprentice engineer on the railways and you'd see him coming in with his dirty hands and dirty face. When you met him half an hour later, he'd be immaculate from head to toe, clean in every respect, thanks to his mother who took pride in her lad."

Looking back, **Billy J. Kramer**[424] admits that he overdid things. "I was known for being the guy who dressed nice, the boy-next-door type of image. Now that I'm older and can look back, I think that if I'd gone on in a pair of jeans and a T-shirt or a denim jacket and rocked them, they'd have loved me. I must have been a bit crazy to appear in the Cavern in a gold lamé suit or a mohair jacket."

Jimmy Justice[425]: "We played the Cavern and it's ironic that, a year later, those kids had put paid to my career. We had suits and short hair and they had long hair and leathers. We thought that, coming from London, we would be leading the fashion world, but we weren't."

Tuesday 10 July 1962

Lunchtime session with the Beatles and a view from the snack bar from **Betty Fegan**[426]: "Paul's father worked in the Cotton Exchange and he used to keep tabs on him. I can remember him saying to Paul, 'Have you put some money in the bank?' and Paul asked, 'Why does he take it out on me?'"

Tuesday 17 July 1962

Frankie Connor[427]: "The first time I went to the Cavern was when I sagged off school to see Gerry and the Pacemakers one lunchtime. Paddy on the door said, 'Are you still at school, son? And I said, 'No' but he said, 'What's that prefect's badge?' He let us in and it knocked me out."

Not yet sixteen, **Edwina Currie**[428] was going to the Cavern: "I used to go to the Cavern in my lunchtime from school as I was at Blackburne House, up on Hope Street. I got permission to be off the school premises as I said I was having lunch with my father because we were kosher. Of course, I went to the Cavern. It cost 1/6d to get in and I would take a black, polo-neck sweater and put it on over my school uniform. To be able to go a gig at lunchtime was amazing. I would see two bands and maybe Cilla would be singing 'Fever'. Because of the acoustics in the place, it was extremely noisy and I would come out with my head vibrating. I wouldn't hear very much for the rest of the day, but it was a wonderful experience. I knew that the Beatles were bound to be very, very big—they were seriously talented—and I loved Billy J. Kramer—I thought he was gorgeous. When I got back, I might have double chemistry and I would go into a lab that stunk of sulphur but everybody would sniff at me, sniff at my hair and they would say, 'We know where you've been. Who was on?' My hair would reek for the rest of the day and I'd be hoping that my mother wouldn't notice."

Tuesday 24 July 1962

(lunchtime) The Beatles
(evening) Blue Genes Guest Night with Gerry and the Pacemakers, and Mark Peters and the Cyclones

Thursday 26 July 1962

(lunchtime) Joe Brown and his Bruvvers. **Joe Brown**[429]: "I travelled to Liverpool by train and I remember a couple of lads opposite me going on about the Beatles, and I thought that I would like to see them."

Alex McKechnie[430]: "I got a job as an apprentice printer in Tinlings on Victoria Street and the building is still called that, but owned by the Council. I was 500 yards away from the Cavern so when it came to the lunch hour I was able to change out of my jeans and put my suit on and go to the Cavern. They were quite strict about what you wore. I went to see Joe Brown at a lunchtime session and they refused me admission because I hadn't changed out of my jeans. I spent about two weeks coaxing Paddy Chambers to see the Beatles and he didn't like them at all. The thing I liked best about the Beatles was their stage presence and their lack of respect for the audience. They were the first punk band."

Friday 27 July 1962

(lunchtime) Joe Brown and his Bruvvers
(evening) The Searchers with Billy Kramer and the Coasters

Saturday 28 July 1962

The Beatles, the Red River Jazzmen, and Dee Fenton and the Silhouettes

Sunday 29 July 1962

Lee Curtis and the All Stars, Mark Peters and the Cyclones, and the Saints Jazz Band

Carol Loftus[431]: "I went to the Cavern first and saw the Swinging Blue Genes who were good and the next time was Lee Curtis and we just stood there and looked in amazement. We couldn't tell you what he sang. He was like a star and way up there. The Beatles for me were not the top band. I preferred the Blue Genes and the Searchers and the Merseybeats. The Undertakers were brilliant and had a lot of attitude."

Joe Flannery[432]: "Brian Epstein and I were childhood friends and both our parents had family businesses and he was involved with the Beatles around about the same time that I was coming into the city with my brother's band, Lee Curtis and the Detours. He asked me to go to the Cavern and hear his new band, the Beatles. I came down to the Cavern on my own in the afternoon and I sat on the steps and listened to them rehearsing 'Hey! Baby' and I was so impressed by both the Beatles and the place. It was like singing in the bathroom and the acoustics were fantastic. I sat there for a while and then I introduced myself. They played me 'Twist And Shout'. In the early stages, they were covering songs and people could use the Cavern as a rehearsal room in the afternoon."

THE CAVERN - 'TEEN PAN ALLEY'

Another band arrives at the Cavern

The Merseybeats

The Kirkbys

Mark Four

Chick Graham & The Coasters

Bob Wooler with the Four Pennies

Tuesday 31 July 1962

(lunchtime) Gerry and the Pacemakers

(evening) Blue Genes Guest Night with the Dennisons and Group One

Friday 3 August 1962

(lunchtime) Big Three

(evening) Clay Ellis and the Raiders, Alby and the Sorrals, and Ray Malcolm and the Sunsets

That evening there was also the first rock show at the Grafton dance hall, two miles from the city centre. Promoted by Albert Kinder, the bill included the Beatles, Gerry and the Pacemakers and the Big Three. **Gordon Vickers**[433]: "Ray McFall told me that there was a group in Liverpool called the Beatles, whom you booked through the drummer's mother. He said, 'Do you want to book them?' and I said, 'No, no, they're too bloody scruffy for me.'

They did play Chester eventually at the Riverpark and at the Royalty. Albert Kinder who was a promoter at Picton Hall and the Liverpool Empire said, 'Gordon, I made £450 last night at the Grafton. I had four groups including the Beatles and gave them £10 each and it was a choc-a-bloc and we had 1,000 wanting to get in. I knew then jazz was on the wane and beat was the thing. Then Brian Epstein took them on and he would say, 'Gordon, I want the Beatles to do Chester.' I still said that they were too scruffy but I had Gerry and the Pacemakers who were £10 and Billy J Kramer who was £15. And that's how I missed being a millionaire."

Wednesday 8 August 1962

(lunchtime) Gerry and the Pacemakers

(evening) Shane Fenton and the Fentones, Gerry and the Pacemakers, and the Big Three. The Beatles, normally at the Cavern on a Wednesday, played the Co-op Ballroom in Doncaster instead.

Friday 10 August 1962

The Cavern's Riverboat shuffle with Johnny Kidd and the Pirates, the Beatles, and Pete Maclaine and the Dakotas

Wednesday 15 August 1962

(lunchtime and evening) Beatles. A normal day for Pete Best or so he thought. **Bob Wooler**[434]: "Brian Epstein told me that Pete Best was going to be sacked. I could imagine it with someone who was constantly late or giving him problems, but Pete Best was not awkward and he didn't step out of line. I was most indignant and I said, 'Why are you doing this?' but I didn't get an answer."

Pete Best[435]: "Brian Epstein said he'd like to see me in his office the next morning. This was quite normal because, with the family phone, I fixed the bookings and he'd ask me about venues and prices. I went down the next morning without a care in the world and he said, 'The lads don't want you in the group any more.'"

It is often thought that Pete Best was kicked out of the Beatles for being too good-looking, but my wife, a better judge of these things than me, says that Mike Pender was much better looking than Pete Best and he wasn't kicked out of the Searchers.

Ann Upton[436] talks about her boyfriend, Ritchie Galvin, drummer with Earl Preston and the TTs: "Ritch was unhappy at Pete Best being sacked. He thought Pete's playing suited the Beatles, he was 'there' as Ritch would say. Brian Epstein asked Ritch about joining the Beatles and he went to see Ritch's dad as he was still under age. Bob Wooler was with him too. Ritch said that he didn't agree with Pete being replaced and he didn't like John Lennon's sarcasm as he thought that they would fall out. Also, to my credit, he didn't want to be leaving me as they would be working away from Liverpool quite a lot. He never regretted it and he said, 'No, I wouldn't have you and I wouldn't have my kids and I wouldn't have this life.' I was quite surprised when they chose Ringo. He was little and skinny and weedy and had a joke of a moustache. I always thought he needed a good scrub, but it worked out okay."

Sugar Deen[437]: "I remember seeing Ringo, we called him Ritchie then, outside a chemist's and he said that he was going to join the Beatles. I said, 'There's no way they will sack Pete Best, man. He's a moody guy but all the girls would go waah!' It was a shock when Ritchie got the job. The next time that I saw Pete he was managing the Job Centre in Green Lane. I signed on and gave him my dole card and he said, 'Is this your name and address? 'Yes' 'Sign here.' I don't think he wanted to acknowledge me."

Thursday 16 August 1962

(lunchtime) The Big Three with a bizarre support act: four trainee architects who took time out to perform a short set.

Friday 17 August 1962

(lunchtime) Freddie Garrity, laughing and giggling and pulling down the Dreamers' trousers to reveal their short shorts.

(evening) Freddie and the Dreamers with the Del-Renas, Vic and the Spidermen, and Gus Travis and the Midnighters. **Derek Quinn**[438] of the Dreamers: "Liverpool groups used to go and see each other, especially at the Cavern. We would be playing at the Cavern and in would walk some of the Swinging Blue Genes, Gerry and the Pacemakers, the Beatles and the Undertakers. All groups converged on the Cavern, and if you were from Manchester, they wanted to see what you were like. The groups from Manchester didn't spend much time going to see other groups."

Freddie Garrity[439]: "The Liverpool groups had this incessant beat. They were very exciting while the Manchester bands were still following Cliff Richard and the Shadows. We were lucky because we were the only comedy group around."

Sunday 19 August 1962

The Zenith Six Jazz Band, the Swinging Blue Genes and the returning Peppy and the New York Twisters, but everyone was waiting for the Beatles with new drummer, Ringo Starr. **Bob McGrae**[440]: "I wasn't worried about the change in drummers as it wasn't the drummer who made the group for me, but there were girls crying in Mathew Street and saying that they would never support the Cavern again."

George Harrison was given a black eye in the Cavern by a Best supporter. **Ian Edwards**[441]: "They were shouting 'Ringo out, Pete in' and refusing to let them play. There was a big question as to whether this could be the Beatles' downfall. Everyone was talking about it. Ritchie was playing in a group that wasn't taken seriously and suddenly he's in the biggest thing on Merseyside. He was a very good rock drummer, but there were a lot of better drummers around, like Johnny Hutch."

Dave Dover[442]: "I was there the day that everyone was going 'We want Pete.' Ringo was looking sheepish and McCartney was doing his usual, hands in the air, sorry, but trying to be diplomatic.

Lennon couldn't care less but George Harrison was being sarcastic so he got thumped as he came out for the break by Mickey Flynn, who looked like Wayne Rooney."

George Melly[443]: "I think they were right in getting rid of Pete Best and recruiting Ringo Starr. Pete Best was tremendously popular in Liverpool and undoubtedly it was a great tragedy for him to be sacked at the very moment when they were breaking through but, whoever it was, be it Brian Epstein or George Martin, saw that Ringo's personality was the perfect foil. He was plain whereas the others were all rather good-looking. He was thick whereas the others were rather bright. He was working class whereas the others were basically suburban. Ringo completed the Beatles and made them more effective, not just musically but as personalities."

Wednesday 22 August 1962

Bob Wooler[444]: "The Beatles recorded two numbers at the lunchtime session for Granada TV's *Know Your North*. The sound engineer ran me off an acetate of 'Some Other Guy' and 'Kansas City', and he gave another to Ray McFall and a couple to Brian Epstein. I kept mine in my box of records and I should have been more careful. When the Beatles became famous, the record disappeared. In 1993, a copy turned up at Christie's and was sold for £15,000. I don't know if it was my copy and anyway, I couldn't prove it if it was."

Dave Boyce[445]: "Ringo tried to comb his hair forward into a fringe but he had had a greasy, ducktail job and it didn't work as it was flicking up all the time. He looked rather odd."

Dennis Fontenot[446]: "I just went for the women. My mates would be telling me about this place in town and there would be loads of women there. If you couldn't cop off, you were nobody. I think it was 1/6d to get in and I used to go in the dinner hour. I never sweat but sweat was pouring off the walls. The session would be over in a minute, and it was brilliant. It was a great place. The women there had jobs! I had a Beatle haircut and I got battered when I got home. Everyone else had Afros. I thought the girls would go for it."

Johnny Hamp[447]: "They made their first appearance on television at the Cavern doing 'Some Other Guy'. Ringo had only just joined them and you can hear the crowd shouting, 'We want Pete' at the end if you listen carefully. As a contrast, they also shot the Brighouse and Rastrick Brass Band and the films were never shown for two reasons. The Beatles film was too grainy but more importantly, the brass band wanted union rates for their members. There were 50 of them so the whole thing was dropped! Brian Epstein rang me and asked me to get some pressure to bear on showing the film. The grainy quality of that film doesn't matter now. If you had a piece of film of the sinking of the Titanic, it wouldn't matter that you couldn't hear the band. It is history."

Monday 27 August 1962
Return of Mike Berry with the Beatles, Red River Jazzmen and Blue Genes

Tuesday 28 August 1962
Blue Genes Guest Night with the Beatles and Gerry Levene and the Avengers from Birmingham. They cut "Dr Feelgood" for Decca at the start of 1964 but it got nowhere. This was to be the Blue Genes' final Liverpool appearance as a quasi-jazz band, although they didn't know it. They were off to Hamburg. **Ray Ennis**[448]: "Our first night at the Star-Club was terrible. We had done about 15 minutes and the audience was whistling at us, which is an insult in Germany. They shut the curtains on us and the owner of the Star-Club, Manfred Weissleder said, 'You must change your music. They only like rock'n'roll.' We rehearsed a new act the next day and Paul Moss, our banjo player, went on the organ. Les Braid borrowed Jackie Lomax's bass guitar, and we've never looked back."

Geoff Davies[449]: "The Swinging Blue Genes were neither here nor there to me. I couldn't understand what they were doing. They were doing country things, but it was not really country. A bit of folk, but not really folk. Rock'n'roll things, not really rock'n'roll. Then they changed and jumped on the rock bandwagon. I'm afraid I didn't like them really."

John McNally[450]: "I would go to the afternoon sessions and get the bus back to work. I went plenty of times. At first it was Terry Lightfoot and the Blue Genes, and then I knew that the banjo would be getting the heave-ho. The double bass had to go too and become electric. Give the Blue Genes their due: they spotted that they would be left behind if they didn't turn to rock'n'roll."

Wednesday 29 August 1962
(lunchtime) The entry of the Gladiators as Nero and his chums play in the hall of the mountain king. (evening) Nero and the Gladiators, Clay Ellis and the Raiders, and Group One. **Dave Williams**[451]: "Nero and the Gladiators had a tremendous act. They all wore togas and Mike O'Neill who came from Bolton said, 'I come to dig Caesar not to bury him.' The drummer did one instrumental that was eight to the bar on the bass drum which was unbelievable."

Dave Dover[452]: "Nero and the Gladiators were dressed like Roman centurions but their skirts looked the blinds that you buy for your windows. The bass player wiggled his hips and moved from side to side. When the Beatles came on, McCartney was skitting him and he got it totally right. He did his act and the whole of the Cavern was in bulk as this guy had looked so stupid. The Beatles were brilliant but that band was awful."

Friday 31 August 1962
(lunchtime) Big Three
(evening) Ian and the Zodiacs, Johnny Templar and the Hi Cats, Kirk Daniels and the Deltas, and Mark Peters and the Cyclones

Sunday 2 September 1962
The Beatles, Kingsize Taylor and the Dominoes and the Zenith Six Jazz Band. **Alex Young**[453]: "The Beatles were just another band to me. I was not a Beatles fan until they became famous as I found them self-centred. They played for themselves. Frank Ifield was on top with 'I Remember You' and I remember George Harrison singing it. That wasn't within his range, especially the falsetto."

Dennis Conroy[454]: "I loved them doing 'Some Other Guy'. Their harmonies were exceptionally good and they had such excitement. George Harrison was my hero. He used to do a lot of Joe Brown songs and of course Joe Brown was a great guitar player. George could do all his licks and the Chuck Berry ones too. When they did their own songs, the solos were very tuneful in themselves and, although he never had the credit, he was really contributing to their songwriting. He was great."

Saturday 8 September 1962

Kingsize Taylor and the Dominoes, Dee Young and the Pontiacs, and Tony Smith's Jazzmen.

Sunday 9 September 1962

Cyril Preston's Jazz Band with Clinton Ford, Beatles and Billy Kramer and the Coasters

Tuesday 11 September 1962

(lunchtime) Joe Brown and his Bruvvers
(evening) Joe Brown and his Bruvvers, Merseybeats and Gerry and the Pacemakers

Wednesday 12 September 1962

The Beatles, Freddie and the Dreamers, Vic and the Spidermen, Group One and Simone Jackson. Freddie and the Dreamers heard the Beatles perform James Ray's 'If You Gotta Make A Fool Of Somebody' and stuck it in their own repertoire. **Bob Wooler**[455]: "Nearly all the groups played their own instruments, but the Chants needed instrumental backing. The Beatles sometimes backed them, although Brian Epstein was not happy about that. I also recall the Beatles backing a new girl from Manchester, Simone Jackson, who was with Kennedy Street Enterprises, but this was Brian's doing as he had done some deal to give her exposure."

Tuesday 18 September 1962

Instrumental band, the Flee-Rekkers, who had a hit with "Green Jeans" in 1960, supported by Billy Kramer and the Coasters, and Lee Curtis and the All Stars. **Lee Curtis**[456]: "You could say I was unemployed as I used to sign on. I joined the line one day and on the desk was a stack of *Mersey Beats* and I was on the front page. I was asked, 'Do you know this person?' and I said, 'I think so', and they told me to go to the interview room. We were getting a fiver for working but they were lots of expenses and my brother arranged the cover of *Mersey Beat*. I don't know what it cost but it came out of the group's money. I told them, 'We are losing money, not making it. Somebody else has paid for that.'"

Lee's new drummer was Pete Best. **Lee Curtis**[457]: "When Pete joined us, he said, 'Curtis,' he would call me Curtis, 'let's see who gets the most fans now.' First off, I thought he meant between him and I but he meant between the Beatles and Lee Curtis and the All-Stars. He played with us exactly as he had played it with the Beatles: very heavy

on the bass drum and head down, not looking at the audience. The moody guy side of Pete wasn't anything he worked upon. He was just a very shy person and a nice guy."

Saturday 22 September 1962

Zenith Six, Lee Curtis and the All Stars, and first appearance of Mike and the Thunderbirds. Mike was **Mike Byrne**[458], who founded *The Beatles Story* at the Albert Dock: "We didn't get on the Cavern until September 1962. We were on with Lee Curtis and the All Stars. He had such a big voice, he loved the big ballads, and Pete Best was with him. They were a great band, but I thought they were all great. We were first on and I don't think we were very impressive as it was a year before we got invited back. We were much better the second time. Mike and the Thunderbirds wore white shirts and black ties and sometimes because I liked Elvis and Cliff, I wore a black shiny shirt. At one time I changed my name to Jet Black, Jet Black and the Thunderbirds. That lasted a week and then I bumped into Rory Storm at the Grosvenor Ballroom and he suggested the name, Mike and the Thunderbirds."

Friday 28 September 1962

(lunchtime) Beatles
(evening) Billy Kramer and the Coasters, Big Three, Ian and the Zodiacs, and the Merseybeats. Also the Cavern has promoted another Riverboat Shuffle. This was the Beatles' third and final time on the Royal Iris and they are supported by Lee Castle and the Barons.

Norman Killon[459]: "I had started working in George Henry Lee's as a commis chef and the head commis chef who was three years older than me said that they were going to the Cavern to see this group called the Beatles: they weren't called bands then. They were about to have a record released. I was short and only 15 and I was only able to get in because I tagged along with them. I was used to hearing records—Neil Sedaka, Del Shannon—great records but this was four people with guitars belting out songs that I didn't know about like 'A Shot Of Rhythm And Blues', and it was quite an introduction. After hearing these songs a few times, I went into NEMS to get the originals. I then knew what I was listening to. Very few groups wrote their own material and so if you heard a song you liked, you could go into

NEMS and ask for the song, and in Brian's shop, they always had the originals."

Saturday 29 September 1962
Gerry and the Pacemakers, Grant Tracey and the Sunsets, Four Jays and Group One

Tuesday 2 October 1962
John, Paul, George and Ringo at lunchtime: Pete Best with Lee Curtis and the All Stars in the evening.

Was **Norman Killon**[460], later a DJ at the Sink and Eric's, influenced by Bob Wooler? "In so far as the things that he picked, yes, but I have always avoided boring people with a microphone when I DJ. I have been to far too many dos where the DJ thinks he is the star and gets on your nerves. I rarely use a microphone and I don't take them out to gigs but Bob was not one of those. He talked but he had interesting things to say whereas a lot of DJs have absolutely nothing to say and say it at great length. His records were magnificent. Where would you have heard these records before? Bob had an entrée into areas that you could never have when you were 15. He borrowed a record from a friend of mine and it was Chan Romero's 'Hippy Hippy Shake' and my friend never got it back."

Earl Preston[461]: "Without Bob Wooler, the Beatles wouldn't have made it, but nobody would. He was the driving force behind us all. He would instil confidence. I doubt if there would have been much of a scene without him. He would be in Aintree Institute and Hambleton Hall as well as the Cavern and it was his idea to feature four or five groups in a night. He was also a great DJ and we were all influenced by his choices."

Wednesday 3 October 1962
The organ-based group, the Echoes, had backed Gene Vincent and Conway Twitty on package shows and so many Cavernites had seen them before. With shades of Acker Bilk, their drummer wore a bowler hat on stage. **Dennis Conroy**[462]: "I had seen the Echoes backing everybody on a package show and they were like the Shadows with lots of echo and reverb. They were on the Cavern one Wednesday night when the Beatles normally topped the bill. They had the main spot and they were okay, but everybody had come to see the Beatles who came on after them. I have a vivid memory of seeing the Echoes standing

there with their mouths wide open. They had no idea what was going to follow them and they had never heard anything like them."

The Echoes were so influenced by what they had seen that when they toured with Joe Brown and the Tornados in January 1963 and came to the Liverpool Empire, they included 'Love Me Do' in their set. Their current single, 'Sounds Of Winter' was written by Mitch Murray: hard luck, lads, you got the wrong song.

Friday 5 October 1962
The Flintstones (an art school band taking their name from the TV series) with Ken Dallas and the Silhouettes, Mark Peters and the Cyclones, and Dee Young and the Pontiacs. A recording of two instrumentals by the Pontiacs has been discovered: Dee Young isn't singing because he was holding the microphone.

Sunday 7 October 1962
The Beatles launching their first Parlophone single, "Love Me Do", the Swinging Blue Genes, back from Germany, Red River Jazzmen, and Ian and the Zodiacs. **Ray Ennis**[463]: "That would be the first time I heard the Beatles play 'Love Me Do'. It wasn't rock'n'roll, and it sounded quite skiffley to me. I know that EMI had wanted Paul McCartney to play a string bass on it at first and Paul had a word with Les Braid about playing a string bass. Paul said, 'How do you do it because there are no frets on a string bass?' Les showed him how to get the octave with his left hand, and the two of them were huddled around the bass working it out. I think they did try it with a double bass but it wasn't released."

Meanwhile, the Blue Genes themselves, following their escapades at the Star-Club, had returned a rock'n'roll band. **Ray Ennis**[464]: "Our fans were dumbfounded at first and didn't like what we were doing at all, but the whole scene had changed in the month we were away. Jazz had almost vanished from the Cavern and we knew that we were right to continue with rock'n'roll. Our banjo player, Paul Moss, left but that didn't matter as he wanted to be a policeman. I can remember Ray McFall putting on Paul's sweater and getting up with us for a song."

Rogan Taylor[465]: "In October 1962, I was seventeen and in the army as a junior soldier. The missile crisis in Cuba was a few weeks old. Missiles were on boats crossing the Atlantic from the Soviets and Kennedy had said that he was going to stop and disarm the boats. The two world superpowers had enough nuclear energy to fry us all 50 times over. We were face to face and nose to nose for the only time in the whole of the Cold War. Most of us thought that really could be it. There I am stuck in this artillery camp in North Wales, thinking if the world is going to be blown to bits, I might as well be in the Cavern. I went over the wall, my first AWOL. When the Beatles' record came out, I had been caught and was back in the camp with 14 days in the guardhouse. I remember 'Love Me Do' wafting down the corridor of the nick. I told someone that I knew them but that they sang a lot better songs than that as I didn't think it was particularly good. It didn't match up to the classic rock'n'roll that I'd been hearing in the Cavern."

Monday 8 October 1962

(lunchtime) Pete Maclaine and the Dakotas standing in for the Beatles who are recording the *Friday Spectacular* for Radio Luxembourg.

Tuesday 9 October 1962

UK's answer to Buddy Holly, Buddy Britten and the Regents, with the Strangers, the Big Three and the Undertakers. **Brian Jones**[466] of the Undertakers: "The Beatles had their strongholds and we had ours. We used to play at the Iron Door and they used to play at the Cavern. We had our first booking at the Cavern in 1962 and lots of people came out of curiosity. There was a queue down Mathew Street, round the corner, past Frank Hessy's and round another corner to the Kardomah. A few months later there was a photograph of the queue with the caption, 'This is the queue for the Beatles at the Cavern'. If you look at the picture closely, you can see our van being unloaded."

Friday 12 October 1962

The Beatles play the lunchtime session and then head out to Tower Ballroom, New Brighton to support Little Richard. **Joe Ankrah**[467] of the Chants: "We had been to see Little Richard at the Tower and we got to meet him. The Beatles were there, whom we had never heard of, and Paul invited us to one of the lunchtime sessions. We didn't play instruments and so the Beatles played

for us while we sang. We heard that Brian Epstein wasn't happy about them doing this but they liked our style. Brian Epstein signed us for about a year but he was too busy with the Beatles to bother with us. We often played the Cavern and we were backed by the Remo Four, the Undertakers and the Big Three. Just as we were on the verge of breaking up, we got a contract from Pye and Tony Hatch did 'I Could Write A Book' with us. We hated it as it sounded too stiff and too British. 'Come Go With Me' was a good recording as it caught our love of doowop. We always opened on stage with 'Duke Of Earl' and we would have loved to record that."

John Frankland[468]: "The Chants would get round one microphone and people would go mad for them. They also did some vocal backings for us, but really they needed brass behind them. They would have been great backed by Cliff Bennett and the Rebel Rousers. They could do 'Young Boy Blues' and 'Sixteen Candles' really well."

Billy Kinsley[469]: "The Chants have been totally overlooked. I would watch them rehearse in a big old house at the bottom of Upper Parliament Street in Liverpool. They would rehearse all day with just a guitarist to get the keys, and they worked so hard on their harmonies. The Beatles backed the Chants at the Cavern—now, that is a memorable gig. The Beatles had an enormous repertoire so there would always be a couple that the Chants would know. I've seen lists of supposedly every song the Beatles ever did but I could name you another 20."

Wednesday 17 October 1962

Johnny Sandon and the Remo Four (back from six wild, wild months in France) and the Beatles (rushing back from performing two songs 'Love Me Do' and 'Some Other Guy' on Granada's *People And Places*), plus Group One and the Swinging Blue Jeans

Friday 19 October 1962

Nobody knew it but B. Bumble and the Stingers were fakes: none of them had played on "Nut Rocker". **Dave Boyce**[470]: "I remember standing in Frank Hessy's the night B. Bumble and the Stingers were on at the Cavern as they wanted to borrow a double-bass. They were travelling around on trains and they had no equipment with them. The drummer had a snare drum and the pianist played the Cavern piano."

Billy Hatton[471]: "The most disappointing band I ever saw at the Cavern was B. Bumble and the Stingers, but it wasn't all their fault. They featured a piano on 'Nut Rocker'. There was an old upright piano against the wall at the Cavern and no one had tuned it. It wasn't even miked up. The sound wasn't right and you could tell that they weren't into it. I said to the guitarist, 'Do you want someone to stand by the piano with a microphone?' and he said, 'No, he's got such a strong left hand, he'll be all right.' They didn't even have a bass player. All the lads were knackered and they could have been going to another gig too. I was thinking about going professional at the time and when I saw them, I thought, 'No thank you.'"

Actually, the Four Jays that night had become the Fourmost. **Billy Hatton**[472]: "The Four Jays to the Fourmost was just a natural progression but we did lock into the pop stuff, and the comedy stuff went on the back burner. It was very useful though as we had something to do in cabaret when the hits stopped. We did a lot of Coasters' songs and 'Ubangi Stomp' and we had a lot of fun with 'Monster Mash'. We didn't have a single lead singer and that was one of our strengths. I think Mike Millward had the best voice in the band. A lot of bands did the Coasters' 'Along Came Jones' but they did it in a major key which didn't work for me."

Saturday 20 October 1962

Another sting from B. Bumble, plus Ian and the Zodiacs, the Merseybeats and Cavern debuts for the Memphis Three and Tommy Quickly and the Challengers.

Billy Kinsley[473]: "I remember playing with B. Bumble and the Stingers and every other song they did was 'Nut Rocker'. They didn't have a large repertoire. They had to keep reminding the audience of their hit. It was piano, drums, saxophone and guitar and I don't think that they had a bass. They were one of the first American bands we ever played with."

The Memphis Three had come out of Ricky and the Red Streaks and included drummer Gibson Kemp and the guitarist **Brendan McCormack**[474]: "There is a moment during the *Let It Be*

sessions where John Lennon tells Paul McCartney that 'You're not talking to Ricky and the Red Streaks now' so they remembered us. At first we didn't have amplifiers and so you had to be scientifically minded or curious to make your own. I was both and I had a Dansette and I rationalised that if I removed the pickup arm and got a lead to my guitar, I could be amplified, and I was amplified, admittedly with a small speaker of two watts. Then I looked at the family radio which was as big as a kennel and it weighed about 60 pounds. There was an input lead in there, which was very curious for the 1950s, and then I did this same cannibalised thing with my guitar. We progressed to a very posh 10 watt amplifier and that is even less than an average radio today. We became the Memphis Three and I think us and the Big Three were the only trios around."

Friday 2 November 1962

Fourmost, Vic and the Spidermen, Dennisons, Johnny Martin and the Tremors

Sunday 4 November 1962

Joe Simon's Dixielanders, Big Three, Blue Jeans, Johnny Sandon and the Remo Four

Tuesday 6 November 1962

Freddie and the Dreamers, Undertakers, Alby and the Sorrals

Saturday 10 November 1962

Joe Simon's Dixielanders, Merseybeats and Dennisons

Sunday 18 November 1962

Beatles, Merseybeats, Pete Hartigan's Jazz Band

Friday 23 November 1962

(lunchtime) Johnny Sandon and the Remo Four. The Remo took over from the Beatles on the lunchtime gig as the Beatles had gone to London for a BBC-TV audition, which they failed.

(evening) Johnny Sandon and the Remo Four, Del-Renas, Merseybeats, and Johnny Martin and the Tremors

Wednesday 5 December 1962

(lunchtime) The Beatles

(evening) Gerry and the Pacemakers (back from Germany), Johnny Sandon and the Remo Four, Statesmen

Ray O'Brien[475]: "When they had their first hit with 'Love Me Do', I lived in Newsham Park and I would go to Liverpool FC which was a mile away. I would walk over there and I used to have a little transistor radio I would play and I remember hearing 'Love Me Do'. I felt proud because I had seen them at the Cavern and because George and Paul went to my school and also because it was so different. I would buy things like 'Johnny Remember Me' and 'Come Outside' at the time and the harmonica on it was great. I imagined them with their black polo-necks singing it. Their hair was so different then. They sounded rough. I felt good about it."

Friday 7 December 1962

(lunchtime) Beatles

(evening) Gerry and the Pacemakers, Fourmost, Merseybeats, and Ian and the Zodiacs

David Crosby[476]: "I started going to the Cavern when I was still at school and when I could afford it. I mainly went to the lunchtimes because it was a shilling to get in, but it was three shillings in the evening. I was at Wallasey Grammar School which was in Withens Lane and we got an hour and a half for lunch. At half past 12 I would race down Manor Lane and jump on the No.1 bus, I had it all timed, I would then jump on the ferry, be first off the gangplank, up the ramp and I would run all the way to Mathew Street, which kept me fit. I would stay 20 minutes and make the same run back, just to return for 2pm."

Sunday 9 December 1962

The Beatles, Fourmost, Blue Jeans and Zenith Six Jazz Band. George Martin was wandering around the Cavern, seeing if the club might be suitable for a live recording. He decided against it, but he did like the Fourmost's comedy and thought of signing them. Not one to miss an opportunity, Brian Epstein asked them to join his organisation. Drummer **Dave Lovelady**[477]: "We nearly blew it as George invited us to London and we worked up 'Happy Talk' for the audition. It's a tricky piece and we were pleased with ourselves, but George Martin said that we were playing the wrong chords."

Tuesday 11 December 1962

The Swinging Blue Jeans, Freddie and the Dreamers and the Lee Eddy Five. **Ray Ennis**[478]: "The fact that it was a small stage didn't stop Freddie Garrity at all. He leapt about all over the place.

He was pretty small so didn't take up much room anyway."

Wednesday 12 December 1962

It's a day of sub-zero temperatures and blizzards in Wales, and the Cavern's bill of fare combines the folk singers, Robin Hall and Jimmie MacGregor, with the Beatles, the Fourmost and the Merseybeats. **Bob Wooler**[479]: "In December 1962, the folksingers from the *Tonight* programme, Robin Hall and Jimmie MacGregor, were booked to appear with the Beatles at the Cavern. I went on stage and said, 'I have got some dreadful news for you. Because of this terrible weather, one of the acts is not able to appear tonight.' There were gasps, I was milking it of course, and when I named the act that couldn't make it, Robin Hall and Jimmie MacGregor, everyone applauded."

Tuesday 18 December 1962

Billy Fury's backing group and 'Telstar' hitmakers, the Tornados, made four appearances (two on Tuesday, two on Wednesday) and were the first group with a US No.1 to come to the Cavern. They'd have been better served by going to the US, but the gigs went well.

Ritchie Galvin[480], drummer with Earl Preston and the TTs, was on the same bill on the evening of December 18. "I've never liked using anybody else's drums as every time I do I break something. The Tornados put their gear on stage and said, 'We'd rather you didn't bring your gear on.' Clem Cattini said, 'You can use my drums—brand new Ludwig—and you'll have a good workout on them.' I said, 'Okay' and when we did our first number, I put his snare drum through his bass drum skin."

Billy Butler[481]: "The first song I ever heard in the Cavern was Cy Tucker singing 'Lend Me Your Comb' and I loved hearing versions of songs that I had in my collection but had never heard anyone do. The girls were doing the Cavern Stomp. It was a compressed space so you held each other's hands and moved sideways very slowly."

Ann Upton[482] tells of life on the road with Earl Preston and the TTs: "I was the only steady girlfriend with the band. There was no comfortable seating in the van, nothing like the airport seats that you get now. The drivers for the groups wouldn't hump the gear: that would be up to the group. Loading the gear at the Cavern was absolutely awful: you had to duck your head and the stairs were steep. The drivers would take them there and back, maybe a double in a night, and they would sit at the back and have a couple of drinks. It was nothing for me to be sitting in the back of the van after a gig with the boys all sweaty and horrible. They'd be trying to carve £5 into 17/6d a head for the band and 30s for the driver. One time we were going to the Mersey View and the van hadn't been packed well and everything started to slide. Ritchie's drums rolled out of the door on a hill."

And did Ritchie ever go to bed? **Ann Upton**[483]: "Ritch was a milkman for Reece's initially so quite often if they were playing two or three gigs in the night, it was hardly worth going home. It was so late that he would go straight to work. If he wasn't playing a lunchtime gig, he would go to bed for a few hours. Then it would be the evening gig. He was out every single night but they were all so young then and were able to do it. Of course there were some helpers around like Prellies or purple hearts."

Friday 21 December 1962

(lunchtime) Big Three

(evening) Johnny Sandon and the Remo Four, Del-Renas, Mike Foster's Jazzmen and Vic and the Spidermen

David Crosby[484]: "Mostly I had the American originals, or certainly had heard the originals, but there were some songs I didn't know. I knew Richie Barrett's 'Some Other Guy' but I had never heard the B-side 'Tricky Dicky'. The same with Arthur Alexander's 'A Shot Of Rhythm And Blues' which I'd heard, but I'd never heard 'You Better Move On'. Most groups did 'You Better Move On': the Big Three did 'You Better Move On': one group would do it and the others would follow. The Big Three did the definitive version of 'Some Other Guy', even better than the Beatles. In concert, it was totally different to the record. Just multiply their record by five to imagine the excitement of it live. It had a very long 12 bar intro before the vocal came in whereas it comes straight in on the record. They were doing it like 'What'd I Say' and there was a very long guitar solo in the middle. The whole thing was about five minutes long and very exciting."

Monday 24 December 1962

(lunchtime) The Big Three with Gerry and the Pacemakers. **David Crosby**[485]: "I went to that lunchtime show because my family had gone to Edinburgh to spend Christmas there and I said I would catch them up later. It was with the Big Three and Gerry and the Pacemakers for a shilling. There was a lot of excitement in the Cavern around that time as the Beatles had made the charts, and this was our group and our club. I thought Gerry and the Pacemakers were excellent. They had a jingly piano like Russ Conway or Winifred Atwell but it was still rock'n'roll and they did American pop records by Bobby Vee and Tony Orlando very well. Gerry had an exciting throaty tone to his voice and I also liked Freddie Marsden's simple but very solid rhythm."

(evening) The Flintstones, Johnny Sandon and the Remo Four, the Merseybeats, and Tommy Quickly and the Challengers. **Tony Crane**[486] of the Merseybeats: "When we were on the Cavern, nobody used any effects. You had to use the house PA system because there was no room to put your own system there. There was a 30 watt amplifier, three 12 inch speakers around the place, two Reslo mikes and everybody used them. We didn't mind the Cavern being grotty as the feel and the atmosphere was so great. With the archways, it was great acoustically, like a recording studio. I had never heard a bass guitar so loud as when you went down and listened to it in the Cavern. It used to vibrate all the walls. Griff made coffins for all the bands. He would put an 18 inch speaker in a big box and it would look like a coffin, you would carry it in like a coffin and it would stand at the back of the stage. The Big Three were first and then the Beatles had one and then we had one. The whole sound of the band changed because you had a big deep bass going and it would vibrate all the walls and the chairs would vibrate too."

Tuesday 25 December 1962

The Beatles have Christmas dinner with the Dominoes at the Seaman's Mission in Hamburg. **John Frankland**[487]: "The minister attached to the Mission said, 'Would anyone like to say grace?' and George in his wonderful deadpan way said, 'Yes, thank Christ for the soup.' The minister said, 'Any more of that and you're all out.' We ate steaks and we found out later that they were horse steaks. We'd eaten a horse for Christmas."

Monday 31 December 1962

(lunchtime) Gerry and the Pacemakers

(evening) All nighter with Del-Renas, Big Three, Johnny Sandon and Remo Four, Fourmost, Vic and the Spidermen, Escorts and Flintstones.

Sam Hardie[488]: "I never thought that the Beatles was the best band from Liverpool. I always thought the Big Three was better, but the Beatles sounded different. They did 'Clarabella' better than the Jodimars as they changed it from a shuffle to a four beats to the bar, Little Richard thing. Epstein stuck the Big Three in suits and gave them those dreadful songs, but for me, Merseybeat finished the day Gerry and the Pacemakers released 'How Do You Do It'. That had nothing to do with Merseybeat, which was American rock and roll."

5

RISE AND McFALL

Cavern owner:
Ray McFall
final years, 1963-1966

One lot at the Beatles auction at LIPA in 2005 was a 1963 Cavern club membership card signed by Paul McCartney together with a lock of John's hair and a letter of authenticity from its original owner. From John himself? Well, no, it was from a hairdresser who gave John a trim and kept what she removed. How can you value that? It fetched £500 but more could have been obtained from a scientific convention with an interest in DNA.

Monday 7 January 1963
Bobby's girl Susan Maughan is supported by Gerry and the Pacemakers and the Fourmost. **Dave Boyce**[489]: "There were some oddball acts at the Cavern like B. Bumble and the Stingers and Susan Maughan. She had a skirt that filled the whole stage as she had about 26 petticoats on, but she went down very well."

Friday 11 January 1963
Celebrating the release of the "Please Please Me" single, the Beatles have a lunchtime session with Kingsize Taylor and the Dominoes. They drive to the Midlands for an evening show at the Plaza Ballroom, Old Hill, Dudley but blizzards prevent them from making it three in a day at the Ritz Ballroom, King's Heath, Birmingham. Back at

the Cavern, Gerry and the Pacemakers are bopping away with the Fourmost, Sonny Webb and the Cascades and the Del-Renas.

Friday 18 January 1963
Billy Kramer and the Coasters

Wednesday 23 January 1963
The Beatles could have been excused for not making it, but there they were. The previous day they had recorded three different BBC radio shows in London and returned to Liverpool that morning in freezing fog. (I know this isn't a book on climate change, but the winter weather was much worse in 1961/2/3 than it has been in recent times.) Neil Aspinall wasn't well and Mal Evans was driving them for the first time. The windscreen was damaged by a small stone, so Mal put his hat over his hand, punched the window out and drove on. When they got into Liverpool, Mal dropped them off, had the windscreen replaced and went to his day job. The Beatles were so impressed by his efficiency that they offered him a job as their roadie.

The Beatles were on with Freddie Starr and the Midnighters, and John Lennon could be as outlandish as Freddie Starr. Asked to do an impression, he sang hoarsely and said it was of a dying singer. **Faith Brown**[490]: "I can remember John Lennon swearing when he broke a string on stage. It horrified me at the time as nobody swore in our house."

Sunday 27 January 1963

The Marauders from Stoke-on-Trent

Sunday 3 February 1963

An eight hour marathon with the Beatles, the Fourmost, Kingsize Taylor and the Dominoes (with "Swinging Cilla"), the Hollies, the Merseybeats, the Roadrunners, Earl Preston and the TTs and the Swinging Blue Jeans. Sue Evans, wife of Mike, kept a diary: "Danced with four gorgeous beat types. Sat on one's shoulders to see the Beatles. They are the most FAB fellows—heavenly time."

Graham Nash[491]: "They were calling the Hollies 'Manchester's answer to the Beatles', which I never liked. You don't like being compared to anyone, particularly a band as great as the Beatles. I didn't sense the intercity rivalry much. There were a lot of great musicians and great bands in both cities."

Allan Clarke[492]: "At the time, I didn't like being called Manchester's answer to the Beatles but now I'm quite proud about it. We can claim to be a Mersey band as Stockport is on the Mersey."

Eric Haydock[493]: "The Mersey bands tended to be more raucous than the Manchester ones. They had a strong, macho, Teddy Boy type of image, whereas the Manchester bands were more glitzy. We wore white suits and that was aimed at the women. Club owners would tell us that if we got the women in, we would get the men and they would book us again." What was that Bob Marley hit? "No Women, No Men"?

Terry McCusker[494]: "Mike Hart of the Roadrunners was a canny guy and he knew how to hold an audience and get everybody's attention. He didn't have the world's best voice but it was one of those voices that had soul and it got to you, and the Roadrunners were a really good blues band. Part of the strength of the band was that they would drag up old blues numbers that I'd never heard of and make them their own."

Billy Hatton[495]: "Mike Hart had an amazingly strong voice and I didn't know he was asthmatic until one day he was doing this song and really belting it out and he turned to one side, took out

an inhaler and had a few whacks. If you don't get your air out properly, you are going to sing flat or the note is going to drop, and to be able to sing like that with asthma is amazing."

Mike McCartney[496]: "I can see Mike Hart with his big lips now and his eyes closed going (Sings) 'Cry Cry Cry'. I haven't heard that for years, but it was my favourite. He always gave it the welly in terms of soul. Whenever he sang that, you were crying, it got to you."

Friday 8 February 1963

Unusually, a country music lunchtime session with the Blue Mountain Boys. They had just signed with Oriole and their single "Drop Me Gently" was released in April.

Saturday 16 February 1963

The Saints Jazz Band, Johnny Sandon and the Remo Four, Vic and the Spidermen, and the Roadrunners. **Frankie Connor**[497]: "I was 16 and worked for Ethel Austin's, and Vic Wright of Vic and the Spidermen was my boss. He had red hair, good looks and a good voice. He took me down to the Cavern and they wore silver suits and were very smart. They were like Cliff and the Shads, but it was the Roadrunners who impressed me. Mike Hart was a great front man and I went back to see them. I would wait for Mike to do 'Cry, Cry, Cry', which was absolutely tremendous: worth the admission fee on its own."

Mike Evans[498]: "The Roadrunners were doing standard R&B stuff but Mike Hart had a most powerful voice and his star number was 'Cry, Cry, Cry'. He sang 'Roadrunner' and he did James Brown and Muddy Waters and he also played a honking tenor sax. It was this powerful voice that came over: he would stand with his eyes tight shut and his cowboy boots and he was really charismatic."

Drummer **Dave Boyce**[499]: "I was still at school when I joined the Roadrunners. I was leading a double life: a schoolboy by day and a rock musician by night. I used to pretend to my mother that I was going to school and I would take my civvies in my satchel and change in the loos at Hamilton Square station. I would come over to the Cavern for the lunchtime sessions, sometimes playing and sometimes watching. I was 17 and I had no sense that I was going to get caught. The school eventually got in touch with my mother and I had the option of staying in school or staying with the band. Effectively, I had already left school."

Sunday 17 February 1963

The Dennisons, the Nomads, Freddie Starr and the Midnighters, and Tommy Quickly and the Challengers. **Geoff Davies**[500]: "Freddie Starr was a good singer and he did a brilliant Billy Fury. He would sing 'Halfway To Paradise' as 'Halfway To Birkenhead' and this was hilarious to us at the time."

John Cochrane[501]: "When I was with Gus Travis and the Midnighters, Freddie Starr would do a spot with us and our manager could see his potential. Freddie had this comedy routine where he would slag off the rest of the band and we would all shout at him. Our manager said that we were doing the Cavern and doing it with Freddie. We weren't sure about that as we had to follow Freddie and the Dreamers. We told Freddie that we couldn't let him do his comedy routine this time as it would have looked sad after seeing Freddie and the Dreamers, who were crazy and very funny and had worked it at much more than anything we were doing. Freddie Garrity is like Lee Curtis, in that respect—they are both showmen with real personalities and they have the audience in their hands. I didn't care for Freddie and the Dreamers' music but I liked to watch Freddie as I wasn't sure what would happen next."

Tuesday 19 February 1963

The Beatles, Lee Curtis and the All Stars, the Pathfinders, and Freddie Starr and the Midnighters. A rare occasion where the Beatles encountered Pete Best on the same bill—and they were never to see him again. The queue for the show had formed the night before and to make it worse for Pete, Bob Wooler read out a telegram sent c/o The Cavern Club just as the Beatles were going on stage. It was from Brian Epstein and it confirmed that "Please Please Me" had climbed to Number One on the *New Musical Express'* chart. The audience went quiet: they sensed that the Beatles no longer belonged to them. The Beatles already knew they were Number One. There are photographs of them that day in Brian's office and by Liverpool landmarks (Pier Head, Water Street, Derby Square), taken by Michael Ward: only one

has been published to date, but they are about to appear in a Genesis book.

Sunday 24 February 1963

Blasting off with Dean Stacey and the Detonators

Sunday 3 March 1963

The launch of Gerry and the Pacemakers' first single, "How Do You Do It", supported by the Swinging Blue Jeans and Earl Preston and TTs. Mitch Murray's song had been offered to Johnny Angel, Adam Faith and the Beatles before it got to Gerry. **Mitch Murray**[502] says, "It makes me cringe to think that George Martin told the Beatles to come up with a song as good as mine, but he knew that I was a professional songwriter and he liked the song. Brian Epstein suggested that Gerry and the Pacemakers should do the song and he told me that Gerry was a Liverpool Bobby Darin. George Martin asked me to hear Gerry at the Cavern but I said, 'I don't care what he sounds like, it's the record that counts.' Arrogant little sod, wasn't I? They made the record, I loved it and it delighted me when it got to Number One."

Sunday 10 March 1963

A Twist And Trad Night with the Swinging Blue Jeans, Johnny Sandon and Remo Four, the Zenith Six and the Merseybeats. Not much twisting in a congested Cavern.

Saturday 16 March 1963

Another Twist And Trad Night, this time with Pete Harrigan's Jazzmen, Vic and the Spidermen, Johnny Templar and the Hi Cats and the Memphis Three

Tuesday 19 March 1963

Jon Anderson[503]: "I lived in Accrington and I went to the Cavern for a lunchtime session and saw the Big Three. I was smitten and knew what I wanted do with my life." Yes indeed.

Geoff Loftus[504]: "When I was a young lad, I saw the Beatles and the Undertakers at the Cavern. I think it was the Big Three I saw first. I would go with my mates and we looked old enough to get in. They were an excellent band and I saw the Undertakers and the Beatles. Ringo was with them. They did 'Long Tall Sally' and 'What'd I Say'. They were excellent but there was no echo in the place and water ran down the walls. Still, the atmosphere was fantastic."

Friday 22 March 1963

Gerry Marsden[505]: "Even when we had a hit with 'How Do You Do It', we had to play the Cavern cheaply because we'd signed the contract six weeks before we'd hit the charts."

Wednesday 27 March 1963

(lunchtime) The Hollies

(evening) The Karl Denver Trio, the Big Three, the Hollies and Earl Preston and the TTs. Earl Preston and the TTs were doing three new songs— "Let's Turkey Trot", "Watch Your Step" and "Good Good Lovin'". A young EMI A&R man, Ron Richards, was at the Cavern and he gave the Hollies a recording contract. A week later they were recording their first chart single, a cover of the Coasters' "(Ain't That) Just Like Me".

Monday 1 April 1963

Clean-cut harmonies and clean-cut looks from the Irish hitmakers, the Bachelors. Their double-bass almost touched the ceiling. **Dec Cluskey**[506] recalls, "It said in our diary, 'The Cavern, Liverpool' and we didn't know anything about the place. It sounded like another night club. When we found it in a little back street, we couldn't believe it. The sound was sensational, because anyone sounds good in a place like that. However, we were a sane and rational act and I don't think the crowd wanted that." The audience still had Ian and the Zodiacs, the Escorts and the Nomads.

Con Cluskey[507]: "I had bought a Gibson guitar and had a little sling that clipped into the hole in the middle, but it kept slipping out. I hated playing that night, though I loved the atmosphere."

John Stokes[508]: "I know that we were in the midst of all the beat groups, but we had no worries about that. It sounds conceited but we always felt that we could get up and do it anywhere." The two Cluskeys later dismissed Stokes and claimed that he couldn't sing. When the matter came to court, they likened his voice to a drowned rat's. There aren't many opportunities for hearing rats sing but the Cavern could be one of them.

Wednesday 3 April 1963

(lunchtime) Rory Storm and the Hurricanes. Johnny Guitar records in his diary, "Played okay, packed." **Judd Lander**[509]: "Rory Storm and the Hurricanes was the first group I saw at the Cavern. Rory should have been a film star. He was larger than life and always had a camel-haired coat draped

around his shoulders. Johnny Guitar had a little narrow guitar that I loved. He was a terrible guitarist but he would be playing it aggressively and got away with it."

(evening) Sonny Webb and the Cascades, Vic and the Spidermen, the Citadels and the Crusaders. The Crusaders, later known as the Kruzads, had a falling out. The bass player used to take the equipment home and when he didn't get paid one night, he sawed the corners of the Vox amps so that they were octagonal.

Friday 12 April 1963

A Good Friday "R&B marathon" from 4pm to midnight with the Beatles, Fourmost, Dennisons, Nomads, Panthers, Flintstones, Roadrunners, Group One and Faron's Flamingos. **Eddie Parry**[510] of the Dennisons: "You had to wait about five hours before you went on stage but I didn't mind as I was watching my idol, John Lennon. Steve McLaren and I got the idea for a song that night and that was our first single, '(Come On) Be My Girl'."

Sunday 28 April 1963

Billy J. Kramer, now signed with Epstein and teamed with Manchester's Dakotas, is on the same bill as the Coasters. Billy's first single, "Do You Want To Know A Secret", had been released two days earlier. **Dave Howard**[511]: "I saw Billy J Kramer with the Dakotas, who were excellent. On the whole, the Manchester bands like the Hollies didn't have the bottom end and the guts of the Liverpool bands. I had no money and it hurt me to see Graham Nash with an acoustic Gibson Jumbo that wasn't even plugged in and it was so annoying. He was just miming with it. He certainly could play the guitar later on. I didn't like Herman's Hermits, but the drummer had an elliptical bass drum, a Trixon. I suppose I noticed the gear more than anything else."

Freddie Starr showed his displeasure by vandalising Graham Nash's guitar. Years later, I was with Michael Snow, who wrote "Rosetta", at BBC Radio Merseyside and we ran into Freddie Starr. They greeted each other warmly, and Michael said, "Freddie, I haven't seen you since you crapped in Graham Nash's guitar."

Monday 29 April 1963

(lunchtime) Gerry and the Pacemakers. **Gerry Marsden**[512]: "Brian Epstein asked us to stay on and make a tape with Cilla Black that he could take to George Martin. At the time, I didn't think she had a great voice, but I was wrong there." Cilla's version of "Fever" with the Pacemakers was included on the box set, *Cilla Black, 1963-1973, The Abbey Road Decade.* Gerry is right about her voice: it was piercing and shrill back then and it was transformed by the time of "Anyone Who Had A Heart".

Joey Shields[513]: "We used to laugh at the trill in Cilla's voice. She did 'Lavender Blue' and it was a very untrained voice. She sounded like an old person but she had stage presence."

Ray O'Brien[514]: "I still went to the Cavern when I was at the shipping office and the office was in the Cunard Building. My mother would say, 'Have you found anywhere to have your lunch?' and I said I was going to the Cavern and she thought it was a restaurant. We would get luncheon vouchers and she said, 'Can you use your luncheon vouchers at the Cavern?' Talk about Aunt Mimi: these people didn't know what was going on."

Saturday 4 May 1963

Johnny Sandon and the Remo Four, the Silhouettes, the Del-Renas and Joe Simon's Dixielanders. Some of this was filmed for a TV programme, *Rave Wave.*

Sunday 5 May 1963

The Cavern is becoming so hip that even religious programmes are interested. Their R&B marathon was filmed for ABC-TV's *Sunday Break.* A varied bill of fare with the Zenith Six, the Dennisons, the Escorts, Earl Preston and the TTs, the Merseybeats, Faron's Flamingos, the Nomads, Derry Wilkie and the Pressmen, and Tommy Quickly and the Challengers

Sunday 12 May 1963

The Red River Jazzmen, Mark Peters and the Silhouettes, and Tommy Quickly and the Challengers. Four coach loads of beat fans come from Sheffield, the first of many coach parties from around the UK. **Bob Wooler**[515]: "When the coaches arrived in 1963, I would say on the mike, 'Welcome to so-and-so and we hope you enjoy yourselves tonight.' The Cavernites would

say, 'What's the idea?', and I thought at times that they might hammer them. They didn't, but they resented outsiders coming in. That was it really. Some of the regulars stayed but not enough to sustain the club. People were coming because the Cavern was a curiosity. One solution would have been to market souvenirs and to turn it into a Memphis on the Mersey."

Friday 17 May 1963

All aboard the Royal Iris for the Big Five Jive with Freddie and the Dreamers and Johnny Sandon and the Remo Four.

Sunday 19 May 1963

Rock'n'roll legend, Gene Vincent with the Hollies and Tommy Quickly and the Challengers.

Friday 24 May 1963

(lunchtime) Freddie Starr and the Midnighters. **Bob Wooler**[516]: "I was always hoping that Ray McFall wasn't around when Freddie Starr was on stage. He worked in the fruit market and he once put an enormous carrot in his trousers and pulled it out slowly. If Ray had seen that, he would have remonstrated with me—'How could you have let him on stage?' I remember being with Freddie in the Grapes and he saw an attractive girl go into the Ladies. He produced his willie and flopped it on the table. When she came out, he shouted, 'Try this one for size.' Ray McFall hated him and that's not too strong a word."

Billy Butler[517]: "Ray was very staid and if any of the groups made sexy remarks on stage, he would be on them like a ton of bricks. Freddie Starr did an impression of Jim Reeves once by lying on the ground and Ray didn't find that funny at all."

Colin Middlebrough[518]: "Freddie Starr was totally uncontrollable. He would unzip his trousers on stage, put a bread roll around his willy and say, 'Would anybody like a hot dog?' He would do very good impersonations of Billy Fury which he did with a very long four foot comb and his collar up, and he did an excellent Elvis Presley too. Beryl Marsden joined us for six months and what a front line that was. I had the dubious task of taking Freddie home as he lived in Central Avenue in Speke. I was the only one with transport, I had a mini-van, and he would open the window and moon people. I would get home and I might be locked out as my father would lock the front door at midnight whether I was in or not. I spent many a happy night in the van, thanks to Freddie Starr. Freddie was fun to be with, but he would go over the top so many times."

Sunday 26 May 1963

The return of Johnny Kidd and the Pirates, supported by the Dennisons and Lee Curtis and the All Stars

Tuesday 28 May 1963

The Hollies, Faron's Flamingos, the Decibels and Sonny Webb and the Cascades. **Eric Haydock**[519] of the Hollies: "Condensation used to drip down on everything and our guitar strings were alive with static. We always came out stinking but we did like the atmosphere there."

Saturday 8 June 1963

Tommy Steele's brother, Colin Hicks, with his group, the Top Spots. Also on the bill are the Golly Golly Boys.

Wednesday 12 June 1963

The Hollies with Vince Earl and the Talismen. Vince Earl became a club comic and then Ron Dixon in *Brookside*.

Friday 14 June 1963

Gerry Devine and the City Kings with Tommy Quickly and the Challengers and (get this) Gay and the Guys.

Sunday 16 June 1963

Gravel-voiced R&B from Alexis Korner, plus the Big Three, Sapphires, Red River Jazzmen and Johnny Sandon and the Remo Four. **Zoot Money**[520] was playing keyboards for Alexis Korner: "I thought the Beatles were a nice little group but I found that everybody in Liverpool was talking about them. At the time my ego was bigger than all four of theirs combined. The Cavern was hot and heaving and they seemed to like our variety of blues and R&B. Alexis was a great performer: he would really be telling you stories while he sang. He was a joybringer."

Tuesday 18 June 1963

Rory Storm and the Hurricanes, Mark Peters and the Silhouettes, Faron's Flamingos and Southport's top band, R&B Inc.

Friday 21 June 1963

Bob Wooler had been beaten up by John Lennon at Paul McCartney's 21st. On the day he received an apologetic telegram from John Lennon (but written by Epstein), Bob was at the Cavern and for once, he took the stage. **Billy Kinsley**[521] of the Merseybeats: "We were topping the bill that night and Bob was wearing dark glasses. He took them off to reveal his black eye and he said to the audience, 'I got this at Lennon's Supermarket.'" Lennon's supermarkets were prevalent in Liverpool at the time, the Morrisons of the day.

Alex Young[522]: "There was a lot of Scouse banter when he made the stage. They were shouting 'Eye, eye' and 'Are you smoking Nelson?' He was a great compère and he used the black eye to his advantage."

Tuesday 25 June 1963

As Tommy Quickly has left the Challengers and joined the NEMS Organisation, his group teams up with one of the best soul singers on Merseyside, Steve Aldo.

Wednesday 26 June 1963

The Hollies, Vic and the Spidermen and Ted Knibbs' new discovery, Chick Graham. Having lost Kramer to Epstein, Knibbs put his former group, the Coasters, with Chick Graham. **Bob Wooler**[523]: "Chick Graham was a good singer but he quit because he wasn't prepared to put up with the jibes and the snide remarks. He was small and people kept calling him a dwarf, which he wasn't." So why on earth did he agree to the stage name of Chick?

Friday 28 June 1963

(lunchtime) Faron's Flamingos

(evening) Sonny Webb and the Cascades, the Escorts, the Panthers and Some People

The Big Three released a single, "By The Way", on 28 June 1963 and the B-side was their own composition, "Cavern Stomp". "By The Way" made the Top 30 but it is "Cavern Stomp" that is remembered. **Bob Wooler**[524]: "Brian Epstein invited Ray McFall and me to his office to hear the Big Three's new single, 'Cavern Stomp', as he knew we would be fascinated by a song which mentioned the Cavern. I'm not very good at PR, I suffer from foot in mouth disease, and I said, 'Brian, it doesn't tell you how to do the dance. All the American dance records like 'The Locomotion' and 'The Twist' tell you what to do.' He changed the subject completely because I had

The Big Three;
Brian 'Griff' Grif-
fiths, Johnny
'Hutch' Hutchin-
son and Johnny
'Gus' Gustafson
The live EP (left)
that should have
been an album

'Sign my arm
Gerry'
Gerry Marsden
with fans at the
Cavern (left)

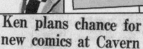

Ken plans chance for new comics at Cavern

BY A "DAILY POST" REPORTER

Comedian Ken Dodd, who suggested last month that Liverpool University should establish a Department of Giggleology, has decided to do the job himself. At Liverpool's Cavern Club lunch-time session, yesterday, during which he was made first honorary life member, Ken said that he intended to do all he could to help young up-and-coming Liverpool comedians.

Pointing out that Liverpool has long been the home of famous comedians ("You have to be a comedian to live here," he quipped) he said his plan was to keep the country well supplied in future.

Hopefuls looking for a break

"I am often contacted by young comedians looking for a break, and until now I have not been able to do much to help them. Now I can send them along to the Cavern where they will be given a lunchtime spot. They will be with youngsters of their own generation, os if they have any talent it should show here."

Ken's partner in thescheme is Cavern Club owner Mr. Ray McFall who said: "We've been wanting to broaden the scope of our entertainment, and this looks like being a good way to do it."

What does Ken Dodd think of the Cavern? "It's bubbling over with vitality and exuberance—and that just suits me fine.

"As far as the Mersey Sound is concerned, I think the real sound is the sound of laughter, and we should have plenty of that round here in future," he said.

BIG! BIG! SESSIONS
FOR YOU AND YOUR FRIENDS AT
THE CAVERN
PRESENTING TOP RECORDING STARS plus FABULOUS SUPPORTING GROUPS

SUNDAY, 2nd FEBRUARY, 1964
THE CHANTS (Pye)

MONDAY LUNCHTIME, 3rd FEBRUARY, 1964
THE BIG 3 (Decca) plus
DAVE BERRY & THE CRUISERS (Decca)

MONDAY EVENING, 3rd FEBRUARY, 1964
THE DENNISONS (Decca) ★ THE FORTUNES (Decca)
LEE CURTIS & THE ALL STARS (Decca)

TUESDAY EVENING, 4th FEBRUARY, 1964
THE CRESTERS (HMV)

WEDNESDAY LUNCHTIME, 5th FEBRUARY, 1964
THE ESCORTS (HMV)
COLOUR FILMING SESSION FOR "LOOK AT LIFE"

WEDNESDAY EVENING, 5th FEBRUARY, 1964
UNDERTAKERS (Pye) ★ THE ROAD RUNNERS (Oriole)

THURSDAY LUNCHTIME, 6th FEBRUARY, 1964
THE MARAUDERS (Decca) ★ BERYL MARSDEN (Decca)

THURSDAY EVENING, 6th FEBRUARY, 1964
HEINZ (Decca) ★ VIC & THE TTS (Fontana)
BERN ELLIOTT & THE FENMEN (Decca)

FRIDAY LUNCHTIME, 7th FEBRUARY, 1964
THE MERSEYBEATS (Fontana)

FRIDAY EVENING, 7th FEBRUARY, 1964
THE REMO 4 (Pye)

SATURDAY AFTERNOON, 8th FEBRUARY, 1964
JUNIOR CAVERN CLUB SESSION — 1 p.m. to 4 p.m. for 12 to 16 year olds - VISITORS WELCOME
THE ESCORTS (HMV)

SATURDAY EVENING, 8th FEBRUARY, 1964
THE ESCORTS (HMV)

12 EXCITING SESSIONS · 17 TOP RECORDING ACTS
In One MAMMOTH STAR-STUDDED Week at the WORLD-FAMOUS
CAVERN CLUB 10 MATHEW STREET (OF NORTH JOHN STREET) LIVERPOOL, 2.
NEW MEMBERS & VISITORS WELCOME · · · · TELL YOUR FRIENDS !!!

Freddie(Fowell)
Starr

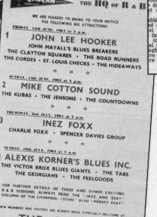

Fans at
the Cavern dis-
cuss the new stage
with Escorts'
drummer Pete
Clarke

dared to criticise something he was involved with, and he didn't play it to us again. To be honest, I didn't care for 'Cavern Stomp' very much: it hadn't got much of a tune."

And what exactly was the Cavern Stomp? **Bob Wooler**[525]:"The Cavern Stomp, if there really was such a thing, was a cramped version of jive dancing. To do the Cavern Stomp properly, you need a lot of space to swing your arms, and you wouldn't get that at the Cavern. I did have a boy and a girl do it for a photographer one Saturday morning when the club was empty. I had visions of releasing the shots to a magazine with dance step diagrams, rather like the Madison. However, nothing came of it."

Norman Killon[526]: "I loved dancing and I liked the Cavern stomp. It was a truncated version of the jitterbug and the jive but you couldn't do the fancy bits because it was so crowded. All you could do was swing your arms, left to right, either over arm or under arm. If you had a bit more space you could do some filigree work and go over the head and around the shoulder. The Big Three's 'Cavern Stomp' reminds me of those times. Bobby Comstock's original recording of 'Let's Stomp' was a wonderful record to dance to and is another great memory."

I wondered why the Beatles never wrote directly about the Cavern in their songs. **Willy Russell**[527]: "Oh, they were too canny for that. When they do take something specific like 'Penny Lane', they transcend the place and it is much much more than that little thoroughfare. It begins with something specific and goes to something gloriously general. It may be that they toyed with the idea of writing a song about the Star-Club or the Cavern but their instincts would have told them not to do anything with it. Look at 'All I Want For Christmas Is A Beatle' and 'Cavern Stomp': they are iffy novelty records. They would have kept away from that, but it may have found expression in due course. George Harrison did 'When We Was Fab', which is a lovely song."

Saturday 29 June 1963

The Merseybeats back from a recording session for Fontana

Sunday 30 June 1963

Love letters straight from the heart with Ketty Lester, supported by the Hollies, the Red River Jazzmen, and Vince Earl and the Talismen

Friday 5 July 1963

Pete Maclaine does both sessions with his new group, the Clan.

Tuesday 9 July 1963

Your chance to do the Cavern stomp with the Merseybeats and a competition judged by Bob Wooler. The winners receive Oriole's new *This Is Mersey Beat* LPs, which had been recorded at the Rialto Ballroom.

Sunday 14 July 1963

Merseybeats, Memphis Three, Tributes and the Red River Jazzmen. Bob Wooler's ad welcomes you to the Cavern "The Teen Pan Alley of Liverpool".

Saturday 20 July 1963

Steve Aldo and the Challengers, Sonny Webb and the Cascades, the Four Just Men and the Panthers

Sunday 21 July 1963

The Hollies, the Chants and the Del-Renas. Tickets went on sale at 1.30pm for the Beatles' appearance at the Cavern on August 3. The show was sold out by 2pm.

Tuesday 23 July 1963

The Hollies did both the lunchtime and the evening sessions. The evening show also featured Alexis Korner's Blues Band, Denny Seyton and the Sabres, the Motifs and the Bob Ross Group. Bob Ross, a double bass player, was to join the Merseysippi Jazz Band. **Ritchie Galvin**[528]: "We were on the same bill as Alexis Korner and they had an absolutely tremendous drummer in Phil Seaman. Unfortunately, he was on drugs and he had to be taken to the Royal Hospital. Alexis asked me to join the band but my dad was a bit strict and said no. I do have a card from Alexis which says, 'Thanks to the greatest rock'n'roll drummer I have ever seen.'"

Friday 26 July 1963

(lunchtime) Searchers
(evening) Rory Storm and the Hurricanes, Wayne Fontana and the Mindbenders, Nomads and Panthers. **Wayne Fontana**[529]: "We were doing

songs by Elvis Presley, Brook Benton and Chuck Berry. One of our big songs was Gene Chandler's 'Duke Of Earl'. It's a crazy song but people loved it because it is four voices all doing something and so it was fabulous to watch. When I saw the Beatles, they were doing 'Some Other Guy', 'Twist And Shout' and some great songs by Arthur Alexander, which would have been perfect for me. I wish I'd been in the Beatles! George Harrison gave me a demo of 'Love Of The Loved' and I was practising it for a record, but Brian Epstein wanted it for Cilla."

Sunday 28 July 1963

Dennisons, Merseybeats, Valkyries and Red River Jazzmen

Wednesday 31 July 1963

(lunchtime) Earl Preston and the TT's
(evening) Dennisons, Escorts, Black Knights, and Mark Peters and the Silhouettes

Saturday 3 August 1963

The Beatles made their final appearance at the Cavern, bringing their total number of appearances to 275: no one is totally sure and it also depends on how you're counting. **Bob Wooler**[530]: "That August appearance only came about because Brian Epstein couldn't pull them out of an appearance at the Grafton the night before. Les Ackerley said 'I've got them under contract', and Epstein was furious because, by then, he had other things in mind for them. He was calling Ackerley all sorts of names, but he didn't use four-letter words as he never did that. Ackerley had a barring clause preventing the Beatles appearing in Liverpool before but not after that appearance, so Brian asked us to take the Beatles for the Cavern on the following night, which was a Saturday. I resented this as he was only doing it to get at Ackerley, and anyway, I had booked all the groups for Saturday 3 August. If I'd said no, he would have gone to Ray McFall, who would have said, 'Of course we'll take them.' The Beatles were paid £300, which was quite a bit of money then, and Brian restricted the audience to 500. I can't blame Brian as he had seen how crowded the Cavern got and he had to think of the Beatles' safety. The admission price was 10 shillings and so that meant that we collected only £250 on the door. All the staff had to be paid, and the other groups on the bill too, so we made

no profit that night." Wooler is mistaken as the Grafton concert was for Albert Kinder, but the fee of £100 for August 2 was agreed on 14 January, 1963.

Brian Farrell[531]: "There was no way I could get in but the crowds in Mathew Street were phenomenal. It was like a high pressure hose coming out of the door. God knows what it was like inside. About three nights later the Beatles were doing a cinema in Conway Street in Birkenhead and I could get in there."

Paddy Delaney[532] was on the door. "The crowds outside were going mad. By the time John Lennon had got through the cordon of girls, his mohair jacket had lost a sleeve. I grabbed it to stop a girl getting away with a souvenir. John stitched it back on. They may have altered their style elsewhere, but they didn't do it at the Cavern. They were the same old Beatles, with John saying, 'Okay, tatty-head, we're going to play a number for you.' There was never anything elaborate about his introductions."

Faron[533]: "I was on the bill for the last show that the Beatles did at the Cavern. I was performing in a pool of water and it was so crowded that two members of my band collapsed and had to be carried outside."

The seats at the front of the stage were invariably filled by girls. A brave lad got a seat on the front row and when the girls frowned at him, he offered them his knees and remained seated. At the end of the evening one girl asked how his knees were. He said, "What knees?"

Because a full evening's entertainment had already been booked for that night, the show went from 6pm to 11.30pm. **Bob Wooler**[534]: "It was more Mercenary Beat than Mersey Beat that night. The Escorts and the Merseybeats still wanted paying for the night: the kudos of being on with the Beatles wasn't enough for them. When I told them that we would be starting the evening an hour earlier, the first thing they said was, 'We're still getting paid, aren't we, Bob?' The Beatles were very professional: there was no larking around and they got on with it. We all felt it was their swan song and that we would never have them at the Cavern again. Brian Epstein still owes the Cavern six dates for the Beatles as he kept pulling them out of bookings by saying,

'You wouldn't stand in the boys' way, would you, Bob?'"

The Beatles were hampered by a loss of power and light, but they gave a memorable performance. **Bob McGrae**[535]: "The reaction was incredible. I didn't think at the time that it was going to be their last night, but now I look back on it, it's obvious. The Cavern could never have afforded them."

Tony Crane[536]: "It surprised us that the Beatles had decided to come back for a show at the Cavern in August 1963 and we had just recorded 'It's Love That Really Counts'. We were on just before the Beatles and we were delighted with our reception as everybody was cheering and going mad. The Beatles all had long faces and John Lennon was saying, 'We never should have come back here.' Everything was sweaty and wet and we told them to make sure that they didn't slip on stage. Once the walls got wet, all that condensation came down onto the stage and it was dangerous. This was proved as they fused the electrics and the lights went out. Normally, John Lennon would have cracked jokes while somebody got it right but he was in such a bad mood that he came off stage."

Billy Kinsley[537]: "John and Paul were singing 'When I'm 64' while they were waiting for the electricity to come back on and they didn't record it for another four years."

Wednesday 7 August 1963
Rockin' Henry and the Hayseeds, Four Sounds, Nomads, and Earl Preston and the TT's

Friday 9 August 1963
Coming from Sheffield, Dave Berry and the Cruisers, supported by the Chants, the Defenders, Johnny Sandon and the Remo Four, and Vince Earl and the Talismen

Saturday 10 August 1963
Supertight harmonies from local heroes, the Easybeats

Friday 16 August 1963
(lunchtime and evening) Jet Harris' former group, the Jetblacks with John Paul Jones on bass. Evening support from the Dennisons, Vic and the Spidermen, and Karl Terry and the Cruisers

Saturday 17 August 1963
The Mojos, Group One, Chick Graham and the Coasters, and Derry Wilkie and the Pressmen

Sunday 18 August 1963
Johnny Sandon and the Remo Four, Ian and the Zodiacs, the Hy-Tones and the Rainy City Jazzmen

Wednesday 21 August 1963
(lunchtime) Wayne Fontana and the Mindbenders (evening) The Merseybeats with their first single, "It's Love That Really Counts", being released on the Friday, plus Wayne Fontana and the Mindbenders, Escorts, Bachelor Boys and Defenders

Thursday 29 August 1963
Noel Walker must be praised for his initiative in recording the Decca EP, *The Big Three At The Cavern*, helped by his excellent engineer, Terry Johnson. George Martin had, after all, decided that the Cavern was not an appropriate venue for recording the Beatles. **Noel Walker**[538]: "I was only 22 or 23 and I felt that we could do anything we wanted. Dick Rowe was away as otherwise, he would never have let me do it. We brought up a huge mobile recording unit and arranged to do this live recording, with the screaming audience which was so much a part of the EP. All the people who said it couldn't be done were wrong because we did it."

David Crosby[539]: "I got there early in the morning and helped Hutch set up his drum-kit. There were no roadies then and I spent the day hanging around with the guys from Decca. There were a few stops and starts, but it certainly wasn't four takes of each song. They just did their usual show. Decca encouraged the screaming as they thought it would add to the excitement but the Big Three were exciting enough."

Michael Gray[540]: "I felt it was a phony session. They made us clap more loudly than usual and we were bullied by the producer, but the Cavern always made me nervous, being a timid middle-class youth."

The four songs on the EP were "Reelin' And Rockin'", "What'd I Say", "Zip-A-Dee-Doo-Dah" and "Don't Start Running Away". Another 15 songs were recorded but the tapes have been lost or erased: "Long Tall Sally", "Cavern Stomp", "Keep A'Knockin'", "You Better Move On", "By The Way", "Some Other Guy", "Peanut

Butter", "Fortune Teller", "Always", "Please Don't Go", "Money (That's What I Want)", "Lucille", "Domino Twist", "Hippy Hippy Shake" and "A Shot Of Rhythm And Blues". The Rolling Stones, whose appearance at the Tower Ballroom, had been cancelled because of a fire, were in the audience.

Rory Gallagher[541]: "The great guitarist from Liverpool was Brian Griffiths from the Big Three. He was a dangerous player and extremely good. That was different from George Harrison who had some unusual phrasing but he was working within the song. The Big Three did a great version of 'Reelin' And Rockin'' on their *Cavern* EP and that original song, 'Don't Start Running Away' is also extremely good. Griff plays a great solo on 'Don't Start Running Away', but I don't want to detract from Hutch and Gus—they were great players and great singers."

John Gustafson[542]: "It's very nice when somebody as good as that likes something you've done. That song was written very quickly. It was following on from 'Some Other Guy'. I turned it upside down, changed the chords a bit and nicked half the intro. I wrote any old words, and we didn't really rehearse it as we never rehearsed. Somehow it found its way onto the EP because it was one of the tracks that they didn't erase or lose. That EP should have been an album."

Bob Wooler[543]: "The Big Three's recording was on a Thursday. The Cavern wasn't normally open on a Thursday and the whole evening was devoted to the recording session for Decca. There were 600 people in, not quite capacity, although that was still a hell of a lot, and the place was steaming. I knew my introduction would be an ordeal and I am not satisfied with what you hear on the EP. I say, 'Welcome to the best of cellars' and 'the' is prolonged when it shouldn't have been. I was searching for words and I did it better on some other takes."

Johnny Hutch[544] recalls, "Over 1,000 people were screaming and shouting, and I don't think there had ever been so many people in the Cavern. The sweat was pouring off the walls. I was here and the crowd was there and I couldn't hear what I was playing. However, the EP didn't turn out too badly."

Bob Wooler[545]: "The Big Three were taking 'bennies' that day and Hutch said to me, 'Come on, Bob, have a benny'. Johnny Gus would say, 'Go on, man, have one.' He was always saying 'man'. I was drinking like mad when they made that EP but I didn't have any bennies. That's why I announced them as 'The Boys with the Benzedrine Beat' and I'm amazed that Decca kept it on the record. I cringe at my sleeve notes—they are so OTT and so American—'I was there, were you?' You lose some and you wince some. They offered me a percentage of that EP but I took £25 cash instead, which was clearly a mistake on my part."

Noel Walker[546]: "I was very naïve. I thought Benzedrine was something you stuck up your nose if you had a cold. Bob's voice was just lovely, supersmooth and not really in keeping with the times."

Frankie Connor[547]: "What makes that EP for me is Bob Wooler's voice. I could listen to that introduction over and over and it is as good as the music. The Big Three had loud speakers which had been made by Adrian Barber and I liked watching Gus play. He used a plectrum instead of fingers and so he was playing it like a rhythm guitar."

Willy Russell[548]: "I was never a fan of the Big Three. I would leave if they came on. I have never been a fan of lead doubling as rhythm, I suppose."

John Gustafson[549] continues the story: "The cover of *The Big Three at the Cavern* is quite ramshackle. We looked like rain-sodden idiots. Anyone who was at the Cavern will know it was a sweaty hole. Our suits were wringing wet. We took them off and slopped them in a corner. The photographer had forgotten to take our picture and we were told to put our wet rags on again as though we were playing."

Bob Wooler[550]: "*The Big Three At The Cavern* was good musically and very raw. It was much better than what George Martin could have envisaged, but the drums are not properly assembled for the cover photograph. Hutch had already dismantled his drums when the photographer from Decca said, 'Hang on, we haven't taken our pictures yet.' Hutch said, 'Do we have to do this after all we've been through?' You can see that he hasn't bothered to reassemble them, he is just propping them up."

Friday 30 August 1963
(lunchtime) Launch of Mojos' first single, "They Say". 25 copies are given away.
(evening) Mojos, Panthers, Vince Earl and the Talismen, and Ian and the Zodiacs

Saturday 31 August 1963
Marauders, Nocturns, Young Ones, and Chick Graham and the Coasters

Monday 2 September 1963
(lunchtime) Faron's Flamingos. Bob Wooler told patrons to watch *Tonight* (BBC) as it would include a feature about the Cavern

Wednesday 4 September 1963
The guest group was an instrumental unit often working on the theatre package shows, The Sons Of The Piltdown Men

Sunday 8 September 1963
Sonny Webb and the Cascades, the Dennisons, the Master Sounds and the Rainy City Jazz Band

Thursday 19 September 1963
The Swinging Blue Jeans with free photographs!

Saturday 28 September 1963
Alexis Korner's Blues Inc with Derry Wilkie and the Pressmen, and Dean Stacey and the Detonators

Thursday 3 October 1963
A documentary by Don Haworth, *The Mersey Sound,* was shown between 10.10pm and 10.40pm on BBC TV. It included footage of the Beatles (filmed in Southport), Rory Storm, Faron, Group One and the Undertakers. The programme was only shown regionally but its success led to a national repeat. **Dave Williams**[551] from Group One: "Don Haworth had asked Ray McFall about a cooperative, melodious band that he could use and he suggested us. We were filmed on Sunday mornings at the Iron Door and the Cavern. We were interviewed as though we had just come off stage and the make-up girl gave us artificial perspiration to make us look suitably bedraggled. The interview took place in our minibus, which was on the owner's driveway with the windows blacked out and with someone bouncing it up and down to look as though we were moving."

Tuesday 8 October 1963
(lunchtime) The Mojos
(evening) The Escorts, the Roadrunners, the Paladins and the Cracksmen. Bill Harry, writing in *Mersey Beat*, says, "The Roadrunners are considered to be the finest group of their kind in the country. Their rhythm and blues style is unique and they deserve a recording contract."

Jean Catharell[552]: "I had my likes and dislikes. I loved the Beatles from the word go as they were always brilliant. They had fun and if they recognised people they would wave to them. I loved the Escorts as they were like Liverpool's answer to the Everly Brothers, but they also did rock'n'roll songs like 'Little Piece Of Leather'. I didn't like Freddie Starr as his humour didn't appeal to me. He was a brilliant impressionist but if you were at the front, you might be picked on. I would leave or do something else when he was on."

Saturday 12 October 1963
Mel Turner and the Souvenirs, Mission Men, Del-Renas, Mark Four, and Bobby and the Bachelors

Sunday 13 October 1963
Merseybeats, Dennisons, Kubas and the Zenith Six Jazz Band. The Rolling Stones and the Hamburg band, the Rattles are in town, playing the Odeon Cinema on a package show with the Everly Brothers, Little Richard and Bo Diddley.

Monday 14 October 1963
The Merseybeats missed a train back to Liverpool and would be arriving late for the lunchtime session. Ray McFall rang up the Escorts and they were there within the hour. Meanwhile, the Rattles had come into the club and the Escorts invited them to do a couple of numbers. The Merseybeats completed the lunchtime session. By then the Rolling Stones had arrived and they all had a drink after the show. **Michael Gray**[553]: "I didn't see the Beatles at the Cavern but I did bump into Mick Jagger. This freckly, gingery youth was standing around giving out autographs and I said, 'Who are you?' He said, 'Mick Jagger. Who are you?' and I said, 'Michael Gray' (Laughs)."

Saturday 19 October 1963
The Kubas, the Panthers, the Mission Men and Vince Earl and the Talismen. The Cheynes with Mick Fleetwood on drums decided on a whim that they must play at the Cavern. They had their

first single, "Respectable", due for release. **Mick Fleetwood**[554]: "My father came from Liverpool and while I never lived there, my sister Susan, who was an actress, spent a lot of her early career in the city so I would go and hang out there. We had a little band in London called the Cheynes with a dodgy manager who hoped to turn us into a big rock'n'roll band. He hired a limo which he never paid for and we got stuck with the bill. We came to the Cavern, almost banging on the door and asking if we could play. We didn't exactly die the death but one of the local bands got hold of our instruments and detuned them before we went on stage. They only gave us 15 minutes to get on stage and play. We returned to London with our tails between our legs."

Tuesday 22 October 1963
Danny Havoc and the Secrets, Mojos, Clay Ellis and the Landsliders, and the Karacters

Sunday 27 October 1963
Jimmy Powell and the Fifth Dimension (with Rod Stewart on harmonica and backing vocals), Del-Renas, Notions and the Zenith Six Jazz Band

Wednesday 30 October 1963
The Hollies, the Hustlers, the Beatcombers, and Bobby and the Bachelors. Gerry and the Pacemakers reached the top with "You'll Never Walk Alone" and **Gerry Marsden**[559] commented, "The groups we knew and had good times with in the Cavern don't have the same spirit anymore, and the new ones that have come up have all gone big-time. They don't want to know you because they think they are stars themselves."

Monday 4 November 1963
Back to old-time rock'n'roll with Derry Wilkie and the Pressmen. This is the day of the Beatles' appearance on the Royal Variety Performance at the Prince Of Wales Theatre, London. John Lennon remarked, "Those of you in the cheap seats, clap your hands; the rest of you can rattle your jewellery."

Tuesday 5 November 1963
It's 4/6d to see the Rolling Stones, supported by the Master Sounds, the Escorts and the Roadrunners. **Bob Wooler**[556]: "Brian Epstein was putting on a promotion at the Tower Ballroom, New Brighton called *Southern Sounds '63* with the Rolling Stones and Jet Harris and Tony Meehan. The

Beatles had taken off to such an extent that he no longer had the time to do it. He was farming out the acts to appear elsewhere and he asked me if I would be interested in taking the Rolling Stones at the Cavern and I said, 'Yes, of course.' The contract was for £60 and so I took them. They were overawed to play here as it was the place where the Beatles started."

Betty Fegan[557]: "The bouncers came down the stairs and said, 'I think we're going to have trouble, there is a group coming down here and I don't like the look of them.' It was the Rolling Stones and they looked like scruffy troublemakers. It was a contrast to Gerry and the others who were always very smart."

Bill Wyman[558]: "We were great friends with the Beatles, but we were in enemy territory, rather like Max Miller playing the Glasgow Empire. We did well as there was a long queue of people wanting to get in. When I was in the forces in 1956/7, I was in a group with Casey Jones, Cass of Cass and the Cassnovas. I've never spoken to him since and he should have stuck with me."

The Rolling Stones allowed the Roadrunners to use their equipment. All went well until they did Bo Diddley's 'Roadrunner', when smoke billowed from a borrowed amp. They sorted it out, but the Stones were not happy. **Beryl Marsden**[555]: "I remember the Rolling Stones at the Cavern and they were fantastic, but to me, the best nights were always when the Beatles were on."

Photographer **Steve Hale**[560]: "The Rolling Stones were good but I wasn't that impressed: the Beatles were much better."

Dave Boyce[561]: "The Roadrunners played with the Rolling Stones when the Stones played the Cavern, and Bob Wooler threw a party for us afterwards. Charlie Watts said to me, 'You know, when they are going on about E flat major and all that crap, do you know what they are talking about?' I said no and he said, 'Neither do I. I just sit at the back and fucking hit things.' That was the drummer's sensibility really: we hit things while this great carnival was going on at the front."

Sunday 10 November 1963
Alexis Korner Blues Inc (with Graham Bond, Jack Bruce and Ginger Baker), Vic and the Spidermen and the Four Musketeers. **Ian Edwards**[562]: "Alexis

Korner was excellent, absolutely superb. He was completely different from the other bands that night and the sound balance was perfect. A lot of people came unstuck because they didn't know of the echo in the Cavern and the sound coming back off the walls. No one did soundchecks then—it was 'Is the mike working? Let's go'—but the balance for Alexis Korner was perfect." Ginger Baker was so far gone that the roadies carried him on in a sitting position.

Tuesday 12 November 1963

The Shouts, supported by Tempos, Beatcombers, Panthers and Shondells

Friday 15 November 1963

Standup comedy at the Cavern with Jimmy Tarbuck, supported by Vic and the Spidermen. **Bob McGrae**[563]: "Tarby was a right Liverpool scallywag and he got up at the Cavern several times."

Friday 22 November 1963

Derry Wilkie and the Pressmen, Escorts, Beatcombers and Asteroids. **Hank Wangford**[564]: "I came to Liverpool in November 1963 as I wanted to see this Merseybeat. As I arrived in Liverpool, I saw this big sign saying, 'Kennedy assassinated', so I know what I was doing when Kennedy got shot. I went down to the Cavern and I remember the Escorts, who were really good. I also went on Saturday and Sunday and I loved the Big Three. Everyone was playing a very funny kind of R&B, very fast and frenetic. I heard 'Fortune Teller' and 'Some Other Guy' over and over again." A party of 36 Cavern fans flew to Hamburg to sample the music in the Star-Club. They took with them a greeting from the Lord Mayor of Liverpool to the Burgomaster.

Sunday 24 November 1963

An R&B marathon with the Big Three, Merseybeats, Escorts, Roadrunners, Astrals, Panthers, Notions and Derry and the Pressmen

Saturday 30 November 1963

Jimmy Powell and the Fifth Dimension, supported by the Mark Four

Tuesday 3 December 1963

Chick Graham and the Coasters, Roadrunners, Mighty Avengers, and Roy and the Dions

Thursday 5 December 1963

The Hamburg group, the Rattles started a series of bookings at the Cavern—nine over the next week. **Dicky Tarrach**[565] from the Rattles: "We are the only band to play the Cavern for a whole week and we played lunchtime and evening and it was amazing, so many people came to see us. I have never sweated so much in my life; you even sweat when you came in. It was very very nice and on the last day, the girls had presents for us like cakes with our name on, and the stage was full. *Mersey Beat* wanted us to pick the girl who gave us the best present and she spent a day with us. They loved our German accent on (sings) 'There is a rose in Spanish Harlem'. We couldn't get the 'r' right and the girls would scream. All the girls were after the band. We asked why and some girl said, 'We want to sleep with a Nazi as maybe it is different from an English guy.' The German Ziegfried, is he bigger or not? It was a nice experience, okay. We were kept pretty busy. (Laughs)"

Joey Bower[566]: "I saw the Rattles a couple of times and they went down well, but I thought that they were a poor imitation of a Liverpool band."

Alan Lewis[567], now editor of *Record Collector*: "I hitchhiked to Liverpool with a mate in the hope of seeing someone famous at the Cavern, if not the Beatles then maybe the Searchers or the Big Three. When we got to the Cavern, the band on that night was the Rattles, but we still had a great time. The club was much smaller than I had expected and the condensation was streaming down the walls. I passed out while I was chatting to a girl and I slowly slid down the wall. We did get off with a couple of local girls but 'getting off' didn't mean quite so much in 1963, despite what everyone says about the Swinging Sixties, or maybe it was just our luck."

Tuesday 10 December 1963

Alan Price[568] of the Animals: "We came down from Newcastle to Liverpool in a little van in 1963 and we carried our own gear into the Cavern for a lunchtime session. We were very nervous about playing there and I said to a girl in a duffle coat who was watching us, 'Do you think they'll like rhythm and blues here?' 'Like it?' she said, 'We invented it.'"

Mike Brocken[569]: "There were very good bands around Glasgow, Newcastle, Birmingham, Richmond but the genres of music did differ. The scene around Newcastle had developed because someone had started a blues club. Alan Sytner started a jazz club which became a rock'n'roll club and so the music in the Cavern was more rock'n'roll than rhythm and blues. Newcastle was a different thing, it was an R&B club, and also in Richmond with Giorgio Gomelsky's club. You have different generic variations of sound. It was not because of anything to do with the city—the Liverpool sound, the Birmingham sound—but to do with the venues and the type of the music that the owners wanted to be played in those venues. The Animals played R&B in the Club A Go Go. They went down well at the Cavern but they sounded very different. They were much heavier, more R&B and more akin to the Hideaways or the Almost Blues, the second wave Liverpool groups."

Eric Burdon[570]: "It was just another hot, sweaty gig to us, but we knew it was the home of the Beatles and it was an audience of hardcore music fans. Our van was covered in telephone numbers written in lipstick, and the radio aerial and the wing mirrors had been taken, and the windscreen wipers had been ripped off. We took it as a compliment—'Oh, they must have liked us.'"

The evening session featured Cliff Bennett and the Rebel Rousers, Mojos, Shondells, and Chris and the Classics. **Frank Allen**[571]: "I never played on stage with the Searchers at the Cavern but I did play with Cliff Bennett. We had trouble finding Liverpool, but Roy Young was in the band and you would think that he would know his way around. We set off for Liverpool in the van and we had no idea where the places were in Liverpool. We stopped on the A580 and asked somebody where the Cavern was and they looked as though we were mad as we still had miles to go. We had trouble finding Mathew Street as it was tucked away around the back but when we got there it was pretty much as we expected. It wasn't a good night as brass is always difficult to keep in tune, especially with the temperature at the Cavern, but the audience thought we were okay. The Undertakers came along to see us and they liked it."

Friday 13 December 1963

(lunchtime) **Mike Gregory**[572] of the Escorts: "Bob Wooler saw us at the Majestic Ballroom and took a liking to us. He wanted us to replace the German Beatles, the Rattles, who couldn't make it one lunchtime. We got on the Cavern, but I got the sack for not going back to work. I was going on holiday at the end of the week and while I was away, they sent me my notice. That meant that I was a professional musician."

(evening) Fourmost, Derry and the Pressmen, the Mark Four and the Easybeats

A new publication, *Merseyside Playland*, has a feature on the "small but cosily furnished sanctum of Ray McFall".

Friday 20 December 1963

The Rattles' Farewell Show with Vic and the Spidermen, the Valkyries and the Young Ones

Thursday 26 December 1963

Escorts, Vic and the Spidermen, Notions, Riot Squad and Beatcombers

Saturday 28 December 1963

Derry and the Pressmen, Mark Four, the Panthers and the Beathovens

Tuesday 31 December 1963

All night session including the Riot Squad with Jon Lord on keyboards and Mitch Mitchell on drums. Rest of bill—Shondells, Detonators, Easybeats, Remo Four, Big Three, Escorts, Mark Four, Vic and the Spidermen, Derry and the Pressmen and Chick Graham and the Coasters. Hey, isn't it a bit after Chick's bedtime? Good value for 9 shillings, but with so many groups performing, how much space was left for paying customers? The Big Three saw in the New Year by playing 'Auld Lang Syne'.

The Cavern's secretary, **Beryl Adams**[573] lived with Bob Wooler in an on/off relationship. "There was one New Year's Eve where Bob had promised to take me for a meal. Instead, he had been drinking in the White Star and he said to the writer, Stanley Reynolds, 'Stan, will you take Beryl for a meal?' I was annoyed but we went for the meal and we came back to the Cavern. Bob was drinking Dubonnet and whiskey. I had a bottle of Dubonnet for him and I flung it down the band room steps. Ray McFall went bananas as I might have injured his precious DJ, but I didn't mark him. However, the accounts of his drinking are exaggerated and generally speaking, he was not obnoxious when he was drunk. He was just more theatrical. He had insomnia in that he would work late and then be up and out early in the morning."

Bob Wooler[574]: "I did drink but not as ridiculously as some people have made out. I would never have lasted seven years at the Cavern if I had. In that respect, I'm like Dean Martin—he was able to drink and yet still maintain a professional attitude."

Wednesday 1 January 1964

Escorts, Notions, Casuals (soon changed to the In Crowd), and Gerry De Ville and the City Kings. "Britain's Beat HQ will be bigger and beatier in 1964," predicts Bob Wooler.

Friday 3 January 1964

(lunchtime) Undertakers

(evening) Escorts, Notions, Casuals and Herman's Hermits

Manchester is only 30 miles from Liverpool and yet the approach to music was different. The few beat clubs in the city were lavishly decorated; groups performed in front of a Swiss chalet set in the Jungfrau. Most groups gained their experience in working men's clubs or cabaret, and they might be the entertainment between the bingo sessions. This was very different to the Cavern where the punters wanted nothing but music. **Derek Leckenby**[575] from Herman's Hermits said, "The Liverpool groups had much more aggression. When they played rock'n'roll, they forced it on you, especially the Big Three. I'd go anywhere to see the Big Three. I don't think the Manchester groups had as much energy, although they had the musical abilities."

John Cochrane[576]: "We saw the other bands from Manchester. That seemed miles away. Some of us hadn't even been to Manchester."

Saturday 4 January 1964

Cavern debut of the Liver Birds with the Mastersounds, Mark Four and Chick Graham and the Coasters. This is the final show on the old stage and the Dark Ages, as a three piece, are the last group to play on it. **Sylvia Saunders**[577] of the Liver Birds: "We started off here and we were the first girl band to play instruments since Ivy Ben-

son's band. We played the Cavern but we weren't accepted as so many of the fans were girls."

Val Hausner[578]: "John Lennon said that an all-girl outfit would never stick together, so we set out to prove him wrong." The Liver Birds went to Germany and became successful at the Star-Club.

Sunday 5 January 1964

During the day the stage was demolished and a new one was installed. The old stage was cut into 1,000 pieces and sold as Beatlewood at five shillings a time for Oxfam. Ray McFall commented, "We have got to keep the stage's present whereabouts a secret because we don't want fans to raid it before we get it to London." To foil timber touts, each piece is being marked individually. In its place was a slightly bigger bandstand. Shortly, the floor space will be increased by knocking down a brick wall and the incorporation of an extra cellar in the premises.

The new look Dark Ages, now a five piece, was the first band to play on the new stage and also performing are Ian and the Zodiacs, Mojos, Panthers, Notions and Shondells.

Saturday 11 January 1964

Escorts, Herman's Hermits, Johnny Anger and the Wild Ones, Savva and the Democrats—the names are starting to get ridiculous. (Sorry, I'd forgotten about Wump and his Werbles.)

Tuesday 14 January 1964

(lunchtime) Mark Peters and the Silhouettes

(evening) Cadillac and the Playboys, Take Four, Diamonds and Georgians. The Georgians are a local blues band, specializing in Howlin' Wolf and Chuck Berry songs.

Lord Derby's house guests at Knowsley Hall included Chris Clark, the 16-year-old son of Lady Bridget Garnett. Chris wanted to see the Cavern and so Lord Derby asked the Deputy Chief Constable to arrange it. I would like to think that the police force had better things to do.

Wednesday 15 January 1964

(lunchtime) The Harlems included Sugar Deen and Lawrence Areethy (brother of Colin) in their line-up as well as the guitarist, Brendan McCormack. They were the closest the vocal group, the Chants came to having a regular backing group.

(evening) Country Gentlemen (from Manchester, who played an instrumental 'Greensleeves'),

Denny Seyton and the Sabres, Boys (from Warrington) and Caverners. **Denny Seyton**[579]: "Bob Wooler was always coming up with something new and one night it was 'Satan on the Sabbath'. When we had 'Tricky Dicky' out, it was Mr Tricky back in town'."

Friday 17 January 1964
Fortunes, Mastersounds, Connoisseurs, Bobby and the Bachelors.

Saturday 18 January 1964
Four Pennies, Panthers, Stereos, Valkyries

Wednesday 22 January 1964
The weather was terrible: ice and fog all over Britain and several multiple pile-ups on the M1. The visibility was down to 10 yards and some motorists abandoned their vehicles. Many roads were closed. The Yardbirds were playing the Star and Garter Hotel in Windsor on 21 January and set off north straight after the gig. **Chris Dreja**[580] of the Yardbirds: "I remember travelling for hours to reach the Cavern. The M1 had just opened and it was very foggy when we set out. We were going north and that was like a foreign country to us—it might as well have been Bolivia. We got lost and we arrived feeling like dog's death. The Cavern was like an underground toilet but I loved the marvellous Liverpool girls, who dressed in long black leather coats."

Billed as Merseyside's first genuine R&B show, Sonny Boy Williamson is backed by the Yardbirds, who also did their own set, plus the Master Sounds, the Pawns and the Champions. **Kenny Johnson**[581]: "Sonny Williamson sent somebody to get him a hot dog and a coffee from the snack bar at the back of the Cavern. When he got it, he said, 'Man, you call this a hot dog? Back in the States we got hot dogs one foot long with chili chili sauce.'"

Sonny Boy Williamson did what no one else had done at the Cavern: he drank openly on stage. **Sue Ellison**[582]: "Sonny Boy Williamson was a big disappointment. He kept changing key on his harmonica and the Yardbirds panicked, and I am sure he was doing it on purpose. Clapton played a few solos and I was very impressed and at the end of the set, Williamson stumbled off. I am sure he had had a few."

Asked about other blues musicians, Sonny Boy would call them "a load of shit". **Geoff Davies**[583]: "My girlfriend got Sonny Boy Williamson's autograph and he wrote 'Fuck off' and the initials 'SBW', so he was not in a great mood. He permanently looked in a bad mood. A few months later I saw him on the Empire with the Chris Barber Band and he wasn't as good, but the show with the Yardbirds was amazing. I had never heard this kind of treatment of R&B before as it was so loud and guitar driven. I knew the guitarist was a bit of a name and it was Eric Clapton."

Jim McCarty[584] of the Yardbirds; "We stayed in an appalling B&B. There were bed bugs, newspapers for tablecloths and the owner cooked us breakfast in his pyjamas."

David Deacon[585]: "Sonny Boy wore a suit and a trilby and carried an umbrella and he had a great, lifeworn face. It looked as though life had been tough on him. He was great."

Tony Crane[586]: "Sonny Boy Williamson was great at the Cavern as I was getting into what he was doing. He was fantastic, a great harmonica player and a great singer and I don't think he had any teeth. And he was blind drunk as well!"

Ray Ennis[587]: "I was standing at the back for Sonny Boy Williamson. That was called the Deep End as the toilets flowed down there. The busier the place got the more it overflowed. It could be six inches deep. The place could never be open today."

Ian Edwards[588]: "We never used the toilets at the Cavern as they were absolutely foul. The urine was always all over the floor. We would go to the Grapes."

The London impresario and manager, Giorgio Gomelsky, had brought Sonny Boy Williamson and the Yardbirds to Liverpool and he found himself deep in conversation with Bob Wooler about the growing popularity of rhythm and blues music. They contacted a Birmingham promoter, Brian Postle, and booked Birmingham Town Hall for the First British R&B Festival on February 28.

Friday 24 January 1964
(lunchtime) Ken Dodd comes on stage with an electric guitar and says that new comedians are going to be given a break at the lunchtime sessions. "The Mersey Sound," he quips, "is the sound of

laughter." Doddy is made the Cavern's first honorary life member.

Saturday 1 February 1964

(afternoon: 1pm to 4pm) Following the lead of the Cubic club in Birkenhead, the Junior Cavern Club opened with the Mark Four and the Notions. Although not performing as such, Billy J Kramer made a personal appearance to promote his new single, "Little Children". Huge crowds queued at the Cavern and 500 were admitted. The police said of the rest, "In the end, we hope they'll get tired and go home." Adults were welcomed provided they were accompanied by a teenager. "We don't want them sliding past the door on their own," a spokesman tells *Liverpool Echo*. There was an adult Cavern Stomp contest for the mums and dads.

Both Bob Wooler and Ray McFall were delighted that Billy J had returned. Said Ray McFall: "I feel like a father feels when his older children leave to follow exciting careers. I'm proud of the Beatles, the Searchers, the Pacemakers and the rest, but like a father, I'd love to see a little more of them at home in the Cavern."

Monday 3 February 1964

The first of two days in which Decca recorded a live LP at the Cavern, produced by Noel Walker and engineered by Terry Johnson and Gus Dudgeon. The lunchtime session featured the Big Three and Dave Berry and the Cruisers, and the evening was with Lee Curtis and the All Stars, the Dennisons and the Fortunes. **Dave Berry**[589]: "I am known as a ballad singer but my roots were in blues and R&B music and you can hear that on this LP. The Cavern was a smoky, hot and sweaty hole but it was a great place to play rock'n'roll. By then each big city had its equivalent to the Cavern—we had the Esquire, the Mojo and Club 60 in Sheffield—but the Cavern was the best."

Steve Hale[590]: "The Dennisons came along after the Beatles had gone to London and I thought they were fantastic. They did a very good version of 'Some Other Guy' but my favourite was 'Walking The Dog' which featured very heavy drums and bass. It really rocked along."

Ray Scragg[591] of the Dennisons: "We did 'You Better Move On' with Steve McLaren singing, but the recording didn't come out too well, and we

had to go up to London to record on top of what we'd done."

Billy Fury never appeared at the Cavern but his audience did. The producer Noel Walker thought that the applause at the Cavern should have sounded fuller and livelier on their tapes so he dubbed some from the album, *We Want Billy!*

Tuesday 4 February 1964

Kubas, Cresters, Nashpool Four, Sundown Valley and the Boys. The Kubas became Cavern regulars, recording 'Magic Potion' and Gracie Fields' 'Sally' for singles, touring with the Beatles, playing at the Saville Theatre with the Who and Jimi Hendrix and in 1969, as the Koobas, releasing an album of original material for EMI.

Wednesday 5 February 1964

The Rank Organisation is recording a documentary in the *Look At Life* series with the Escorts

Thursday 6 February 1964

A second day of recording for Decca's live album. At lunchtime, it's the Marauders, the Four Just Men and Beryl Marsden and, in the evening, Bern Elliot and the Fenmen, the Marauders and Heinz. **Beryl Marsden**[592]: "The Cavern album was recorded in hot and sweaty conditions. It was really good fun because it was a great atmosphere for recording. I preferred doing live performances, recording as opposed to going into a studio. I used to be a little bit scared of studios."

Bob Wooler[593]: "That wasn't a bad album but Decca included outside acts like Heinz who had nothing to do with the Cavern. It was simply exploitation for Decca recording artists. Noel Walker put some echo on my voice and I recorded my introductions separately. He came down to the Cavern with a tape recorder and I had worked on my intros like 'It's Dennison time' and 'Here's the bouncy bubbling Beryl Marsden'. They thought that a tinge of echo would add brightness to my voice, and it did."

Producer **Noel Walker**[594]: "The Big Three EP did wonderfully well but the album bombed. I suspect it was Dick Rowe's fault as he made me put on Heinz, who had nothing to do with Merseybeat. I hated the idea and I think that took the essence out of the album, but there is some bloody good music on it. Beryl Marsden was marvellous and I don't know why she never had hit records.

CELLARFUL OF NOISE

WELCOME TO THE CAVERN CLUB

EVENING SESSIONS 7·30 TO 11·15 ON TUESDAYS · WEDNESDAYS FRIDAYS · SATURDAYS & SUNDAYS

FIVE LUNCHTIME SESSIONS 12 NOON TO 2·15PM MONDAYS TO FRIDAYS

NEW MEMBERS WELCOME · JO

NOTE: NO ADMISSION RE-ADMISSIONS BY PASS OUT AFTER

THE BIG 3 AT THE Cavern

Cavern chicks digging the sounds

Ray McFall with Sonny Boy Williamson

Gerry Marsden & Cilla White doing the Twist

The Best of Fellas; Bob Wooler

Bob Wooler with Chick Graham

I would like to have produced Beryl Marsden in the studio as I don't think Decca did Beryl justice. I would have liked to have produced the Dennisons as well, but I wasn't allowed to. Straight after the Cavern LP, the Fortunes' contract came up for renewal and Decca didn't want them. I said, 'Hey, they sing wonderfully and they should be recorded like they are on the Cavern album.' They gave the Fortunes another lease of life and I did 'You've Got Your Troubles'. It was one of the few records that turned out exactly as I wanted it and it sold a million. Dick Rowe didn't like it, so he was wrong again."

Friday 7 February 1964
The Merseybeats and a Salvation Army band from Carlisle, the Messengers. The Messengers wore their uniforms on stage, and their leader, Captain Rodney Smith, said that they were trying to reach teenagers with religious songs put over in a pop style.

Meanwhile, the Beatles have just arrived in America for appearances on *The Ed Sullivan Show* and concert dates. **Bob Wooler**[595]: "When I first met him, Brian Epstein said he was desperate to get the *Liverpool Echo* to write an article on the Beatles. George Harrison was a popular columnist, a typical old-time newspaperman, and he used to frequent the city centre pubs, drinking their contents and picking up stories for his column, *Over The Mersey Wall*. I suggested to Brian that a bottle of Scotch might do the trick, which it did, but the article was not complimentary as George had no time for beat groups and thought that they were all scruffs, but he soon realised how fortunate he was to share a name with one of them. Not long after that, the whole world was going Beatle crazy and they went on their first tour of America in 1964. Who embarks from the plane with them, to report to the folks back home about their world-beaters from Liverpool? George Harrison!"

Ray McFall[596] was invited to New York for their Carnegie Hall concert: "Brian booked me on the flight and into the same hotel, the Plaza. I was on the fifth floor and they were on the seventh floor and the place was like a fortress. It was crawling with detectives in addition to the hotel staff because the fans were trying to get in. One young lady packed herself in a laundry basket and got delivered to the hotel but they rumbled her right away. I have still got the programme from their gig at Carnegie Hall and it was extraordinary. The entrepreneur took a chance, and everyone in New York wanted to be there—high society people, politicians, everybody. The audience went mad and it was unforgettable."

Saturday 8 February 1964
Junior Cavern Club with the Escorts and Chick Graham and the Coasters. **Raphael Callaghan**[597]: "I was a member of the Junior Cavern Club, which sounds very uncool. I could have got into the adult sessions when I was 15 but I was very young-looking for my age. I went there every Saturday for a long time and I saw both the Escorts and Chick Graham and the Coasters who were fantastic."

Dave Jones[598], who came to own the Cavern in 1990s: "I loved it when the Junior Cavern opened and I would go down there on a Saturday afternoon. I was devastated when they stopped doing it, but I've got over it now that I own the Cavern. That's taught me something too: you should always view your decisions from the audience's point of view."

But **Dave Jones**[599] was soon following the groups as a young adult: "The Escorts and the Hideaways were my Beatles and my Pacemakers. I followed them both round Liverpool for about two years. The PA and the band equipment were rudimentary but it didn't matter. You were listening to their numbers and wondering if their rendition was better than Earl Preston's or anybody else's."

Wednesday 12 February 1964
(lunchtime) Undertakers
(evening) Merseybeats, Escorts, Valkyries, Georgians and a Fiedler on the Hoof. Arthur Fiedler, the conductor of the Boston Pops, is in Liverpool for a concert at the Philharmonic Hall and he looks in on the evening session.

Thursday 13 February 1964
The Vernons Girls, Johnny Mike and the Shades

Saturday 15 February 1964
(Junior Cavern Club) Escorts, Panthers, Deans
(evening) Escorts, Mark Four, Panthers, Executioners

Tommy Flude[600]: "My dad was a local councillor and I was only 13 when I was in the Deans and as my dad was worried about me playing places where there were beer and cigarettes for sale, he decided to be our manager. We said, 'If you're the manager, you've got to get us some bookings.' About four days later, he said, 'You can play the Cavern on Saturday.' He had gone to see Bob Wooler and he said that he was a councillor and wanted to take a look at the place. Bob naturally was very obliging, and my dad then said, 'I am managing a band. Can they appear here?' and so we were on that Saturday! We had a trailer with our gear in and we went down in the car, pretending we were stars and that fans would want to know what we had for breakfast. It was empty when we got there but it still had the atmosphere and once the kids came in, it was throbbing. It was fantastic and was our first memorable gig. We were doing hits by the Beatles, the Searchers and the Swinging Blue Jeans. In fact, we knew all the songs off the Beatles' first album."

Any reason why the Deans didn't play there again? **Tommy Flude**[601]: "Yes, my dad left the Council! Even though Bob did the booking as a favour to my dad, I would still say that we justified ourselves. We were all twelve or thirteen and the average band age was eighteen so we did our job and I went back a few years later with Solomon's Mines. The Deans lasted about eighteen months and we did a charity gig at Walton Hospital that meant walking from ward to ward and setting up the drums and the amplifiers in each of them. Some of the patients were chronically ill and we were blasting out 'Long Tall Sally'. We also did the Moulin Rouge in Formby with Rory Storm and the Hurricanes, and as Rory's microphone broke, we lent him ours and he said, 'I'll get it back to you, give me your address.' We were kids and had to be back home tucked up in bed by 10.30pm and at about 2am, there was a knock on the door, and my dad went down. It was Rory Storm dropping the microphone off on his way back home. Tomorrow would have done."

Friday 21 February 1964

(lunchtime) Those Muswell hillbillies, the Kinks, travelled up in an old ambulance and washed in the toilets at Lime Street station before heading for the Cavern. The Kinks befriended some girls and took them in their ambulance to their next gig. **Steve Hale**[602]: "I thought the Kinks were

brilliant. They had a driving beat throughout their set and they didn't talk much between numbers. They didn't let up at all and I was particularly impressed with the way they did 'Long Tall Sally'."

Sunday 23 February 1964

Alexis Korner's Blues Inc record a live album, *At The Cavern*, produced by Geoff Frost and released by Oriole in October 1964. It is a companion to *R&B From The Marquee* (1962). The vocals are shared by Alexis and a black American serviceman, Herbie Goins, and the tracks include a fantastic 'Hoochie Coochie Man'. **Frankie Connor**[603] of the Hideaways: "The band had to do a lot of retakes as the recording wasn't right, but the audience didn't mind. Alexis was very nice to us backstage and very supportive of what we were doing. He was very erudite and very knowledgeable."

Raphael Callaghan[604]: "I consider Alexis Korner's live album from the Cavern to be one of the greatest live recordings of all-time. Nobody mentions it and yet it is the most amazing record of British blues. It easily ranks alongside Georgie Fame's *Rhythm And Blues At The Flamingo*, *Five Live Yardbirds* and those by John Mayall and Graham Bond. It is a classic, classic record and it is long overdue for recognition."

Monday 24 February 1964

Losing your shirt at the Rael Brook Contest Night with the Fortunes, the Escorts, the Hawks, the Defenders, the Interns and the Cavels

Wednesday 26 February 1964

(lunchtime) Sonny Boy Williamson, Yardbirds and Undertakers

(evening) Sonny Boy Williamson, Yardbirds, Roadrunners, Mersey Blue Beats, Valkyries, St. Louis Checks.

Steve Hale[605]: "I'd been told that the Yardbirds were a great R&B band from London, but it didn't gel when I saw them with their bright yellow jackets. Their lead singer, Keith Relf, was very blond with a Beatle haircut. It looked a bit like pantomime, but they were excellent. Eric Clapton had a very short haircut and looked American."

Lawrence Swerdlow[606]: "I remember seeing Eric Clapton in the Yardbirds as a very skinny young man at the Cavern playing phenomenal guitar. Even in those days, he was way ahead of anyone I had ever seen in terms of ability."

After less than a month, Sonny Boy Williamson made a return visit, playing both lunchtime and evening sessions. **Bob Wooler**[607]: "Sonny Boy Williamson was backed by the Yardbirds, and Sonny Boy came into the bandroom with a suitcase and I said, 'Is that for your harmonicas?' He opened it up and there was a bottle of Johnnie Walker inside. He offered me a drink and I asked a lad for some paper cups and we drank some. He said, 'Let's finish it off', and I said, 'I've got an evening session.' They were staying at the Lord Nelson Hotel, so I joined them there. Another bottle came out and I had to show restraint or I would have been legless. It didn't affect him at all—in fact, it exhilarated him."

Ray McFall[608]: "Sonny Boy Williamson came to the Cavern at lunchtime and did a lunchtime show and he sat in the bandroom, with bottles in each hand, simultaneously swigging some Scotch and some Coke. He wasn't a young man and I thought he mightn't get on stage, but he played for an hour. He came off stage and finished the Scotch, and went to his hotel and got another one and drank that in the same manner, and I remember saying to Bob that he was going to be flat on his back when he is due to come on stage in the evening, but I couldn't have been more wrong. He was there on time and he sang and played for the best part of two hours. He must have had a cast-iron stomach and he was marvellous."

Ian Edwards[609]: "It became a thing to have old bluesmen playing harmonica and singing in gravelly voices. I loved them and I felt it was going back to the roots. We were already doing his song, 'Good Morning Little Schoolgirl', but in Liverpool not many people wanted to hear the blues as the blues. We gave it a dance beat as most of the places like the Jive Hive were dance halls. It was different at the Cavern as people would be listening: it was more like a theatre in that respect."

Judd Lander[610] of the Hideaways: "Sonny Boy Williamson was an inspiration as 'Help Me' was a track to die for. I was a terrible player then as I could never get the vibrato I wanted. The first time I tried to talk to him, he was too entranced with some young lady to notice me. I had noticed that he drank whisky. I brought in some whisky

and I said, 'I'm desperate. Your technique is brilliant and I would learn a few things from you, and I have got a bottle of whisky here.' 'My, my,' he said, 'You're on my side. Let's sit down and talk about this.' He taught me how to do the vibrato and also some techniques with the hand—I am talking into the mike now and if I push my hand backwards and forwards between the microphone and my mouth, I will sound different. It is the same with the harmonica. I used to speak to him every time he came over until it got to the stage where he told me to bugger off. He was a great mentor and he taught me how to play the harmonica properly."

Meanwhile, a replica of the Cavern had been created for an exhibition of men's wear at Earl's Court.

Friday 28 February 1964

The Escorts were at the Cavern but Bob Wooler and the Roadrunners had gone to Birmingham Town Hall for the First British R&B Festival featuring Sonny Boy Williamson and the Yardbirds. This was incompetently recorded for a live album as Bob Wooler sounded as though he was in the pub next door and the start of the Roadrunners' "You Can Make It If You Try" was missing.

Monday 2 March 1964

Back to the Rael Brook competition with six bands including Derek's Bohemians

Tuesday 3 March 1964

First recording session for the Radio Luxembourg series, *Sunday Night At The Cavern*. Bobby Sampson and the Giants, Dions, Panthers, Roadrunners and Rockin' Rivals were performing.

The Panthers were from Kirkby and when Bob Wooler introduced them, he mistakenly called them the Kirkbys (that is, if Bob Wooler ever did anything by mistake). The name stuck and they recorded "It's A Crime" for RCA in 1966 and acquired a following in Finland after a tour with Herman's Hermits. In 1967 they became 23rd Turnoff (the numbered exit from the M6 to the East Lancs Road) and made the classic psychedelic single, "Michael Angelo" (sic). Campbell made three solo albums and worked in Rockin' Horse with Billy Kinsley: all good stuff.

Bob Wooler[611]: "In 1964 Geoff Baker from Kennedy Street Enterprises came over from Manchester and said he could arrange a series at an excellent time on Radio Luxembourg, 10.30 on Sunday evenings. It would be called *Sunday Night At The Cavern* and there would be a group and I would play a few records. More importantly, the programme would be interspersed with plugs for Curry's, the sponsors. *Sunday Night At The Cavern* was made by a production company, Ross Radio, and their owner, Monty Bailey-Watson, would drive up the new motorway to the Cavern in a superduper E-type Jag. Despite that, perhaps because of it, Ross Radio made the series on the cheap by recording four 30-minute programmes in a day because they didn't want the expense of staying in Liverpool overnight. It was two shows at lunchtime and two in the evening, and when they switched to one at lunchtime and three at night, it was no better. They hated retakes and they would say, 'Try not to make any mistakes.' It was in front of a paying audience, so there could be no delays as we would lose the audience. I was quaking and doing them that fast was ridiculous. The programme was being broadcast across Europe on 208 and I was only being paid £10 a show. I had to get Ray McFall on to them when they hadn't paid me for a while."

Ray McFall[612]: "Bob worked hard on that programme. He would select the groups, write the script and present the programme. It worked out very well but Bob suffered from last minute-itis. He would be writing his links for one show while he was recording another."

Pete Frame[613] recalls, "I was working for the Prudential as a surveyor and I came to Liverpool one week in four. I only went to the Cavern once and they were recording the first *Sunday Night At The Cavern*. They were having difficulties with placing the microphones correctly and the Remo Four did 'Sugar Shack' six times. I remember the darkness and the ambience and I felt very lost, a little boy lost from the south, but a local lad asked to me go on the dance floor with him and split up a couple of local lasses. I must have been intimidated as I retreated as soon as the song was over."

Ken Testi[614]: "I first became aware of the Cavern in the sixties listening to Radio Luxembourg's *Sunday Night At The Cavern* with Bob Wooler on board. I was tantalisingly close as I lived in Widnes but I was too young to be let in

and far too timid anyway. It was very frustrating to have that hotbed so close and yet out of reach. I was excited to get in when I was eighteen but I did find it a very difficult place to work when I was the road manager with Ibex. There was a queue of bands waiting to get on stage and a queue waiting to get out and moving around was very awkward."

Thursday 12 March 1964
Rael Brook Competition with guests, the Cresters

Saturday 14 March 1964
(Junior Cavern Club) Herman's Hermits, Mark Four, Fallons
(evening) Herman's Hermits, Mark Four, Pilgrims, L'Ringos

Sunday 15 March 1964
Saints Jazz Band, Mersey Blue Beats, Feelgoods, Hideaways, Georgians and Chequers. **Frankie Connor**[615] of the Hideaways: "We were only seventeen or so and we stood in the band room and we were so nervous about being on the Cavern. We got £6, that's £1 for each of us and £1 for our roadie. It was a tremendous night and it began our Cavern career as we played here more often than the Beatles."

Ozzie Yue[616] of the Hideaways: "My family had a Chinese restaurant and we could use the basement when it was closed to rehearse. I remember Judd Lander sitting at the cash-desk with a little Dansette player, learning to play the harmonica parts on Cyril Davies' 'Country Line Special' and Sonny Boy Williamson's 'Help Me'. He persevered and became one of the country's top players. Looking back on it, the Hideaways were a good band but we played too many of the songs hell for leather."

Judd Lander[617]: "I was desperate to learn a track called 'Candy Man' which was the B-side of Roy Orbison's 'Cryin'. There is a little run on there and I was practising on this chromatic harmonica, which is one that has a button on the end and plays the full scale including flats and sharps, in other words, the black and white notes on a piano. I should have been using a diatonic harmonica, which is a blues harmonica that has no black notes so I have to bend the note to make a flat or a sharp. I was using the wrong instrument and for ages I was thinking, 'How the bloody hell did they do that?' It wasn't until I met a few other people who played the blues harmonica that I realised what it was."

Tuesday 17 March 1964

Ian Crawford and the Boomerangs, Sonny Kaye and the Reds, Lee Paul and the Boys, the Jokers. A party of eight London-based foreign correspondents came to Liverpool to see Ford's car factory at Halewood and spend an evening in the Cavern. Mr V. Dushenskin from the Soviet news agency, Tass, said, "The car factory was very impressive but in Russia we place more emphasis on lorries than cars." No comments about the Cavern, sorry.

Saturday 21 March 1964

(Junior Cavern Club) Denny Seyton and the Sabres, Earl Preston's Realms, Four Aces

(evening) The Kirkbys (pronounced Kirbys), Secrets, Georgians, Skeletons, Group One. **Frankie Connor**[618]: "Jimmy Campbell of the Kirkbys was a highly original songwriter. I like 'Leanna' which is about a girl he knew in Germany and I like 'In My Room' too. They did a kind of Stones-meets-the-Beatles number, 'It's A Crime' in 1965."

Tuesday 24 March 1964

Riot Squad, Earl Preston's Realms, Secrets, Photons, Country Gentlemen

Wednesday 25 March 1964

The *Liverpool Daily Post* asked teenagers at the lunchtime session, "Who has made the greatest contribution to contemporary society—Ernest Marples or the Beatles?" 55% voted for the Minister of Transport and his attempts to improve the UK's road system. Terry Sylvester of the Escorts commented, "The Beatles are great, but Mr Marples is helping to cut down road deaths and in the end, that's the kind of thing that really matters in this world." Also, 75% did not know what was on at the Playhouse (*Hindle Wakes*); 45% did not know which team was top of the First Division (Everton), and 15% did not know the name of the Lord Mayor of Liverpool (John McMillan).

Saturday 28 March 1964

The Mike Cotton Sound, Nashpool Four, Acoustics, Mark Four, JJ and the Executives. **Tom Jones**[619]: "There was a great band, the Mike Cotton Jazz Band, and virtually overnight it became the Mike Cotton Sound. He turned from out and out jazz to rock, all the same guys but with huge speakers and the decibel level was fantastic. I asked Mike how he managed with such a noise. He said, 'We wear these' and he pulled out some rubber earplugs that Ack-Ack Gunners used to wear during the war. He put them on a string round his neck and popped them in."

Sunday 29 March 1964

Earl Preston's Realms, Billy Butler and the Tuxedos, Secrets, Hideaways, Pilgrims and Chick Graham and the Coasters. **Frankie Connor**[620] of the Hideaways: "We came on the second wave, we were sixteen and seventeen, and we found Bob Wooler very trustworthy, and he was putting an agency together with Dougie Evans, the keyboard player from the Blue Angel. They had ourselves, the Clayton Squares, Michael Allen Group and the Masterminds and they were building a stable like Epstein. We were going to Carlisle once a month for three or four days at a time, and we did well on the east coast of Scotland. We were very visual and we were playing R&B, and we weren't a Beatle group. Bob had stopped his 'hi-fi high' stuff by then and simply introduced us by saying, 'R&B as you like it with the Hideaways'. Paddy Delaney had a wonderful voice too and they used to fight in a mock way about introducing us. Bob gave us some advice: he said, 'I don't think you should learn too many difficult chords because the girls don't come to watch you play diminished chords and augmented chords. They are interested in what you are wearing and how your hair is cut. The image is important and should come first.'"

Tuesday 31 March 1964

Sham rock (no, that's cruel): the start of a five day stint for the Irish showband, the Green Beats. John Keogh, the leader of the Green Beats, has been leading Full Circle. The webside for Kielys pub in Mount Merrion, Co. Dublin says that Full Circle is "the best party band in the world."

Sunday 5 April 1964

My girl lollipop, **Millie**[621], says, "I was only a little girl doing silly things and I don't think I did more than three or four songs. The Cavern was very damp and dark, but I can't remember much about it." **Betty Fegan**[622]: "Our Billy was with me and oh, Millie fell in love with our little Billy. He was only a little boy and her next record was 'Sweet William'."

Saturday 11 April 1964

Millie with the Five Embers at both the Junior Cavern Club and the evening sessions. **Kenny Parry**[623]: "There was a fella in my class who sagged school at dinnertime, his name was Brian Dickens, and he told us about how great the Cavern was. I didn't have the nerve to sag and I didn't go to the Cavern until I played on a Junior Cavern session with the Scribes, my first little band from Garston. We tuned up our guitars two days before the gig but I had been to the dentist and had lockjaw."

Sunday 12 April 1964

A definitive collection of second generation Liverpool bands: the Roadrunners, the Kirkbys, the Hideaways, the Clayton Squares and the Escorts.

Tuesday 14 April 1964

The Rattles (back in Liverpool for the week), Earl Preston's Realms, Blackwells, and Denny Seyton and the Sabres.

Thursday 16 April 1964

The Rattles with Billy Kinsley's new group, Kinsleys. **Billy Kinsley**[624]: "I left the Merseybeats because of our management. I knew we were getting ripped off and six months later, the lads knew as well. It was announced that I was leaving to get married but I was only seventeen and there was no way I was doing that. The Kinsleys were a very good band and we found a great song, 'Goodbye' by the Cinderellas. We had four good singers in the band so we could do harmonies. Dave Preston the drummer had a great Little Richard voice and we did 'Long Tall Sally' and 'Bama Lama Bama Loo'."

Friday 24 April 1964

(lunchtime) The Four Pennies, who are climbing up the charts with 'Juliet'.

(evening) Clayton Squares, Notions, Griff Parry Five, Feelgoods, Chessmen. **Brian Griffiths**[625]: "The Griff Parry Five was managed by Spencer Mason, who had the Mojos, and it was a terrific band. There was Steve Aldo singing, myself on guitar, Ron Parry on drums, Vinnie Parker on organ and Frank Galway on bass. Rhythm and blues in Britain was being played too smoothly

and we gave it a few rough edges. Our single of 'Can I Get A Witness', which was released under Steve's name, was pretty good too."

David Crosby[626]: "Bob Wooler used to play the records as soon as they came out and I can remember rushing to the band room and saying, 'What was that one, Bob, that record you just played?' It was 'I Can't Stand It' by the Soul Sisters and I had to have it."

Monday 27 April 1964

An unusual day at the Cavern. In the afternoon, the Cavern's management held a cocktail party to celebrate the opening of its suite of management offices next door to the club. They were further plans to build a recording studio. Being a private party, it marked the first time that drink was served officially on the Cavern's premises. During the evening an American guitarist, Jimmy Webster, held the first of three clinics at the Cavern. He created a stereo effect by having one amplifier connected to the bass strings and another to the treble. He told them, "Most people who buy a guitar only get about ten per cent of the possibilities from it."

Sunday 3 May 1964

Alexis Korner's Blues Inc, the Cordes, the Tempests and the Clayton Squares. The Cordes was a Liverpool Institute, R&B band, and they included Lonnie Donegan songs in their set, "Betty, Betty, Betty" and "In The Evening".

Tuesday 5 May 1964

(lunchtime) Herman's Hermits

(evening) Norrie Paramor judging the *Sounds Of 64* Big Beat competition, plus Merseybeats and Dolly Mixtures

After hearing of a Russian balalaika band, the Candid Lads, performing their own songs at the Kremlin, Ray McFall in a gesture of goodwill offers them honorary membership of the Cavern. From Russia With Love—the group accept their honorary membership in June.

Wednesday 13 May 1964

(lunchtime) Tony Rivers and the Castaways plus the Trends

(evening) Notions, Redcaps, Kirkbys, Renicks, Vic and the TT's

Monday 18 May 1964

From 3.30pm to 11.30pm, it was *Beatrama* with the Clayton Squares, the Roadrunners, Billy Kinsley, the Centremen, the Mastersounds, the Hideaways, the Nashpool Four, Freddie Starr and Flamingos, the Spidermen, St Louis Checks, the Georgians, the Blackwells, the Coins and Schatz.

Bessie Braddock, the Labour MP for Liverpool Exchange, went to the Cavern and was made the club's second life member. (Who was the first? Keep up now.) She said that if there were more clubs like the Cavern, there would be fewer difficulties with mods and rockers. **Judd Lander**[627]: "Bessie Braddock was a very short fat lady and she had a Rover with blocks on the pedals so that she could reach them. A lot of what she was doing was for political ends rather than doing something from the heart."

Gerry Marsden visited the Cavern with the production team for his film, *Ferry Cross The Mersey*. Lee Almond, the associate producer, tells *Mersey Beat*: "In the script, Gerry enters a beat competition and this will give us the opportunity to present three other Mersey groups. Gerry, of course, wins the competition." Not sure if it's a compliment or not, but they hear the blond Blackwells and sign them up.

A *Liverpool Daily Post* reporter writes, "The Coins are now thundering down the Mississippi to New Orleans. Dancing begins, quietly, unfrenzied. Things seem to have become more sedate since the Twist. That concrete warehouse floor still vibrates though with the sound from those throbbing guitars."

Lawrence Swerdlow[628]: "I saw the St Louis Checks play on one of their group nights at Hope Hall and I was particularly impressed with the sound. They had a very good lead guitarist, Terry Kenno, who had that little bit of extra ability, and he had a shiny red Gibson guitar which was a big deal in those days. They all had very good instruments and the lead singer, Eric Savage, had quite a bit of charisma. I thought of managing them. I talked to them about it but they said to me, 'We're looking for an organ player.' A lot of the groups had Vox Continental organs which were bright red, plastic cased organs on chrome plated stands and they looked stunning on stage. Instead of the standard keys being white with small black

keys, it was the reverse. The guys said to me, 'If you want to buy a Vox Continental organ, you are in the band.' I knew about nine chords, but I went to Frank Hessy's and I ordered one on the drip. When it was delivered, I was in the band. I increased my nine chords to twelve and I seemed to get by, playing 'Green Onions' and the like, but I was just bluffing my way through it. I left in the end because they needed a better player."

Thursday 21 May 1964

Denny Seyton[629]: "I used to like the lunchtime sessions as they were always packed and we would go to the White Star and the worst thing about that was having cheese and pickled onion sandwiches and then singing with John Boyle on the other side of the mike."

Sunday 24 May 1964

Kinsleys, Ian Crawford and the Boomerangs, Connoisseurs, Premiers and Them Grimbles. **Sue Ellison**[630]: "Them Grimbles was a really good band with a sax player and they did a lot of Chuck Berry and early Motown." **Mike Byrne**[631]: "Them Grimbles were totally different to any of the other Merseybeat bands. It was started by Chris who was a keyboard player and he had a Hammond L100, the same as Georgie Fame. I was listening to Ray Charles and so we had a Georgie Fame styled band with a sax, and we did 'Get On The Right Track, Baby, 'Mary Ann' and 'Watermelon Man', which was a bit jazzy. We did the Cavern but mostly we played in the basement of the Blue Angel for Allan Williams."

Dennis Conroy[632]: "I was about fourteen when it was all happening and I was in the Premiers. We became the Mersey Gonks as were told that Jimmy Savile was going to push the Gonks. We were gigging in Scotland at the time and someone suggested the name to us. It seemed a good idea at the time. Then we ended up with saxophone and Hammond organ as Chapter Six. We thought we were a soul group. We weren't really but we had fun. Guys came and went."

Wednesday 27 May 1964

(lunchtime) Wayne Fontana and the Mindbenders (evening) Long John Baldry and Hoochie Coochie Men (with Rod Stewart), Clayton Squares and Griff Parry Five

Wednesday 3 June 1964

Dave Lee and the Staggerlees, Hideaways, Ivan D Juniors and the Elements

Friday 5 June 1964

Mickie Most and the Gear, Vic and the TT's, Georgians, Triumphs, Kris Ryan and the Questions

Tuesday 9 June 1964

Freddie Starr and the Flamingos, Dions, Mysteries and Elektons. A party of 60 youngsters from the Wavertree School for the Blind visited the Cavern. A Cavern spokesman said, "They were the happiest people we have had here. There's always laughter down here of course, but somehow their laughter was much brighter." **Betty Fegan**[633]: "The children from the blind school came down one lunchtime. At the time there was bother with some lads and I said, 'Listen, these kids from the blind school can show you how to enjoy yourselves without causing any trouble.' They gave them a marvellous lunchtime session and made it memorable for them. It is all about approaching people the right way. I had to take a girl to one side because her mother had been down as she was skipping school. I said, 'I can't let you in. Your mother has been down and you have got to go to school. If you don't go to school, you won't get in at night either.'"

Friday 12 June 1964

John Lee Hooker with John Mayall's Bluesbreakers, St Louis Checks, Clayton Squares, Cordes and Hideaways. **Billy Butler**[634]: "The only artists who didn't interest me were Alexis Korner and the American blues stars as their music was too repetitive and too melancholy. That was the kind of music I didn't like it and I would go and chat to my mates at the back of the club. I did try and listen to John Lee Hooker to see what I was missing but he was waking up every morning and finding his girl had gone. Sonny Boy Williamson was a real character—he was in his sixties but he was still able to pull the birds." (Actually, Sonny Boy was in his fifties, but he looked much older.)

John Mayall[635]: "Sonny Boy was amazing. He was able to play no matter what condition he was in. He was mostly inebriated but he was always my favourite of the blues artists."

Dave Dover[636]: "I have John Lee Hooker's autograph on the back of my birth certificate for the simple reason that I could never get served in pubs, so I carried it around with me and it was the only piece of paper that I had. He was very drunk and he had half a bottle of whisky in his side pocket. He could just about write and he played great. He looked old then but he didn't look any older when he was in *The Blues Brothers*."

Steve Lister[637]: "I remember John Lee Hooker being in the dressing room and people handing him things to sign. He had a bemused expression as though he couldn't believe that was going on: why were all these people so interested in him. He had never had such adulation in America."

Saturday 13 June 1964

(Junior Cavern Club) Escorts

(evening) Notions, Hideaways, Spidermen and St Louis Checks

A two-day conference was taking place for youth leaders, organised by the National Association of Youth Clubs. After formal study sessions, the youth leaders visited the Cavern, the Iron Door and other city clubs. They preferred "the smartness and chic of the Liverpool boys and girls" to the Mods and Rockers in London. Bob Wooler, Bill Harry and Geoff Baker (manager of Freddie and the Dreamers) were part of their panel on the opportunities and dangers of performing professionally. Bob said that the groups must be protected from "briefcase merchants who have nothing in their briefcases but empty promises."

Sunday 14 June 1964

Mike Cotton Sound, Countdowns, Jensons and back from their Spanish dates, the Kubas

Wednesday 17 June 1964

Country Gentlemen, Georgians, Kruzads and Jacobeats. Bob Wooler tells *Liverpool Echo*: "We feature about 40 groups a week, and the first spot in each session is reserved for a new group making their first appearance here. They play for 30 minutes, and I see how they are received by our members. If they shape well, they will nearly always get another booking. Once a group can say they have played at the Cavern, they won't find it difficult to get more bookings."

The lucky group that night was the Jacobeats from Crosby. They had been together five months and their leader, 22-year-old Malcolm Nixon, had a high-tech job: he was a computer programmer. Seventeen-year-old Laurence Ashley of the Georgians revealed that his parents would rather he was studying for a university place.

Tuesday 18 June 1964

The Yardbirds, Freddie Starr and the Flamingos, Jimmy Powell and the Five Dimensions

Saturday 20 June 1964

(lunchtime) Arrow and the Archers, Chick Graham and the Coasters, Kinsleys

(evening) Riot Squad, Kinsleys, Cordes, Paladins, Connoisseurs

There was a profile of 22-year-old Joey Bower of the Connoisseurs in the *Liverpool Echo*. The group had been playing in Carlisle and he had got back home at 2am, only to be up at seven to work as a painter and decorator. (The Liverpool bands often went to Carlisle: clearly, Bob Wooler had some dealings with a local promoter.)

Dick Heller, a London travel agent, was running regular weekend coach trips to Liverpool. He had been getting one-off bookings from fans and "It suddenly dawned on me that Liverpool is where the Beatles come from."

Thursday 25 June 1964

Gerry and the Pacemakers, Kris Ryan and the Questions and the Pretenders.

Wednesday 1 July 1964

The Escorts, Mark Four, the Mersey Four, the Notions, and Bobby and the Bachelors. A police sting was in operation. Four witnesses saw over 100 people enter the club and pay their admission fees. At the end of the night, there was a discrepancy of £8 and the 35-year-old cashier is arrested.

Thursday 2 July 1964

Inez and Charlie Foxx, backed and supported by the Spencer Davis Group (with Steve Winwood). **Spencer Davis**[638]: "My memories of playing the Cavern are vague as we were working seven nights a week with two shows on Saturday. Inez Foxx was a beautiful lady, stunningly beautiful, and it was a pleasure to be backing them."

David Crosby[639]: "Inez and Charlie Foxx were very good at the Cavern. Their problem was that the only song that everybody knew was 'Mockingbird'."

Billy Butler[640]: "The heat made no difference to the looks as a gorgeous woman is a gorgeous woman. Inez Foxx was really glamorous and so were the two girls in the Exciters."

Frankie Connor[641]: "Steve Winwood was only sixteen but he had an extraordinary voice and he sang 'Georgia On My Mind' like a black soul singer. He would do this tremendous song and then come off stage and say in a Birmingham accent, 'All right, Frankie, how are you?'"

Thursday 9 July 1964

Kingsize Taylor and the Dominoes, Griff Parry Five, Hideaways and St. Louis Checks

Friday 10 July 1964

(lunchtime) Undertakers

(evening) Billy Butler and the Tuxedos, the Feelgoods and Savva and the Democrats. **Clive Epstein**[642], Brian's brother, recalled, "There was a wonderful occasion when the Beatles came back to Liverpool for the première of *A Hard Day's Night*. The streets of Liverpool were lined all the way from the airport to Castle Street. It was exactly the same as if Liverpool had won the Cup Final."

More than 20,000 people lined the streets for the Beatles. **Jean Catharell**[643]: "My brother got me a ticket for the premiere of *A Hard Day's Night* but I had to go on my own. I sewed my ticket into my jacket because I was terrified of losing it. The streets were crowded and the Beatles sat on the front row in the balcony, and I sat with my back to the screen watching the balcony. I had to go back a couple of days later to find out what the film was about."

Billy Butler[644]: "The only time the Tuxedos got top billing at the Cavern was when the Beatles came to Liverpool for the première of *A Hard Day's Night*. The whole of Liverpool was lining the streets but none of them came to the Cavern. We got about 80 people and I wouldn't be surprised if that booking wasn't one of Bob Wooler's jokes."

Thursday 16 July 1964

Since their last visit, the Four Pennies have had a Number One with 'Juliet'.

Saturday 18 July 1964

The Merseybeats and the Hideaways top the bill at the Junior Cavern Club, but they are supported by the Flyaways. This five-piece group has an average age of nine, and three of them are Ray McFall's children—Peter, Stephen and Susan.

Monday 3 August 1964
Bank Holiday special with Prince Khan and the Babes, Savva and the Democrats, Valkyries, Dions, Earl Preston's Realms, Kubas, Them Grimbles, Strangers and Smoke Stacks. The Valkyries get booked for American bases in France and they back both the country star, Little Jimmy Dickens, and a very fat Egyptian stripper for whom they played 'The Sheik Of Araby'. The original Valkyries were female goddesses so maybe the band had been booked by accident.

Tuesday 4 August 1964
Tell me when. It's lunchtime for the Applejacks.

Thursday 6 August 1964
Launch party for the latest publication in Panther Books, *On The Scene* series. This one is *On The Scene At The Cavern* by Alistair Griffin (Tony Barrow under a pseudonym). Peter Adamson (Len Fairclough from *Coronation Street*) performs 'Got My Mojo Workin" with pianist Doug Evans (the Cavern's office manager) and the Hideaways. Peter Adamson demanded to play the drums and almost wrecked them in the process. The guests include George Harrison's parents and members of Liverpool and Everton FC. **Frankie Connor**[645]: "George Harrison's mother, Louise Harrison, liked us and thought we could become as famous as the Beatles. She became an honorary member of our fan club and we also roped in Ken Dodd. Louise Harrison would come to the Cavern to see us and sit in the front row. She loved the Motown songs that we did and she would give us wine gums, dolly mixtures and Everton Mints. She was a lovely lady." The Hideaways' big moment is the tick-a-tick Timex advert, filmed at the Cavern one Saturday morning before Junior Cavern Club.

Saturday 8 August 1964
Jimmy Nicol and the Shubdubs play the Junior Cavern Club and the evening session. Nicol was the Beatles' stand-in drummer when Ringo Starr had his tonsils removed, but the only Beatles-related number in his set was "Twist And Shout", sung by their vocalist, Tony Allan from Leigh.

Monday 10 August 1964
(lunchtime) The Kinsleys, plus Cavern finals for the Rael Brook Contest

(evening) The Cavern presents the Rolling Stones at the Tower Ballroom.

Tuesday 11 August 1964
Tiffany and the Four Dimensions, Escorts, Vampires

Forty members of the Commonwealth Youth Movement on their *Quest Of 1964* made a detour from the Town Hall to the Walker Art Gallery with an unscheduled visit to the Cavern. John Nicholson of the Royal Commonwealth Society told the *Echo*, "I didn't even know my own son was a member until he produced his card."

Thursday 13 August 1964
Alex Harvey Big Soul Band, Hideaways and Clayton Squares. **Mike Evans**[646] of the Clayton Squares: "Quite coincidentally, we were in tune with what was going on in London. That Chicago R&B sound was still quite underground and the Clayton Squares did a bit of that, but because we had two saxophones from the start we were doing Ray Charles and Fats Domino and the new soul stuff from Otis Redding and Wilson Pickett. The Roadrunners once they got saxophones were quite James Brown oriented. It was a different bag to the three guitar and drum groups from the Merseybeat era. In that sense, we were new wave, and so were the Hideaways who were doing a Chicago harmonica R&B."

Monday 17 August 1964
Luncheon beat with Rory Storm and the Hurricanes. A telephone link was set up with WROD in Daytona Beach, Florida as the station was broadcasting a 24-hour *Salute To The Beatles*. The station spoke to George Harrison's parents, Ray McFall, Bob Wooler, Frieda Kelly and, from her holiday in Scarborough, Bessie Braddock. The station placed random calls to those in the city's telephone directory for off-the-cuff comments about the group.

Thursday 20 August 1964
The jazz-based singer/songwriter Mose Allison had a new following amongst the British beat groups with his songs "Parchman Farm" and "Young Man Blues" as well as his versions of Willie Dixon's "I Love The Life I Live" and "Seventh Son". Listen to his voice and you'll know why Georgie Fame sounds the way he does. Mose Allison came to the Cavern on a UK tour, backed by the T-Bones.

Mose Allison[647]: "I was very glad when the British acts like Georgie Fame picked up on my songs as otherwise, I mightn't have found enough work to keep myself going. I remember the Who doing 'Young Man Blues' and I got a cheque in the mail that was a lot more than I was used to getting. I can remember coming to the Cavern and those stairs were pretty steep. I was backed by the T-Bones and we were doing a lot of blues, which was what the audience wanted. Someone remarked that I looked very proper and certainly I wasn't as bizarrely dressed as some of the performers of that time. To be honest, it was just another job but it was a good one and I wouldn't mind playing the Cavern again although I am not up to the travelling these days and mostly I stay in London when I come to the UK."

Terry McCusker[648]: "I joined Rip Van Winkle and the Rip It Ups which was just a stupid name. We played the Cavern on a mid-week summer evening in 1964. We were all from Birkenhead and we went and picked up Freddie Starr who was living on the Woodchurch estate. We got him in the van and we didn't stop laughing all night. He didn't get up that evening, but he might have been under orders not to because everything degenerated when Freddie got on stage. Getting instruments in and out of the Cavern was horrendous. I've seen cabinets come crashing down the stairs many times. The Cavern was a very dangerous place and a fire in there would have been awful—and the groups were right at the back with no fire escape."

Monday 7 September 1964

(lunchtime) **Raphael Callaghan**[649]: "The Bluesville Bats from Hamburg were playing at my first adult session at the Cavern. They were just another beat group doing bluesy covers—nothing to get excited about."

The Cavern was holding *Beat Week* for Oxfam's *Freedom From Hunger* campaign, but the week was off to a bad start as thieves broke into the office early in the morning and used explosives to blow up the safe. They were unsuccessful and its contents of £200 remained intact. As they worked, they drank the gin and whisky that they found in a drawer. £25 was stolen from a briefcase but a signed photograph of Paul McCartney was untouched.

Tuesday 8 September 1964

Herman's Hermits, Denny Seyton and the Sabres, and the Notions. **Denny Seyton**[650]: "We were doing Earl-Jean's 'I'm Into Something Good' before Herman recorded it. It was one of our best numbers and it went down very well. He did it as a single and we didn't, and he was in charts with it when we did this show."

Saturday 12 September 1964

Kris Ryan and the Questions. The Lord Mayor of Liverpool, Louis Caplan, was unrecognised as he made his way through the stomping crowd to the stage. He wanted to thank the Cavernites for raising £50 for Oxfam and to denounce the Hastings magistrate who had referred to Liverpool youths as 'drifting scum'. He said, "Liverpool should be proud of the city's youngsters, and so should the country." He expresses surprised that no beat group has yet called itself the Kopites or the Goodisons. What's wrong with Sonny Kaye and the Reds?

Thursday 17 September 1964

Blues night with Jimmy Powell and the Five Dimensions, Clayton Squares, Hideaways and the Music Students

Sunday 20 September 1964

This eight hour session starred Jimmy Witherspoon, supported by the Cordes, Mark Four, the Experts, Mark Anthony and the Avengers, the Bluesounds and the Abstracts. **Frankie Connor**[651]: "We did 'Baby, Baby, Baby' in the Hideaways so I was looking forward to seeing Jimmy Witherspoon. I knew that he sang both blues and jazz, but he was definitely on a blues kick that night and was very good." Witherspoon was markedly different to most of the touring bluesmen, who had usually seen better days. His refined baritone contrasted with their lived-in, gravelly voices.

Wednesday 23 September 1964

The Escorts, the Hideaways, and a Manchester band, Ivan D. Juniors.

Sunday 27 September 1964

Radio Luxembourg's show, *Sunday Night At The Cavern,* with live music from Denny Seyton and the Sabres and hosted by Bob Wooler. Seyton performed "Hands Off", "Funny How Time Slips Away", "Rag Doll", "On Broadway", "The Way You Look Tonight" and "Tricky Dicky". The show also featured records from Zoot Money, blues man Jimmy Rogers, the Rustiks, Little Eva and Bobby Bland.

Wednesday 30 September 1964
(lunchtime) The Escorts
(evening) The Notions, the Kirkbys and Brian Epstein's new signing, the Rustiks

Thursday 1 October 1964
Come on, come on and do the Locomotion with Little Eva.

Sunday 4 October 1964
Mark Peters and the Silhouettes are featured in *Sunday Night At The Cavern* on Radio Luxembourg.

Friday 9 October 1964
John Lee Hooker with the Groundhogs, plus the Abstracts, the Clayton Squares, Power House Six, TL's Bluesicians, the TTs (without Earl Preston) and Savva and the Democrats. The Bluesicians were a local band, originally called the Groundhogs, although the visiting Groundhogs had something to say about that. **Bob Wooler**[652]: "It was a bonus for me to have American acts performing at the Cavern. I was very impressed by the blues musician, John Lee Hooker, who played one Friday night. The audience wanted him to stay on the stage but there was a Merseyside group ready to go on. I should have said, 'Sorry, fellas, you'll get paid but there's no time for you tonight.' As soon as he came off, nearly everyone went and the group played to an empty house."

Tony (T.S.) McPhee[653] of the Groundhogs: "John Lee Hooker was illiterate and could hardly write his name. If he was asked for an autograph, he would be struggling. We would help him out by saying 'Bad pen, John' and things like that. Once he got the hang of it, his signature got longer and longer and the n's were always backwards. He is to be congratulated for working out how to do it, not like Big Joe Williams who just wrote 'XXX'. John liked the girls over here and he would be fondling them in the band room. He was a fabulous guy but you would have to watch him on stage as he could switch in the middle of a bar."

Mike Evans[654]: "John Lee Hooker said to me, 'Where can I get some drink?' I told him that the White Star was round the corner as the musicians

had been banned from the Grapes at that juncture. This, I think, stemmed from John Lennon's time as they had behaved so badly. Hooker gave me some money and asked me to get him something. There was no drinks licence for the Cavern and it was like Prohibition. I could go out with my saxophone case empty and fill it with bottles and bring it back to the band room. I remember bringing this bottle of Scotch in for Hooker and getting it past Paddy Delaney on the door. Hooker and various musicians were sitting around through the night, finishing this bottle of whisky and as the bands on stage were so loud, you could jam quietly in the band room. I remember that the Chants came along and one of them said to John Lee Hooker, 'Did you ever sing in a vocal group?', and John Lee Hooker looked a bit puzzled and said, 'Well, man, I sang in front of a bunch of chorus girls once.'"

Sunday 11 October 1964
The Alex Harvey Big Soul Band, Clayton Squares, Abstracts and St Louis Checks

Thursday 15 October 1964
The day of the General Election with the Abstracts, the Hideaways, the Sheffields, St Louis Checks and the Tabs. Harold Wilson wins, but only just.

Monday 19 October 1964
Folk night with the Spinners, the Green Ginger Four, the Silkie and Luke Kelly from the Dubliners. Bessie Braddock lent her support: "I like this kind of music very much." Tony Davis commented, "We don't think our audience here is any less intelligent than the one we play to at the Philharmonic." **Mick Groves**[655]: "The place was heaving and Luke Kelly came on stage with his banjo over his shoulder and sang 'Plough The Rocks Of Bawn' unaccompanied. The whole club listened in silence."

Thursday 22 October 1964
Yardbirds, Aintree Four, Clayton Squares and Abstracts

Thursday 29 October 1964
Little Walter, TL's Bluesicians, Hideaways, Sheffields and Abstracts

Tuesday 3 November 1964
Amos Bonney with the TTs, Sett and Cresters

Friday 6 November 1964

Cavern opens a Pop Record Inn for selling records and offering free haircuts by Romanoffs. Music from Kris Ryan and the Questions and the Road-runners

Saturday 7 November 1964

All night session—Long John Baldry and the Hoochie Coochie Men (with Rod Stewart), St. Louis Checks, Excelles, Clayton Squares, Earl Preston's Realms, Abstract Minds, Hideaways, Riot Squad and TL's Bluesicians

Tuesday 10 November 1964

Sonny Boy Williamson, Moody Blues, Hidea-ways and Easybeats. **Frank Townsend**[656] of the Easybeats: "The Moody Blues were excellent and Denny Laine brought the house down with his lead vocal on 'Go Now'. I'm not really into the blues but Sonny Boy Williamson was tremendous and he looked about the oldest person I'd ever seen. His entertainment value was tremendous and I went home smiling."

Billy Butler[657]: "Denny Laine said, 'We will bring on Sonny Boy very soon, but here's a song we have just recorded and they went into 'Go Now'. Those opening bars stick in my mind as much as when the Beatles introduced 'Please Please Me' at the Majestic on the *Mersey Beat* awards night."

Frank Townsend[658]: "I was interested in west coast music but I didn't get into the Beach Boys until 1964 when 'I Get Around' came out. Radio Caroline came into the bay and they opened up with 'I Get Around'. I was in the Easybeats and we were about to do four days in Scotland. The lads had come to my house for breakfast and all the band was there. We heard the Beach Boys and we knew we wanted to do that. We didn't leave for Scotland right away. We went up to NEMS in Great Charlotte Street and we bought everything they had by the Beach Boys like *Shut Down, Volume 2* and *Surfin' USA*. By the time we had been in Scotland two days, we were doing a whole Beach Boys set. Nobody else was doing the songs in Liverpool although Bern Elliott and the Fenmen and Tony Rivers and the Castaways were doing that elsewhere."

Tuesday 17 November 1964

The Hideaways, the Notions, Billy Butler and the Tuxedos, and one of the first tribute acts, the Strolling Bones. Mostly, Billy was working as a DJ at the Cavern, getting £2.50 for organising a lunchtime and an evening session.

Thursday 19 November 1964

(lunchtime) **Mike Evans**[659] of the Clayton Squares: "Because we were managed by the Cavern Agency, we could rehearse before the lunchtime session and Terry Hines sometimes arrived in his pyjamas: he would get out of bed at the last minute and he would put his jeans and his jacket on over his pyjamas. He even did gigs in his pyjamas if he hadn't time to change."

(evening) Folk night with Spinners, Silkie, Leesiders, Billy Boys, and Tina and Mardi

Saturday 21 November 1964

Junior Cavern Club and evening shows from the Soul Agents, a Southampton band with Rod Stewart as vocalist.

Sunday 22 November 1964

Recording of *Sunday Night At The Cavern* for Radio Luxembourg with Cordes, Secrets, TL's Bluesicians, Hideaways and New Chariots. The Secrets had spent £2,000 on their instruments and equipment.

Tuesday 24 November 1964

The Hollies, who'd had five Top 20 hits, supported by the Kirkbys and Earl Preston's Realms, and their set was recorded for Radio Luxembourg.

Sunday 29 November 1964

Recording *Sunday Night At The Cavern* for Radio Luxembourg with the Merseybeats, the Excelles, the Notions, and Amos Bonney with the TTs.

Thursday 3 December 1964

(lunchtime) Rory Storm and the Hurricanes. The bands that had made it had left the Cavern but Rory Storm and Earl Preston were still around. I asked **Mike Evans**[660] if they felt bitter about it. "It was only a year or so after the Merseybeat explosion, so the time difference wasn't that great, and anyway, a new band like the Escorts was very much in that tradition. Some years later when the Hurricanes had packed in, I was doing a gig with one of the last versions of the Clayton Squares and we were at the Wooky Hollow and Rory Storm was the DJ. He said, 'Can I get up for a song in the second set?' We said yes, and before he came on to do his number, he said in my ear, 'Just tell them that the Golden Boy is here.' I thought that was very sad and it showed that he was past it."

The Cavern opens Cavern Sounds Ltd, a recording studio, the first one of a professional standard in Liverpool and there is a door from the Cavern into the studio. On the face of it, it should have been an immediate success, but it is under-used.

Sunday 6 December 1964
Recording *Sunday Night At The Cavern* for Radio Luxembourg with Kubas, Georgians, Litter and Harpos.

Monday 7 December 1964
The Mojos, returning after three hit singles.

Wednesday 9 December 1964
If there was anywhere better to be on 9 December 1964, I don't know of it. The Chess blues star, Howlin' Wolf with Hubert Sumlin and T-Bones, supported by the Hideaways, the Michael Allen Group and St Louis Checks. **Sue Ellison**[661]: "I had Howlin' Wolf's album, *Moanin' In The Moonlight*, and he lived up to it. His guitarist, Hubert Sumlin, was brilliant. Wolf was a giant in every sense and he had the biggest feet I had ever seen. His shoes were split because he hadn't been able to get a pair that was big enough."

Thursday 10 December 1964
Long John Baldry

Sunday 13 December 1964
Recording *Sunday Night At The Cavern* for Radio Luxembourg with Steve Aldo, the Jokers, the Griff Parry Five, the Fontanas, the Kubas and St. Louis Checks

Monday 14 December 1964
The Cavern was full and the Cavern was in darkness. There was an explosion, girls screamed while the lights flickered, and the Clayton Squares broke into Ray Charles' "Danger Zone". Welcome to Adrian Henri's Bomb Event (very much in the tradition of the Happenings in the New York). Adrian Henri commented on a Civil Defence pamphlet and then it was "Atomic Talking Blues" from the Clayton Squares. Bob Wooler satirised TV commercials with "PAD—Prolongs Active Death." As Adrian read another poem, a monster, played by Pete the Papers, strangled him. The Clayton Squares accompanied Adrian doing "Tonight At Noon". The Excelles sang "Don't Say Goodnight And Mean Goodbye" and went into

"Silent Night". The four-minute warning was given over the PA. There was another explosion and a false ceiling made of paper and powder and representing fallout collapsed. Then two mutants, dressed in black, wandered round the audience to the accompaniment of eerie organ music.

Mike Evans[662] of the Clayton Squares: "We took part in *Bomb* with Adrian Henri, Brian Patten and Roger McGough. It was a multi-media thing as the band played in the middle where the chairs normally were and all kinds of weird things were happening on the stage. We played Charlie Mingus' 'Oh Lord Don't Let Them Drop That Atomic Bomb On Me' and Ray Charles' 'Danger Zone'. They were warnings about the nuclear holocaust and Brian Patten came on wrapped in bandages. He looked like the Invisible Man and he was a post-Bomb zombie. There was an explosion at the end and paper fell down on the audience like confetti. It represented fallout. It was all very pre-psychedelic and it was revolutionary in its own way."

John Gorman[663]: "We were trying to change the mood and we never explained what we did. I can remember recording the adverts off television and playing them in the dark, just the sound tape. They just sounded so stupid so people would be laughing. We played them all the way through, and then we played them again 20 minutes later and some people laughed. Then we did it again and nobody laughed. Dave Midgeley said, 'When you played those adverts, they were really funny but why did you keep repeating it?', and I said, 'Because that's what happens on television.' I think the people at the Cavern thought, 'What they are they doing here, what's going on? Is this a dream?'"

Tuesday 15 December 1964
Twin nights—all twins got in free! (Hardly Bob Wooler's finest hour) They heard Earl Royce and the Olympics, the Cresters, the Pretenders and the Stormers

Wednesday 16 December 1964
Just like 1962—the Chants, Rory Storm and the Hurricanes, and Earl Royce and the Olympics

Saturday 19 December 1964
All night session with Undertakers, Riot Squad, Pawns, Kirkbys, Hideaways, Tabs, Georgians,

Nightwalkers and Michael Allen Group. **David Crosby**[664] of the Tabs: "Tab collars were very popular then, rather like Cuban heels, hence the name. We wanted to be like the Clayton Squares but not as bluesy. When we added sax and trumpet, we were doing James Brown stuff. One of our favourites was Otis Redding's 'Mr Pitiful'."

There were Christmas greetings from Cavern Artistes Ltd in *Mersey Beat*. According to their ad, they represented the Michael Allen Group, Clayton Squares, Excelles, Hideaways, Kubas, Notions, Earl Preston's Realms and St Louis Checks.

Sunday 20 December 1964

Recording *Sunday Night At The Cavern* for Radio Luxembourg with Hideaways, St Louis Checks and Hipster Image

Thursday 31 December 1964

All night session with Escorts, Notions, Earl Preston's Realms, Kirkbys, Clayton Squares, Pretenders, Hideaways and Kinsleys

Tuesday 5 January 1965

A review in the local beat paper, *Combo* said, "The Roadrunners filled the Cavern with a rich, gutsy sound—and more than impressed an executive of a major recording company. Mike Hart's raw voice has lots of soul and sincerity—and he received a wave of applause for his scat solo in 'Got My Mojo Workin'. Throughout their act a Tony Sheridan influence was apparent, caused no doubt by their several appearances in Hamburg."

Sunday 10 January 1965

The Brian Auger Trinity, the Clayton Squares and the Almost Blues. **Brian Auger**[665]: "The Cavern had the worst toilets I had ever seen. I have stopped halfway across the desert in the UAE near Dubai and even that didn't compare. Still, the music that came out of the Cavern was incredible. Part of it is due to the northern cities being so friendly, quite different from London. We drove back to London in a hellish rainstorm and we were going through Kirkby and saw an old man and an old lady. She was laid out on the pavement and he was trying to pick her up. We stopped the van and got out to give them a hand and they were totally plastered. She was lying on the pavement, laughing her head off. I'd got totally wet for nothing.

Sunday 17 January 1965

Recording *Sunday Night At The Cavern* for Radio Luxembourg with Earl Preston's Realms, the Notions, the Hillsiders, the Feelgoods and the Hoboes

Friday 22 January 1965

Return visit for Boston Pops conductor, Arthur Fiedler. Since his last visit, the Boston Pops had been recording Beatle songs, the first classical orchestra to do so. They had made the US charts with "I Want To Hold Your Hand". Fielder visited the lunchtime session at the Cavern and saw the Undertakers. Fiedler told the crowd that he loved the Beatles' music and he became the first (and only) person to dance the Cavern Stomp in an overcoat and scarf. "It's a bit suggestive," he said, but surely not when you're wearing an overcoat and scarf. The next night he conducted the Royal Liverpool Philharmonic Orchestra through a classical repertoire and concluded with 'I Want To Hold Your Hand'.

Father Edwyn Young, the Rector of Liverpool, was also spotted at the Cavern. He was showing it to his seventeen-year-old daughter but he said that he popped in once a week anyway "to see if there is anything I can do for the groups." Indeed, part of the official role of his chaplaincy was to get involved in city life, but there was no Cavern Stomping in a cassock for him and indeed, he organised the Cavern's annual carol service. He had, incidentally, been the pastor for Raymond's Revuebar, which must have been more of a challenge. No wonder he named his autobiography, *No Fun Like Work*.

Sunday 24 January 1965

Recording *Sunday Night At The Cavern* for Radio Luxembourg with Kris Ryan and the Questions, Victor Brox Blues Train and Rory Storm and the Hurricanes

Sunday 31 January 1965

Recording *Sunday Night At The Cavern* for Radio Luxembourg with the Johnny Gus Set (Gus has left the Big Three), the Undertakers, the Blues Syndicate and the Clayton Squares.

Monday 1 February 1965

John Winton wrote "The Cavern In The Town" for *Lancashire Life*. Ray McFall said, "It's no longer good enough for four young men with long hair and guitars to get up on a stage and play." So what were they doing now? Bob Wooler said, "We've had everybody here but Pinky and Perky", which is a bit of a porker. Winton wrote, "It is too easy to laugh at the Cavern club and its zoo noises," and then went on to do so. He thought that there would soon be more musicians in the Leece Street Labour Exchange than the Cavern.

Sunday 7 February 1965

Geoff Davies[666]: "I loved hearing bands like the Roadrunners and the Clayton Squares as they did their songs with so much excitement and emotion. Around this time, I saw Muddy Waters at the Philharmonic Hall and he was very disappointing. He threw his songs away as though he were going through the motions."

Rumours that the Cavern was in financial trouble were starting to appear. Ray McFall told the *Liverpool Daily Post*, "It is true that the bonanza years are over. Attendances are less than they were, but they are still very good…and we are not losing money." Whatever the situation, Bob Wooler and Dougie Evans were setting up Bob Wooler Productions Ltd, and transferring the groups from the Cavern's company to their own agency.

Monday 15 February 1965

Adrian Henri organised a second Event, *The Black And White Show Against Apartheid*. **Mike Evans**[667]: "*The Black And White Show* was a race relations, anti-apartheid event. The audience was split into two, they were either black or white as they came in and they were physically divided in the actual club, one side black and one side white, and there was a team of girls dressed in gymslips building this wall between the two sides of the audience. The only reason they were dressed in gymslips was because Adrian preferred that to a gang of brickies building the wall."

Pete Brown[668]: "Well, Adrian's schoolgirl fixation was a part of his personal culture. The thing about Adrian Henri and Liverpool pop culture is that they managed to relate it to what was happening locally. They made it uncosmic and down to earth. It could have been pretentious with other people and certainly, some of the London manifestations were. They were much less humorous than the Liverpool version of it. There were amazing audiences in Liverpool. They were completely open to these things and would enjoy them. They

would not be prejudiced and go, 'That's a load of arty-farty pricks poncing about.'"

Bob Wooler[669]: "The most unusual nights were the avant-garde ones arranged by the Liverpool poet and artist, Adrian Henri. He hired the Cavern one Monday night and mounted *Bomb*, which was about CND, with the Clayton Squares Some of the audience were bandaged for that performance, and *The Guardian* quoted me as telling the audience, 'This is not for the feet, it is for the head.' He also did one about anti-apartheid and I remember them singing, *I'm Dreaming Of A White Smethwick*."

Saturday 20 February 1965

Alexis Korner's Blues Inc, Hideaways, Notions, Roadrunners, Spidermen and St. Louis Checks

Friday 5 March 1965

Brendan McCormack[670]: "When I joined Tom O'Connor for a comedy duo, I was playing both classical and jazz guitar and he had a whole menagerie of things he could do as well as comedy monologues. We played at the Cavern in March 1965, a Friday I think. We were in the Cavern studios and we were being recorded by Peter Hepworth. Tom was recording some country and western songs for Decca and we were also doing tracks for a Keele University rag record for Jimmy Savile. It was late morning and whoever was playing that lunchtime session wasn't coming and so Bob Wooler asked us to perform. We did monologues, comedy, blues and Irish jigs. I must be the first solo guitarist to have played Bach at the Cavern, and they were quiet too: that was lovely. Tom and I did some theatre work and we did a Blackpool season. It was great fun. He packed in teaching and then he went back to teaching and I became a solo player and then he came back as a comedian."

Saturday 6 March 1965

Pete Best Combo, Easybeats, Poets and Feelgoods

Sunday 7 March 1965

The Lawbreakers, Denny Mitchell Soundsations, and Amos Bonney and Karl Terry with the TTs

Friday 12 March 1965

Phil Brady and the Ranchers, Coins, Hideaways, Tiffany and Four Dimensions

Sunday 14 March 1965

Annette and the Riverdales, Sheffields, Masterminds and Blue Angels. **Joey Molland**[671] of the Masterminds: "We did 'She Belongs To Me', 'Nowhere To Run', 'Dancing In The Street' and some stuff from the Velvelettes and Arthur Alexander. I didn't hear too many groups doing Bob Dylan songs at the Cavern but 'She Belongs To Me' is pretty routine by his standards. Andrew Loog Oldman heard us at the Blue Angel and then we started recording for his Immediate label, 'She Belongs To Me' was a nice thing to do with easy guitar parts."

Tuesday 16 March 1965

Clayton Squares, Warriors and the US Limited. **Jon Anderson**[672] of the Accrington band, the Warriors: "I had been down the Cavern and seen a lunchtime session and I was determined to play the place and when we got a booking, it was a dream come true. The atmosphere was amazing and we did a lot of Everly Brothers songs and could sound quite like the Beatles. I turned professional and I've never done anything else since then. We also recorded the Beatles' 'Every Little Thing' in a very mod version with an extended structure."

Sunday 21 March 1965

Two Earls, Preston and Royce.

Wednesday 31 March 1965

Battling against the odds, a French TV station broadcast a live show from the Cavern. It was compéred by Petula Clark and featured Gene Vincent backed by the Dyaks, Gerry and the Pacemakers, Manfred Mann, Sandie Shaw (miming as she walked down the stairs) and the Clayton Squares. Petula sang "I Know A Place", a Tony Hatch song with a reference to "a cellarful of noise". **Ray McFall**[673]: "That was a daring enterprise as there was no satellite television then and connecting the Cavern in Liverpool with a French studio was a monumental task, and the Post Office engineers needed two or three days to set up the landlines. Happily, it went well and Petula Clark sang 'I Know A Place', which could have been written about the Cavern."

Mike Evans[674], who played sax with the Clayton Squares, recalled: "Being managed by Bob Wooler meant that we were on every big event that went on at the Cavern. We were on a French television show and the London manager, Don Arden, was there. When he saw our following, he asked Bob for a 50% share in the band and he would see to it that we recorded the following week with Andrew Loog Oldham. We recorded an amazing version of 'I've Been Lovin' You Too Long' which, with double and triple tracking sounded like a huge soul orchestra. However, Oldham fell out with Arden and it never got released. We made another record and Don Arden said he wouldn't promote it unless we signed over the other 50% of our management commitment to him. We voted by four votes to two to oust Wooler which was very much against our better instincts and I feel guilty even talking about it today. It did us no good at all as Arden didn't promote the record and moved on to something else."

Wednesday 21 April 1965

(lunchtime and evening) Dave Dee, Dozy, Beaky, Mick and Tich

Wednesday 28 April 1965

(lunchtime and evening) Downliners Sect

Saturday 8 May 1965

All nighter with the Merseybeats, the Terry Hines Sextet, the Clayton Squares, Earl Preston's Realms, the Blue Lotus Jazzmen, the Easybeats, the Defenders and the Blues Angels. Billy Butler introduced the Merseybeats dressed in pyjamas at an all-nighter. Bob Wooler told him not to and he told Bob to get lost.

Saturday 22 May 1965

All night session with Johnny Gus Set, Hideaways, Roadrunners, Amos Bonney and the TTs, St. Louis Checks, Richmond Group, Experts, Blues Pentagon and Billy Butler and the Tuxedos. **Frankie Connor**[675] of the Hideaways: "We did the first spot at 7.30 in the evening and then went to Queen's Hall in Widnes. We came back and did the Cavern at 3am. It didn't bother us—when you're young, you have boundless energy. Some of the girls would follow us to Widnes and then come back for the late session: incredibly loyal, extraordinary people."

Friday 28 May 1965

The Feelgoods, the Warriors and the Measles

Saturday 29 May 1965

The American poet, Allen Ginsberg, was in the UK for an international poetry reading at the

150 TEENAGERS IN SIEGE AT CAVERN CLUB

Mrs. Braddock Joins Cavern

Mrs. E. M. Braddock, M.P., signs in at the Cavern Club, Liverpool, last night, when she was made a life member and presented with her membership certificate by the owner, Mr. Ray McFall (standing).

Caving in?

Quite attractive at first sight is Paul McCartney's suggestion that "if the City Council looked upon the Cavern as a tourist attraction instead of just an old warehouse, something could be done about the threatened closure of this doyen of beat clubs."

After all, the city was quick enough to jump on the Liverpool Sound bandwagon and if financial assistance can be given to struggling cultural organisations, why not to The Cavern?

But one reason for this club's financial difficulties is that it no longer gets the sort of rave support which made it famous. Times change, and any establishment as fashionable as the Cavern is bound to be a victim of them.

It is hard to perceive the case for extending civic subsidy to an establishment for which public support is obviously waning, and it is precisely because The Cavern is not "just an old warehouse" that its proprietor has been told by the City Council to put his drains in order.

Life Member Of Cavern

Mrs. Braddock's Appeal

AMONG THE MUSTS

Liverpool Attraction For Overseas Tourists

Liverpool is finding its place among the musts in holiday itineraries of American tourists in this country—it is no longer Shakespeare's birthplace, but where the Beatles come from that has the appeal, said Mr. Lewis Edwards, founder and managing director of the Youth Travel Club, at a Press conference yesterday.

String along with Jim

U.S. GUITAR KING SHOWS THEM HOW

By Colin Malam

CAVERN COCKTAILS

THREAT TO CLOSE THE CAVERN: LITTLE WE CAN DO, SAY BEATLES

Make It An Attraction For Tourists—Paul

LETTER FROM GIRLS

INQUISITIVE grannies explored Liverpool's Cavern Club at yesterday's open day, courageous in the knowledge that Mr and Mrs Harold Wilson and their son, Giles, had made it safe for respectability at the official reopening on Saturday.

JOHN O'CALLAGHAN

Courtesy of Mersey Beat/Bill Harry

Royal Albert Hall Before the event, the poet and musician Pete Brown brought him to Liverpool, where Ginsberg proclaimed, "Liverpool is at the present moment the centre of the consciousness of the human universe." Not terribly profound as almost everybody knew that, and Ginsberg had made similar claims for Milwaukee and Baltimore. Maybe he said it everywhere on the grounds that one day he would be right. After visiting the Cavern, he said he was struck by "the beautiful boys with golden archangelic hair." He wrote home, "I spent all week in Liverpool and heard all the new rock bands and had a ball with the long-hair boys—it's like San Francisco except the weather is greyer."

Pete Brown[676]: "I took Allen Ginsberg to Newcastle and to Liverpool, and in Liverpool he was mostly interested in chasing young boys. We did go to the Sink where the Clayton Squares played. Allen did say that the Beatles were going to change the world, and I said, 'No, they're not that good.' I was into modern jazz at the time and was very entrenched in it. Of course he was completely right: he felt those tremors and so he was prophetic. Liverpool was incredible then: it was like a magic city and those manifestations were just part of it. There was nothing like it anywhere else and there never will be. Although people compared it to San Francisco, this was much nicer as it had to do with people getting in touch with each other and breaking down barriers of class and culture."

Wednesday 2 June 1965
The VIPs (later Spooky Tooth)

Tuesday 8 June 1965
The Soul Sisters, Steampacket (Brian Auger, Rod Stewart, Julie Driscoll, Long John Baldry) and the Hideaways. **Mike McCartney**[677]: "I saw Long John Baldry in Steampacket. I invited them back to Heswall but I said, 'You will have to keep quiet as my dad has just got married and he has his wife, her daughter and her mother there. Come back but keep quiet.' They said, 'Great, okay.' There was John Baldry, Julie Driscoll, Brian Auger and this very quiet, young singer, Rod Stewart, oh, and also a young gentleman called Freddie Starr. We got into the lounge, quiet, sssh. Freddie Starr saw the velvet curtains at the end of the lounge and he thought, 'Right, I am going to do a striptease.' John said that he would play piano. He

said, 'Don't worry, Mike, I shall keep the lid shut, and he goes 'Da, da, da, da, da', that is, David Rose's 'The Stripper'. Freddie is opening his own curtains doing his striptease, and at the end he jumps out in his undies. We burst out laughing and it woke the whole house and we all had bacon butties at two in the morning."

Friday 11 June 1965
Kris Ryan and the Questions, Hideaways, Georgians.

Friday 18 June 1965
Dave Dee, Dozy, Beaky, Mick and Tich, plus Richmond Group and Dekkas

Wednesday 23 June 1965
Earl Preston's Realms, Fritz and Startz. **Earl Preston**[678] with the Realms: "Long John Baldry came in one night when he wasn't billed to appear. I was backed by the Realms who had sax and organ and they were a very good group. He asked if he could get up and sing and he took over—he did the whole show. I didn't mind. In fact, we were knocked out that he liked us so much that he wanted to stay on."

Saturday 26 June 1965
Johnny Gus Set, Blues Angels, Dimensions, Earl Preston's Realms

The Cavern was in trouble. Their telephone has been disconnected by the GPO and a builder has obtained a writ against them for unpaid work. Ray McFall told the *Daily Mail*, "This kind of thing is enough to start a stampede among creditors. As far as I am concerned, everyone is snarling, hungry for information. They want to announce the death of beat. It seems to me that I am being singled out."

Monday 12 July 1965
Geno Washington and the Ram Jam Band, Richmond Group, Exit

In a feature in the *Liverpool Weekly News*, Ray McFall insists that the Cavern is a viable proposition but he has made some mistakes including pouring £10,000 into the *Mersey Beat* newspaper to keep it going.

Friday 16 July 1965
The Four Just Men, the Pretenders and Tiffany's Thoughts

Tuesday 20 July 1965

Coming from London, The Thee. Nothing new about The The then.

Saturday 24 July 1965

All night session with Steampacket (Brian Auger, Julie Driscoll, Long John Baldry and Rod Stewart) and Seftons, Richmond Group, Exit, Clayton Squares, Hideaways and Tarantulas.

Monday 26 July 1965

Phew! A 24-act benefit show for the Cavern from noon to midnight with Steve Aldo, Blue Secrets, Boomerangs, Clayton Squares, Connoisseurs, Cresters, Dimensions, Escorts, Five Aces, Hideaways, Hobos, Lancastrians, Manchester Playboys, Masterminds, Measles, Power House Six, Earl Preston's Realms, Richmond Group, Kris Ryan and the Questions, Scaffold, Spinners, Undertakers, Hank Walters and the Dusty Road Ramblers and the Warriors. The groups waived their fees and the session raised £400.

Friday 30 July 1965

The Spencer Davis Group with Clayton Squares and Richmond Group. John Peel went to the Cavern for the first time and was impressed by the Richmond Group as well as a young Stevie Winwood. **Kenny Parry**[679]: "Stevie Winwood was jumping between piano and guitar and he was so young and so talented. He had listened to blues records and he had a black voice and he played great piano, but all the band was good. I copped off with my wife that night. I wanted to chat her up but couldn't think of anything to say so I offered her a Polo."

Sunday 8 August 1965

An unlikely pairing—Dave Dee, Dozy, Beaky, Mick and Tich, supported by Alexis Korner's R&B Band

Saturday 14 August 1965

An all night session with Earl Preston's Realms, Steve Aldo, Hideaways, Bumblies, Dimensions, Richmond Group, Masterminds and, having split from the Roadrunners, the Mike Hart group

Friday 20 August 1965

Clayton Squares, Easybeats and country/rock band, the Hillsiders

Sunday 22 August 1965

The Nashville Teens, Black Knights, Hideaways

Ken Gilmore[680] of the Dark Ages: "We played a few times at the Cavern and at some point Bob had a little office upstairs. We walked in and Bob put his finger up and said, 'Ah, Ken, Dark Ages, I am sending you to Carlisle and you are on with the Kinks.' We used to do four or five Kinks' songs so we needed an emergency rehearsal to sort out the act. We got £5.10s for playing the Cavern as a three piece, so if you went out and got an LP, you didn't learn one song but three or four songs. We went to the Cosmopolitan Club in Carlisle and we did a Saturday and Sunday for £25 and we had to find somewhere to stay. We did the job with the Kinks. Ray Davies asked me how many were in the band. I said, 'Only the three of us.' He said, 'Only Scousers would do that', meaning that we had a lot of bottle as we were down to bare bones. We wore what we stood up in but they had hair-driers and were getting ready to go on. There was another band on who knew the Kinks and they had a chip on their shoulder about them. 'Oh, the Kinks aren't very good, and all that.'" The Dark Ages returned to Carlisle in the winter and the problems of having a van with no heater kicked in, not to mention an oil leak. "I'd got a five gallon drum and we had to top it up while we were still on the move so that it wouldn't seize up," says Ken.

Monday 30 August 1965

Eight hour session with Fourmost, Silkie, Hideaways, Clayton Squares, Masterminds, Richmond Group, Aztecs and Aarons

Friday 3 September 1965

Action, Masterminds and Fritz, Mike and Mo (that is, the Four Pennies minus one)

Saturday 11 September 1965

Gary Farr and the T-Bones, Clayton Squares, Dark Ages, Hideaways, Masterminds, Richmond Group, Tabs and Scottish band, the Resistance. **Norman Killon**[681]: "Gary Farr was the son of the boxer, Tommy Farr, and he was a very good harmonica player as well as a vocalist. I couldn't get in that night but I was outside the Cavern listening to what I could hear."

Tuesday 14 September 1965

A standard night for the Clayton Squares and the Hideaways or so they think: there in the audience is a young folk singer touring the area but with a night off, Paul Simon.

Sunday 26 September 1965

Four Blues, Richmond Group and Crescendos. **Glenn MacRae**[682] of the Canadian band, the Crescendos: "We came over stone cold and we didn't know a soul. We landed on the Liverpool docks and all our equipment and our luggage was dumped on the side. We hailed a taxi and the driver took us to a bed and breakfast. The Cavern was where it was all happening and so that was the first place that we had to visit. We befriended a group that was playing there that night, the Easybeats. They were excited about meeting musicians from Canada. They were an absolutely fabulous group, a Beach Boys group, and they became good mates of ours and helped us immensely. For the first five or six months that we were there, we hooked up with a taxi driver named Brian Kelly and he and his father in law were would-be impresarios and wanted to market us. We wound up playing a lot of working men's clubs, fairly low key venues, murky clubs with bingo, and it wasn't getting us into the mainstream. We were disappointed about that and we thought that we were wasting our time as they were dives but in retrospect it was a good taste for us of what it was like for the up and coming groups. We did our time doing that before we were able to get into the Cavern."

So what happened when they first played? **Glenn MacRae**[683]: "It was an unbelievable feeling. We had a number of friends in the groups by then. The musical community was so helpful to each other that it was an eye-opener. In Canada it had been very competitive. Everyone wanted to steal gigs from each other. We persuaded Bob Wooler to give us a chance and the Easybeats and others came down. It was wonderful. We felt that if we all died the next day, we had at least accomplished our dream of playing the Cavern. We played again after that and it was always an exhilarating experience."

Friday 1 October 1965

The Silkie, the Richmond Group and the Hideaways. **Mike Ramsden**[684] of the Silkie: "We had been formed at Hull University and our bass player came from Liverpool, which is how we came to be at the Cavern. We did make a demo

tape in their studios. We were playing the Cavern with the Spinners and a guy from Fontana offered us a contract. When we went to London, we called in at Brian Epstein's flat and he signed us up. The first single was 'Blood Red River' and then 'You've Got To Hide Your Love Away' was a hit. John phoned Eppy after the session to tell him it was a Number One." The Hideaways would perform the song at the Cavern as "You've Got To Love Your Hideaway".

Saturday 9 October 1965

An all night session with Cliff Bennett and the Rebel Rousers, David John and the Mood, Clayton Squares, Hideaways, Roadrunners, Blues Angels, Richmond Group and the Klubs. The contract asked Bennett and his band to arrive at midnight for a 45 minute spot: payment £70. The five Klubs received £4 between them: enough for fish and chips on the way home.

The Klubs, sometimes known as the Wild, Wild Klubs, came from Birkenhead and they had been formed for a TV discovery programme in the Isle of Man which they won in September 1965. They were signed to Cavern Enterprises and played the Cavern regularly as well as some key London clubs. The long-haired boogie boys are way ahead of the game, wearing make-up and dresses long before David Bowie and Glam Rock, and organising primitive but effective light shows. They did record some demos for Decca, but by then, record companies were wary of Liverpool bands.

Dave Donnelly[685]: "I saw the Klubs about six times and they were very different from other bands I used to see. They used Triumph amplifiers which were a forerunner of the transistorised amps of the late sixties. They were very tall amps though and they had lights on the top, which were very impressive. They had long hair and a guitarist who looked like Ray Dorset and ran amok with a tin of talcum powder."

Alan Devon[686] of Solomon's Mines: "The Klubs were great on stage. Their lead singer looked like the guy from the Pretty Things and they wore make-up and they said, 'This is what we're about and we don't give a monkey's.' It was heavy music for its time and they could produce the goods."

Saturday 16 October 1965

Gideon's Few from Yorkshire, Earl Royce and the Olympics, Hideaways, Masterminds, Du Fay, Notions and then, attempting a world record for non-stop playing, the Merseybeats. **Billy Kinsley**[687]: "We wanted to play for 12 hours non-stop as a publicity thing, but we had a previous gig in Bridlington and we did that first. We started at the Cavern at about 5am and did about eight hours before our drummer John Banks collapsed from exhaustion. We went on for another half-hour with just the three of us. There were people who had been at the Cavern the night before, had gone for a good night's sleep and then returned to watch us finish. It was a nice party atmosphere as they were cheering us on, and I think we would have done the 12 hours if John had taken it easy and we had been more relaxed."

Sunday 17 October 1965

Wynder K. Frog with the Easybeats and the Dresdens

Wednesday 20 October 1965

A full day for Ben E. King—Granada's *Scene At 6.30*, the Cavern and an unscheduled appearance at the Blue Angel. He performed both his solo hits and the ones with the Drifters. **Frankie Connor**[688]: "Ben E. King arrived wearing a white mac which I thought looked very cool. We got to back him later in the evening at the Blue Angel."

David Crosby[689]: "Seeing almost any American artist was a dream in the sixties and especially as close up as this. Ben E. King had a wonderful baritone voice and I loved it when he hit the low notes."

Billy Butler[690]: "Ben E. King would put his hands out over the stage but he was very aware that the girls who were holding his hand might just be after the ring with his initials on it. They couldn't see him at the back and so he stood on a box to finish his act. Colin Areethy harmonized with him on one song. After the show, Ben went to the Blue Angel and he did an hour on stage for Allan Williams for nothing, which didn't make Bob Wooler very happy."

Bob Wooler[691]: "I remember taking Ben E. King to the Blue Angel after the Cavern session at 11.30pm, and I left him at the bar as I had a Cavern lunchtime the next day. I learnt the next day that Ben had thoroughly enjoyed himself at the Blue Angel and even sung there. I was furious about this—we had paid him £120 to play at the Cavern and there he was playing for Allan Williams for nothing. Allan Williams said, 'Well, I didn't charge him to come in.'"

Colin Areethy[692]: "I was in the In Crowd, which had been called the Casuals. We played the Cavern with Ben E. King and we did 'Amor' in our act. Ben stood there watching me from the side—he looked very cool in sunglasses and a white mac with the collar turned up, and we became good friends."

Ben E. King told *Record Mirror*: "Now I know how the Beatles feel. In all my years of singing, I've only ever been afraid of fainting twice, and that was one of them." **Joey Molland**[693]: "I saw Ben E. King at both the Cavern and the Blue that night and he was great. I've still got the autographed photograph he gave me."

Wednesday 27 October 1965

Two guitars worth £350 together were stolen from the Cavern, and they were sold to two youths for £20 each. The purchasers thought that they might be stolen property and took them to the police. The sixteen-year-old responsible was sent to Borstal and told that he must have training in citizenship.

Sunday 31 October 1965

The Who, supported by the Aztecs and the Big Three. Richie Routledge of the Aztecs was also part of the Bumblies, who had just changed their name to the Cryin' Shames. **Bob McGrae**[694]: "The Who were louder than the other groups and had a lot of speakers. Pete Townshend would break his guitars on stage, but he would have special ones made for that. He made a mistake at the Cavern and someone destroyed his best guitar. He was in a right temper backstage."

Bob Wooler[695]: "I felt that the Who didn't put a lot of effort into their performance that night. You know, 'We're not going to be in awe because this place was the launching pad for the Beatles.'"

Earl Preston[696]: "The Who were on with the Big Three, and the Big Three blew them away. They were far superior. The Who didn't have the right sound. Keith Moon was a very good drummer technically but the Liverpool drummers relied heavily on their bass drums. As a result, the

Who lacked the driving rhythm that the Liverpool groups had."

Saturday 6 November 1965

Was it a good news week for Hedgehoppers Anonymous? "Even by then the Cavern has a mystical aura about it," says **Billy Butler**[697], "because the Beatles had come from there and Hedgehoppers Anonymous were terrified to be in the Cavern. They thought they would go down badly but they did okay as they had excellent harmonies."

The all night session also included the Fourmost, Almost Blues, the Verbs, the Drifting Sands, the Richmond Group, the Dresdens, the Harpos, the Masterminds and the Baskerville Hounds. **Mike Haralambos**[698] of Almost Blues: "We were a five piece band and we only wanted to do original blues material: we didn't want to rock them up like the Yardbirds. We were unique on Merseyside in that respect. We found that it was the white kids who liked our music as the black kids didn't regard it as their heritage and thought of it as Uncle Tom music."

Saturday 13 November 1965

All night session with John Lee Hooker, Earl Preston's Realms, Rory Storm and the Hurricanes, Earl Royce and the Olympics, the Escorts, the Crescendos, the Dimensions, the Sect, the Hideaways and the Big Three.

Sunday 14 November 1965

Earl Royce and the Olympics, plus a Cavern debut for the Bootleggers. **Dave Howard**[699] of the Bootleggers: "We copied most of the Roadrunners' set and one night when we opened for them at Hope Hall, one of them said, 'That was excellent, just like us, only in tune.' We achieved our ambition of playing the Cavern in November 1965, and it was an audition for Bob Wooler. We had to tune to the saxophone as it had a reed on it that was variable depending on how it was put in and the temperature. We did R&B, Little Richard and Slim Harpo songs and we were told that we had passed the audition. The drummer who did the bookings for us said that we were not coming back for £6.10s. Bob refused to pay more. We had done it once and achieved our ambition."

Friday 19 November 1965

Spencer Davis Group, the Fix, and from Manchester, the Cymerons

During the day, the Health Committee on Liverpool City Council discussed the Cavern. A routine inspection discovered that toilets were connected to a catchpit acting as a cesspool in violation of the Public Health Act, 1936. Ray McFall was unaware that the toilets were not connected to the sewers. Statutory notice was served on him to provide adequate toilet accommodation and satisfactory means of drainage. The cost was estimated at £3,500 and McFall, lacking the resources, wanted the Health Committee to implement the work, which he would pay back over time. He pointed out that he had already enacted the previous requirement which was to install a fire escape a year earlier. However, that £4,000 bill was largely unpaid.

The original drainage system was designed only for drawing water from melting ice in the cold store. The toilets were installed by the Ministry of Food in 1948/9 and had been connected to the existing drainage system. The cost of reconstruction was high because the toilets were below the level of the sewers. As these problems had been revealed at a routine inspection, how come that they weren't spotted before the Cavern opened? Incompetence methinks, and in retrospect, perhaps Ray McFall could have issued a counterclaim against the Council and possibly won the day.

In any event, the Committee was not prepared to carry out the work. Ray McFall said that he would sell the club. The *Liverpool Daily Post* suggested that the Beatles should pay for the improvements.

Saturday 20 November 1965

Wilson Pickett with the Tony Colton Big Boss Band, Earl Preston's Realms, Almost Blues, Hideaways, Verbs, Richmond Group and Tiffany's Thoughts. **Billy Butler**[700]: "There isn't a lot to say about Wilson Pickett and Stevie Wonder and some of the soul stars who played the Cavern. They were doing a double with the Twisted Wheel in Manchester and they were always backed by good musicians. They would usually be on early here and we would get them in and out as quickly as possible: it wasn't a problem as we had the back entrance by then. Wilson Pickett certainly made an impression. He could scream as well as he could on the records."

Al Peters[701] of the Almost Blues; "Wilson Pickett wanted more horns behind him and so he asked our sax man, Tommy Huskey, to play a certain riff. He was happy with the results and Tommy joined him on stage." Tony Colton's song, "I Stand Accused", had just been recorded by the Merseybeats.

Saturday 27 November 1965

Steve Day's Kinsmen (the return of Wump!), the Secrets and the Principals

Saturday 4 December 1965

An all night session with Georgie Fame and the Blue Flames, Masterminds, Cryin' Shames, Richmond Group, Hideaways, Big Three, Cordes, Crescendos and Earl Preston's Realms.

The Beatles played the Liverpool Empire on 5 December 1965 on what was to be their last Liverpool appearance. **Bob Wooler**[702]: "The Beatles were accosted by the press when they were playing the Liverpool Empire. They had just done *Help!* but they weren't giving any. The press was asking punchy questions such as 'The Cavern is on the ropes, so what are you going to do about it?' They said they couldn't help out but they could have done, they were rolling in cash. The key is in something John Lennon said. He said, 'We owe nothing to the Cavern. We've done them a favour and made them famous.' You can't argue with that, but where was their generosity? It would only have been £2,000 a Beatle." Paul McCartney commented, "If the city council looked upon it as a tourist attraction instead of just an old warehouse, I'm sure that something could be done about it."

Saturday 11 December 1965

The Dark Ages appeared at the Cavern for £5.10s. I doubt that the Aztecs or the Detonators were getting much more and possibly Earl Royce and the Olympics merited £15: in other words, a complete evening's entertainment could be booked for £30. How come the Cavern wasn't making money?

Wednesday 15 December 1965

The Rector of Liverpool, Edwyn Young, held his second carol concert in the Cavern using the Signs and the Klubs. Bob Wooler read the lesson. "Grown-ups will be just as welcome as the youngsters," said the Rector, "last year 'Silent

Night' most definitely wasn't but they put across 'The Holly And The Ivy' as beautifully as I've ever heard it played."

Friday 17 December 1965

All night session with Zoot Money's Big Roll Band, the Hickory Six, the Richmond Group, the Hideaways, the Kirkbys, Earl Preston's Realms, Earl Royce and the Olympics, Paul Williams, the Fix and the Sect. **Andy Summers**[703] was part of the Big Roll Band: "We had a very tight, slick rehearsed show and we played every night of the week. We were thrilled to play the Cavern and I can remember walking in there and thinking, 'Blimey, this is incredible, this is where the Beatles started.' The truth is though, it was just a club like anywhere else. It was what the Beatles did in there that made it special."

Sunday 26 December 1965

Nine hour session hosted by DJ, Billy Butler and with Big Three, Escorts, Earl Preston's Realms, Hideaways, Fix, Masterminds and Richmond Group.

Tuesday 4 January 1966

The Alan Price Set, the Fix and the Power House Six

Saturday 15 January 1966

An all night session with the Exciters (US group who did original of 'Do Wah Diddy Diddy'), Freddie Starr and the Delmonts, the Almost Blues, the Dresdens, the Fix, the Masterminds, the Calderstones, the Cryin' Shames and the League Of Gentlemen (with Robert Fripp on guitar). **Kenny Parry**[704]: "I was eighteen years old and I saw the Exciters. The two girls wore skin-tight silk dresses and they were shapely girls. They danced and they sang and the harmonies were great and the backing band was good. I was watching from the side and one of the dresses started to split and it was one of the best shows I've ever seen."

Bob Wooler[705]: "Ironically, I view the end of Merseybeat with a record called 'Please Stay'. 'Please Stay' was a Burt Bacharach and Bob Hilliard song that had originally been recorded by the Drifters. Zoot Money covered it but his version didn't take off. The record producer, Joe Meek, excelled himself by copying Zoot's arrangement and making an excellent record with the Cryin' Shames. The Cryin' Shames released 'Please Stay' in 1966 and so I take the span of Merseybeat as being the decade from 1957 to 1966. The Cryin' Shames were the last of the squeal and scream groups. Paul Crane had a very winning 'little boy lost' personality, ideal to be mothered by the girls. It was a cryin' shame that the Cryin' Shames came apart at the seams."

Thursday 20 January 1966

Lee Dorsey, Crew, Fix, Earl Preston's Realms. **Al Peters**[706]: "I don't think that Lee Dorsey was making much money. When he finished his UK tour, he went back to working as a car mechanic in the US."

Liverpool City Council asked the Health Committee to reopen the matter of loaning the money to fix the Cavern's toilets. They again said no, and again in February.

Saturday 22 January 1966

Karl Terry and the TTs, Almost Blues, Roadrunners

Sunday 23 January 1966

Starting in the afternoon and going through the evening with 16-year-old Little Stevie Wonder, Aztecs, Sidewinders, Almost Blues, Cryin' Shames, Earl Preston's Realms, Fix, Richmond Group and Hideaways.

Al Peters[707] of the Almost Blues: "I remember the girls shouting, 'Are you really blind?' and of course he was. His MD stood him in the middle of the dressing room and got him ready for the stage. He played drums, piano and harmonica and he was absolutely wonderful, especially when he did 'Fingertips'."

Colin Areethy[708]: "Stevie Wonder wore an awful red suit and it only fit him where it touched. His MD, Clarence Paul, had boss gear and he was only playing the tambourine. I thought, 'There's something wrong there', but Stevie himself was tremendous."

Bob McGrae[709]: "Little Stevie Wonder was tall for his age and he was swinging his head back and forth and to and fro. He didn't realise that the roof was curved and he caught it on the wall."

Sugar Deen[710]: "Colin Areety and I went to the Cavern when Stevie Wonder was on. We wanted to be there early so that we could sit at the front. We knew all his songs and when he got going, I said, 'I can't contain myself, man, I'm going on

that stage.' Colin said, 'I'm with you, man.' We snatched the mike away from his guitarist and did some harmonies. Bob Wooler came out and said, 'No, no, no, get off the stage', but Stevie Wonder said, 'No, that's cool, man, that's all right.' We stayed on for four songs and it was brilliant."

Saturday 29 January 1966

An all night session with the Drifters, Earl Preston's Realms, Plain and Fancy, Aztecs, Richmond Group, Fix, Sect, Trendsetters and Hideaways. The Drifters played the Victory Memorial Hall in Northwich, then the Jigsaw in Manchester and ended up at the Cavern's all night session. They were Gerhart Thrasher, Bobby Hendricks, Bobby Lee Hollis and Bill Pinkney, none of whom had been on the Drifters' recent hits. They performed "Up On The Roof", "On Broadway", "Stand By Me", "Only You", "The Night Time Is The Right Time", "If I Had A Hammer" and "Shout". **Bob McGrae**[711]: "Billy Butler and I had to find the money to pay the Drifters as the Cavern was bankrupt. Billy and I really wanted to see them and we took the money from the takings on the night, but it was touch and go."

Wednesday 2 February 1966

(lunchtime) Comedian Mike Donohue, supported by Plain and Fancy
(evening) Plain and Fancy, Hideaways

Sunday 5 February 1966

Mock, yeah, In, yeah, Bird, yeah—have you heard that Inez and Charlie Foxx played the Cavern?

Monday 7 February 1966

A knight to remember—Bluesology with Elton John, Doris Troy, The Fix and Earl Preston's Realms. Asked many years later about the Cavern, Sir Elt can only remember the drains. **Bob McGrae**[712]: "It was almost the standard thing for the Gents to be overflowing. I remember Rod Stewart complaining about it. And no matter what they did, the Cavern was always full of rats. You could see them scattering if you went close."

Earl Preston[713]: "Two nights with the American artists stand out for me—Ben E. King and Doris Troy—and in both cases it was the sheer brilliance of their voices. Two great shows."

Tuesday 8 February 1966

Disco night with Bob Wooler, Bob McGrae and doorman Pat Delaney as DJs

Saturday 12 February 1966

An all night session with Fortunes, Fix, New-towns, Hideaways, Dresdens, Richmond Group and Solomon's Mines. **Alan Devon**[714] of Solomon's Mines: "We took our name from the film with Stewart Granger. We had looked at birds' names like the Ospreys and warlike figures like Zeus. We thought Solomon's Mines was good as it was not a 'the' name like the Shadows or the Beatles. We told everybody that we were playing at the Cavern but it was an all-nighter and we weren't on til 3am."

Thelma Hargrove[715]: "At 4 o'clock in the morning, Ray McFall told me that I had done enough. It was seven until seven for an all-nighter and working in all that heat. He took me to a café in Dale Street and he told me that the Cavern was due to close down. He was broken up. He was a marvellous boss. I know he was a blooming fool. I was a bit older than him and I had my head screwed on a bit more."

Saturday 26 February 1966

The Mersey Boys, the Dresdens and the Crescendos

Sunday 27 February 1966

Rory Storm and the Hurricanes, the Big Three, the Cryin' Shames, the Kwans, the Rekords, the Richmond Group, the Dark Ages, the Sect, the Hideaways, Rigg, the Runaways, Earl Preston's Realms and the Pro-tems. **Billy Butler**[716]: "We were told on the Sunday night by Ray McFall that this was going to be the club's last session. My first thought was that we can't shut without a fanfare and Chris Wharton, who was a partner of mine at the time, and myself went round the Liverpool clubs and said that the Cavern was shutting, 'If you want to come down and play, this could be your last chance.' The momentum built up and about half-past eleven, I said, 'Let's block the stairway with chairs and stay here as long as we can, and anyone who wants to leave can go down the side alley. The bailiffs came at nine in the morning and couldn't get in. I went down the alley and went to work at one o'clock because I was working during the day, and, as far as my boss knew, I was at Gladstone Dock doing customs work. I phoned up a few mates, did a little bit to show I'd been there, and then went back to the Cavern, but by then the bailiffs were in."

Bob Wooler[717]: "Ray McFall had been expecting the bailiffs and it happened on Monday morning, 28 February 1966. He had been told that this time it was for keeps, and the groups played there from three o'clock on Sunday afternoon to eight o'clock on Monday morning. They played the whole night through for free, but to no avail. The Cavernites barricaded the stairs with chairs but they were soon cleared away and if you see photographs, they are either bewildered or laughing: they are not crying."

One of the groups at that final session was Rory Storm and the Hurricanes. **Jimmy Tushingham**[718] recalls, "As soon as we had finished our show, Rory went up to Bob Wooler and said, 'Have you got the money, Bob?' He said, 'I'll get it for you.' Next minute chairs and tables had been stacked at the bottom of the stairs and nobody could get in or out. Ray McFall had gone bust and we were one of the creditors trying to obtain our £15. We never got it."

He should have asked **Thelma Hargrove**[719]. "Chris Kelly who was Paddy's brother in law and Bob McGrae walked us out. They took us into the office. Ray said the kids could have anything. Bob McGrae had the money from the night and he had put it in the safe. He gave me a briefcase and asked me to keep any of the takings that I hadn't given to him earlier. He told me to pay the bar staff and cloakroom girls as the Receiver would take it off us otherwise. And that's what I did."

The bands played all night and continued into the morning. Ray McFall went to Liverpool County Court where a receiving order in bankruptcy was made against him. The bailiffs then went to the Cavern where 100 teenagers had locked themselves in. Ray McFall went to Mathew Street and spoke to Paddy Delaney, who was in the street, and told Paddy that they must not resist the police. Paddy went in through the fire escape. The music continued with the Cryin' Shames' 'Please Stay' lending an additional poignancy.

The police arrived with their dogs at 1pm and although the teenagers were singing 'We Shall Not Be Moved', they left peacefully, assembled themselves together and marched to the Town Hall carrying a banner. The club's doorman,

Paddy Delaney[720]: "We let the police in when they arrived and the kids were escorted outside. I was kept back because the kids felt I should be the last one to leave. I made my way out of the Cavern into Mathew Street and that was it: the Cavern was officially closed."

Ray McFall[721]: "I had nothing to do with the siege. I was outside looking like a bloody undertaker. I went down in the morning and I was dressed immaculately in black"

Ken Gilmore[722]: "Vinny and I were hoping that there were no TV cameras capturing us as we were supposed to be in work."

Kenny Parry[723], then with the blues band, the Rigg: "When the bailiffs came in, we sneaked out round the back. We were carrying Ozzie Yue down Mathew Street on our shoulders. We went to St George's Hall and we had our placards saying 'Save the Cavern' and there was a march on the other side with protestors saying 'Close the Cavern'."

The final group to play at the Cavern, that is, the group that was playing when the bailiffs were allowed in, was the Hideaways. In March, John Donaldson, their eighteen-year-old leader, was elected chairman of a Cavern Cooperative of beat groups and fans to save the club. A strange piece in the *Liverpool Echo*: Jimmy Savile contributes £1 and invites all the Caverngoers to buy shares at £1 each. One of Bob Wooler's ideas: don't think this would impress the *Dragons' Den* but the Lord Mayor of Liverpool, David Cowley, lent his support. Bob Wooler signed up some "quid kids" at a dance at the Hoylake YMCA. Cilla Black said that she was very sorry to see the club go, but as she was buying a new Rolls-Royce at the time, it gave out a confused message.

On Saturday March 5, beat fans assembled at St George's Plateau with banners and placards and marched to Mathew Street . **Billy Butler**[724] was the organiser. "I remember us all walking up Lord Street singing 'Still I'm Sad', the Yardbirds' song which was popular at the time, and we laid a wreath over the Cavern's doorway. Everyone got down on their knees for a minute's silence and that wreath stayed over the doorway until the flowers died. A few weeks later we handed a petition to Harold Wilson at Lime Street Station, and this led to him reopening the Cavern." The

papers reported that Harold Wilson was met by 500 teenagers who gave him the names of 5,000 youngsters who wanted his help in re-opening the club.

An American youth leader, Frank Patrick, was keen to purchase the club: he had a string of Daniel's Den clubs in the US. Bessie Braddock made an appeal to show business personalities and music publishers in the hope that the Cavern could be reopened. The former bandleader Bill Gregson, who ran the Royal Tiger Club in Manchester Street and had been a director of the Tower Ballroom at New Brighton, said that he was prepared to outbid any offer for the control of the club. None of these projects materialized.

The £1 share appeal did not generate funds and Bessie Braddock announced an all-out drive to raise £15,000, the estimated cost of the lease plus the work on the drains. If sufficient cash was not forthcoming, the money subscribed so far would be refunded, a nightmare scenario if they were £1 donations. Bessie Braddock said, "When I met Harold Wilson in Manchester, he said, 'What is happening about the Cavern?' amidst all his other worries and troubles." Good heavens, there couldn't be a General Election in the offing could there and these events couldn't be related, could they? No, no, no, that's far too cynical but Harold Wilson did agree to reopen the Cavern if the funds were found.

Bob Wooler[725]: "The Cavern was in Bessie Braddock's constituency and she was jumping on the bandwagon by saying she would get the Prime Minister, Harold Wilson, who was also the MP for Huyton, to reopen the club if the necessary work could be done. She was true to her word, and she saw the Cavern as a youth club, which in a way it was. We were selling bits of board from the original Cavern stage and I had an expression culled from the Milk Marketing Board's 'Drinka pinta milka day'. I said, 'Buy a bit of Beatle board'."

Tuesday 5 April 1966

The start of Ray McFall's bankruptcy hearing. With shades of Alan Sytner, we are told that he threw money around 'like confetti'. His debts are around £11,000. The turnover for his tenure was given as £207,000, which seems low to me. **Ray McFall**[726]: "I made a dreadful mistake by not making the Cavern a limited company so that the creditors came after me personally, but it's history and very personal too. My solicitor was surprised that the lease fetched as much as it did. If he had taken a lien on it, he could have defrayed his costs, but instead he had to stand in line with everybody else."

Bessie Braddock's consortium was given until April 14 to put forward an offer. If nothing was forthcoming, the trustees would accept the highest offer. Alderman Harry Livermore said on her behalf, "It has not been possible to raise the required cash. The effort by Mrs Braddock to get the Cavern open quickly and run on proper business lines by an independent board of directors has therefore not proved successful." The good news was that four offers had been received.

Billy Butler[727]: "I would be getting my wages from the Cavern net of tax and when the Cavern closed, I was amazed to get this bill from the Inland Revenue for tax that I owed them. They hadn't paid anything."

6

DO IT AGAIN

Cavern owners:
Joe Davey and Alf Geoghegan
1966-1969

Q: When did Liverpool die musically?
Bob Wooler: It went to seed in the flower power year.
(Melody Maker, 25 August 1973)

On 18 April 1966 the Cavern club was sold by the court receiver after bankruptcy proceedings. The leases on 8, 10 and 12 Mathew Street plus the very name of the club were purchased by Joe Davey of King Street, Wallasey for £5,500. The land was owned by British Rail and rather tellingly, the lease would expire in 1972.

52-year-old Joe Davey was the owner of Joe's Café, which was open through the night and many of the groups would go there for curries and receive a 50% discount and free bread. Early in the Beatles' career, Paul McCartney was there with a girlfriend and Joe didn't know he was in a group. "I should get a discount on the curries," said McCartney when he got the bill, "and you shouldn't have charged me threepence for the bread." I'm sure his girlfriend was well impressed.

The quality of the food was probably the best there was for three in the morning in Liverpool, which isn't saying much. Cy Tucker, a postman by day, delivered mail to a lady in the most rundown house in the most rundown part of Liverpool. She told Tucker that she recognised him. "I don't think so," said Tucker. "Yes, I do," she said, "you're in a group and I'm the cook at Joe's Café."

For the Cavern, Joe Davey brought in a partner, 57-year-old Alf Geoghegan, the man with the most inexplicable name in Liverpool. It was pronounced Gay-gan. He had done well with his butchers' shops—admittedly, losing a couple of fingers in the process—and he had a club act as Alf, the Lightning Cartoonist. He was always asking groups to record his songs, but as they were trite moon and Juners, he found no takers. In effect, Joe and Alf were a more unlikely combination for the management of a beat club than Ray McFall and Bob Wooler.

Joe Davey announced, "We'll be reopening it just as it was before—after we've finished correcting the drains." The Health Committee refused to offer any help with the cost. The new owners gave the club a facelift without destroying the atmosphere and some poor souls did resolve the drainage for the toilets. The toilets were designated "Cave Girls" and "Cave Men", but despite the psychedelic times, the Emergency Exit had not been labelled "Way Out". In the foyer, there was the Fame Frame.

Down the stairs, the Cavern itself was left very much as it was. A café was introduced at street level, capable of serving 200 at a time, but only

Save Our No. 10 Plea By Cavern Fans To Premier

An appeal to save No. 10 will be made to Mr. Wilson when he arrives at Lime Street Station, Liverpool, later to-day, on his way to his adoption meeting at Huyton.

As he steps from the train, three regular young visitors to No. 10—Mathew Street, Liverpool, not Downing Street—will present him with a 3,000-name petition seeking his help in saving the Cavern Club, which closed on Monday.

Arrangements have been made for the deputation to go on to the platform just before the Prime Minister's train is due.

A procession to the station was being led by John Fisher, of 7 Mace Road, Croxteth, and Graham Maitland, of 26 Lovelace Road, Garston.

The petition has been organised by Mr. John Graham and by former Cavern disc jockey, Billy Butler.

Save the Cavern —says travel club chairman

BY A "DAILY POST" LONDON REPORTER

The Beatles have turned Liverpool into a tourist attraction for overseas visitors, Mr Lewis Edwards, a Liverpool magistrate and chairman of Y.T.C., the international travel club, said in London yesterday. The city was now a must for young people visiting Britain.

The Beatles and the Cavern have spread the fame of Liverpool and we have found this has had an effect upon our European tours," said Mr Edwards. "We think it would be a great disaster if the Cavern were closed," he added. "It is a magnet for bringing young people to the city."

Americans, particularly, were coming in increasing numbers.

Hope to bring more than ever

A group from a radio station in Detroit wanted to see the home of the Beatles and beat and arrived with tape recorders to record programmes for transmission over their own network.

Mr Edwards' firm arranged for them to visit the Cavern and some of the streets where the Beatles and their families live.

We hope to bring more people than ever to Liverpool during the coming season." he said.

The Rattles from Germany

Courtesy of Mersey Beat/Bill Harry

SPIKE WEIGHS UP THE CAVERN

Spike Milligan, who is currently appearing in his play 'The Bed Sitting Room' at the Royal Court, was among the guests at a Charity Show at the famous Cavern club last Thursday evening.

The show, which was organised by the Variety Club of Great Britain in conjunction with the Cavern, featured a number of Liverpool beat groups, an Army group from Cyprus called the 'Kingstones' and the very first appearance there of the celebrated Scaffold—John Gorman, Roger McGough and Mike McGear.

The other guests included some of the cast from Spike's play, Valentine Dyall, Bill Kerr and Denise Stafford.

Said Spike: "This is the fourth time that I have been to Liverpool, and my first visit to the Cavern. I have always wanted to look it up, and now that I have, it completely lives up to my expectations.

"I can't say that I am too struck on this beat type of music as I am very fond of modern jazz," he added.

The money collected from the show will be distributed throughout various charities.

THE CAVERN

BRITAIN'S No. 1 BEAT BASEMENT

NOW HAS A NEW 30 MINUTE RADIO PROGRAMME ALL ABOUT ITS

GALS, GUYS, GROOVES AND GROUPS

EACH SUNDAY AT

10-30 p.m. on Radio Luxembourg

"SUNDAY NIGHT AT THE CAVERN"

YOU MUST NOT MISS IT !! Tune in to the trend! TELL YOUR FRIENDS !!

ALL REQUESTS FOR POSSIBLE INCLUSION IN THIS PROGRAMME TO BE SENT TO BOB WOOLER

Lyons showing interest in the Cavern

By a STAFF REPORTER

THE nationwide caterers and confectioners, J. Lyons & Company Ltd., together with pirate Radio London, have shown an interest in acquiring Liverpool's famous Cavern Club.

Wilson may get Cavern petition

If two young Liverpudlians have their way to-day, even the Prime Minister will be drawn into the fight to re-open Liverpool's Cavern club, which was closed down on Monday.

John Fisher, of 7 Mace Road, Croxteth, and Graham Maitland, of 26 Lovelace Road, Garston, are planning to lead a procession this afternoon which will meet Mr Wilson on his arrival at Lime Street Station. They will present a petition, signed by about 3,000 teenagers, pleading with him to use his influence to get the club re-opened.

The petition is being organized by John Graham and the former Cavern disc jockey Billy Butler.

U.S. Conductor Hears Liverpool Sound

Mr. Arthur Fiedler, United States conductor of the Boston Pops, visited the Cavern yesterday to hear the famous Liverpool sound. He is seen here (extreme right) with the Merseybeats on the stage of the

with soft drinks and refreshments. No intoxicants. "That's something we are definitely barring," said Joe. Inspired by Carnaby Street, there was a boutique and a souvenir shop selling Cavern memorabilia. Their closed circuit TV was an innovation: you could see what was happening on stage.

In May, *Punch* published the results of a competition in which readers had been asked for a newspaper report to turn the Cavern into a shrine for teenagers. The results were highly inventive: "Already, many teenagers claim to have seen Visions, but we have now confiscated their Purple Hearts." There was talk of the sacred Starrsticks, the Cilla Chapel and the chamber reserved for Lennon's tomb. A vicar is quoted as saying, "Liverpool churches only opened on Sundays. For the rest of the week, there was just nowhere for the kids to desecrate."

While the Cavern had been out of action, Bob Wooler had been promoting dance hall dates as *Cavern Hits The Road* with the Hideaways, the Big Three, Earl Preston's Realms and the Fix, which featured saxophonist Albie Donnelly. On Whit Sunday, May 29, Wooler and Les Lydiate promoted a concert at the Liverpool Empire with two houses featuring Ben E. King, the Mindbenders, the Cryin' Shames, the Hideaways, Tiffany, the Dark Ages and the Thoughts. This was followed by the All Night Beat Boat, an overnight show on the Royal Iris with the Graham Bond ORGANisation, Freddie Starr and the Delmonts, Billy Butler and Blue Angel Go-Go Girls.

Ken Gilmore[728] of the Dark Ages: "Our manager and Bob Wooler put on a show at the Empire called *A Groovy Kind Of Show* with Ben E. King and the Mindbenders. It was our original three piece band. We did two shows, one at 5.40pm and one at 8pm, and after that we were to do the Riverboat Shuffle with Freddie Starr and Graham Bond, who was top of the bill. Fred Hall, our lead guitarist, was very nervous that day, concerned about two houses at the Empire and then the Riverboat Shuffle. One of the girls that followed us round suggested that he took a few tablets and she gave him three Prellies. Fred took them and nothing happened, so he thought, 'I'd better take another three.' Still, nothing happened. Then he took another three and things started to happen. He couldn't keep still and he couldn't shut up. We

did the first house and then the second house and we went down to the Royal Iris and we played twice as it was an all-nighter. We were driving away at 10 in the morning, so we had been on the go since 3.30pm and Vinny and I were dead to the world. Fred is behind the wheel of the old Bedford van and saying, 'Where are we going now?' His dad worked nights. He would come home from work and he would roll a ciggie and he would have it with his breakfast. Fred's dad could talk the leg off anybody except for that particular morning. His dad said to him, 'Are you okay, son? Have you been taking anything?' And he said, 'No, no, of course not.' He didn't shut up for a week but he played wonderfully on Prellies."

Saturday 23 July 1966

The Cavern reopened with three events in one day, but there was almost a disaster. A fuse had blown and the electrician who had put in the fuses had forgotten to label them. Technicians struggled to get enough light into the club, and most of the lighting for the opening ceremony was provided by television lights. Even so, there was a blackout during the opening ceremony during which Ken Dodd said in a loud voice to Bessie Braddock, "Get your hands off my sausage."

Even now, there can't be many beat clubs that have been opened by Prime Ministers, but at noon on 23 July 1966 the Cavern was officially reopened by Harold Wilson. His wife Mary, his son Giles, Bessie Braddock, Ken Dodd and the Lord Mayor of Liverpool were alongside him on the stage. For his trouble, he was presented with a pipe made out of wood from the Cavern's original stage. Harold Wilson, showing his firm grasp of economics, suggested that each group booked by the club should agree to appear annually for the next 25 years for the same fee. Obvious, I suppose, from the man who coined the phrase, "the pound in your pocket". The PM beat a hasty retreat at 1pm: did the wooden pipe even make his car?

Edwina Currie[729]: "I don't think Harold Wilson needed any persuading to reopen the Cavern, either from Bessie Braddock or anyone else. There was a general election in 1964 which he had only just won and another one in 1966 which he had won with a bigger majority. If you ask why politicians do anything, just ask first, 'When's the vote?' Reopening the Cavern also fitted in with Harold Wilson being one of us, a Liverpool MP and a man of the people."

The Cavern had an arrangement with Jimmy Duggan of Radio Caroline North to feature the club and so they broadcast a special on the reopening of the Cavern. This may have been a little embarrassing for the PM, who was trying to shut down the pirate stations.

The local musicians included the Chants, the Fourmost, Tony Jackson, Billy J. Kramer and Scaffold as well as local comic, Johnny Hackett. The Merseybeats' invitation did not arrive in time. The out-of-towners included the Bachelors, Georgie Fame, Dave Dee, Dozy, Beaky, Mick and Tich, Jonathan King and Marty Wilde. There were also the DJs Jimmy Savile and Simon Dee, the boxer Brian London, who was about to fight Muhammad Ali, and members of Liverpool and Everton FC.

The afternoon session featured the Pete Best Combo, the Hideaways, the Signs, the Escorts, the Dark Ages, Georgia's Germs, the Excelles, the Strandmen, the Seftons, the Prowlers, the Dollies, the Tremas and a family group, the Carrolls, with Billy Butler as DJ. Frankie Connor told me how voluptuous the lead singer of the Carrolls was, but **Faith Brown**[730] says, "No, I wasn't. The walls were saturated, the air was smoky and my white clothes became filthy. I looked more like a drowned rat."

The Hideaways played the opening notes and before they started, Bessie Braddock asked them if they knew anything by Bing Crosby. Ozzie Yue replied, "No, we do R&B" and she said, "I like him as well."

Tony Davis[731]: "We only ever did two or three nights as the Spinners at the Cavern, and although we were at the reopening, we didn't perform. I like to think that Harold Wilson was genuinely interested in what the young people were doing and I hope it wasn't just to cash in on the youth market. Bessie Braddock, I am certain, didn't give a damn about opportunism and she was a great woman. She thought that the Cavern was a very important venue for the youth in the area as it wasn't licensed."

The Seftons supposedly had their supporters outside the Cavern as fans carried placards, which

also said, "Where are the Beatles today? We don't need them—Stay in London."

Yianni Tsamplakos[732] of the Seftons: "That was a scam by Allan Williams, who managed us for a while. When he knew that we were playing at the opening of the Cavern, he had these posters done. He got a crowd of people to carry the banners and we got a lot of good promotion."

There was an all night session in the evening with many of the same bands plus the American soul men, Solomon Burke and Rufus Thomas, as well as the Senates, the Dions and the Rockhouse Band. **Geoff Davies**[733]: "I was in and out of the Cavern all day and I used to drink in the Grapes. I was disappointed with Solomon Burke as I felt he was trying too hard to get the audience involved. He had a hit at the time with the Bob Dylan song, 'Maggie's Farm', and I didn't like his version much: well, I resented it really. I was prejudiced. I should have liked him more."

Solomon Burke[734]: "The Cavern was a great place to play. The groove was there, the people were there, and it was wonderful. I remember them selling hot Pepsis. What a mistake—you gotta put ice in those things. Think of how many more they could have sold with ice in them."

Billy Butler[735]: "I vividly remember seeing Solomon Burke in the entrance to the Cavern with his long red robe with white fur and a crown on his head. He was about to appear and Bob McGrae had been told to announce him as 'The King of Rock'n'Soul, Solomon Burke'. Rufus Thomas had come 300 miles from his last gig and his band hadn't made it. A couple of the lads from the Cavern said that they would play for him, and the makeshift band was pretty good. He did 'Jump Back' but he largely entertained us with jokes."

Al Peters[736]: "We were down for a spot about one in the morning. Rufus Thomas was being backed by Georgie Fame and his Blue Flames but they were stuck on the motorway. Vans were forever breaking down in the 60s. Rufus Thomas asked us if we knew 'Walking The Dog'. It was in our repertoire but he did it in E, which was great. He said he would crack a few jokes first and it was like a medicine show in the States. The band did arrive but Rufus had done his set by then. They did something in the early hours of the morning."

Monday 25 July 1966
Billy Butler with a DJ evening, 'The Platter Parade'.

Tuesday 26 July 1966
5am Event, actually our Canadian friends, the Crescendos. **Glenn MacRae**[737]: "We started at the Cavern and then had been in New Brighton and Manchester and we wound up back in Liverpool at the Iron Door at 5am. Chris Curtis was there and he approached us after our set. He was working as an A&R man for Pye Records and he invited us to London for an audition. He wanted us to cover 'Hungry' which was coming out by Paul Revere and the Raiders. He had a vision as to how he wanted us to sound and the record was more his sound than ours. He was trying to shape us into a heavier version of the Searchers. Pye thought the name Crescendos sounded dated and Chris called us the 5am Event because that is when he saw us."

Saturday 30 July 1966
All night session with Pete Best Combo, the Escorts, the Hideaways, the Signs, the Dark Ages, Becket's Kin, Georgia's Germs and at last, a band called the Kop.

Brian Gilmore[738]: "When there was a band on stage, you would set up your kit in the arch ready to go on. This particular night this guy was getting ready to do that and I had set mine up in the band room further down. He was lethargic about it, not really interested, and it was Pete Best. I could sense that he felt he had missed out on everything. He was in another world and it was quite moving. The Pete Best Combo was very good though."

The same names are recurring because it is now estimated that there are now only 100 groups on Merseyside. "Too much HP chasing HP—hire purchase chasing hit parade," said Bob Wooler. "I call it Rock and Dole now, and the biggest crowd some of these musicians will see is at the Labour Exchange."

Sunday 31 July 1966
Local band Carol and the Memories have a CBS recording contract and their single is "Tears On My Pillow". **Carol Loftus**[739]: "They invented a story that I had turned up at the Empire when the Walker Brothers were on, got past the doorman and gave a tape to Gary Leeds. He liked it and said that I reminded him of a little Liver Bird. They were going to follow it up with Gary and I becoming an item but it didn't happen. 'Tears On My Pillow' had been done by Little Anthony and the Imperials and many years later, Kylie Minogue got to it. I prefer the B-side, 'Crying My Eyes Out', which is more like a country ballad and has some of the Walker Brothers sound. I did a lot of songs like 'Love Potion No 9', which should be done by males because I thought the songs for girls were a bit wishy-washy. The only one I remember doing was Kathy Kirby's 'Secret Love' and we whacked that up."

Tuesday 2 August 1966
From London, art school rock from the Creation.

Tuesday 4 August 1966
The Cryin' Shames, Countdowns

Saturday 6 August 1966
All night session with Ike and Tina Turner's backing vocalists, the Ikettes, supported by the Excelles, the Fix, the Dions, the Hideaways, the Kop and the Signs. Several people have told me how Ike and Tina Turner played the Cavern, but they definitely didn't. It was their backing group, the Ikettes, who included P.P. Arnold and made the sassy solo records, "Fine Fine Fine" and "Peaches 'n' Cream". The Ikettes then joined Ike and Tina for a UK tour with the Rolling Stones.

Monday 8 August 1966
The Monday Show with Billy Butler with 100 free tickets for a film show on Wednesday

Tuesday 9 August 1966
Classy harmonies from those Essex boys, Tony Rivers and the Castaways

Wednesday 10 August 1966
Afternoon showing in the Cavern of the concert film from the Santa Monica Civic Auditorium in California, *Gather No Moss*, sometimes called *The TAMI Show*. The performers included Chuck Berry, James Brown, the Rolling Stones and Gerry and the Pacemakers. This had been arranged with the Scala cinema on Lime Street and it continued there throughout the week.

(left)
Scaffold

(left)
Chuck
Berry;
Sweet
Little
Rock'n
'Roller

AT THE CAVERN
To-night — FRIDAY — To-night
SIGNS
KOP & MAJORITY PLUS
MORROW NIGHT SATURDAY 7.30
TYME & MOTION
MULTIVATION
TOP
n't Miss This Big Saturday Show
This SUNDAY — This SUNDAY
KLUBS
BEECHWOODS
KEGMEN
Everybody's Talking About The
Fantastic Monday Night Show
AT THE CAVERN
When The King of Rock'n'Roll
CHUCK BERRY
will make his only Liverpool
appearance on stage about 9 p.m.
THIS YOU MUST NOT MISS!
ADMISSION IS ONLY 10/- FOR
FOUR TOP GROUPS PLUS
THE TRULY FANTASTIC
CHUCK BERRY
mply pay at the door — 7.30 start
PLEASE. PLEASE BE EARLY!
FREE MEMBERSHIP TO
ALL AGED 18 AND OVER
THIS MONDAY FEBRUARY 27
AT THE CAVERN

Mr. Chuck Berry, pop singer from Missouri, holds his young audience captive
number called "Memphis Tennessee."

The Hideaways at the Cavern.

HIDEAWAYS PLAN CAVERN COMPANY

By a "Daily Post" Reporter

The Hideaways, a Liverpool beat group, yesterday joined the Cavern crusaders when they came up with a fresh move to save the famous club.

Their idea is to form a limited company with shares in denominations of £1 which the public are invited to buy. And their appeal for shareholders is not confined to just this country, but goes out all over the world.

These plans were revealed yesterday in the dimly-lit coffee lounge at the Everyman Theatre where the five long-haired group members called a Press conference presided over by their legal adviser Alderman Harry Livermore.

Alderman Livermore said that the company would be called the New Cavern Ltd.

"We are getting in touch with the Official Receiver to ascertain the possibility of acquiring leases of the Cavern and to acquire fixtures and fittings," said Alderman Livermore.

Too young to be directors

"If this can be done then the new company will be formally formed and share certificates will be issued."

Money will be refunded minus a modest sum for bank charges if it was not possible to get the leases, fixtures and fittings.

A board of directors would be formed, although Alderman Livermore stressed that he would not be a member, and Bob Wooler, former Cavern disc jockey, and Bob McGrae, former club manager, would play an important part in running the new Cavern.

John Donaldson, aged 18, of 10 Cockshead Way, Woolton, leader of the group, explained that the five boys had discussed the plan about three months ago when it was realised the Cavern was running into trouble.

He added that none of the Hideaways would be able to sit on the board of directors as they were too young.

MAMMOTH MARATHON
P.M. TO 11 P.M.—EIGHT HOURS
Starring, direct from the U.S.A.
THE VERY FABULOUS
THE VERY SENSATIONAL . .
ALVIN CASH
AND THE CRAWLERS
They're very young and
they're very, very dynamic,
YOU'LL BE SORRY IF YOU MISS 'EM !
ALSO ON STAGE AT THIS
FABULOUS POP PARADE !
THE KLUBS
THE KIDS
THE PRINCIPLES
SOLOMON'S MINES
MAJORITY PLUS
Plus, by overwhelming popular demand,
Special Guest Stars
SIGNS !
ALL THESE FANTASTIC ACTS FOR
YOU, THIS SATURDAY, AT 3 P.M. AT
CAVERN

CAVERN

Edge Hill College Students Union
with
Kirby Fields College Students Union
presents
ZOOT MONEY   THE ORIGINAL DRIFTERS
HERLOCKS ROCKHOUSE   THE FIX
THE KONDA GROUP   THE ALMOST BLUES
Friday June 30th 8-00pm until Saturday July 1st 8-00am
Bar open until later than late
Admission by Ticket only   12/6

Saturday 13 August 1966

The US band, She Trinity, who covered "Yellow Submarine", plus Outrage from Manchester.

Liverpool Daily Post carried a story that a ghost had been seen by the cleaners at the Cavern. He was male and possibly in his twenties. Sounds like someone who had got locked in to me.

Tuesday 16 August 1966

Paul and Ritchie and the Cryin' Shames: bizarre billing as the two front men pushed themselves forward.

Tuesday 23 August 1966

John's Children (but Marc Bolan had not yet joined the band)

Saturday 27 August 1966

A day of legends but nobody knew it. Jimmy Page, Albert Lee and Vic Flick together at the Cavern— backing the pied piper, Crispian St Peters. Also, Ian Anderson took the vocals for John Evans' Smash.

Monday 29 August 1966

Paul and Richie and the Cryin' Shames, Times, Mommie's Darlings (Manchester) and the Iveys (who became Badfinger)

Willy Russell[740]: "When we first saw the Beatles at the Cavern, Tommy Evans and I determined to get guitars and I got a plank with some wire for 19/6d and it would have been better used for cutting cheese. It certainly cut my fingers. I didn't see Tom for about three weeks and he had got something for £2 and was already playing bar chords using all the fingers. It was obvious that he was a naturally gifted guitarist in the way that I would never be. Tom very soon got into playing in a band and I tried to find some kind of role for myself and was an unofficial roadie for a couple of gigs. My young dignity wouldn't allow me to wear that. If I couldn't be really involved, I didn't want to be near it. I pulled away and then I discovered girls. I had left school and I had begun work as a ladies' hairdresser. To all intents and purposes, I was going nowhere in life other than a salon and 50 years of perms and shampoos and sets. Tommy had a group before the Iveys and they played a Christmas gig at Knowsley Village Hall and I went to see them play and my emotions were so tangled. I was fantastically proud that this person I knew was up there on the stage. I was devastated because I could see that Tommy was going places and I wasn't going with him. I was going back to the perm trolley."

Saturday 10 September 1966

All night rave with the Rockin' Vicars, Eddie Cave and the Fix, Mack Sound, Kop, Hideaways, Seftons

Saturday 17 September 1966

All night rave with the UK soul band, Jimmy James and the Vagabonds.

Thursday 22 September 1966

Coming from Leeds, the Dawnbreakers.

Saturday 24 September 1966

All night rave with Neil Christian and the Crusaders—that's nice.

Saturday 1 October 1966

The Mad Lads from the US, the Knack from London, the Iveys, the Bojacs, Chapter Six and the Prowlers

The guitarist from Chapter Six, **Dennis Conroy**[741]: "We were doing a gig with the Iveys and we had done our set. I looked down the tunnel into the audience and I was aware of a red Fender Strat flying through the air behind me and dropping on the floor right next to me. Pete Ham got hold of it, put it across the step and snapped its neck. He was furious and he was telling everyone that it had gone out of tune. I was horrified as I had a guitar that was exactly the same and I thought it was mine, but when I realised it was his, I was relieved. Then his manager asked me if they could borrow my guitar but I said no. I thought he might have smashed mine as well. It wasn't done for effect. It wasn't done in front of the audience: he was just so angry."

Saturday 8 October 1966

All night rave with the Wheels from Belfast.

Thursday 13 October 1966

The Warriors and Look Twice

Saturday 15 October 1966

All night rave with Southport's Rhythm And Blues Inc, Fix, All Night Workers, Klubs, Seftons. The Klubs travelled to gigs in an old Black Maria and they painted flowers and anti-war motifs on the sides.

Sunday 16 October 1966

A 3pm to 11pm marathon with Lee Dorsey, the Dark Ages, the Hideaways and the Gates of Eden.

Tuesday 18 October 1966

Return of the painter men, the Creation with the Hideaways. **Billy Butler**[742]: "The back of the stage had been repainted and they had gone over all the names that had been on it. The Creation used spray paint as part of their act and they painted over the walls. The idea had been that the back of the wall would look smart and it no longer did anymore."

Saturday 22 October 1966

One of the earliest appearances from Roger Chapman's classic rock band, Family.

Tuesday 25 October 1966

Although the Searchers were billed for the night, it never happened.

Saturday 29 October 1966

All night rave with Motown star, Edwin Starr, Steve Aldo and Fix, Prowlers, Impact, Senate, Signs, Times, Talismen and Fix.

Friday 4 November 1966

John's Children (still no Marc Bolan, who never played the Cavern)

Saturday 5 November 1966

All night rave with R&B singer Alvin Robinson ('Down Home Girl'), Herbie Goins and the Night Timers, Hideaways, Prowlers, Quiz And Query, Sect, and Johnny Breeze and the Atlantics.

Wednesday 16 November 1966

Personal appearance from *Top Of The Pops* compère, Samantha Juste.

Saturday 19 November 1966

All night rave with the Original Coasters. Many of the soul acts came from the promoter Roy Tempest, whose first concern was not authenticity. Everybody knew the Drifters and Coasters' records, but few could identify the performers. The Original Drifters' lineup had been suspect but the three Coasters were even more so as only Cornell Gunter had been on any of their records. The other so-called Coasters were Bobby Stegar of the Shields and Nat Wilson. The clowning and highly camp Cornell wore a silver-green pyjama suit with vivid nail polish. He told the audience that he was prettier than both Muhammad Ali and Little Richard. Nat serenaded Cornell with the Temptations' "My Girl".

Paul Nicholls[743]: "I was in a band called the Elcorts and we were a really good band in the sixties. We played Manchester and then we went to the Cavern to be on with the Coasters and we didn't get on until four in the morning. I was sixteen and the place was buzzing and the sweat was dripping off the walls. I met this girl who lived in Anfield and she let the entire band come back to her house for something to eat. Her mum and dad even let us stay there."

Sunday 20 November 1966

Soul singer, Barbara Lynn, who had a US hit with "You'll Lose A Good Thing".

Saturday 26 November 1966

An all night rave—Ben E. King and the Senate, supported by the Joy Strings, Mommie's Darlings (Manchester), Signs And Times, Beechwoods and Reaction. Ben E. King had been on ITV's *Ready, Steady Go!* the night before and he was so taken with the Senate that he wrote and produced a song for them, "Can't Stop". The Joy Strings were a Salvation Army beat group and everyone was waiting for the collection box to come round.

Frank Townsend[744] of the Beechwoods: "In the Easybeats, we were doing the Beach Boys' harmonies with three voices, but in the Beechwoods, we had five singers. Billy Butler was on stage one night and we had an oscillator to get that sound in 'Good Vibrations' and he was delighted about it. Talk about psychedelic as I got it all wrong and it went all over the place. It might have sounded more psychedelic than we intended."

Saturday 3 December 1966

They must be popular as Tony Rivers and the Castaways keep coming back.

Sunday 4 December 1966

It's December but it's sunny with Bobby Hebb, supported by Lynne Randell, Beechwoods, States, Hideaways, and Chapter Five.

Lynne Randell was born in Liverpool in 1950 and her family emigrated to Melbourne. She had her first Australian hit with "I'll Come Running Over" in 1965 and did some UK dates on the strength of that success. She had her biggest hit with 'Ciao Baby' in 1967 (Number Five 5, Australia, Number One, Hawaii) and toured the US with the Monkees. Unfortunately, someone remarked that she looked big in the yellow dress she was wearing for a TV appearance and as a result, she became addicted to slimming pills (effectively, speed). Her amphetamine addiction continued, on and off, for many years but she returned to performing in the 1990s. By 2007, she had had enough, wrote letters and sorted out gifts for her family and friends, and committed suicide.

Saturday 17 December 1966

All night rave with the US singing group, the Orlons ('The Wah-Watusi' and original of 'Don't Throw Your Love Away') plus Normie Rowe, another Australian chart-maker.

Saturday 24 December 1966

Early sixties instrumental group, Peter Jay and the Jaywalkers with the Klubs

Saturday 31 December 1966

Renowned vocal group, the Soul Sisters, noted for 'I Can't Stand It'.

Bob Wooler[745] didn't like talking about the later years, in his case, the years after 1966. "I was a drained person by 1967, a spent force, as the novelist Graham Greene would say, 'a burnt-out case', although that refers to leprosy. I was at the end of my tether, nothing interested me and I was blasé and looking for some new excitement or enchantment. It was not forthcoming at the Cavern as the rock'n'roll years had finished as far as I was concerned. I had pushed Billy Butler forward and Brian Kelly used to say to me, 'Why are you pushing Billy Butler? You should be doing this yourself.'"

Saturday 7 January 1967

Peeps, Principals, Prowlers, Solomon's Mines and All Night Workers

Saturday 14 January 1967

Alvin Cash and the Crawlers supported by Victor Brox and the Brox Band, Solomon's Mines, Tremas, Majority Plus, Klubs and the Pro-tems

Tommy Flude[746] of Solomon's Mines: "We had a fan following, about 30 or 40 girls who followed us around, so even though Victor Brox was the main attraction, we would still have our fans there. We never had a bad night at the Cavern except when we shorted the lights doing a Hen-

drix number. You had to get up close to those Reslo mikes and sometimes you would get a little belt off it. You could sense that there was a break in the electrics. I was meant to be singing 'Excuse me while I kiss the sky' but I sang 'Excuse me while I kiss this guy' and I lent over and kissed the bass player for a laugh. We were both sweaty and we ended up in total darkness. It took half an hour to get the lights back on."

Tuesday 17 January 1967

If you were starting a group, would you think of calling yourself the Dodos? And what's more it's the tenth anniversary of the Cavern. You might say it's a post-modernist joke but post-modernism hadn't been invented.

Sunday 22 January 1967

Alvin Cash, known for his dance records, "It's Twine Time" and "The Philly Freeze".

Solomon's Mines took part in a beat competition organised by a chain of ice rinks. They won the heat at Silver Blades in Liverpool but lost to Mud in the final, who received a recording contract with CBS. However, their hits were a few years off. Solomon's Mines manager had been so confident that his group would win that he had accepted no future bookings as he was sure they could command higher fees. Disillusioned by not winning, the group broke up.

Sunday 29 January 1967

Return of Motown performer, Edwin Starr

As well as Liverpool's St. Louis Checks, there was also St. Louis Union. **C.P. Lee**[747]: "St. Louis Union was a Manchester group who had a hit with 'Girl'. They were with Kennedy Street Enterprises and they split up leaving Kennedy Street with some future bookings. Rather than cancel them a few of us were asked to become St. Louis Union and we had a booking for £50 at the Cavern where, amongst other things, we did a shambolic version of 'Girl'. We were booked for two 45 minutes sets and the person who was running the evening was at the side of the stage with a stopwatch. He said, 'You were tuning up for four minutes. You introduced the numbers for so long and we pay you to sing and not talk, and you had the audience laughing instead of dancing.' He made all these deductions and we ended up with £16."

Thursday 9 February 1967

Country night with the Millers

Sunday 12 February 1967

The Hideaways and Tyme and Motion, plus a light show from Carl King

Monday 27 February 1967

Chuck Berry backed by the Canadians with support from Motivation, the Klubs and the Tremas. Chuck was not happy about having the audience so close to him and so some makeshift bars were put across the stage. **John Seddon**[748], then an advertising executive for Radio Caroline: "When Chuck Berry was at the Cavern, he treated Bob Wooler terribly. He made Bob stand in the rain while he was in the car talking to him."

Bob Wooler[749]: "Chuck Berry appeared at the Cavern in February 1967. I don't know whether it was a massive comedown for him or if he was in a state of going up to Cloud Nine, but he cut dead Kingsize Taylor who had known him from playing in Germany. Kingsize was very, very annoyed. The vibrations were extremely bad so I was glad when Chuck Berry left the band room. He did his act but he only did what was required of him. He wasn't forthcoming like Sonny Boy Williamson or John Lee Hooker, who communicated with the crowds."

Steve Hale[750]: "People were shouting out and passing him notes asking him to do this and that and he ignored them all. He was a very handsome man but he held his head aloof and had this air about him." *Liverpool Weekly News* published a photograph of Chuck Berry on stage with Ray Scragg of the Dennisons at the front of the crowd, mesmerised by his hero.

Billy Butler[751]: "I was at the Mardi Gras the night that Chuck Berry was on at the Cavern. His roadie came and in and said, 'Billy, get me a drink as I might go back and kill him.' Chuck Berry was a difficult man. He wasn't cooperative and his band didn't know what he was going to do next, and there was always the hassle for the money."

The Klubs left some equipment in the Cavern and it was vandalised. Their drummer, Kenny Marshall, was so disheartened that he left the band.

Sunday 12 March 1967

Lee Dorsey supported by Friendly Persuasion, Gale Blues, Hideaways, Signs and the Times, Rogues, Michael Henry Group and the Ox. **Colin Hall**[752]: "My friend Simon and I had been talking to Bob Wooler about a band on the Wirral that we were co-managing called the Ox. We told him that they had a Tamla sound with a bit of the Small Faces about them and he said that they could perform on the same show as Lee Dorsey, but I don't think that he was all that bothered. I didn't realise until later that he had invited them for an audition and so they weren't going to be paid. The band did very well and I was very impressed by Lee Dorsey. He came through the crowd, resplendent in his white suit and jumped up on the stage and did his act. I hadn't seen a soul performer close to before and his energy and his dynamism were mesmerising. Everything was spot on as his band was much sharper than anything I'd seen and he was a showman as well as a great singer. When he finished his act, he jumped off the stage, ran through the club and was gone. The Ox evolved into Hurley's Jinks and I'm pleased to say that both bands have bricks on the Cavern wall."

Sunday 19 March 1967

Return of the Drifters. *Record Mirror* showed a photograph of the group to their former lead singer, Ben E. King, who didn't recognise any of them. They were Herman Coefield, Bobby Rivers, Gary Gant and Bobby Morris, actually the soul group, the Invitations. This kind of thing, sadly, became commonplace. **Bob McGrae**[753]: "Some of our artists came from Don Arden and one of the problems was whether it was going to be the true artist. Someone came in and wondered whom he was going to be that night. He was a young boy and he was meant to be Clarence 'Frogman' Henry. Don Arden told us that it was a mistake and promised faithfully that it would never happen again and how he couldn't understand how it had happened in the first place."

Thursday 23 March 1967

Chris Farlowe and the Thunderbirds, supported by the Fix and the Klubs. Farlowe gave a great show although he had a hacking cough and looked extremely ill. The *Liverpool Echo* ad for the Cavern listed Bo Diddley and Jimi Hendrix as forthcoming attractions. Bo didn't come until 2001 while Hendrix didn't appear at all and it's an unlikely appearance as he is playing the Empire on April 9 (see entry).

EXCLUSIVE How great White House Presidential hope Clinton came to Ringo Starr's rescue

BILL'S BEATLE BUST-UP

THE MAN battling to be the next American President once won another battle — in Liverpool.

For Bill Clinton is revealed today as the man who once saved Ringo Starr from a beating in a city centre pub.

Ex-Cavern Club bouncer Paddy Delaney today studied photographs of White House front-runner Bill and declared:

"His face is definitely familiar."

Paddy believes the young American student he saw saving Ringo from an iron bar attack in the Grapes pub could well have been Clinton.

And excited American newspapers have now sent teams over to Liverpool to investigate the story for themselves.

By Will Rolston   Picture: Martin Birchall

The Democrat hopeful was a young Oxford University student in Britain in 1969 — when the incident happened.

The young American leapt into action when a German nationalist — who complained about the impact the Fab Four were then having on the world — went at Ringo with the iron bar.

Paddy, now 61, recalled how Ringo was in The Grapes, Mathew Street, talking to an American and others when the German came in and shouted: "You've screwed the world."

The German then pulled a metal bar from his sleeve, ready to attack the drummer.

Paddy, who now lives in Netherley, explains: "This American grabbed the German and held him down.

"I know — because I me in at that moment d said: 'I'll take care this.'

"I then took hold of e German and kept m there till the police rived and carted him f."

Paddy recalls the ght clearly.

But he was only told bout the Clinton link hree weeks ago, after n Irishman wrote to wo American papers.

Paddy said today: "It s a long time ago.

"The face is definitely familiar — although he's a lot older now.

"The Irishman who wrote to the papers aying it was Clinton ertainly knew all bout me.

"I remember him — ut I don't know his ame."

Mr Clinton's ampaign office told he Echo they had no formation that their andidate has never set Ringo.

Still Rockin' at
The Cavern
(Above)
The Dark Ages
(Right)
The Klubs

Sunday 26 March 1967

Klubs, Tyme and Motion and a quick return of the Ox.

The Cavern was running into difficulties. The club could be packed at weekends but as there was not much interest during the week, it was hired out for private functions. The shop windows were full of former beat musicians selling equipment at bargain prices.

Thursday 30 March 1967

Scaffold plus the Kingtones, an army group from Cyprus, take part in a charity show for the Variety Club of Great Britain. Spike Milligan, Valentine Dyall and Bill Kerr visit from *The Bed Sitting Room*, which is at the Royal Court. Milligan sings a song for a bottle of Blue Nun. **Bob Packham**[754]: "I joined the army in late '62 and I was there until '68. I played on the Cavern with the army group I had, the Kingtones, from the King's Regiment, which was a north-west regiment, and we did a Variety Club show. The army organised it and we played in uniform. Diana Dors was supposed to come but she didn't, and we backed Spike Milligan. He said, 'Can you play "London Bridge" in C?' and we did that. It was a good gig. We went down very well but we were roasting in our uniforms."

Monday 3 April 1967

A celebrity night in support of Young Christian Workers with footballer Ian St John, MPs, councillors and clergy. A band from the Unity Boys Club, the Fingers, makes its debut at the Cavern and there is also music from the Klubs. A press photo shows three priests at the front of the stage talking while the Klubs are playing so the music can't have been too loud. The evening raises £100. The Cavern is not licensed so the celebs are drinking tea and coffee. This becomes a turning point in the Cavern's history.

Sunday 9 April 1967

Ben E. King and the Senate, supported by Tremas, Klubs and Candy Choir. Jimi Hendrix is supporting the Walker Brothers and Engelbert Humperdinck at the Liverpool Empire. He dedicates *Electric Ladyland* to Joy, an eighteen-year old from Liverpool. He is finished by 9pm and he could theoretically have visited the Cavern.

Norris Easterbrook[755] of the Klubs: "We were on that night at the Cavern. Some of our fans

went to see him at the Empire and came down and told us what he had played, but Hendrix didn't come himself."

Saturday 6 May 1967

Jackie Lomax of the Undertakers is back with a new band, the Lomax Alliance.

c. 17 May 1967

A private party to launch the book, *The Liverpool Scene*, edited by Edward Lucie-Smith, and alcohol is permitted. **Maurice Cockrill**[756]: "The launch of Edward Lucie-Smith's book was held at the Cavern and it was a really big party. It was extremely lavish as they had cases and cases of champagne, which was almost unknown in Liverpool at the time as people drank beer or occasionally spirits. There was endless free champagne and it was a completely drunken affair but very, very happy. When the champagne ran out, the publishers sent out for another 100 bottles, so you can imagine the scale of the thing. It was a terrible evening in some ways as everything went wrong in everybody's personal lives. Relationships were shattered and it was like something from Thomas Hardy as everybody was out of their minds with alcohol. All their inhibitions faded and they would do very rash things. They would leave their wives and go off with somebody else's girlfriend. There were endless stories for days afterwards. It was too much to cope with."

Saturday 10 June 1967

A mixed bag for an all-nighter—Scaffold, Escorts, Merseysippi Jazz Band, Klubs and poet Brian Patten. The Bonzo Dog Band turned up but didn't perform. Their lead singer, Viv Stanshall said that the place smelt and he refused to play despite Alf buying all the Bonzos fish and chips.

The club was shut during July 1967 for improvements, although one of them could be criticised. The premises were licensed when the club reopened on Wednesday 9 August. This created a problem for younger members, and new members had to be over eighteen. **Bob Wooler**[757]: "There was a lot of ballyhoo and hype, but it was a different scene. It became just another club and I hated the way they served the drinks. It wasn't fashionable in those days to drink out of the bottle. The bottle was poured into a plastic container, which could easily give way. You needed both hands on them and I thought how crude it was. It was done because it was safer that way: it stopped people being 'glassed', as they call it."

On 19 August 1967, at the height of the Summer of Love, Bob Wooler and Beryl Adams were married. **Doug Evans**[758]: "It was a marriage of convenience and he didn't seem the marrying type to me. I knew Beryl from the Cavern. She was a very nice girl but highly strung, which meant that they argued endlessly, a bit like himself and Allan Williams."

Wednesday 30 August 1967
All girls admitted free until end of September.

Thursday 31 August 1967
The start of the Search For Talent and the Songwriters Night with the winner to be recorded by Chart Records. Music from the Klubs

Thursday 14 September 1967
Country night with Hillsiders, Ranch Hands, String Dusters and Carl Fenton Trio. **Alex McKechnie**[759]: "I was in the band Carl Fenton Country and we headlined every Saturday night for six months. I was Carl Fenton and I pinched half the name from Shane Fenton and thought Carl was just a cool name. We did country and western, and we also sang 'The Ballad Of John And Yoko' and 'Some Other Guy'."

Thursday 21 September 1967
Country night with the Blue Mountain Boys

On 26 September 1967, Yoko Ono staged a Happening, called *Music Of The Mind*, at the Bluecoat Chambers. **Bob Wooler**[760]: "Jimmy Duggan, who was connected to the pirate station, Radio Caroline North, invited me to a Happening at the Bluecoat. I had read of the Happenings in New York, but the name meant the reverse as nothing really happened, and I was curious about the whole thing. Yoko Ono had a shock of black hair down to her waist and she hardly said a word—her husband, Tony Cox, did the explaining. I was bewildered by the evening. I spoke with her afterwards and she was told I was connected with the Cavern. I'm sure she'd heard of the Beatles, but she didn't show any interest in seeing the place."

Friday 29 September 1967
Jazz night with the Savoy Jazzmen

Friday 6 October 1967
More jazz with Max Collie's Rhythm Aces

Friday 17 November 1967
Billy Butler's Midnight Phonographic Soul Explosion with Detours, Earl Preston's Reflections, Spare Tyres, Bicycle

Wednesday 22 November 1967
For the opening of BBC Radio Merseyside, the station joined the Cavern on the Royal Daffodil. The DJs are Tony Wolfe, Keith Macklin and the Detours, Tremas, Excelles, King Bees and Jerry Shaw's Background performed.

Friday 24 November 1967
DJ Billy Butler with go-go girls. **Billy Butler**[761]: "On Fridays and Saturdays, I used to work at the Paradise club in Wigan until 11.30 and then I would drive down from the Paradise club with these two girls, Big Yvonne and Little Yvonne, and I would do the disco upstairs at the Cavern, I did it downstairs on the other days, and I brought these two girls with me and they went down very well. We took the girls to Oswestry when I was opening a store there. They danced on the overhang of the shop and all the traffic stopped. It was total chaos. They were very attractive girls and we had a big PA blaring out. There was a big American wrestler at the time called the Mighty Chang and his car was stuck in it. He got out of his car and he shouted at us, 'You take those girls off or I will come up and take them off.' And we did."

Saturday 2 December 1967
The Mojos, Tee Time Shock, Fred Lloyd's Bicycle

Friday 8 December 1967
Motown soul from The Temptations, but no. The Temptations were the Fabulous Temptations, a bogus act who normally worked as the Fascinations.

Friday 15 December 1967
Start of Cavern Lounge evenings with Gerry Shaw and the Bare Essentials with Locomotive Soul Band, Good Times, Equadors and Ronnie Pimlott.

Joe Davey had decided that running the Cavern wasn't for him and after some health problems, he sold his interest to Alf Geoghegan, so Alf owned the club completely, but much of the day to day management was carried out by his daughter.

Norris Easterbrook[762] of the Klubs: "Because we were signed to Cavern Enterprises, Alf had forced us to play the Cavern nearly every night in 1967 and we were sometimes replacing people who hadn't turned up. We had grown our hair and Alf thought we were reprobates and he told us that we had to have our hair cut and play what he told us. We were then ostracised from the Cavern and we got involved with Don Arden and played down south. Don Arden told Tony Blackburn to get down to Carnaby Street and see him. He said that we would be Number One with his help in February 1968 with 'Blue Suede Shoes'. 'No problem, Mr Arden,' said Tony Blackburn. But nothing happened."

Friday 19 January 1968
Country night with the Westerners

Friday 26 January 1968
Herald's Angels (from Bolton)

Saturday 27 January 1968
Kasper's Engine, the Driftwoods and the Texans

Saturday 3 February 1968
Country band Idle Hours

Thursday 29 February 1968
The Chants, Granny's Attic, the Hideaways and Curiosity Shoppe, who despite their name were more rock than psychedelic.

Thursday 7 March 1968
Faron and the TTs, Mike Hart and the Moon Dogs with DJ Billy Butler. **John Cornelius**[763]: "I place Mike Hart on the same pedestal as Bob Dylan and John Lennon. He was that good. He let himself down in the way that he conducted himself but in my opinion he was the genuine article, a Woody Guthrie who led a rolling stone lifestyle. He was a very gifted songwriter, a great singer and a great, charismatic performer, but he didn't give a damn. It made no difference to him that there was only a handful of people there. On a bigger, more organised show, he might fail to turn up or give a very desultory, perfunctory performance, but he was a genius."

Wednesday 10 April 1968
Start of a weekly residency for Liverpool Scene, which features Adrian Henri, Andy Roberts, Mike Hart, Mike Evans, Percy Jones and Brian Dodson.

Friday 26 April 1968
Shady Lane (Tamla-sounding band from Wales)

Sunday 5 May 1968
Football match between Cavern Kickers and Merseybeat XI at Longview Playing Fields.

Saturday 1 June 1968
The Iveys

Friday 26 July 1968
Bernie's Buzz Band. Bernie Wenton won a TV talent contest as Nat 'King' Cole.

Friday 16 August 1968
The Merseys, the Hideaways and Curiosity Shoppe

Saturday 17 August 1968
Magic Lanterns (London) and Libra (Manchester)

Friday 6 September 1968
"Two floors of non-stop entertainment" with the Tremas and Spoken Word

Thursday 12 September 1968
21-year-old Boja Christovova, the secretary of the Beatles fan club in Czechoslovakia, managed to leave the country on a tourist visa after the Russian invasion. She was the guest of honour at the Cavern that night, which featured Curiosity Shoppe.

Wednesday 25 September 1968
Following his success with "Keep On", a tour was arranged for Bruce Channel, who returned to the Cavern after six years, this time backed by Dr Marigold's Prescription. Supported by Curiosity Shoppe and Baltimore Switch

Friday 4 October 1968
US singer/songwriter Tim Rose with John Bonham on drums

Thursday 10 October 1968
Colonel Bagshot's Incredible Bucket Band

Friday 18 October 1968
Gary Walker (from the Walker Brothers) with his band, the Rain

Friday 25 October 1968
By the late sixties, it was thought that the Beatles had little interest in their roots and indeed some vilified them for leaving the city.

They had no choice but "all these places that you mention" still had great significance to them and, in October 1968, Paul McCartney visited the Cavern to show Linda around. The Curiosity Shoppe are rehearsing downstairs and the Hideaways upstairs. **Frankie Connor**[764]: "We were upstairs and he wandered in unannounced. We were rehearsing and he said, 'All right, lads' and we said, 'All right, Paul'. That's about it as they went downstairs." Alf Geoghegan hadn't got a camera with him when Paul visited the Cavern and so he went round the corner to buy one. He had trouble with it so Linda took the pictures of Paul at the Cavern.

Saturday 30 November 1968
House Of Lords (from London, naturally) with the Original Soul Brothers Boogaloo Band

Friday 6 December 1968
Third Stone From The Sun

Saturday 28 December 1968
Great band Sinbad featuring Beryl Marsden, Paddy Chambers and Albie Donnelly.

Tuesday 31 December 1968
Kenny Parry[765]: "We did the Cavern on New Year's Eve with the Mojo Band and we had a Hammond organ. Half way through our set, we opened the back of the organ and drinks were in there. We gave them to the audience. My memory is a bit hazy because my life has been a river of lager ever since."

Friday 7 February 1969
East Of Eden, Smokestack

Saturday 8 March 1969
Chapter Six, Sunshine

Saturday 15 March 1969
"Quite like old times at Liverpool's Cavern Club, when hundreds had to be turned away from seeing return of former local group, the Perishers, formerly the Seftons." (*Disc And Music Echo*). I think not.

Saturday 5 April 1969
Billy Munder and the Liquid Umbrellas

Friday 11 April 1969
'She's Not There' with the Zombies

Thursday 17 April 1969
Joey Shields[766]: "I saw Jackie Lomax when he came up from London with Heavy Jelly and they were brilliant, doing rock and blues, but all original material, Jackie's voice was impeccable and still is."

Thursday 8 May 1969
Bunker's Bubble Gum with DJs Billy Butler and Robbie Rave. Robbie Rave was **Bob McGrae**[767], who didn't care for Alf Geoghegan's new name for him, especially when he was advertised as "Robbie Rave, The Pop Slave". "I came in one night and it said, 'And introducing Robbie Rave' in the paper and I asked who it was. Alf said, 'It's you.' I was doing the DJing to save money for the club as it was just another of my duties."

Saturday 17 May 1969
House Of Lords

Saturday 26 July 1969
Frank and the Countdowns, Dimensions

Monday 28 July 1969
Scaffold backed by Business

Thursday 14 August 1969
Guthrie's Klokke

On 19 August 1969, two young married Canadians, Alan and Susan Mayer made a pilgrimage to the Cavern. Nineteen-year-old Alan had played in a Beatles' styled band in Toronto and he tells the local paper, "The Beatles were the first group to question the way things were. They have been the forerunners of student protest." Susan adds, "From our point of view, coming here means more than visiting the Tower of London."

President Kennedy was a war hero on PT 109, but, in October 1992, the *Liverpool Echo's* front page headline revealed that the White House hopeful, Bill Clinton, had saved Ringo Starr from a beating. Clinton was at Oxford University in 1969 and he visited Liverpool and walked down Mathew Street. Ringo Starr, also visiting Liverpool, was talking to an American fan in the Grapes when a German shouted at him, "You've screwed up the world." He pulled a metal bar from his sleeve and was about to attack him. Clinton grabbed hold of the German and held him down. Paddy Delaney walked over to Clinton and took charge, holding the German until the police arrived. 23 years later, when Paddy saw photographs of the Democratic candidate, he said it could have been President Clinton that he had met in the Grapes. Yes well…

Friday 22 August 1969

Petrus Booncamp, Frisby Dyke

Thursday 4 September 1969

Clayton Squares

Monday 8 September 1969

Scaffold

Thursday 18 September 1969

St James Infirmary (London)

Monday 29 September 1969

Underground night with the Klubs

Thursday 2 October 1969

Colonel Bagshot

Friday 24 October 1969

Coconut Mushroom, Anton Farmer

A police officer from the vice squad offered to let Alf Geoghegan know when the club might be raided for drugs in return for £5 a week. Geoghegan informed his superiors and a sting was set up. The police officer was jailed for fifteen months and the judge remarked that the sentence was relatively light because he would be in the company of those would not take kindly to having a former policeman in their midst.

Monday 17 November 1969

Arnold Greenyard

Friday 28 November 1969

Golliwog and Strawberry Blues. **Bob Wooler**[768]: "When the Cavern reopened, I spent most of my time working in the office. The window outside the Cavern had been boarded up and we would paste posters on it. One poster from a London agency advertised a group called Golliwog, and no-one thought anything unusual about it. Suddenly there was a commotion and someone had thrown a brick down the hallway. There were three lads in the street and they said, 'Get that poster down. It's offensive.' So we covered it up."

Saturday 20 December 1969

Baby (from London) with Warm Dust. **Paul Carrack**[769]: "My first band was Warm Dust and we played the Cavern. We were a dreadful, Frank Zappa-inspired band and we thought that we were in the forefront of modern music."

Monday 19 January 1970

Simon Dupree and the Big Sound. Admittedly, 'Kites' was a hit in 1967, but this was the first name act for some months.

Monday 2 February 1970

Mike Brocken[770]: "I was very impressed with Wishbone Ash at the Cavern as I hadn't seen twin lead guitars before."

Thursday 5 February 1970

Half Scouse, half Welsh Badfinger with their single, 'Come And Get It', written by Paul McCartney

Monday 9 February 1970

With two Top 10 hits, welcome to Status Quo. Their road manager and harmonica player, **Bob Young**[771], recalls: "It was freezing cold and getting the equipment in and out was really difficult. The stage was far too small for Quo to run around as they tended to do, but we were happy to say we'd played on the same stage where the Beatles had played so many times. We couldn't do it a second time because we were carrying more and more equipment and those bloody stairs were a pain in the butt."

Thursday 16 April 1970

Rob Luke[772] of local favourites, Zelda Plum: "We were a trio at first but we did a gig with Steve Marriott and he suggested that we added a keyboard player. We were loud and noisy and very visual. We would slide our guitars down microphone stands to get feedback. The heavy bands went in for marathon performances then. If someone said, 'One more song' to us, it could last for fifteen minutes."

Saturday 25 April 1970

The psychedelic band, Rupert's People, released "Reflections Of Charles Brown" and "A Prologue To A Magic World" in 1967, but both the line-up and management of the band were in disarray. For a time, John Banks (ex-Merseybeats) played drums and Mal Evans produced a session. This was one of their final gigs. The name is a nod to the contentious, schoolkids' issue of *Oz*, which divided the nation.

Friday 15 May 1970

Three years before the hits, Nazareth

Saturday 6 June 1970

Perfumed Garden with support from Kansas Hook, who once backed Gene Vincent.

Tuesday 21 July 1970

Brian Farrell[773], lead vocalist with Colonel Bagshot: "I am lacking in patience and I can't watch something on the telly twice, but I saw *Hair* fourteen times. For a time, half the Bagshot's act was *Hair* and the other half was our normal repertoire. *Hair* was good as we had a bit of theatre and we would get out in the audience. It was great at the Cavern. You could be at the other end of the club and yet be involved in what was going on. We would use any props and improvise with anything we could, and we would gather flowers from a field and take them to a college. One night we got two girls on the stage and taught them what to do, and one of them worked for Robert Stigwood who published *Hair*, so what are the odds of that? We got a letter from his solicitors to stop doing *Hair*."

Saturday 25 July 1970

Barbed Wire Soup, Galliard

When a Liverpool youth was charged with submitting forged prescriptions to Boots in Whitechapel, a probation officer said that it was probable that drugs were being sold in the Cavern. The club dismissed these claims as "absolutely ridiculous".

Friday 7 August 1970

Klubs, Uncle Sam

Friday 9 October 1970

Trapeze, Bram Stoker

Saturday 31 October 1970

With help from his father, Brian May made his first guitar when he was sixteen and although he graduated in astronomy at Imperial College, London, he wanted to be a rock musician. In the late sixties, he formed Smile with drummer and biology student, Roger Taylor. In 1970, they formed Queen with art school graduate, Freddie Mercury and bass player, Mike Grose. Their first public appearance as Queen was in Truro on June 27. They wore jewellery and black and white stage costumes and their set was a theatrical mixture of new songs and rock'n'roll standards.

Ken Testi[774]: "I was the social sec at St Helens College and I saw Freddie Mercury when he got with a local band, Ibex, at the Bolton Octogon. Then Freddie formed Queen with Brian May and Roger Taylor and I wanted to put them on at the college but we needed somewhere else to make the trip pay. Alf Geoghegan very kindly gave us a gig at the Cavern as he had had Ibex in the past. Billy Butler was in charge on the night. I got the impression that he resented bands coming in as it interfered with him playing records, but nonetheless he put it up with it and we did get paid. I can't remember a great deal about the gig, but it was pretty much a selection of the material that went on the first album. There were also a few songs from an album by Smile which Brian and Roger had recorded with Tim Staffell prior to Queen. They were excellent songs, but the album never got released in this country. I had seen Clapton and Hendrix and all the big boys and thought I had read the book on guitar playing, but I knew that Brian had something new to offer. We passed a terrible road accident on the way back to St Helens, somewhere round Dovecot, and I remember how much Roger and Freddie were badly shaken by the scene of people being loaded into ambulances."

7

ROLL OVER BEAT OVEN

Cavern owner:
Roy Adams
1970-1976

Alf Geoghegan wanted to retire. He was finding the Cavern a bit much as he also had his butcher's shops and a taxi business with 100 cabs. He knew that Roy Adams was making a success of the Iron Door, now the Egyptian-themed Pyramid, 400 hundred yards away. **Roy Adams**[775] also owned pubs in New Brighton and Birkenhead and he was the first owner of the Cavern to have a background of club life. "Anyone who takes over a club has his own ideas and wants to enhance it. It is nearly always better to say that it is a new club opening rather than an old one reopening, but the Cavern was the exception to that rule."

By then the Cavern's regular DJs were Bob McGrae (Robbie Rave), Daniel Boon, Gray Donna and Joey Wall. **Bob McGrae**[776]: "The Cavern never had an owner who got it completely right. Alan Sytner didn't realise that rock'n'roll was happening and even though Ray McFall was trained as an accountant, he spent money like it was going out of fashion. Joe and Alf were out of their depth and Alf would put on a group even if they weren't going to make money from it. Roy Adams knew a lot about the running of clubs. He kept a good check on what was going in and what was going out. Unfortunately, we were restricted

on the amounts we could spend and we had to rely on local talent or on Beggars Opera and other rock bands from Scotland."

Mike Brocken[777]: "The Cavern didn't book many name bands as they were only booking what they could afford, and by 1970 the Stadium had taken over. The Stadium's great gig of Free with Mott The Hoople was like a gathering of the tribes for my generation. After that, Roger Eagle's gigs took over from the Cavern as he could afford the Steve Miller Band while they could only afford second division outfits like Stray. Economics had become the be-all and end-all of everything."

Roy Adams[778] disagrees: "We had no competition with the Stadium as the Cavern was very busy all the time that I was involved with it. It was licensed for 400 and if you got in 800, it would be packed. We got 1,600 some nights, but that is using all the floors. I was in the process of expanding the basement when I found out it was going to be knocked down. The noise would be deafening if you had to cross in front of the stage."

Monday 30 November 1970
Rob Luke[779] of Zelda Plum: "Zelda Plum used a domestic tape recorder to put down twelve songs

SOUVENIR PROGRAMME - 10 P.

THE 1st MERSEYBEAT REUNION

The Chants

SOUNDS OF THE 70'S
AT THE CAVERN

Merseyside's Lettermen

Status Quo

Ex-Big Three Guitarist Paul Pilnick

Vinegar Joe

Phil Lynott

Petula Clark

Suzi Quatro

Roy Young

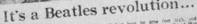

It's a Beatles revolution...

A SMALL plaque as a tribute to a big slice of Liverpool history is to be unveiled next week for the whole world to see.

It will be placed outside the newly opened Revolution Club in Mathew Street—the former Cavern Club—to commemorate the nightspot made famous by the Beatles.

Inside the club is a massive fibreglass sculpture of the Beatles. The sculpture, admired above by Sheila Farrell, from Aintree, and Eileen Fletcher, from Crosby, is

14 feet long by nine feet high, and was designed by Liverpool artist David Webster.

Managing director of Cavern Enterprises, Mr Roy Adam, said the plaque and sculpture were primarily to explain to the tourists what had happened in the club since the 60s.

"The club has become a bigger tourist attraction than both the city's cathedrals," he said.

at the Cavern and I am surprised at how the quality has remained over all these years. People have heard a Hendrix influence in our sound, but they were my songs and no copying was intended. I must have been influenced by the Small Faces though as they were my favourite band. Like all the heavy bands, our songs were marathons and they could last for 20 minutes. The band's name came from a Juicy Lucy album as the girl on the cover was named Zelda Plum."

Monday 7 December 1970
Bluto

Thursday 17 December 1970
Peaceful Nature

Friday 1 January 1971
Explosion, Birth

Saturday 2 January 1971
Crazy Mabel

Thursday 7 January 1971
Uncle Sam

Friday 22 January 1971
Stackwaddy

Monday 1 February 1971
Ozzie Yue is back with Confucius

Friday 19 February 1971
Bilbo Baggins Band, Kansas Hook
  Bob Wooler hosted the first Merseybeat Reunion Event at the Jacaranda. Bob asked, "Is the Mersey brand of rock the real thing—does it have Liverpool all the way through it?" In an interview with Pete Halligan, Bob said that the Beatles EMIgrated.
  To tie with the court case to dissolve the Beatles' partnership, BBC's *24 Hours* ran a feature on the decline of Liverpool music. The reporter was Bernard Falk, who had been in the Bohemians when a junior reporter on Merseyside. A Cavern bouncer likened the present scene to a graveyard "but like the Resurrection, it will happen again."

Saturday 6 March 1971
Gentle Giant, Gass

Friday 19 March 1971
Perfumed Garden had keyboards and included ELP material in their repertoire.

Saturday 20 March 1971
Northwind (from Scotland), Nothin' Ever 'Appens

Friday 26 March 1971
"Hold Your Head Up", it's Argent.

Saturday 27 March 1971
Strife was a heavy metal trio who emerged from Clayton Squares and was managed by the Cavern. **Mike Brocken**[780]: "A lot of second or third division rock bands who were playing the college circuit might play the Cavern on a Friday or Saturday night. Strife was a good hard rock three-piece but a bit turgid, rather like Taste."

Friday 30 April 1971
May Blitz (from America), Axis

Friday 7 May 1971
Dada, a 12 piece band with Robert Palmer and Elkie Brooks, plus Gravy Train

Friday 14 May 1971
Tear Gas (from Scotland), Ronno

Monday 24 May 1971
Alan Bown Set

Friday 28 May 1971
Fairfield Parlour, Cottage
  On 6 June 1971, John and Yoko appeared on stage with Frank Zappa at the Fillmore East in New York. John introduced a song he used to do at the Cavern, the Olympics' "Well (Baby Please Don't Go)".

Friday 18 June 1971
British country-rock band, Cochise, featuring B.J. Cole. **Raphael Callaghan**[781]: "Cochise was great and I always warm to a band that is doing original material."

Saturday 10 July 1971
Scottish prog rock band, Beggars Opera

Friday 17 September 1971
Blonde On Blonde, Wave

Saturday 25 September 1971
Smokestack, Crumble, Klubs. By now the Klubs are cross-dressing and Dusty Springfield's make-up had nothing on them. Glam Rock starts here.

Friday 1 October 1971
Renaissance

Friday 8 October 1971
Sutherland Brothers and Quiver

Friday 19 November 1971

Vinegar Joe (with Robert Palmer and Elkie Brooks)

Saturday 4 December 1971

Hackensack (from Glasgow), Greasy Bear

Friday 31 December 1971

Confucius, Strife

British Rail owned the Cavern and surrounding properties and they served notices to quit as they wanted to create an extraction duct for the underground rail loop. The letter to the Cavern was addressed to Alf Geoghehan, who kept quiet about it. When selling the club, he had not informed Roy Adams that this was a possibility, and who could blame him? *Caveat emptor*, and all that.

Rolling Stone published a feature on Liverpool music on 20 March 1972. It talked of Allan Williams, Bill Harry and Ray McFall and their problems with bankruptcy. Roy Adams' sister, Freda Mullan, managed the Cavern. On the ground floor, which was bare with black and white linoleum, skinheads danced to reggae and soul, and in the basement there was heavy metal. Her daughter, Maureen, worked on one of the bars and her son-in-law Tony on another. She commented, "Upstairs is a discotheque for the skinheads who like bluebeat and reggae. They're a tough crowd and do a lot of fighting, and sometimes we have trouble between them and the younger, heavy crowd that we call Troggs. They don't mix which is why we serve all the drinks in paper cups. Sometimes we might put on a Beatles record and the kids really like them because they've never heard them before."

Roy Adams had kept Paddy Delaney as he was a very effective doorman, rarely getting into scrapes and knowing how to resolve a problem diplomatically. He added six foot eight Barry McLelland, who had been Sonny Liston's sparring partner and was very good at resolving drug issues. The problem was largely cannabis. Paddy Delaney was not happy with the music as he commented, "The stuff they play here now is rubbish, just rubbish."

Roy Adams[782]: "We had big overheads—twelve doormen and a large staff. All the drink was served in paper cups—we were too busy to wash glasses—and it would have been too dangerous to have them anyway as apart from breakages, they are too handy as weapons when there is trouble. We kept a row of chairs in the passage way by the door, and when the girls fainted, they were passed over the heads to sit on the chairs. The punters loved it as that was the way they wanted it."

Saturday 15/ Sunday 16/ Monday 17 April 1972

Smith, Perkins and Smith from the USA

On Wednesday 19 April 1972, Allan Williams' second Merseybeat reunion at the Top Rank Suite featured Kingsize Taylor as well as Beryl Marsden's new group, Minnesota Fats.

Roy Adams[783]: "At the Cavern, the police's duty jeep would pass down Mathew Street with the back door open and a member of the Cavern staff would put a tray of pints of beer in there. On the return patrol, the empty tray and glasses would be collected in the same way. The police in the main were allies who often had to help out during trouble."

Friday 21 April 1972

Stoke's finest, the Living Dead

Saturday 20 May 1971

Judas Priest, Unicorn

Bulldozers moved in as the Mardi Gras in Mount Pleasant was the subject of a Compulsory Demolition Order.

Thursday 8 June 1972

Gary Wright and the Wonder Wheel

Thursday 15 June 1972

The Pretty Things

Liverpool Echo reported that Roy Adams had been welcomed in Australia as the owner of the Cavern. It was a leading heavy metal venue and he had plans to extend the capacity to 2,000. The restaurant upstairs is doing good business with its unfussy menu, the most expensive meal being steak and chips for 50p. The club was said to be the only one in the country with special treatment for overseas guests as they were given instant membership rights.

Thursday 29 June 1972

Budgie (Wales)

Thursday 6 July 1972

Vinegar Joe, Gravy Train

Thursday 27 July 1972

Brinsley Schwartz (including Nick Lowe)

Beatles 'shrine' comes down...

...for a railway

(Right) Demolition man offers some typical sentiments as he tears down some of Liverpool's history

Bricks crumble and timbers crash in Liverpool's city centre as demolition boss Terry Balmer makes history, for he has the task of demolishing the world famous Cavern Club in Mathew Street.

But as the giant caterpillar vehicle clawed at the warehouse, Terry, aged 32, said: "It's just another job."

The cellar that saw the birth of the Beatles will vanish to make way for an underground railway ventilation shaft.

And Terry, a director of the firm given the job of flattening the site, will be carrying bits of the one-time Mecca of pop music home to Parliament Street, Toxeth, Liverpool.

He said: "My 11-year-old daughter, Donna, has asked me to get her whatever I can as a souvenir."

Another director, Sid Fishgold, aged 44, of Carkington Road, Woolton, has had orders from his daughter, Jeanette, aged 15.

"She wants a brick from the back of the stage because it was nearest to the Beatles," he said.

The Cavern has now moved across Mathew Street to premises opposite the condemned cellar.

(Left)
Cave-dwellers,
how they long for
yesterday

Sid saves memories of the Cavern
— 5 JUN 1973

SID FISHGOLD
— Just another job

DEMOLITION boss Sid Fishgold took some of his work home with him yesterday.

The father of four has got the job of knocking down Liverpool's world-famous Cavern Club.

And his children, Jeanette, aged 15, Marilyn, aged 13, Terry, aged 9, and Paul, aged 7, pleaded: "Bring us some souvenirs."

So Sid, aged 44, agreed to take home to Carkington Road, Woolton, chunks of brick and wood from the Mathew Street cellar.

Jeanette wants a brick from the back of the stage because it was nearest to the Beatles.

All the lads will be taking bits and pieces home as souvenirs. But as far as we are concerned it's just another job," he said.

Sid is one of the directors of the demolition company given the task, started yesterday, of tearing down the old warehouse, to make way for an underground railway ventilation shaft.

The Cavern has moved to premises opposite.

Said club owner, Mr Roy Adams: "I am just looking ahead to the future. I have finished crying about the past."

He said there had been a steady stream of visitors over the past week, wanting a last look at the Cavern before it disappeared.

The Immortal **CAVERN** In Matthew Street

Wishbone Ash

New Lease Of Life

Roy Wood

CAVERN
GOES
COUNTRY

WANTED
THE HILLSIDERS

Amazing but true! The news that the Cavern Club was to commence country and western shows on Thursday evenings at first amazed the C&W fans who had always considered the Cavern to be the home of a rather less tuneful sound than country andwestern. After the initial shock reaction, the possibilities offered by such an evening at the Cavern seemed endless.

Here was a large club with a big stage capable of presenting the really great names in country music. Situated in the centre of Liverpool—a club of renown throughout the world —this obviously had to be a big step forward in the progress of country music on Merseyside.

Right from the start the management of the Cavern showed that they intended to go wholeheartedly into country music when they announced the bills for their first shows. The first show on May 9, features three really top acts — Countryside, Hartford West and the James King Duo. Acts for future shows incl,ude Hank Walters and the Dusty Road Ramblers and the Stringdusters on May 16, from America, Jo Anne Steel and the North Country 4 on May 23, and on June 6, a really big scoop for the club in the form of the Hillsiders' 10th Anniversary Party.

The Hillsiders decided to use the Cavern to celebrate their tenth anniversary together, for they considered this to be a really big breakthrough for country and western music in Liverpool. This feeling is also shared by a great number of artistes and others concerned with country music on Merseyside.

Having spoken to Mrs McMullen, the manageress of the Cavern, I know that, with the support of the country fans, she will endeavour to make the Cavern into the country music scene on Merseyside, thus filling a void in the entertainment field in Liverpool. She told me that she would like country fans to let her know which artistes they would like to see, and she will do her best to get them. They need not just be local acts for Freda hopes to present top international artistes as well. She already has high hopes of introducing Marvin Rainwater to the Cavern.

A special country and western membership for Thursday evenings has been opened at a cost of 25p per year, which is very reasonable indeed. Certainly the aims are big and enterprising like this deserves success, certainly hope that the fans rally round for this is a great chance for a big country club to develop on Merseyside.

ROBBY RA

Thursday 17 August 1972

Patto (featuring Southport's great guitarist, Ollie Halsall)

Friday 18 August 1972

Frump (Belfast)

Thursday 24 August 1972

Thin Lizzy

Thursday 7 September 1972

Gary Glitter and the Glitter Band. **Roy Adams**[784]: "When Gary Glitter came on stage, the place was packed although he was playing a different music to what we had at the time. He turned his back to the audience—I seem to think that there was a curtain then—he had his hand stretched up and he turned round and said, 'Do you want to rock?' and they went, 'Yeah.' He went down a storm but they were dancing on the benches and the benches collapsed, which didn't please me."

John Allen of Kirkby told *Liverpool Echo*, "I went into town on the day of the concert to buy some suede boots. It was jam-packed at the Cavern and when they took to the stage, we stood on benches to get a better view. Unfortunately, our bench gave away and I got my ankle stuck underneath. I lost one of my boots and I had to go to hospital with a badly sprained ankle."

Thursday 14 September 1972

Roy Young from BBC-TV's pop show *Drumbeat!* was one of the first musicians that the Beatles met in Hamburg. He came to the Cavern with his own band.

Thursday 21 September 1972

Flamin' Groovies, Bilf Slat

Thursday 5 October 1972

Back to the 50s with the Rock'n'Roll All Stars with Mal Grey

Thursday 12 October 1972

Supertramp

Friday 13 October 1972

Judas Priest, Graphite

Friday 20 October 1972

Jericho, Clear Blue Sky

Thursday 26 October 1972

Just before they broke big, Focus from Holland, supported by the Living Dead. **Bill Heckle**[785]: "I was seventeen and I saw a little advert that said that Jan Akkerman of Focus was playing at the Cavern and I was blown away by them. It was the only time that I went to the old Cavern and I went with George Guinness, another of the directors of Cavern City Tours. I've always been a big Focus fan and I am so pleased to have booked Jan Akkerman myself for the Cavern."

George Guinness[786]: "Being born in 1956, I was too young to go to the Cavern when the Beatles were there. The first time I went was to see Focus with Bill Heckle and a couple of other friends. It was a strange night as they had a discussion about the Beatles before Focus appeared. It was very dingy and poky with a little bar. The walls were whitewashed and they were very wet."

Roy Adams learnt at last that British Rail wanted the Cavern to be closed at the end of January. He told the *Echo* that this was a tragedy as the Cavern was a tourist attraction and he had had eight film crews in the last past year. What's more, he had spent £10,000 creating a new fire escape and other improvements.

Also, Roy Adams had commissioned large, fibreglass heads of the Beatles. They were briefly in the old Cavern and then they went over the road to the new Cavern. They were joined by giant heads of Che Guevara and Jimi Hendrix when it became the Revolution. When that closed, Roy Adams put the heads in a stable attached to his home. The Cavern's owners purchased them in the nineties and they were used both upstairs and at the back of the Cavern. They are currently in the Cavern's administration offices and another public appearance is likely. They are the only artifacts to have appeared in all Cavern locations.

Thursday 2 November 1972

Trying out the UK clubs, Suzi Quatro

Thursday 9 November 1972

Blackfoot Sue

Thursday 16 November 1972

Atacama (South America), Holy Mackerel

Wednesday 22 November 1972

Ro-Ro recorded for EMI and even though they worked with John Entwistle in Rigor Mortis in 1972, he was not with them on this date.

Thursday 30 November 1972

Brinsley Schwarz, Confucius

Thursday 7 December 1972

Geoff Davies[787]: "Amon Düül II was a German rock band and I was buying their albums at the time. I liked them anyway and they didn't disappoint, but that was the last time that I went to the Cavern."

Monday 11 December 1972

Smart suits from local band, the Lettermen and their act betrayed their Wooky Hollow look with Wishbone Ash and Jimi Hendrix songs in the repertoire.

Friday 12 January 1973

Fraternity, a 17 piece rock band from Australia

Thursday 25 January 1973

Geordie, enjoying their first hit, "Don't Do That"

The Cavern was scheduled for closure on 30 January 1973, but British Rail allowed the club to keep going until 5 February. Roy Adams said that all Cavern membership cards would be valid at the Pyramid until a new home was found.

Wednesday 31 January 1973

A special night for teenyboppers—a disco from 6.30pm to 9.30pm for twelve to sixteen year olds so that they too could say they had been to the Cavern. In the event, they let in children of all ages and served Coca-Cola and hamburgers.

Thursday 1 February 1973

Glen Cornick's Wild Turkey

Still threatened with demolition, the Cavern was granted a three month reprieve. Roy Adams was hopeful that the basement could be saved, even though the top buildings would be demolished. He said, "We are thinking about putting a concrete ramp across the top of the premises, which would support the lorries when work starts on the site. The problem is that it will cost us several thousand pounds."

Thursday 8 February 1973

Babe Ruth, Jerusalem Smith

Saturday 10 February 1972

Strife and Hiroshima. As the evening drew to an end, Roy Adams in evening dress took the stage, "We have heard today that we have a three month extension on the Cavern." Cheers all round.

Thursday 15 February 1973

Glencoe, naturally from Scotland

Thursday 22 February 1973

Capability Brown

Sunday 11 March 1973

Harpoon, who performed "Not With You" for the film of *Little Malcolm And His Struggle Against The Eunuchs* starring John Hurt and David Warner and produced by George Harrison.

Thursday 15 March 1973

Alex Harvey Band, Tear Gas

Saturday 17 March 1973

Tasavallan (Finland)

Thursday 22 March 1973

Supersister (Holland)

Thursday 29 March 1973

String Driven Thing

Editorial in *Liverpool Daily Post* for April 9: "Any city other than Liverpool would, by now, have become a tourist Mecca. As the Beatles have themselves learned, there's no surer investment than a touch of yesterday." Photographer **Steve Hale**[788] says today, "Can you imagine anyone knocking down the Sun Studios, the Brill Building or Gracelands? Whoever took the decision to demolish the Cavern should be certified. Okay, we have a replica now and tourists love it, but it's not the original."

Paul McCartney told the *Echo* in 1983: "They should never have pulled it down. It was the most maniacal move possible. I think there was a bit of an attitude going around at the time which was, 'Well, the Beatles left us. They hate Liverpool anyway.' We used to get an awful lot of that. If someone's got to live somewhere else, it doesn't mean he hates Liverpool. Not for me anyway."

Thursday 19 April 1973

Jonesy featuring Alan Bown

Saturday 21 April 1973

Supercharge

Friday 27 April 1973

Al Quin (from Holland), Jerusalem Smith

Paul McCartney, playing at the Empire with Wings, said, "If it had been physically possible, I would have gone to the old Cavern to kiss it goodbye. I wanted to take the group with me on a surprise farewell visit but there wasn't the time." Allan Williams advised tourists to take a ferry cross the Mersey while they're here. "They'll be getting rid of that next."

Friday 25 May 1973
Supercharge

Sunday 27 May 1973
All-night festival. Tickets were £1.25 and the publicity said, "One last attempt to bring this famous roof down will be made tonight by Strife, Hackensack, Harpoon, Supercharge, Bilf Slat, Caliban and the Yardleys." The DJs were Billy Butler, Robbie Rave, Ricky McCabe and Joey Wall. The Yardleys, a band from Long Island which worshipped the Beatles, came over especially for the night. Unfortunately, the group was detained at Heathrow for not having work permits. **Roy Adams**[789]: "The Yardleys were held up at the airport. They came along anyway and they still played without the permit. That would be down to me, 'Oh, stick them on anyway.' My sister lived with my mum in Crosby and as the Yardleys had nowhere to stay, they put them up. They had sleeping bags and slept on the floor in the lounge."

Bob McGrae[790]: "The day after the Cavern closed I went with Liverpool FC to Hungary. It was the first time that any supporters had been allowed behind the Iron Curtain. It was a nil-all draw."

For the next week, there was a steady stream of visitors having a last look at the Cavern. Then the demolition company moved in and both Sid 'Curly' Fishgold and Terry Balmer told the press that it was "just another job". The fact that the team posed in front of the Cavern before they started work and took home souvenirs for their families meant that it was anything but that. Roy Adams said, "I have finished crying about the Cavern. I am looking ahead to the future."

Roy Adams had been running the old Cavern with three or four other clubs. He thought that if he went across the road as the new Cavern, he would get publicity and it would offer improved facilities as the old Cavern was never a great place for that. So Roy Adams moved the Cavern across the road, namely 7 to 15 Mathew Street, the ground floor and the basement of the old Fruit Exchange. Some of the cellars had been built by French prisoners during the Napoleonic wars. The walls were incredibly thick, and metal filings had been mixed into the bricks. The drills made little impression and Adams had to call on the demolition expert, Blaster Bates. Without any financial help from the Council, Adams ploughed £35,000 into the project. He wanted to create a similar atmosphere, but this was a much bigger space, which could hold 2,000 people.

Frieda Kelly[791]: "When the old Cavern closed, they moved to the other side of the road and said, 'This is the Cavern'. Of course, it wasn't and the whole thing became very confusing for visitors. I blame the Council as they were far too late in recognising the tourist potential in the Beatles."

Judd Lander[792]: "Of course politicians are out of touch with reality but how on earth could they destroy the Cavern? It was criminal. It is like burning a Van Gogh and then painting a copy and sticking it next door."

Mostly the new Cavern was a heavy metal venue. The fans came at first but then they fell away, although local band Strife now recorded for Chrysalis. The Cavern booked the all girl American band, the Runaways (with Joan Jett), the Chi-Lites, Redwing and Wizzard, but Status Quo said that the stage would be too small for their equipment. **Roy Adams**[793]: "I had an army of bouncers across the stage to keep it calm while the Runaways were on but the girls were geeing the crowd up: they were beckoning them to come to the stage. They were only around sixteen. That was very successful. Wizzard was the worst act of all as far as I was concerned. Their equipment was delayed and they had to hire equipment to do the gig and they weren't happy. They were supposed to do an hour, they didn't wear their outfits, Roy Wood didn't have any makeup and they only did 45 minutes. I went to the dressing room for Roy Wood's autograph for the kids, 'What do you want?' I said, 'I'm the owner, I want to see Roy Wood.' This skinny little feller was sitting with his head down between his knees looking like a wrung-out rag. I wondered what he was on. I walked out disgusted. I paid them £1,000 plus VAT and that was the early seventies."

The DJ and club entertainer, Pete Price, recognised that there should be a statue to the Beatles in the city and he raised the funding for a work by the Communist and Catholic sculptor, Arthur Dooley, one of the most controversial characters in a controversial city. In April 1974, Dooley erected his tribute to the Beatles on the outside wall of the new Cavern. The gold-coloured Madonna represented Liverpool with the Beatles as her babies—at least, I think that's what it means. The inscription is "Four lads who shook the world". Dooley also created a new sign saying, "Beatle Street". He said, "I think it would have been rather staid if I had just done four statues of the Beatles." He described it as a symbol of hope for the city.

Remember the Liverpool band, Nutz with their provocative LP covers? **Keith Mulholland**[794]: "Our band was essentially a live band and it was very difficult to make the transition when we were in the studio. We did Cream songs in our set and sometimes we did 'Far As The Eye Can See' live. We started to develop after the first album and we were going into heavy rock with harmonies and good chord structures. Later, we couldn't get a deal as punk had slaughtered us and we became Rage."

Thursday 9 May 1974

The first *Cavern Goes Country* with Countryside, Hartford West and the James King Duo

Thursday 16 May 1974

Cavern Goes Country with Hank Walters and the Dusty Road Ramblers, Stringdusters and Tom and Jean

Thursday 6 June 1974

The Hillsiders' tenth anniversary party

Attendances at the new Cavern venue were not good, not enough to sustain the business, and Roy Adams said at the time, "Most youngsters on Merseyside are on the dole and don't have the money to go to clubs." The new Cavern was on two floors so, in 1975, Roy split it into separate premises. Gatsby's was on the ground floor and had access from Victoria Street, and the Revolution Club in the basement, which had access from Mathew Street. The revamp as the Revolution didn't work out until Roger Eagle and Ken Testi came along. **Ken Testi**[795]: "Roger Eagle and myself had decided to do something together. I had been touring with Deaf School and I wanted to come off the road, while Roger was doing his last shows at Liverpool Stadium. We decided to do one night a week and we wanted a club owner who

was prepared to play ball with us. We approached Roy Adams and he offered us Gatsby's and we did our first shows there including, notably, the Runaways. The Runaways was an all-girl band with Cherry Vanilla and Joan Jett. They were hot Californian girls, and the show was always going to sell out as there had been some good marketing. As luck would have it, the *News Of The World* carried a double page spread on the Sunday before our show. It not only showed hot pictures of the band but also showed the police with a water cannon. The police had been using this to clear the streets outside the Glasgow Apollo, and we only had them in a small club. That was the first occasion that a queue has gone out of Mathew Street, up Temple Court, along Victoria Street, North John Street and back in Mathew Street. It was sensational and it was our second gig."

The final night of the Revolution club was on Saturday 17 April 1976. One of the last bands to play was Confucius, which means that Ozzie Yue was on stage when the Cavern closed in 1966, 1973 and, as the Revolution, in 1976. Roy Adams still had the lease on the property and he sold part of that lease to Roger Eagle, who was the motivator for a new club, Eric's which he purchased with Ken Testi and Pete Fulwell. Although they prided themselves on being a venue for new music, the licensing certificate shows that they were the Cavern Club trading as Eric's.

Ken Testi[796]: "Roy Adams perceived us from the Runaways night as an exit strategy and he wanted to sell half of the club to us. It appeared that we might be able to generate enough payments to meet the mortgage payments. We asked Pete Fulwell to have a look at a business plan. Pete had good strong business skills which wasn't our forte at the time. He came in with us and we became co-owners of what had been the Revolution Club and was now Eric's. I wanted a name that would be the antithesis to names of clubs at the time. Everything was like Tiffany's and Annabel's and I wanted something male and Anglo-Saxon. I thought 'Eric's' would do."

The music appealed to the disaffected in the area and it became one of the key clubs of the punk era. Although Eric's disassociated itself with the music of the past, it is ironic that it was born out of the Cavern. Eric's started 1 October 1976 with the Stranglers, and the groups who played at Eric's included the Sex Pistols, Ian Dury and the Blockheads, Ultravox, Dave Edmunds, the Police, the Pirates, and Elvis Costello and the Attractions. The Cavern site opposite was fenced off and at the time of Costello's appearance was covered with life-size posters for his first album, *My Aim Is True*. When the Ramones played Eric's, they were such Beatle fans that they were photographed on the original site. Eric's closed in March 1980, after it ran into problems with the police and the licensing authorities. The premises reverted back to Roy Adams as he had guaranteed the mortgage in the first place.

Norman Killon[797]: "That building that they called the new Cavern, had the Cavern sign outside but it had nothing to do with the Cavern that the Beatles played in. Every time I walked up Mathew Street, I wanted to get hold of the tourists and say, 'Stop taking photographs there. The Cavern is by that waste ground.' When Roger Eagle took the building as Eric's, he didn't want anything to do with the past at all and he wanted it completely new. Much later when the Beatles released the *Hollywood Bowl* album, EMI held the launch at Eric's."

8

THIS EMPTY PLACE

Increasing numbers of tourists were coming to Liverpool by 1976 but what was there to show them? Visitors would walk down Mathew Street and see a flattened space where the Cavern was. Admittedly the Cavern sign was still displayed, but that was across the road and even that club had closed down or rather, had been transformed into Eric's. Even the fruit trade had moved away to a new market in Fairfield. Also, there was no annual event on the calendar to celebrate the Beatles, so the tourists were spread throughout the season.

The most regrettable aspect of the demise of the Cavern was that it did not need to be closed at all. British Rail had switched their proposed ventilation shaft to a different area: the shafts were never sunk and the flattened area where the Cavern was became waste ground which was used as a car park. Pete Halligan, one of the city's more eccentric characters, ran a hippie market, Aunt Twacky's in Mathew Street and he recognised the potential of the site for tourists. He asked British Rail about reinstating the Cavern but his plan was turned down.

Ron Jones[798]: "It's unbelievable to think of what they did, but that's Liverpool. They also knocked down the seaman's home in Canning Place. They were acts of civic vandalism and the sculptor Arthur Dooley applied to be City Planning Officer in protest. I first got involved in tourism in Liverpool in 1972. You couldn't even buy a picture postcard of the Beatles and you couldn't go on a tour of Beatle sites as nothing was published. One of the first things I did was to get together with Mike Evans for a souvenir Beatles pack in the shape of a double LP and it included a map of Beatle sites, and it came out in 1974. The booklet said why Liverpool was the only place that could have produced the Beatles. I never told the councillors what I was doing, and that was my philosophy for the whole ten years, although they did catch up with me in the end. I was getting a lot of press. The local journalists loved it, and the politicians wanted to be in on it. They set up a tourism committee and made me report to it. Of course, things then started to slide then but I had done what I wanted."

In 1976, Dave Chisnell organised a small Beatles Convention in Norwich. This did okay, and so Dave and Allan Williams booked the Alexandra Palace for two days and what was billed as Europe's First Christmas Beatle Convention. **Bob**

Recorded for posterity,
Sounds of The Cavern

Courtesy of Mersey Beat/Bill Harry

WW Associates,
Bob Wooler and Allan
Williams, organisers of
the first Beatles
Convention
'Williams - Wooler
Worldwide Promotions'

ECHOCOMMENT

The voice of the people

NEARLY twenty years ago there emerged from the teenage clubs of Liverpool a new form of music which reverberated around the world.

It was the Mersey Beat—the unmistakably new sound which had its birth in a city which already had a long and proud musical tradition.

At the very forefront of this exciting new wave of creativity was one group of young musicians who rose above all others and whose special talent is now indelibly written in the history of popular music.

The Beatles.

The songs and sounds that were of their creation have been adopted and adapted by musicians whose styles and talents range from jazz to the classical. The world's top orchestras and finest bands find the music of the Beatles as irresistible to play as audiences find it a pleasure to hear.

The full measure of the impact of Lennon and McCartney, Starr and Harrison, undeniably is a considerable one and a lasting one.

Isn't it rather more than a little sad, then, that in the city that saw it all begin, a group of elected representatives should vote down a plan to erect a statue in recognition of what the Beatles meant to so many people?

Councillors debating the issue in committee last night spoke of the group "not being able to sing" and suggested that they had made no real contribution to the city.

How narrow minded, how short sighted—and how typically out-of-touch with what people think and feel!

The Beatles were a brilliant manifestation of a grassroots movement, the contribution of which should not be measured in material terms but in the sense of excitement and involvement and pride which it gave to the people of Liverpool.

That is something that the councillors, in their remote ivory tower, cannot take away—even though they seem set on denying the city a Beatles monument, paid for by private subscription and at no charge to the ratepayers.

There is time for a change of heart, though. Perhaps the full City Council will change this committee decision and show that the voice of the people can still be

(Above) Article from Liverpool Echo which includes a quote from Liverpool Council about The Beatles

ELEANOR RIGBY
DEDICATED TO
"ALL THE LONELY PEOPLE..."

This statue was sculptured and donated to the City of Liverpool
by Tommy Steele as a tribute to the Beatles.
The casting was sponsored by the Liverpool Echo.
DECEMBER 1982

Wooler[799]: "It was forlorn, dreadful and a total disaster. One reporter said that I was walking round in an alcoholic haze, and who could blame me? I did get my money, £35, but I had to wait several months. The image that sums up the Convention has to be of the four inflatable Beatles, each about 30 feet high, which started leaking and beginning to droop. One photographer caught the Beatles hanging their heads in shame as so few people were attending the Convention in their name."

Despite the setback, Allan Williams felt that there was mileage in Beatles conventions and he teamed up with **Bob Wooler**[800] to create them. "The Liverpool Beatles Conventions started in a very modest way in the late 70s with Allan Williams and myself. Allan wanted to call us Williams—Wooler Worldwide Promotions, but I wanted something more sedate. We settled on WW Associates, and you can decide for yourself whose 'W' comes first. We called ourselves 'entertainment entrepreneurs' but we didn't have a phone in our office. We would take our papers to the main post office in Victoria Street and use their call-boxes. We would load in the coins to prevent people from knowing it was a call-box and we would say, 'I'm making this call very quickly as I'm due to meet somebody.'"

This first Liverpool Beatles Convention was held at Mr. Pickwick's Club in Liverpool in 1977 and inside the programme, they included the English Tourist Board's guide to Liverpool. Considering Wooler and Williams' experience in organising events, it was an amateur affair, starting late and sometimes offering no more than a video as entertainment. There were further events in Liverpool at Mr Pickwick's and the Top Rank and in Sheffield, the final WW promotion being in May 1980. **Bob Wooler**[801]: "We weren't getting good attendances and the interest in the Beatles was largely negative, especially from the Merseyside area. Most people who came to the Conventions were from outside Liverpool."

In October 1977 a London businessman wanted to donate £500 for a life-sized statue of the Beatles. The rest of the finance would be through private funding. The Council dismissed the idea. Some councillors maintained that the Beatles were "not able to sing" and suggested that they had made no real contribution to the city's culture. Others were indifferent as to what the Beatles had achieved. The chairwoman condemned the Beatles for introducing their generation to drugs and said that if there was a statue of a Liverpool entertainer, then it should be of someone who had an unblemished character and had made a major contribution to British culture. Her suggestion was Arthur Askey. Whilst it is staggering that nobody challenged these nincompoops, it does reveal one significant point, namely, that the Beatles were never totally popular, even in Liverpool. The histories often tell you that everybody loved them, but that was far from the case.

The editorial in the *Liverpool Echo* said, "How narrow minded, how short sighted and how typically out of touch with what people think and feel." It continued, "The Beatles were a brilliant manifestation of a grass roots movement, the contribution of which should not be measured in material terms, but in the sense of excitement and involvement and pride which it gave to the people of Liverpool. That is something that the councilors in their remote ivory tower cannot take away—even though they seem set on denying the city a Beatles monument, paid for by private subscription and at no charge to the ratepayers."

Ron Jones, the city's Tourism Officer, said that if the Cavern could be opened again it would be a major boost for the city. A taxi driver wrote to the *Echo* in support: "What other city in similar circumstances would have demolished it in the first place? As a city taxi driver, I recently took three French tourists to Mathew Street. What a sight greeted them! Everything closed on one side and where the Cavern stood was a waste ground full of cars. Like the Beatles or not, that street is a potential goldmine for the city. I just hope that the Cavern is opened up again and used as it should be—a worldwide tourist attraction."

In 1978 a Wallasey couple, Jim and Liz Hughes, opened the Magical Mystery Store in North John Street but the lease ran out in December 1980. They moved to 18 Mathew Street in January 1981 with much support from Beatle fans, both from donations and volunteer help. The centre included a replica of the Cavern stage and local bands could play there. But they never had the funding they required and they couldn't do it on their own.

In 1979, the American DJ and broadcaster, Dick Clark financed a film, *Birth Of The Beatles*, which was largely shot in Liverpool. There wasn't a Cavern to film but the replica was reasonably accurate, although the middle section was too wide and even though Bob Wooler was consulted, the DJ looked nothing like him. In its favour, Nigel Havers is a good George Martin but where did the director get the idea that Pete Best played drum solos whilst the rest of the Beatle left the stage? Oh, I get it now: Pete Best was the technical advisor.

One catastrophic event changed the city's attitude to the Beatles. **Bob Wooler**[802]: "The death of John Lennon at the end of 1980 transformed everything with regards to the Beatles. Everyone became Beatleised. Sam Leach organised a very big candlelight vigil on St George's Plateau in Lime Street. David Shepherd, the Bishop of Liverpool, was there with other luminaries. The weather was kind to us: the event was free and extremely well attended, and it was very touching. I felt then that there was a rebirth, a renaissance of the Beatles. It's extraordinary really but from the moment that John Lennon was shot by a crackpot, the whole attitude towards the Beatles changed. Beatles Conventions have done very well since that date."

Wooler is certainly right in that a growing stream of tourists visited the city from 1981 onwards. It would undoubtedly have been more if the city had not had its own troubles, notably the so-called Toxteth riots, which made some think twice before coming.

A local architect **David Backhouse**[803] wanted to develop the area. "British Rail asked me to look at the Cavern site and at Lime Street Station in September 1980, and it was just before John Lennon's death. We did a scheme for Lime Street Station and then they asked me to come up with ideas for the Cavern site. They didn't create a ventilation shaft for the loop line and they had just used it for the storage of materials and cabins. It wasn't until we did the scrape—a technical expression which means cleaning the site—that we found five wells on the site, and the biggest was about 40 feet below the surface. It was very, very spooky as Christine Ruth and I went with torches in the personnel skip of the crane

and we found ourselves in this vast cavern which had been a reservoir cut in 1850. We had no idea where we were going. We could have come to a waterfall and gone over the edge, but you can see a rope at the back of the dinghy and the lads on the bank were feeding this out to us. As we paddled forwards, they pulled the rope slightly back and so we were going nowhere. Then they let us go and we went round that curve and it was frightening."

Christine Ruth[804]: "I had met David Backhouse socially and he told me that they had found an underground cavern under the Cavern. I asked him to take me down as I was working for the BBC and I just thought, 'Oh well, I will be insured by the BBC if anything happens to me.' Nowadays, it would all have to be checked out with Health and Safety and I doubt if I could have done it. It was very scary as we had no idea how far the water went or how deep it was. I didn't even know how safe the dinghy was and I kept hoping that I wouldn't fall out. It was definitely clean water: there was nothing unpleasant about it. I thought it would make a very interesting item for people to hear on the radio, and it did. We got lots of comments about it."

A natural underground lake had been discovered under the Cavern—a second cavern in fact. This cavern extended across the site and turned up Mathew Street and down Harrington Street. And is the water still under the Cavern? **David Backhouse**[805]: "No, we had to get Cavern Walks finished to coincide with the opening of the Garden Festival and we had to clean it out. It was filled in with concrete. It is a shame as we could have opened up Cavern Walks and made a canal with bridges. That would have been an amazing tourist attraction, but expediency had to rule the day. If we had had more time, I am sure we could have designed the structure around it." It would have been the ideal place for rides in a Yellow Submarine too.

David Backhouse[806] submitted his plans to British Rail. "I was working at the time with the local builder and entrepreneur Ted Spencer and I was embargoed from practising as I had left my previous practice. I couldn't practice for a year and so I was working with Ted. I had the idea of reinstating the Cavern with a modest building

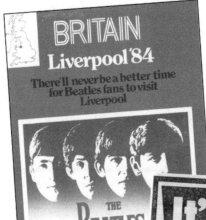

1984 ~ There'll never be a better time for Beatle fans to visit Liverpool

It's been a hard day's night

...and he's been working like a dog

Dejected Beatles curators long for yesterday

By Val Woan

"YESTERDAY, all their troubles seemed so far away"—but today dedicated Beatles fans Liz and Jim Hughes are dreading a future without their Cavern Mecca.

Financial problems have finally forced the closure of this original Beatle museum.

A sign over the door reads "Number 9 Dream". It refers to a John Lennon song but to the two owners of the Mecca, at No. 9 Cavern Walks, it summed up all their hopes for keeping the Beatles memory alive in Liverpool.

Now their dream has faded.

After 12 years of "fighting tooth and nail" to keep the Beatles name going in the city, Liz and Jim have decided they cannot go on any more.

Summer

From the days when their Magical Mystery Store was the only place fans could go to talk about their idols and buy memorabilia, the recent Beatles boom has caused too much big business competition.

Said Liz: "There are too many people jumping on the bandwagon and a little place like us cannot beat them. We had a good summer but now the tourists have gone and we just cannot afford to keep going. It is very sad."

Ironically, the closure comes just as Liz and Jim received the most important praise of all for their work.

"We went to the Freedom of the City ceremony and met Paul and Linda," said Liz. "They said they had heard all about the Mecca, thanked us for our dedication and told us to keep up the good work. Afterwards I cried my heart out."

The museum closed for the last time at the weekend and this week the Hughes', along with their many friends who have helped out over the years, are packing away the memories.

Then, say Liz and Jim, they plan to take a week off and decide about the future.

Jim Hughes packs away the memories of a faded dream at Cavern Mecca.

over it, but the day after John Lennon was killed, I designed Cavern Walks in a very similar state to the way it was built, an atrium with a massive roof, but it was only later when negotiating with the local planning officer Rod Hutchinson that we introduced the warehouse effect with the terracotta on it, but the embryonic building was designed the day after John died." And does that explain why it looks so much like the Dakota building?

Backhouse showed his plans to Cynthia and Julian Lennon who liked what he was doing. Ted Spencer had several other projects to hand and so Royal Insurance was approached for outside finance. British Rail was prepared to sell the land to their subsidiary, Royal Life Insurance. He convinced Royal Life of the validity of his plans and, on the first anniversary of John's assassination, the plans for a seven million pound shopping and office centre with penthouse luxury flats and a roof garden were announced. The ground floor shopping mall would have entrances in both Mathew Street and Harrington Street, and because of the way the streets sloped, both levels of shopping would be entered at ground level. The deal was struck and the building contractors, a local firm, Tyson's, began in October 1982.

Backhouse worked with a team of architects including Dominic McCannon. The flats were not built as Royal Life did not want a mixed development and it became seven floors of offices. The design was not a standard monochrome. If you look down from the skylight to the floor you will see how it goes from a strong yellow to near white. The terracotta was of especial interest to Backhouse, who was a potter and a co-founder of the Liverpool Craft Centre, also on Mathew Street.

The site lay between the main office area of the city and the shopping centre and so it had become a short cut for office workers. This made it a very viable proposition, and it was going to have a unique flavour. Laura Ashley, Culpeper and Next came on board, and then a Japanese retailers and a jewellers. The shops would be completed eight months before the offices to tie in with the International Garden Festival and the Tall Ships Festival and hence, should benefit from the additional trade coming into the city. Royal Life also

bought the Yellow Submarine from the London film première and displayed it on the first floor of the centre.

In June 1982 they found that they could not use the Cavern's original arches. **David Backhouse**[807]: "There was a gas mains on the site and we had to break the tops of the arches so that no gas could build up. If the gas had built up, there would otherwise have been a potential bomb going off. The tops of the arches had been broken but we reclaimed all the bricks that we could."

The original bricks were saved and taken to a warehouse in Kirkby. They had the mortar removed and were cleaned. 5,000 were sold for charity and others were used in the building of the new Cavern. Some metal slots were put in the tops of the arches and an air conditioning system was installed.

Although the dimensions of the original 1957 Cavern were duplicated, there was an extension with a larger stage. The club was deeper than the original club (30 steps instead of 18) and at right angles to the original premises. When you entered the original Cavern, the stage was directly in front of you and now it is to the left.

David Backhouse[808]: "The main criteria was to get the dimensions and the ambiance the same as it had been, but when the bigger gigs are on, they go to the bigger space at the back where the view of the stage and also the sound are a lot better. I've seen quite a lot of gigs on there like Lonnie Donegan. If he had been on the stage in the old Cavern, then only a few people could have seen him. There were 350 there that night but had he been on the front stage, less than 100 would have seen him, although all would have heard him."

The address, 10 Mathew Street, is the same, although the inscription above the door, "Where it all began", is not wholly accurate. The entrance is about 15 yards closer to North John Street than the original club but the fire exit onto Mathew Street is the exact site of the original doorway. With hindsight, this could have been the new entrance, but **David Backhouse**[809] disagrees. "It would have been awkward. When you are designing a large, complex building, it is quite a consideration to knit the whole thing together. We had to get the car parking on one side and the entrances into the shopping mall and the atrium right. In the end, it became impossible with the constraints of the planners and the constraints of the client's needs."

The result was a distinctive building that, admittedly, cannot be fully appreciated as it is so hemmed in. The glass lift, in particular, was very unusual for Liverpool and, for its time, quite exotic. It is worth viewing the building in detail. **David Backhouse**[810]: "There are a lot of idiosyncratic touches on the building. Because of my interest in ceramics, Cynthia Lennon designed a lot of the terracotta, and round the back, on the Harrington Street arch, there is a gorilla with a compact putting on lipstick. On the big arch as you go down into the car park, if you look up on the keystones, you will see the gorilla. As we were designing the building, Baron Foster said that art is to architecture as lipstick is to a gorilla, that is, irrelevant. I thought that was a good quote so we got this sculptor to make it. I made a postcard of it and sent it off to him but didn't hear anything." Baron Foster is often referred to as Lord Wobbly in view of the structural problems with the Millennium Bridge.

The 5,000 bricks from the original Cavern went on sale in August 1983. They were £5 each and the money was to buy a minibus for the Strawberry Field children's home. They were authenticated by Ray McFall but it's a shame he didn't look at the plaque too closely as he was not the 'founding owner' of the Cavern. I bought one and clearly I should have bought a wall as bricks now fetch £300 at auction.

In 1983 a crane driver working on the development caught the Cavern sign across the road and damaged it. This remained in place for another 10 years and caused nothing but confusion. In the 1990s, the Cavern's management did consider a night raid to remove it but they were saved the effort as it blew down in a storm. Now there is a sign for the Cavern Club on one side and the Cavern pub on the other.

Merseyside County Council had started its MerseyBeatle Weekends in 1982. You arrive on the Friday, have a city centre walking tour on the Saturday which included seeing Beatle films in a reconstruction of the Cavern in Cavern Mecca, an Ale Trail in the evening and a Magical History Tour and a ride on the ferry on Sunday. Also, in 1983, the company Cavern City Tours Limited was registered. They started a series of themed weekends in conjunction with the Atlantic Tower Thistle Hotel and tied in with Beatle birthdays. Radio City had opened its own museum, Beatle City, in Seel Street.

Things were moving on the Beatle tourism trail at last. In 1984, a record shop owner, Ian Wallace, opened a souvenir shop, The Beatles Store, in Mathew Street. There was a sculpture of the Beatles above the door. The time was ripe for the Cavern, or at least a Cavern, to open its doors.

9

CAVERN WALKS

Cavern owners:
Tommy Smith and George Downey
1984-1985

Sunday 25 March 1984

Former Merseybeat musicians were invited to sign the wall behind the stage at the new Cavern Club. Many of them went first to the White Star, a pub that looked the same as it had 20 years earlier. Whenever someone aged between 35 and 45 entered, there was widespread speculation: Wasn't he in a group?" Cheering and applause marked Bob Wooler's arrival.

You might have assumed that the musicians would still know or, at least, recognise each other, but this was not so. Many of them were meeting for the first time because there had been so many groups and venues on Merseyside. Norman Kuhlke of the Swinging Blue Jeans was stopped outside the club by someone who said, "You'll get free booze if you go through that door and say you played in a group." Having said that, all the signatures on the wall did seem legitimate.

Observing the signing was like seeing umpteen editions of *This Is Your Life* rolled into one. Musicians who hadn't met in 20 years hugged each other, but every conversation was interrupted by another old friend. There was much catching-up to be done, especially as many had brought along

wives, children and even grandchildren. A lot of Merseybeat musicians had married their fans.

After all this time, some had difficulty in recognising old friends. Clive Hornby was well known as Jack Sugden from *Emmerdale Farm*, so everybody knew him. Another Dennison, Steve McLaren, scarcely looked 25, while age had taken its toll on others. Gus Travis with his sleek black hair had worked on his appearance, while Lee Curtis in white tuxedo and a medallion had the look of a club entertainer. A young boy blocked a photographer's view as Lee was about to sign the wall. He was asked to move and replied, "It's all right. It's only Grandad."

Wherever possible, groups assembled in their original line-ups to sign the coloured squares on the wall. So the Swinging Blue Jeans went on stage, followed by the Dennisons, the Undertakers, the Merseybeats and the Fourmost. Hank Walters went up with his Dusty Road Ramblers and said, "I've also signed for a couple of the lads who've died. They'd have wanted to be included." Very country.

Roy Brooks of Roy and the Dions watched quietly as the better known musicians signed the

Beatle City
The Total Experience

Wish we could show you a picture of Beatle City – but you don't easily put a Total Experience down on paper.

And anyway, when this leaflet goes to press, we'll still be building it. A good few hundred hard days' nights will have gone into planning and creating before we open in January 1984, at Seel Street, Liverpool.

One thing, though, we're certain of. Beatle City will be a Total Experience that's totally new – and quite unique anywhere in the world. An absolute 'must' for Beatle fans. A stunning show for anyone at all.

We could give you some idea of how Beatle City will <u>look</u>. Talk about full-size studio sets, lights, holograms. Clothes and instruments that belonged to the Fab Four. But that might sound more like an exhibition.

We could tell you how Beatle City will <u>sound</u> (as if we needed to!). But that wouldn't tell the whole story either.

What we can't possibly tell you is how it will <u>feel</u> to be absorbed by Beatle City. Because that's the Total Experience – and everyone must feel that for themselves!

Eight days a week, from January 1984!

In fact, we'll be open every day except Christmas Day and Boxing Day. Special rates for groups and parties. Write for details now – to Beatle City Limited, P.O. Box 12, Liverpool L69 1RA, England. Telephone: 051-709 0117

BEATLE CITY
The Total Experience

Arthur Dooley's famous statue (right) in Mathew Street serves as a prominent reminder of The Beatles and The Cavern's importance

Gerry Marsden cuts the ribbon at the Cavern

Liverpool Echo, Wednesday, February 22, 1984   7

Tommy and George in the rebuilt Cavern. Picture by John Davidson.

Tommy tackles the Cavern gamble

By Colin Wright

TOMMY SMITH and George Downey are the chalk and cheese partnership set to turn Liverpool into Beatles City again.

They talk with an assured ease about the re-birth of the world famous Mathew Street Cavern Club . . . an ease which belies the fact that they are putting their reputations on the line with a project which most multi-million pound leisure tycoons would give their right arms for.

Tommy Smith is the "hard man of Liverpool" — the Conservative-voting footballer who has won every major domestic honour.

George Downey is the quietly-spoken staunch Evertonian and one-time Post Office engineer, who supports Labour and will not have a word said against the party.

Together they have formed a business partnership which has stood the test of 15 years and gained the reputation of being solid, dependable and — most importantly — successful in its own small way.

Their slow, steady and unflappable approach to the job has been enough to beat off competition from Britain's top leisure groups and breweries and give them the chance to create what many believe could become one of Europe's top entertainment spots.

Royal Insurance, which is pumping millions into developing Mathew Street as a major shop and office tourist attraction, chose their newly formed Cavern Entertainments company for the project ahead of a host of others.

At least 13 big group's were in the running to win the Cavern lease when Royal first floated the project. In the end it boiled down to just three . . . Virgin Records, Mecca and the comparitively miniscule Liverpool business.

"To be honest we thought we stood no chance against that lot, but there you go, we got it, didn't we?" says George — at 48, ten years the senior partner.

"We had the backing of Tetley and EMI, so we knew we had the muscle and we just slogged on from there".

The slog was worth it. They have cornered the market on a legend which spawned names like The Beatles, Gerry and the Pacemakers, Cilla Black and Freddie and the Dreamers and spread the term "Merseybeat" throughout the world.

Their new Cavern development will be significantly larger than that of the early 1960's when it opens its doors for the first time on April 26.

The original club has been recreated, but this time will feature the new generation of Mersey bands and talent as well as offering nostalgic film shows and disco's.

From there all similarities end. Tommy and George are building a new pub above the underground site, which will sell traditional beers and special label "Cavern" brews available no-where else in the world.

Downstairs the club will be supported by another bar, restaurant and memorabilia shop.

Challenge

The cost to the partnership is at least £350,000 — big beer indeed for a business which started in 1970 with a lower Castle Street bar, which Tommy and George altered themselves in their spare time.

Life since then has been good to both Tommy and George. They are not short of a few bob, they can afford to drive Mercedes cars and take regular trips abroad . . . so why step out to take a big and unnecessary gamble?

"Let's get it straight, if this does take a dive — and we are positive it won't — we will still have other ways to make a crust," says Tommy Smith.

"Businesswise this will be the biggest thing which has ever happened to me. It is a real challenge which we will make work."

For George it is, "the ultimate. It would give me an awful lot of pride to see through a successful — not just for myself, but for Liverpool".

But behind the local pride there is a strong feeling that the massive tourist potential of the Cavern and its appeal to Liverpudlians could make them both rich.

"But if it doesn't . . ." George shrugs his shoulders.

The bands sign the Cavern wall, Above; Swinging Blue Jeans, Ray Ennis, Norman Khulke, Ralph Ellis and Les Braid. Left; Lee Curtis Below; Merseybeats Billy Kinsley, Aaron Williams and Tony Crane

wall. When his turn came, he chose one of the larger boxes and in bold lettering wrote "ROY BROOKS AND THE DIONS", very close to, but bigger than the Beatles' name. That sheer cheek is typical of Merseybeat.

The new Cavern was the same size as the old one, but also had an extension. The passageway from one to the other was like a Liverpool street. A 29-year-old artist, Nicki Palin painted a 60 foot mural to run along the staircase down to the Cavern and it took two months to complete, costing £4,000. It featured full scale figures painted with emulsion. The figures have lasted. They have been over-painted with black emulsion.

Competition to manage the new Cavern was intense. There were thirteen bids including Virgin Records and Mecca. Royal Life gave the lease to two local entrepreneurs, Tommy Smith and George Downey, who had the backing of Tetley Bitter and EMI. 38-year-old Tommy Smith was the former Liverpool and England football hard man and his partner, George Downey, was ten years older. They had opened their first venture, a bar, in Castle Street in 1970 and they had done well, both driving Mercedes.

Smith and Downey formed a new company, Cavern Entertainments, and they ploughed £350,000 into the venture including the Abbey Road pub, which was on ground level above the Cavern and would serve a special Cavern brew. They announced that they would feature the new generation of Merseyside bands as well as nostalgic film shows and discos. There was talk of another city centre club, Bradys, changing its name to the Cavern and Royal Life took out a High Court action to prevent this.

Thursday 26 April 1984
The opening of Cavern Walks. The whole project had cost £9m, but building costs always escalate. A statue by John Doubleday was placed in the new Mathew Street shopping centre called Cavern Walks. As Mike McCartney succinctly said when he unveiled it, "I wouldn't have recognised our kid if he wasn't playing the guitar left-handed."

David Backhouse[811]: "Royal Life had commissioned John Doubleday to do it and he had made the Charlie Chaplin sculpture in Leicester Square. Now that is a very good work: there is tension in the legs and it looks like Charlie Chaplin. We

commissioned him and told him what we wanted. I even posed in the position Lennon used to sing with his guitar high and his legs slightly apart, and we did the marquet and it looked okay, but when the final thing came, it was a disaster. The *Liverpool Echo* thought of running a competition to determine who was who. It wasn't his inability but I think he bottled out. He said that it wasn't supposed to be the Beatles, it was supposed to be a representation of Merseybeat, which was a load of nonsense. Paul Mercer from the Royal was very, very specific about what we wanted and I remember Mike McCartney's face when it was unveiled. He was totally aghast. It was a shame as it was a great opportunity to have a really brilliant piece of sculpture."

Mike McCartney[812]: "Don't remind me! I will never unveil a statue again! I said no at first as this was not my group. They said, 'Look Mike, Liverpool is not in a good way and we would like you to do this.' Okay, I said, I would take my personal feelings out of it as it was good for Liverpool. This big opening was with the world and his dog, and now Mike McCartney is going to perform the opening thingy. I had to pull something and the cover came off the statue. I had not seen it before and I looked at it and thought, 'Oh dear.' Everybody was going, 'Can we have a picture of you with John?' and I'm going, 'Which one's John?' The only way I knew Ringo was because of the drumsticks in his hand."

Tourists overlook that there are also offices in Cavern Walks. **David Backhouse**[813]: "There are 70,000 feet of offices and it took a long time to fill them. Because of the feasibility study the Royal had to achieve a certain level of rental, and that level was not compatible with what was being obtained at the time in Liverpool. They had to wait for the market to catch up and as far as I know, the offices are now all let. Tweeds, who were the quantity surveyors on the project, have their offices there. There has been some refurbishment and Vivienne Westwood has a store in Cavern Walks, so there are some really good tenants."

The opening ceremony was performed by Gerry Marsden. The first band to play at the new venue was Mojo Filter and then Gerry Marsden played with his new Pacemakers. **Tommy Smith**[814]: "He is a great lad and a wonderful feller. He has never lost his Scouseness, he has never lost sight of the fact that he came from Merseyside. What a great lad he is and he really enjoys life. The Beatles weren't interested in football, but Gerry was. I knew Gerry was because he was a Liverpool supporter. It surprised me when he did 'You'll Never Walk Alone' as it seemed out of date for him, but then Shanks got a hold of it. Gerry played in my testimonial."

There was a celebrity opening night and there were performances from Billy J Kramer, Swinging Blue Jeans and the Merseybeats with some lively stand-up from the compère, Jimmy Tarbuck. **John Gorman**[815] of Scaffold: "We were very peeved because Jimmy Tarbuck was compèring and he wouldn't introduce us for some reason. We kept hanging on and waiting to do a turn. Mike hates hanging around and just wants to get on and do it. I think we got on after midnight, which was a waste of time by then."

Bill Heckle[816]: "Their idea was that all the people who originally visited the Cavern were 10 to 20 years older and wanted home comforts when they went out. They installed carpeting and lounge furniture and in a way they were right as since the demise of the Shakespeare and the Wooky Hollow, there was a gap for a cabaret lounge. Blundell Street works like that now, but it has never worked at the Cavern."

For the Beatles fans, Liz and Jim Hughes of Cavern Mecca were offered a place in Cavern Walks from April 1984. David Backhouse designed the premises and the proposed annual rent was only £2,000. Even so, by the end of 1984, Liz and Jim had too much competition and Liz Hughes said, "There are too many people jumping on the bandwagon and a little place like us cannot beat them. We had a good summer but now the tourists have gone and we just cannot afford to keep going. It is very sad."

During the summer of 1984, the Liverpool Playhouse staged *Cavern Of Dreams* written by Carol Ann Duffy and directed by Bill Morrison. This energetic production included Andrew Schofield and early performances from Ian Hart, Michael Starke and Roy Brandon as well as John McArdle as Bob Wooler. It was about a fictitious group, Billy and the Dingles and incorporated

many anecdotes from the book, *Let's Go Down The Cavern.*

Friday 27 / Saturday 28 / Sunday 29 April 1984

Cavern Mecca's weekend party featured Faron's Flamingos, Karl Terry and the Cruisers, Beryl Marsden, the Dark Ages, Cavern and Mojo Filter. The guests include Tony Barrow, Paddy Delaney, Uncle Charlie Lennon, Cynthia Lennon, Pete Shotton and Victor Spinetti. **Norman Killon**[817]: "At first Liz and Jim Hughes had a little collectors' shop in Moorfields and then they did a convention at Gulliver's and every record the DJ played he said, 'Here's another old record by the Beatles.' Even then, any record that you played by the Beatles was old, and I said to Liz and Jim, 'If you do it next year, I'll do it for nothing,' which I did. Then they had a place in Mathew Street, and they never made any money out of it because they were too early. Other people are now making a fortune out of the Beatles, and they lost so many valuable items as well. The one thing I regret not getting, but I couldn't afford it, was the visitors book from the Whitechapel branch of NEMS. Anthony Newley had opened it so he was there and also all the other VIPs who came subsequently. An American bought it for £40. I am kicking myself as I am telling you this. Liz and Jim Hughes would have made Cavern Mecca work in the end, but they needed less of a friendly relationship and more of a business relationship. They welcomed everybody in and you could touch everything and things were disappearing."

Saturday 28 July 1984

The Cavern was open all day for the Box Of Toys appeal and donations were received for needy and sick local children. Over 2,000 toys were collected. There was live music from Box Of Toys and Joey Musker and the guests included Ian McCulloch of Echo and the Bunnymen and Pete Burns of Dead Or Alive. Children were welcomed by someone dressed as the bear, Echo Ted. Less scary than being welcomed by Pete Burns, I suppose.

There was a Beatles auction at Sotheby's in August 1984 which included gold discs, some stage suits (with pockets for plectrums!) and some scribble from John, but Paul McCartney's leather trousers from his Hamburg days were withdrawn. They were apparently too short to be McCartney's. The counter-argument was that he had

□ READY TO ROCK: Bob Wooler, DJ in the Cavern Club in the 60s, left, and former Beatles manager, Alan Williams

THE Cavern Club in Liverpool is once more to be the venue for a Beatles Convention.

The 20th anniversary convention will be held on Sunday and will be hosted by ex-Beatles manager Allan Williams and 60s Cavern Club DJ Bob Wooler, both now 67.

Allan, who managed the Beatles from 1959 until 1961, when a row with John Lennon led to his split with the group, said: "It's fitting that the Cavern should host the event. Everyone knows it's the place where it all started.

"The convention will be a truly international event with Beatles acts from all around the world. It's going to be a great occasion."

Bob and Allan staged Liverpool's first Beatles convention in The Pickwick Club in 1977.

Bob Wooler, who was resident Cavern DJ between 1961 and 1963, said: "We despaired of finding suitable venues for the first four conventions. But in 1980 all that changed. When Lennon was shot there was a real Beatles renaissance and from that moment everyone wanted to jump on the bandwagon."

■ Doors open at 6.00pm and tickets cost £4.

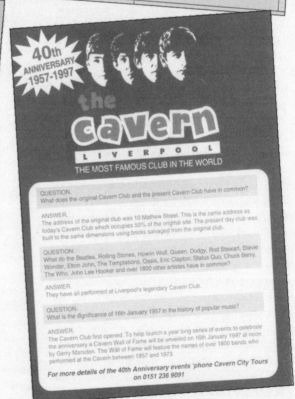

sold the trousers to Faron, and Faron, being small, cut them down. Still, the auction raised nearly £400,000. Kitsch was also a feature of Beatle auctions and no auction would be complete without Beatle stockings, lunchboxes and talcum powder tins.

Beatle memorabilia auctions were already a feature of London life and the first Merseyside one was under the auspices of the auctioneers, Eldon E Worrall, on 31 August 1984. This was a modest affair with the 170 lots fetching £4,000. An autographed photograph of the Beatles fetched £400, but it was evident that there was a goodly supply of material from the Beatles' formative years in the city. A smart dealer would buy in Liverpool and sell in London.

The first issue of *The Cavern Quarterly* said, "How can we cram so much into such a tiny space?" and that was making a virtue of a liability. Cavern Walks was never big enough to become a major shopping experience. There are only around 20 shops and cafés. However, the concept of revitalising Mathew Street was admirable. The Cavern Quarter Initiative was to make the whole area smarter and make it a place that everyone would want to visit.

The opportunity was taken to present new bands at the Cavern, but the owners soon found that there were problems, particularly with the lunchtime sessions where people could just drift in to hear the music. Far too many of them were drifting right out again.

In September 1984, George Downey told the *Echo* that they had fallen out with the booking agents and he would be choosing the acts himself. The lunchtime sessions had been a disaster. "I know you cannot suit all the people all of the time but I do want our customers to come down, have a drink and a bite to eat and enjoy some entertainment. The bands we were getting were not providing that. A lot of them were way out with only a very small following of fans. They used to frighten away the customers."

And then this revealing comment: "Whilst I appreciate that not everyone are big drinkers, I don't appreciate discovering that some of the bands' audiences bought nothing at all or brought their own in with them. We are, after all, in business." Downey was returning the Cavern

to more nostalgic times and he would be presenting rock'n'roll, jazz, folk and poetry readings and a few buskers.

Friday 28 September 1984

A five-hour carnival to celebrate 25 years of the Cavern (not sure how that was calculated) is halted by police after managers complained that their staff were hanging out of windows listening to the music instead of working. The carnival featured several bands along with jugglers, magicians, clowns and dancers. Karl Terry and the Cruisers were stopped from performing.

Sunday 7 October 1984

The start of a weekly talent competition with the prize of a recording session at Amazon Studios and sponsored by Tetley Bitter. It was hosted by the folk singers Jack Owen and Brian Jacques. Among the successful acts are the busker Paul Wilson, Bolton poet Phil Cooper, Widnes poet Jean Wrigley, singer Tony Flynn, country singer Chris Elsom, the bands Annex (Liverpool), Fritzz (St Helens) and the Reasons (Formby), plus Colin the Birkenhead Bass Man. **Brian Jacques**[818]: "It wasn't really the Cavern as it was so much cleaner. They had a fantastic carpet and woven into the design was 'Cavern'. I said to the manager, 'What does 'Craven' mean?" He panicked as he thought it might be wrong."

Everything appeared to be going wrong in Liverpool. Christopher Oakley, editor of *Liverpool Echo*, attended a financial conference in Europe and commented, "The only time potential investors mentioned the city's name was as a joke to lighten the mood." In a 1984 study of the economic health and quality of the European Unions 102 largest cities, Liverpool was placed at 102.

Andy Byrne of *Liverpool Echo* on 5 January 1985 described the décor as "sumptuous". Maybe though the word is out of place as he also says, "The restaurant area is very swish and modern and wouldn't be out of place in a McDonalds." He says that the club is struggling to find an identity but it is "beautifully furnished, well managed and efficiently designed." Not really the Cavern, then.

Tommy Smith and George Downey were always more interested in the Abbey Road pub as the barrelage was going to be greater. **Tommy Smith**[819]: "Once a year we had the Beatles week but people weren't sure whether the Cavern was open or closed. We did some advertising but it never paid for itself. We were fortunate that the Abbey Road pub paid for the two of them, but after a couple of years, we let them go. We should have used it for a different reason, for something other than a night club. We could have done a lot more advertising and put in some memorabilia. All we did was put in seating. Without the Beatles, the Cavern didn't mean much. We should have turned it into a museum."

Alex McKechnie[820]: "It was very difficult to get anyone to go to the Cavern. They had carpets there and they didn't aim at any particular market. The Cavern didn't work as a commercial venture until the students started going there."

Friday 23 August 1985

To kick off the first ever Beatles Festival Week, there is the Beatles Freak Ball at the Cavern with the Fab Four, Mojo Filter and a disco.

10

TROUBLED TIMES

Cavern owners:
Jimmy McVitie and others
1985-1989

In October 1985, the *Liverpool Echo* reported that the Cavern club had been sold in a £500,000 deal. George Downey said, "It was an offer we couldn't refuse." The new manager, Alan O'Donovan, said, "We don't feel that there is any mileage left in the Beatles' name. It's possible that we could get rid of the Beatles flavour altogether." How could someone be so hopelessly wrong? In its place would be an ultra-modern disco with flashing lights and to his credit, contemporary music.

Saturday 26 October 1985
The plans for the club angered Beatle fanatics, and the Liverpool Beatles Appreciation Society staged a protest. They marched from the Cavern to the Town Hall (not much of a march, in all honesty) and handed in a petition (and surely better to hand it in at the Cavern rather than the Town Hall).

Thursday 21 November 1985
The Cavern under new management started promoting local bands. It was the Young Lions and the Bingo Brothers this night with a disco. The popular Ground Pig would appear the following week, but then things went very quiet.

Radio City's Beatle City in Seel Street was packed with memorabilia but the two million pound development dragged the company into a mire. In the winter months, they only had a handful of visitors each day but its failure could be attributed to weak marketing, bad location and poor design. They agreed to sell the business to John Anton of Transworld Leisure in April 1986 but only received £100,000 of the proposed £500,000 purchase price. He had plans to transfer the memorabilia to a new building at the Transworld Garden Festival site. The deal fell through in October 1986 when Anton's other businesses collapsed with debts of three and a half million pounds. In April 1987 Beatle City was sold to London businessman, John Symons. In July the contents were shipped to the West End Market shopping centre in Dallas for four months and there were plans to take it to Canada or Japan.

In February 1987, Goldaden took over Cavern Entertainments and hence, the lease of the Cavern and the Abbey Road pub. They already had Trader Jacks in Berry Street, and they were granted a loan by Tetley Walker to complete the deal. Within a month, Tetley's had called in the Receiver to protect their interests. Steve Foster

SIR PAUL GETS BACK

● We love you . . . fans watch Paul at the original Cavern Club

He's doing his first Cavern gig since he was a Beatle

By Philippa Bellis

THE SCRAMBLE started today for the hottest ticket of the century - to see Sir Paul McCartney back at the Cavern.

The former Beatles star confirmed last night that he will hold his last gig of the Millennium at the place where it all began.

And eager fans were on the phone within minutes of the news being announced early today.

But only 150 tickets will be available for the show and will be distributed FREE via a worldwide raffle.

Filmed

Sir Paul will be the first former Beatle to play the Cavern since the band's last gig on August 3, 1963.

The comeback, scheduled for Tuesday, December 14, will be filmed for posterity by Sir Paul's director, Geoff Wonfor.

Cavern City Tours boss Bill Heckle said today: "It is a dream come true for us and will bring international coverage for the city.

"Because it is such an historic occasion, McCartney wants it documented. There was only ever one-and-a-half minutes of him playing at the Cavern ever recorded.

● Yesterdays . . . at the Cavern

"International TV rights will be negotiated and there is talk of a live link-up with the Internet.

It will be McCartney's 281st gig at the Cavern - but his first for more than a quarter of a century.

Sir Paul said: "Rock 'n' roll has shaped my life and it changed the sound and the thinking of the country. Before the Beatles ever got big they started playing at the Cavern.

"I am going back for just one night as a nod to the music that has always and will ever thrill me.

"I can't think of a better way to rock out the end of the century than with a rock 'n' roll gig at the Cavern."

The scramble for tickets officially starts after the weekend.

Five HMV stores - Liverpool, Birmingham, Glasgow, Newcastle and London - will have entry forms available for 75 pairs of tickets from next Monday.

Fans will fill in an entry form to go into a ballot, but HMV bosses warned that only a limited number of forms will be available.

And they advise the public not to start queuing until Sunday evening at the earliest.

Those who miss out are likely to be able to watch it live on television but that will be little consolation to fans, Sir Paul's spokesman Geoff Baker acknowledged.

"Millions are going to want to be at this gig and the fact is that millions are going to be disappointed," said Geoff. "It's going to be the gig of the century."

● People were urged today NOT to ring Cavern City tours or HMV, but to pick up an application form from HMV stores from Monday. The ECHO has no further ticket details.

John gets a brand new mop top

JOHN Lennon's Mathew Street statue has been given a new head.

Sculptor David Webster (left) swapped the figure's 50s-style quiff for a 60s mop top, as thousands of Beatles fans are set to flock to the area for Sir Paul McCartney's Cavern gig tomorrow.

David said: "It's how I wanted him to look in the first place. But the Cavern owners wanted the 50s version. It was always a possibility that the look could be changed later.

"I always wanted to cast Lennon as most people remember him in the Beatles with his mop-top haircut.

"I copied the expression using photographs. I hope Paul McCartney likes it, I'm one of the lucky ones as I've got a ticket to his concert."

Hundreds of tourists have photos taken alongside the fibreglass and bronze sculpture every day.

ED: Cavern boss Bill Heckle

GIRL fans are offering SEX in a bid to get tickets for Paul McCartney's historic Cavern gig, we can reveal.

It's the first time Sir Paul has played the legendary Liverpool venue since the Beatles last appeared there back in 1963.

And demand for the one-off gig next Tuesday has made it the hottest ticket on the planet.

Bribe

Bill Heckle, manager of The Cavern, said: "Women have been blatantly accosting me in the club, trying to bribe me with their bodies.

"I've been repeatedly offered sex in exchange for a ticket."

Other lures have included a £10,000 all-expenses-paid holiday in California

Pete misses out on reunion as he drums up support in Germany

By Peter Grant

ONE man who won't be there tonight is Pete Best, the Beatles first drummer.

He is on a world tour with his band and will be playing a sell-out concert in Bremen, Germany.

Pete was sacked from the band to make way for Ringo Starr.

His brother and manager Roag said: "I'll be there tonight but Pete can't make it; he is working. — touring the world with his new album Casbah Coffee Club.

"It is a pity Paul didn't make the announcement earlier because it would have been a great opportunity for Pete and Paul to hook up again after all those years."

Roag, who had to pull out of Pete's tour due to a hand injury, added: "It's been a great year for Pete. Earlier in August we celebrated the 40th birthday of the Casbah where the Beatles first played. Pete's diary is booked solid throughout the year 2000.

"Next year he will present his An Audience With type shows in Britain."

City goes Macca crazy

Sir Paul flies in for gig of century — Page 2

It's the biggest gig in the world

By Paddy Shennan

IN five days time it will be Sir Paul McCartney but right here, right now, Bill Heckle is possibly one of the most popular men in Liverpool.

How else would you explain a stranger asking to have sex with him?

"I've been offered all sorts in the last few days," says Bill, one of three directors of Cavern City Tours, which owns the Cavern.

"On Saturday a woman offered to have sex with me – if I gave her a ticket. I said 'No thank you' – and yes I did tell my wife!"

Less glamorously, someone offered him £1,000 for one of the application forms for tickets – and one of the Cavern's draymen asked whether Bill could get him two tickets, adding 'There'll be a tenner in it for you.'

"A tenner!" says Bill, with disgust. "If I was going to be bought, I'd expect more than a tenner!"

The worldwide publicity has even seen what appears to be a genuine long-lost Heckle cousin get in touch for the first time in 40 years . . . from Peru.

"He phoned out of the blue. He spent 20 minutes talking about this and that – and then asked 'Can you get me a ticket?'"

Again, sadly, the answer had to be 'No.'

The 130 tickets going to the public (70 others will go to the world's press and the venue also needs to accommodate a produc-

● Music maestros . . . Cavern directors Dave Jones, George Guinness and Bill Heckle take to the stage at the

Hey, we're playing the Cavern! Wow!

Macca talks to the press inside The Cavern before the gig

The Cavern comeback

Sir Paul McCartney gets back to where he once belonged

Pictures DENIS O'REGAN

Sir Paul McCartney returned to his roots last night when he performed at The Cavern in Liverpool, the club where The Beatles began their rise to fame. *Review: Page 5*

was an accountant in Rodney Street and he had Joe Heuston manage the club on behalf of the Receiver for a while. Somewhere around this time, the leases were split so that the Abbey Road and the Cavern became separate entities. The Abbey Road has been successful in its own right and is now called Flares.

Friday 10 April 1987

The Blue Magnolia Jazz Band had a residency at the Cavern and added some young musicians, the Juvenile Jazz Combo as support. This seven-piece band from local schools won a prize as the top group on *Saturday Superstore*.

Tuesday 2 June 1987

It was 20 years ago today, so there was a *Sgt Pepper* celebration at the Cavern. It featured Scotland's top Beatle band, Ringer, and local heroes, Two's A Crowd (who became Up And Running).

RPMC, the biggest radio consultants in the US, had hired Abbey Road studios to show them to 120 influential Americans and they then came to Liverpool with shock jock Howard Stern. They transmitted a programme to the States. The UK organiser was Bob Young, who co-wrote 'Down Down' and worked as road manager for Status Quo. Bob befriended Bill Heckle and Dave Jones and he forms an important part of the next chapter as he organised several of the main events.

Monday 5 October 1987

Free lunchtime concert with Liverpool Express to celebrate the 25th anniversary of the release of "Love Me Do"

Saturday 27 August 1988

The Bootleg Beatles played the Cavern as part of the Merseybeatle Convention. It was a dramatic convention as there was a book burning of the scurrilous biography, *The Lives Of John Lennon* by Albert Goldman. Dave Jones comments, "Normally fans are quite mild-mannered people but when you get rubbish like this, it provokes people into a response."

A million pound scheme to smarten Mathew Street started with new paving stones for a pedestrian only area.

Mike Byrne[821] had been a manager at Beatle City and seen what Radio City was doing wrong. "In 1988, I was looking a site for The Beatles Story. The first place was in Mathew Street, which is where it should have been but there was no space as I needed 7,000 square feet and there was no parking. I had to have parking space for coaches. I looked at the Albert Dock and I went into the basement which hadn't been used for 50 years and it was a smelly hole. It had arches and my wife Bernie and I thought it had to be there. There had to be a replica Cavern, as well as Mathew Street and the White Room for John Lennon. Our tunnel is within a foot of the original width, it is so close, but, of course, in the original Cavern there are three tunnels."

In February 1989, Paul McCartney announced plans to turn the former Liverpool Institute building into a "Fame" academy, soon to be LIPA.

Jimmy McVitie became the new owner of the Cavern. He brought live music into the Cavern and the Saturday afternoon sessions did well. **Bill Heckle**[822]: "Jimmy McVitie went for a new market with the students. He made it very cheap to get in, reduced the price of the ale and put on dance music, and he turned the fortunes of the Cavern around. His student nights on Mondays would be packed. The formula worked and there were two reasons for that: lots of university places and at the time, not much for students to do." But Jimmy McVitie hated the tourists: he would say that took photographs and didn't spend money. It obsessed him so much that he would sometimes stand at the bottom of the stairs and say, "You can't come in unless you buy a drink."

Saturday 24 June 1989

Jimmy McVitie had made Roy Chin his manager. There was a serious assault on a customer, James Paton. He had been punched by the club bouncer Kurt Hughes—actually, McVitie's stepson—and knocked to the floor where he banged his head. McVitie and Chin carried his body into Mathew Street and when they saw he had not recovered they took him to the Royal Liverpool Hospital and said that they did not know how he had been injured. Paton was left with permanent brain damage.

August 1989

Beatlefreak Ball at the Cavern was part of the Merseybeatle Festival. One of the bands that was performing was a Russian band, Girl, which had been brought over by Allan Williams. **Bill Heckle**[823]: "The following day there was an event

It was a special night, says Sir Paul

AN AUDIENCE of one daughter, 300 invited guests and three million Internet users saw Sir Paul return to his roots for The Cavern Club concert.

The fashion designer Stella McCartney watched as her father and his band played 13 songs, including *I Saw Her Standing There*, a Beatles number he first performed at the club in the early Sixties.

Geoff Baker, Sir Paul's publicist, said an estimated three million people had logged on to watch the one-off performance via the Internet site.

"It's amazing, I think it's the biggest webcast ever," he added.

Sir Paul's set was made up mainly of the rock 'n' roll standards of his recent album *Run Devil Run*, including the Ricky Nelson song *Lonesome Town*, of which both he and his late wife Linda were huge fans in their teens. "This is dedicated to loved ones past, present and future," he said as he introduced it.

After the show Sir Paul said: "I'm elated. I can't think of a better place to be.

"I always knew it would be a special night but this is better than I could have hoped. We wanted to rock out the century — we did it, we rocked Liverpool and the world bopped too."

Now and then: Sir Paul playing at The Cavern last night and, above right, with the Beatles in the early 1960s

MACCA'S NIGHT OF MAGIC AT BEATLES' CAVERN

By IAN DISLEY

PAUL McCartney rolled back the yesterdays last night for a magical night at the club where the Beatles legend was born.

The Cavern had waited more than 36 years for Macca to come back to where he once belonged.

And after a nostalgia-packed gig at Liverpool's most famous music venue it was clear he still belongs.

Sir Paul beamed: "It's fantastic to be back — what better way to rock out the century?"

It was a bit like old times as Sir Paul belted out Fab Four classics like I Saw Her Standing There in front of an audience of just 300.

But only a bit. Around 500million fans logged on to a live music link on the Internet, but found it jammed.

And millions more around the globe tuned into TV and radio broadcasts of the 75-minute show, which

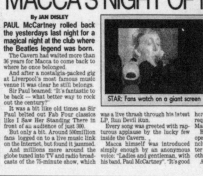

STAR: Fans watch on a giant screen

was a live thrash through his latest LP, Run Devil Run.

Every song was greeted with rapturous applause by the lucky few inside the Cavern.

Macca himself was introduced simply enough by an anonymous voice: "Ladies and gentleman, with his band, Paul McCartney". "It's good

THE PLAYLIST	
❶ Honey Hush	❼ Twenty Flight Rock
❷ Blue Jean Bop	❽ No Other Baby
❸ Brown-Eyed Handsome Man	❾ Try Not To Cry
❹ Fabulous	❿ Shake A Hand
❺ What It Is	⓫ All Shook Up
❻ Lonesome Town	⓬ I Saw Her Standing There
	Encore: Party

here limit" and "We're not doing requests," were about as chatty as Macca got.

But that said, every time he opened his mouth the crowd — including his fashion designer daughter Stella, his brother Mike and 27 other relatives — went wild.

And if the cheers were loud for Paul's version of Elvis's All Shook Up or Ricky Nelson's Lonesome Town, which he dedicated to "loved ones past, present and future," you should have heard the screams for the last song of the main set, I Saw Her Standing There.

The crowd made up of fans, Macca's family and a handful of jour-

nalists went bananas when they heard the intro to the only Beatles number of the night.

With Pink Floyd's Dave Gilmour on guitar and Deep Purple drummer Ian Paice keeping time at the back, the music was superb.

After performing a single encore, Presley's Party, Macca swept off-stage saying: "See you next time."

The only complaint was that the show was too short.

Jane King, 31, Glossop, Derbyshire said: "Paul was looking good and I thought he sounded good. But it wasn't long enough."

The club has been rebuilt since the Beatles' days. But one refurbishment was missing last night.

A leather settee in Paul's private room was removed in case it offended the strict vegetarian, whose animal-loving wife Linda died of breast cancer last year.

● Voice Of The Mirror – Page 6

in the Blue Angel and Allan Williams said that some of the group's equipment had been damaged and the £200 fee had not been paid. Jimmy McVitie said that they should be proud to be playing the Cavern. The *Daily Mirror* had got wind of it and was going to make a story out of it. Their group's manager was Eduard Shevardnadze's granddaughter, and this is before the Wall came down. It was nothing to do with me but I went down and asked him about the payment on Allan's behalf. I explained that it would be a diplomatic incident and that he was are dealing with something outside his league. I said, 'I do know that if you don't pay her, you are going to be slapped all over the papers. I am just letting you know.' He said, 'They can fuck off.' An hour or two later, he relented, apologised and paid the girl."

In November 1989, the Rock Circus opened at the London Pavilion at Piccadilly Circus and it was a rock version of Madame Tussaud;'s. The Beatles were depicted in a reconstruction of the Cavern's stage and some of Beatle City's memorabilia was on display.

Mike Byrne used his experience to devise the perfect site for tourists with The Beatles Story and he had the financial support of the company behind Wembley Stadium. The intention was for visitors to experience for themselves, through music, lighting and displays, the chronological story of the Beatles. In March 1990, the first pictures of the replica Cavern were shown to the press.

Screaming Lord Sutch wrote in his autobiography, *Life As Sutch*: "I was disgusted by the new plastic Beatles Story exhibition set up in the trendy Albert Dock, while the original Cavern had been filled in to make a car park, and I therefore pledged to rebuild it." Come on, it was shut but it was there.

On Saturday 5 May 1990, an all-star tribute concert to John Lennon was televised from a special stage at the Pier Head. Despite the huge list of major performers, only 5,000 fans turn up, probably put off by the £25 ticket price. The following month, though, tickets are at a premium for Paul McCartney's concert at King's Dock.

Paul Hughes, another of McVitie's stepsons, was working as the manager of the Cavern from July 1989 when the club had a turnover of around £10,000 a week. In August 1990, the new pedestrian area around Mathew Street was commended in the Street Design 90 competition for councils. But what would the tourists see? In November 1989, the court convicted and jailed those concerned in James Paton's beating, and the Cavern was closed.

Paul Hughes applied for a licence to run the Cavern and commented on the sentences. He said, "Both of them know that they can have no part in running the club because of being jailed. They are not prepared to ruin my life in the way they have ruined their own." He received a glowing character reference from Allan Williams. The manager of the Adelphi said that "Paul and Kurt are as different as chalk and cheese. Paul fulfilled all my hopes while I let Kurt go because I didn't feel he was suitable." The testimonials did no good and the Cavern remained closed.

11

RUN DEVIL RUN

Cavern owners:
Cavern City Tours
(Bill Heckle, Dave Jones, George Guinness)
1991 onwards

Although I originally drafted this chapter in the same form as the others, it didn't work or, at least, I didn't like it. The policy of promoting new music may be the same, but the Cavern itself is a very different entity from what it was in the sixties. There is so much music at the Cavern and 150 bands can be playing in a month or, indeed, a week if the International Pop Overthrow festival is being staged. Many of the acts are new bands playing for the experience and although the listings have merit as an historical record, they would overwhelm a book like this. Furthermore, there have been hundreds of tribute bands playing over the years and it would make dull reading to list them, except, naturally, the ones with entertaining names.

I. A Surprising Offer

By 1983, it was self-evident that a well-organised tour operator could do well by promoting Liverpool's Beatles heritage. The city was fortunate that this was brought into being by a Beatles enthusi-ast, a former schoolteacher, Gerry Murphy, who worked as the singer/ songwriter Gerry Markey. He had brought a group of Italian tourists to Mathew Street in 1976 when, admittedly, there was precious little to see.

Merseyside County Council was already initiating Beatle Guides, one of them being Murphy, and he recruited two more for the company, both of them teachers: Bill Heckle and Ron Jones, who was also a DJ and the BBC's Rock'n'Roll Brain Of Britain. Taking their lead from New Orleans being the Crescent City, Murphy named the company, Cavern City Tours. Each director invested £200 and they made a flying start by receiving £350 from Granada TV's *Flying Start*. They started Beatle weekends in conjunction with the Atlantic Tower Hotel, which was close to the Pier Head, and soon there was a strong link with tourist organisations in the US and elsewhere. There is no definitive account of what happened next but, for whatever reason, Murphy left the company in 1985.

A legacy of Murphy's time is the homage to John Lennon, "Oh John!" which was issued on Cavern City Records. Another single featured Up And Running's version of "Stand By Me" with a choir of tourists, recorded at Abbey Road. Its B-side was Ron Jones' song, "Let's Go Down The Cavern". Ron Jones was to leave the partnership in 1988, around the time that Cavern City Tours acquired its first office, in Mathew Street as it happens. He was the DJ at the Cavern itself from 1984 to 1994.

Dave Jones, a former cab driver who had become a registered Blue Guide Tourist Guide working for Merseyside Country Council, became a director of Cavern City Tours. Bill and Dave organised regular Magical Mystery Tours on a coach painted in psychedelic colours, annual conventions (which they took over from the Mersey Tourism Board) and Beatle-related special events. Their Beatles Map sold 200,000 copies. They were effectively making money for others by bringing tourists into the city and they thought of buying a bar in Mathew Street.

In 1983, the John Lennon Memorial Club opened, which became the Lennon Bar, although its only real connection to the Beatle was that John's Uncle Charlie drank there. The intention was open the bar all day and hence, it had to be for members only. The rules were flouted and the owner became exasperated with the authorities and wanted to sell. In order to expand their business and purchase the bar, Bill and Dave brought in George Guinness, who owned several suburban shops and was a long-standing friend of Bill's. Through the bank, they raised the capital, but Bill naively revealed his plans to a friend and found himself gazumped. Bill felt that he had been knifed in the back but it was the best thing that could have happened as, within a week, Royal Life, a subsidiary of the mammoth Royal Insurance company, asked Cavern City Tours if they would bid for the lease on the Cavern.

Cavern City Tours had hired the Cavern for special events and brought tourists in during the day, but while the club was closed, two significant events took place in Liverpool: the Lennon memorial concert at the Pier Head and Paul McCartney's concert at King's Dock. These increased Beatle awareness in the city and it was self-evident that the club should be up and running as soon as convenient, but Royal Life had to find the right management. Cavern City Tours had no experience in running a club, but that was outweighed by their enthusiasm and commitment. Bill and Dave brought in George Guinness as a third director.

Bill Heckle[824]: "We started Cavern City Tours in 1983 and we think of ourselves as tour operators, still to this day. Everything we do is related to bringing tourists to the city. We were approached by Royal Life about taking over the management of the Cavern because there had been problems with club owners and they wanted someone from outside the club scene to clean it up. Dave had been against going into the bar business and I had had to push him on that, but he thought we had nothing to lose by seeing what the Royal wanted. There were twelve people in a circle firing questions at us. One thing that we could definitely do was bring in the visitors from the Magical Mystery Tours. We would bring back live music and we would pay tribute to the Beatles. It was what they envisaged in 1984 but the Cavern had degenerated into a disco and we wanted it to be a venue for local, emerging talent. After a brief recess, they wanted us to make a formal offer. They said, 'We have had six offers. We like what you're saying so yours doesn't have to be the biggest bid.' Dave and I went into an anteroom and it was surreal. We knew we could deliver but there was still the problem of going in after Jimmy McVitie. Dave said, 'Leave it to me: I have an idea, but don't laugh.' We went back in and the chairman said, 'What is your offer?' Dave said, 'You're looking at it: we are the offer.' The chairman burst out laughing. Dave said, 'If you want your dream of what the Cavern should be with live music and tourism and non-violence and non-drugs, then we are the people to do it. We will dream up events to bring people to Mathew Street. If you are just interested in the money and you're not bothered about the violence and the drugs, then take any of the other envelopes in front of you. Do you want short-term money or a long term plan?' They asked for another recess and they must have heard us laughing. Dave said, 'It seems a good idea: they definitely want us, and why should we pay a lot for going in after Jimmy? If we don't pay a lot and we even get a tickle from the baddies, then we can walk away. There is little risk for us.' They said that it was a novel approach and they would be in touch. Within a week, we got a letter. We had got the Cavern with the lowest bid, but we had to deliver. We evolved a clear plan which involved the Beatles heritage and also looked forward with new bands from the region."

But they were operating in a community rife with organised crime. **Bill Heckle**[825]: "When we were offered the Cavern one of the things we had to do with the 'due diligence' process was to go for an interview with the police and they tried as hard as they could to deter us from signing. It is a big bad city out there and you don't know what you're taking on: you have got professsions and careers and a successful tour company and you don't need to get involved in clubland. Ostensibly, we still see ourselves as a tour company: we don't socialise or connect ourselves with any other club owners."

Except Jimmy McVitie. He was released from prison early and the new owners owed him £25,000 for the fixtures and fittings. Bill and Dave were worried about his reputation, especially when he came to the Cavern and asked Dave for the money. Dave didn't have that much on hand, but he gave him a couple of grand here and a couple of grand there, and over six months he had received it all. McVitie then became a real gentleman, never bothered them and even remarked that it was more appropriate that they should have the Cavern instead of him.

Bill and Dave discovered that there was no valid trademark for the name, the Cavern, and they registered the name. As a result, they now own the Cavern brand, which is probably more valuable than the bricks and the mortar. Cavern City Tours own the intellectual property rights in 30 countries and they are fighting the Hard Rock Café. The company had heard that they were planning to go into the American market and registered the trademarks. Morally, it was unfair, but the courts are to decide whether Hard Rock has acted illegally.

The club reopened on 11 July 1991 and got off to a good start. After a month, they were doing as much business as they were anticipating after nine months. At first, they continued with the student market to generate interest and revenue. On Mondays, they offered a disco with food and beer for £1 a head. This went well until they tried live music, and the students went elsewhere,

mostly to Cream which also ran a students' night. **Bill Heckle**[826]: "When we re-opened the Cavern we got the benefit of the student market, but then Cream and some other clubs came along and we lost them. We are the first owners post-1984 to appreciate what the Cavern meant to different sets of people. One of the challenges is how to market that as it can confuse people if you have Joe Brown one Monday and a young band trying to break through the next. We pay tribute to its rich heritage but we also look forward to breaking new bands and new talent. The previous owners never understood that there were so many markets within the Cavern itself. The Cavern is a very difficult place to own and a very difficult club to market as it is all things to all people. Since we started in 1991, we have moved more and more towards it being a vehicle for young up-and-coming talent which is what it was in the fifties and sixties. We pay tribute to the Beatles and their legacy with a Beatles night on a Thursday and the annual Beatles week as well. There is a Beatles band on a Thursday night and throughout the week there are 30 or 40 new bands playing the Cavern and you won't hear a Beatles song all night."

Bill and Dave felt that owning a club that was so famous gave them some protection from the heavy brigade. **Bill Heckle**[827]: "One of the things we gambled on was that our profile was not just local, but regional and even international. We had access to the police and to the media which we would have used as the first line of defence. We didn't have that shady background, and maybe they didn't touch us because they had a fear of the respectability and the establishment around us. We were backed by the City Council, Royal Insurance, the police and the media. Now it would need a bigger invasion force than they put into Iraq to get us out."

Around 1999, Royal Life had sold Cavern Walks to Moorfields plc. The new owners didn't invest in the property to any degree and sold it on in June 2002. The Agora Shopping Centre Fund (a joint venture between Warner Estate and the Bank of Scotland) took over Cavern Walks, although it was reported erroneously that they had purchased the Cavern for £13.9m. However, the business of the Cavern and its intellectual property rights belong to Cavern City Tours. By Agora's standards it was a small shopping centre but they had plans for a designer outlet. Cricket Designwear and Drome were already there, and they were joined by a flagship boutique for the internationally known but highly individual Vivienne Westwood. Cricket has been a continuing success story and keeps expanding its retail space.

Looking to overseas, Cavern Adelaide has been doing well since 2004 and now it has been joined by Cavern Buenos Aires. These outposts are obliged to represent what the Cavern itself stands for, both by presenting new music and by acting as embassies for the Cavern itself and its history.

Cavern City Tours took on a new director in 2004: John Lennon's half-sister, **Julia Baird**[828]: "We had gone to Australia for the opening of the Cavern Club in Australia. It was also the 40th anniversary of the Beatles playing in Adelaide and the Council had organised a celebration at the Town Hall. There was Bill Heckle, his wife Diane, and myself and my partner Roger. We were having dinner and Bill wanted new blood to buy into the Cavern. I had just sold a house and the money was going into the bank when we were in Australia. I was looking for another house. I said to Bill that I could be their new partner instead. We talked about it and Bill was then on the phone to Dave and George. I have always been very impressed with the three of them. When I first met them, they were stamping T-shirts in their office above The Beatles Shop, so things have really moved on. It stems from hard work and plenty of good ideas and being really nice people. I love taking part in Beatle week. I love the tribute bands and say, hearing a Mexican band with a different take on the Beatles. The Fab Faux are bloody brilliant. It was difficult at first to accept Beatle week but John Lennon is a world icon and I must go with it. There is nowhere to run so I run with it now. The Beatles are simply going to go on and on."

A Hard Day's Fight, a 40 minute episode in the BBC2 series, *Trouble At The Top*, produced by Alison Millar, was shown in January 2005. The *Radio Times* billing said, "It seemed logical for the owners of Liverpool's legendary Cavern Club to branch out with a Beatles-themed hotel. But their attempted conversion of a crumbling office block brought little more than ten years of misery." The compelling programme put on record the troubles that they faced. It was blisteringly honest and the owners spoke frankly of the hurdles they had to overcome. On the other hand, the producer selected clips where they talked in Beatles song titles. "This is a long and winding road", "Let it be". I know that they don't speak like this all the time and it weakened the end result.

In addition, *A Hard Day's Fight* explained how George Guinness' health had been affected by the set-backs, and that while it was being made, he had sold his shares. This was wrong. George had had pleurisy a couple of times (arguably, the consequences of having an office in the Cavern itself), but he didn't sell his shares.

George Guinness[829]: "I will sell my shares sometime, but there is no rush to do so. I'd like to think we have left a mark on the city. We were never out for the money, and our chief aim has been to enhance the Beatles' name and legacy. In the early years, the Council was not very responsive as for them, Liverpool was all about football and maritime history. They now appreciate what Beatle tourism can do for the city. I would like to think that we will be remembered for the positive things we have done to move the city on in terms of tourism." If George did go now, he would be the first successful person to leave in the history of the club: "That surprises me but I can't see how they could have made any profit in the early years when it wasn't licensed. The admission charges weren't large and you would have to sell a heck of a lot of Cokes to break even."

Also during the filming, it looked as though a £2.3m development grant for the listed building might be dropped. *A Hard Day's Fight* ended on a positive note in that a suitable developer for the 120 room hotel had been found and the hotel was being built, but I got the impression that this wasn't the ending the filmmakers wanted.

The Cavern franchise has some value outside Liverpool and we saw a club being proposed in Spain. The two clowns involved in this project came off really badly: you wondered how anybody would do business with them and, indeed, if they could even manage a shrimp stall on Southport pier. Not surprisingly, Cavern City Tours turned them down.

SOUNDS OF THE CAVERN
FROM AROUND
THE
WORLD

TUNNEL DE TEMPO (BRAZIL)

CAVERN (UK)

THE FABZ (SCOTLAND)

THE PARROTS (JAPAN)

SILVER BEATLES (UK)

ABBEY ROAD (SPAIN)

1964 (USA)

THE BEATLESS (UK)

LENNY PAYNE
(SWEDEN)

II. Beatle Festivals

Starting in 1986, Bill Heckle and Dave Jones organised the annual Beatles Convention in Liverpool. With the years it was becoming more of a festival than a convention and though there were the interviews, the films and the flea market (always a ridiculous name for high-priced memorabilia) at the Adelphi, there was increasing emphasis on concerts and club performances at other city venues. There would usually be a large event at the Empire and now that Bill and Dave had the Cavern, club appearances could be staged throughout the weekend.

In 1993 Joan Knibbs, the manager of Flanagan's Apple, complained about the state of Mathew Street. Jean Catharell of Liverpool Beatlescene said in the *Liverpool Echo* that Mathew Street was a shambles and "a dismal and disappointing place". The response from Bill Iveson of the Cavern Quarter Initiative was that four Cavern Quarter Gateways, designed by David Backhouse, were about to be erected and "We have created a momentum to regenerate the area." The plans were announced swiftly and there was talk of a crystal sculpture creating with special lights "the girl with kaleidoscope eyes" for Mathew Street, which, thankfully, didn't materialise.

Cavern City Tours, on the other hand, was finding that organising the Beatles Festival was taking up a disproportionate amount of time and they wanted to re-establish the Cavern as a leading music venue. The main problem was that the festival was attracting little local interest. 3,000 visitors might come from abroad, but only 500 local fans would attend. Cavern City Tours decided that this would be the last festival but it would go out with the mother of all parties and that groups would be playing in pubs up and down Mathew Street, not to mention on an open-air stage as well, and that all the events would be free. The first Mathew Street Festival had its main stage on the car park to the side of the Cavern and it featured the best local bands of the day:

Cat Scratch Fever, Alternative Radio and Up and Running.

It was the farewell that never was. The festival attracted 20,000 locals and so Cavern City Tours never announced that this would be the last. It had an unexpected knock-on benefit as locals met Beatle fans from abroad and invited them to stay the next time they came. They saw how much their group meant to outsiders and hence, the Beatles were embraced by the city. Although still called the Mathew Street Festival, it became bigger and better and the main stages were erected at the Pier Head.

The potential for the Mathew Street Festival was officially recognised and in 1994, Dave Jones and Bill Heckle received the Special Achievement Award from Scouseology for their efforts. The previous year it had been won by Paul McCartney. Cavern City Tours have also received several tourism awards over the years including an Event of the Year for the same 1993 Mathew Street Festival. The event was expanded in 1994 with 65 bands over 20 stages.

Opposite the Cavern was a disused aerobics studio and Cavern City Tours secured the lease and opened it as the Cavern Pub. **Bill Heckle**[830]: "Our first three years at the Cavern were very successful and we rolled everything over into the Cavern Pub which has been a huge success as we can do things at the pub that we can't do at the club such as the memorabilia display. The Cavern is still hot and sweaty and it doesn't lend itself to that. We got that idea from Sloppy Joe's in Key West: they have got a pub with memorabilia next door to the live music venue."

One of the regular performers at the Cavern Pub for many years was the one-man band, **Billy May**[831]: "I enjoy singing at the Cavern pub as you get tourists coming in and asking for Beatle songs. 'Twist And Shout' and 'A Day In The Life' are very popular, but not 'Yesterday'. I love the songs and I think that must come over. I use a Digitech vocaliser which takes my voice and puts it in harmony. I also like doing 'Bohemian Rhapsody' as everybody joins in with that bit in the middle."

Dave Jones[832]: "Billy May is very good but in my view the greatest artist at the Cavern pub has been Paul Kappa. He has performed in many guises over the years, but his Saturday afternoon shows are absolutely sensational. He does a lot of heavy rock covers from the likes of Free and Deep Purple." I couldn't agree more. The former leader of Cat Scratch Fever is a very exciting performer, someone who knows how to maintain the dynamics between his voice and guitar and the band. He has the confidence to run one song into another so it might be 20 minutes before you have a chance to applaud. His heavy rock version of "Strawberry Fields Forever" is electrifying.

In 1996, there was unexpected controversy surrounding the Mathew Street Festival. It had expanded into neighbouring streets but solicitors realised that the food stalls could break a law from 1786 which did not allow trading in smart city streets like Castle Street and Cook Street. The law was circumvented by moving the caterers to streets built after 1786. The festival did well despite some appalling weather. Walk on, walk on, through the wind and the rain. The pubs and shops had a bonanza but they had not helped with the financing of the festival. This led to Cavern City Tours saying that they would pull out of subsequent festivals unless something was done about it. The Mathew Street Festival was cancelled in 1997 for lack of funding. Cavern City Entertains was put on around the local pubs and clubs.

They also started Cavern Records with the CDs, *Why Don't We Do It In The Road* with some leading Beatle tribute bands in Abbey Road, the *Boom* EP from Up And Running, and *Cavern Days* from Class Of 64, featuring Merseybeat performers from the sixties. The title song from the Class Of 64's album listed the key bands who played the club.

Among the festival events at the Cavern have been the Pete Best band (August 1994), a Beatles samba party for Brazilian fans (August 1996) and an afternoon of Japanese tribute bands for the Japanese fans (1997).

On Sunday 5 October 1997, Allan Williams and Bob Wooler held an evening at the Cavern to commemorate the twentieth anniversary of the first Beatles Convention, an odd thing to commemorate, to put it mildly. It featured Dark Horse, No Reply and Mecca with DJ Stan 'The Man' Livingstone.

In 1998, the Mathew Street Festival was back, bigger than ever. The main sponsor was Cains, a local brewery, but dozens of businesses and the Cavern also supported it. 100,000 fans attended the free festival. On Tuesday 1 September 1998, there was an afternoon concert from the Rutles (Neil Innes, John Halsey) billed as "The Rutles at the Cavern where it all ended." **Colin Hall**[833]: "I enjoyed Neil Innes but I think it would have been better at the Philharmonic where you could sit and take it all in. His bass player has a mane of hair like a lion. Neil Innes is a mesmerising character but the show was more suited to a different venue."

In August 1999, the US Post Office decided to launch their Yellow Submarine stamp 'in the town where I was born', in Liverpool at the Town Hall. The coverage was amazing and a wonderful testimony to the Beatles in their home city. While Apple's managing director, Neil Aspinall was at the Town Hall, he took a call from Ringo Starr. Ringo had seen the celebrations on breakfast TV in LA and he wondered what on earth was happening. **Bill Heckle**[834]: "Paul McCartney's PR, Geoff Baker brought the Postmaster General from the US into the Cavern. It was the first time that they had launched a stamp outside the USA. This rather dumpy, very nice VIP wanted to see the Cavern and it was full with live music. Geoff smiled, 'Now I've seen the Cavern full, I will not rest until Paul plays here. Seeing it like this, he has got to play the Cavern.' Within four months, he delivered."

On Tuesday 26 August 2003, the final concert of Beatle week was with Jackie Lomax and Tony Sheridan at the Cavern. Lomax, backed by the American band, Wonderwall, played songs from his 1969 Apple album, *Is This What You Want?* and from his new MP3 album, *The Ballad Of Liverpool Slim*. His soul ballad "Fall Inside Your Eyes" had been recorded by Percy Sledge.

Imagine when the Beatles first went to Hamburg in 1960. They were used to seeing smart-suited performers with well-structured sets. They came across Tony Sheridan, who played as the mood took him, and they copied his maverick ways. Tony Sheridan hasn't changed and the last time I saw him, he was backed by two South American musicians who knew what they were doing or, more importantly, sensed what Tony would be doing. His set included a powerhouse, ten minute workout on "Skinny Minnie" (hard to believe that this song originated with Bill Haley), "Yesterday" (with new Sheridan lyrics), "Bright Lights—Big City", "What'd I Say" and a frenzied, punk-like "My Bonnie". As Sam Hardie from Kingsize Taylor and the Dominoes remarked, "Now you can see what turned us on."

In 2004, the Pete Best Band was at its best. In the past, they had strayed from what fans wanted to hear: I have even heard Pete doing "Ticket To Ride". This time the entire set was based on songs he'd played during his tenure as the Beatles drummer between 1960 and 1962. The lead vocalist Chris Cavanagh was very good but everyone was watching Pete. The heat in the Cavern was stifling but not a hair on his head was misplaced and he looked great for 62.

By 2005, the event had grown to International Beatle Week, not to mention a Beatles Easter Extravaganza and events to mark John Lennon's birth and death. The Mathew Street Festival included McFly, the Stranglers, Buzzcocks and Tony Christie, but all were on the Pier Head stage. 370,000 attended the festival and it generated a remarkable £32m for the Liverpool economy.. All city hotels were fully booked. 60,000 visitors came from abroad.

III. Tribute Bands

There have been hundreds of tribute bands that have played the Cavern and not just Beatle sound-alikes either. Tribute bands are no longer regarded as naff and their acceptability is demonstrated by the Tribute Conventions, hosted by Rock Off and Soundwave Promotions at the Cavern during 2006. These weekly shows offered a year's worth of tribute acts, along with flea markets and guest speakers such as Marc Bolan's son, Rolan and Klaus Voormann.

Many of the tribute acts also play original material under a different name. One of the bands when Pete Best reopened the Casbah was a tribute band, A Hard Day's Night: it turned out that they were the sixties hitmakers, Ohio Express.

They sometimes worked as A Hard Day's Night in the US and found that this was now their entrée to the UK.

The best Beatle tributes in the early eighties were Cavern and Mojo Filter and the tributes have got bigger and better with the Bootleg Beatles filling national theatres. The Fab Faux is a group of top US session musicians led by Will Lee, the bass player from *The Late Show With David Letterman*. They lovingly rework the Beatles' repertoire in intriguing ways. In 2004, they wore leathers for a Hamburg set. **Will Lee**[835]: "The Cavern, with its roots as a 'civil' jazz club, was totally transformed by the Beatles and their Mersey groove. Since the day they set foot inside the club and created a frenzy for the locals of Liverpool, the place has never been the same. When you walk in, you're bowled over with emotions. To get a chance to play on stage at The Cavern is an unforgettable experience—a career milestone for me and for countless other musicians."

Here are some of the inventive names of tribute bands which have played the Cavern: A Hard Day's Band, Apple Scruffs, Beat The Meatles, Back To The USSR, the Blue Meanies, the Magical Mystery Band, the Len'n'McCartney Band, I Am The Eggman, the Prellies, the Repeatles and Sgt Pepper's Only Darts Board Band from the Beatle world, plus Dylanesque, Guns2Roses, Motley Scrued, the Beautiful Couch, Jeepster (T. Rex), Stayin' Alive (Bee Gees), Gimi Hendrix, Kounterfeit Kinks, Dire Straights, Led Zed, Led Balloon, the Smyths, More Alanisette, Mentallica, Nearly Dan, Pink Fraud, Red Mock Chili Peppers, Into The Bleach (Blondie), Unforgettable Fire (U2), Maximum Who, Who's Next and Dios Salve A La Reina (God Save The Queen).

IV. International Pop Overthrow

Handicapped by a ridiculous and misleading name, the International Pop Overthrow (IPO) presented festivals of new music in various American cities, organised by David Bash and Rina Bardfield from their base in Los Angeles. As one programme says, "The artists who play at International Pop Overthrow do the kind of music you already love; edgy, cool tunes with timeless melodies, the kind of songs that will endure long after all the flavours of the month have left a bitter aftertaste." A band can get on board the IPO if they write their own material, the songs are melodic and David Bash approves. On the whole, backing tapes are frowned upon.

Jean Catharell[836]: "The IPO was something that I wanted to experience, but I didn't really want to go to Los Angeles. For purely selfish reasons, I thought about bringing it to Liverpool and also because it would be good for the city to have a music festival that was nothing to do with the Beatles. David had not thought about it coming to Liverpool, but realised it was a goer, especially as I had suggested the Cavern with the use of its two stages. The Cavern wasn't sure about a festival with unknown bands, but they did have some faith in what I was doing, so it went ahead."

In October 2003, its founder and organiser David Bash presented the first IPO festival outside North America, featuring 90 bands from 23 countries at the Cavern and spread over six days. Liverpool, like every other city, was awash with cover bands and so it was gratifying to hear an evening of 80 new songs from 12 different bands playing on the stages for £5. The quality was variable—it had to be—but all the bands had to find their own way there and were playing for free. In other words, they had to be passionate about their music to set out from across the world. Being able to put the Cavern on your CV is an incentive.

Nearly every band had something to offer and Wendy Ip, Bailey and the General Store were outstanding. The most memorable lyric of the week was "I am a dick, I am a dick, I am addicted to you" from 'Hardcore' by the Piper Downs, a thrash band with Spinal Tap humour. The Liverpool performers that I saw—the Suns and Reece—did very well and in that same year, Reece also won the Cavern's *Battle Of The Bands* competition.

The organisation and the bonhomie between the bands at IPO was impressive. There didn't appear to be any prima donnas and nearly all the bands started on time and their 30 minute sets didn't overrun, which is a credit to the awesome skills of the aptly-named David Bash.

It was gratifying to see Tony Rivers with a reformed Harmony Grass. **Frank Townsend**[837]: "Tony Rivers was thinking of doing a one-night revival of the Castaways and Harmony Grass and he asked me to join him for an IPO gig. We were going to do his son Anthony's set one night, and the Castaways and Harmony Grass the next. The second night would be nearly all Beach Boys. My friend Mike used to entice to me to see the Beach Boy tribute bands and I would always want to leave after three songs as they were never good enough. Tony Rivers though is as high as you can possibly get and Mike never understood this. Mike was in tears after our set and he was stunned."

The return of the IPO came a year later, this time covering nine days and featuring over 100 bands. The veteran surf musicians, Walter Egan and John Zambetti, were part of the Malibooz and it was unsettling to hear 50-somethings singing that "Surfing and driving are the only two things that I know." Walter, a surf guitarist par excellence, included his 1978 US hit, 'Magnet And Steel' and the entire set was hugely enjoyable. The other veteran was Kimberley Rew, who wrote the Eurovision winner, 'Love Shine A Light' by Katrina and the Waves in 1997. He was with Ralph Alfonso in a group called RALPH and their set included a poignant tribute to Billy Fury.

The most impressive of the many bands influenced by the psychedelic Beatles was the Badge from New York and their "Walkin' Down A Brand New Road" was a kissing cousin to "Drive My Car". Also from New York were the Sun Kings and their "Give Me A Reason" could have come from a Badfinger album. In the same vein, Kelly's Heroes from London were striking. If young bands could write Lennon and McCartney songs, why couldn't McCartney?

The Mags playing with Scouse confidence had the compressed sound of Oasis and their songs, "Freefallin'" and "I Feel Freedom", made them a band to watch. Susan Hedges, who was growing in confidence, presented new songs like "Dying Fire", "River City Girl" and a statement about growing up blind, "The Fighting Kind". I enjoyed the melodic songs and harmonies of re: verb from the Ribble Valley, but their fantastic, jazz-based drummer sounded as though he had

Cavern Survivors

Courtesy of Mersey Beat/Bill Harry

JOHN McNALLY (Searchers)

PAUL McCARTNEY (Beatles) & BILL HARRY (Merseybeat)

TONY CRANE (Merseybeats)

RAY ENNIS (Swinging Blue Jeans)

GERRY MARSDEN (Pacemakers)

MIKE PENDER (Searchers)

KARL TERRY (Cruisers)

JIMMY TARBUCK

TED 'KINGSIZE' TAYLOR (Dominoes)

RINGO STARR (Hurricanes & Beatles)

KENNY JOHNSON (Sonny Webb & Cascade)

BERYL MARSDEN

BILLY KINSLEY (Merseybeats)

LEE CURTIS

come to the wrong place. The previous year Tam Johnstone, the son of Elton John's seventies guitarist, Davey Johnstone, played a terrific country-rock set with his band, the General Store, but this year it was just him and his tapes. Nevertheless, he is a strong performer and his current album, *Mountain Rescue*, was first rate.

By the third festival in October 2005, the event had turned into a free festival, but, from my point of view, there was too much grunge. The fourth IPO festival in May 2006 was a massive return to form. During the course of six days, 140 acts played on the front and back Cavern stages, the Cavern Pub and the Lennon Bar and I caught 40 of them.

The new Cavern is deeper than the old one and so you usually cannot hear the music from the top of the stairs, but you can at the Cavern Pub, which is about as deep as the old Cavern. A wonderfully exciting and vibrant sound hit me as I walked into Mathew Street and I descended to see who was making it. The pub was full and the singer was Johnny Lloyd Robbins from Dallas with his musicians. His rocking "Miss Sugar Pie" was a "Mystery Train" for the Noughties. Johnny Lloyd Robbins was playing with the excitement of a young Bruce Springsteen and all his songs combined a strong melody with an intriguing lyric. He wrote about an old whorehouse in "Sulphur Springs Midnight Scatt" and talked about aging with his partner in "One Day At A Time". His torrent of words in "Bipolar Bear Blues" resembled Springsteen's love of language. Nobody had heard of Johnny Lloyd Rollins, but the audience loved everything he was doing. There were music fans who wanted to hear new acts, other IPO performers, goodtime Bank Holiday drinkers and a bunch of people dressed as cartoon characters! Johnny's rapport called for split-second timing. This was a performer who oozed confidence and could excel in any situation.

The key influences for the year's IPO bands were the Who, the Small Faces and the Jam, and the band that embraced them most successfully was the Len Price 3. Wearing striped, mod T-shirts, the powerhouse trio performed a very energetic set with most of the songs coming from their album, *Chinese Burn*. Glenn Page

danced amongst the audience with his guitar and included a Chuck Berry duckwalk.

In the late seventies, the Tasmanian group, the Innocents, created their bright Power Pop sounds in Australia and now they had reformed and released a new album, *Pop Factory*, in the same tradition. They presented a sparkling set, full of jangling guitars and razor-sharp harmonies: it was like hearing the Searchers performing unfamiliar material. Their 1977 single, "I Wouldn't Have It Any Other Way" was magical.

About one in four bands was local and the standard was again impressive. The best of the local bunch was Endbutt Lane, indie Scousers from Crosby (hence the name) with overtones of the Coral and the Zutons. Their quirky songs ("Peas And Carrots", "Sausage Man") revealed their love for food and another song, "Pirates", was about Crosby beach.

Dave Jones[838]: "There is no doubt that it is the magnetism of the Cavern that gets the bands over, and it works out very well for us. We have three stages and normally, we are paying out for bands all the time. The amount we spend in a week is very considerable. We have now come to an arrangement with David Bash whereby he is sponsored for organising the event and the bands play for free. It is going extremely well, and we have expanded with the use of a fourth stage at Lennon's Bar. It is a very exciting event and I know David Bash regards Liverpool as the best venue for the IPO. It is good for us as it is a week that is given over to contemporary music."

The fifth IPO Festival at the Cavern was held in May 2007. The festival ran for a full week and, over the bank holiday weekend, there was over twelve hours of music each day. 150 acts were featured (about 30% local) but as many of them were playing more than once, you can usually see the ones that particularly intrigue you. No one is allowed to play for more than 30 minutes so if you don't like an act, not only will there be another one soon, but you can also go to another stage.

Again Johnny Lloyd Rollins stood out and I was very impressed with the Bongo Beat evening, featuring Canadian artists like Dave Rave and Ari Shine, a spindly guy with lots of hair and jerky movements. Nigel Clark from Dodgy played a solo set but he brought one of his mates along to play drums, who ruined the more sensitive material. Nigel chided him on stage, "Leave off the bass drum. You sound like someone in a foundry." Right, so tell me again, what was he doing there?

By calling themselves Gringo Star, the Atlanta band only had to be halfway good to succeed. They had Merseybeat and psychedelic influences, but the accordion veered them towards the Americana of The Band. Most of the European acts were singing in English even though it was their second language. The Italian band, Il Complesso Di Andrea, stuck to their own language but this was no barrier to the audience appreciating their highly melodic songs which took in several influences including the sixties bands, the Police and old-style Italian Eurovision entries. One of the best of the local acts was Alun Parry, whose cheerful list song, "You Are My Addiction" had such lines as "I can be your night of passion, you can be my flannel nightie".

David Bash[839]: "The history of the Beatles is of course an important factor in making the IPO a success in Liverpool, but there is also the city itself. It is one of the smaller cities in which we stage the IPO and I think that this, ironically, has helped to make it such a success. The word about the Festival can spread so fast and the city is full of the most genuine, down-to-earth people that you could wish to meet. We love bringing the IPO here and we hope it will continue for many years."

Other regular music festivals include Northern Xposure, Liverpool Now! and ones for Ormskirk and Isle of Man musicians. In April 2006, a very successful *Dr. Who* Convention was held at the Cavern with Colin Baker, Frazer Hines and Deborah Watling, and it led to a second one in 2007. The Daleks could never achieve world domination from the Cavern as they could never climb the stairs.

V. Diary

Thursday 10 October 1991

The start of weekly sessions for local talent. The new bands came through Roag Best's Splash Pro-

motions and included Oasis. They came with a party of dope-smoking Mancs, who were evicted by the police. They complained that the police had thrown them out. Subsequently, Noel Gallagher said that playing the Cavern was a disappointment as it was like "a fucking wine bar."

Bill Heckle[840]: "Roag Best had Splash Promotions, and he was putting on bands up to three nights a week. We would always have something for the tourists at the weekend. Whenever we had young bands doing their own stuff, we would empty a full club. Conversely, Jimmy McVitie had packed the place with a seventies and eighties disco. It was a huge commercial dilemma and the more we tried to impose upcoming talent onto Cavern regulars, the more we were losing them."

c. October 1991

Albert Lee with Hogan's Heroes. **Dave Jones**[841]: "The band hadn't told us that they were going to use a smoke machine and anyway we might not have realised what would happen. It was a Sunday and they set off the fire alarms, which were bells and not warblers. Albert Lee was on the main stage and I was in the front part with a CID inspector. The fire alarms went off. Eddie Porter started to unscrew the bloody bells from the wall. He came through to the front of the club with the alarm bells in his hand in full view of the policeman and the fire brigade, who were coming down the stairs. We should have evacuated the club and not taken the bells off the wall, but Eddie knew that it was the smoke machines that had set the alarms off. That was my first encounter with a very annoyed fire officer."

Thursday 9 April 1992 (Election Day)

In February 1992, Screaming Lord Sutch asked the Cavern to help finance his party in the General Election. If they could give him £4,000, he could fund enough candidates to merit a TV broadcast and he would film it in the Cavern, saying that he was about to move from one Number Ten to another. Cavern City Tours had no spare cash at the time but they did give him a gig. Despite the Cavern not funding his efforts, he did stand in the Bootle by-election as the Official Monster Raving Loony Cavern Rock Party and polled 418 votes. Significantly, the SDP candidate only managed 155, which was why the party collapsed when it did. Brilliantly if irrationally, Sutch claimed vic-

"44 Years Ago Today"

Rory Storm & the Hurricanes + Cass & the Cassanovas

25th May 1960 The First Official Beat Night held at
THE CAVERN, LIVERPOOL

25th MAY 2004, the CAVERN CLUB, MATHEW ST, LIVERPOOL

MC FRANKIE CONNOR

**FARONS FLAMINGOS * THE CLAYTON SQUARES * THE BLACK KNIGHTS *
KARL TERRY & THE CRUISERS * THE TUXEDOS * LEE CURTIS & THE MOJOS*
JACKIE LOMAX &THE UNDERTAKERS * DALE ROBERTS & THE JAYWALKERS*
THE KIRBYS * KINGSIZE TAYLOR & THE DOMINOES * ALBERT WYCHERLEY *
KENNY JOHNSON * + SURPRISE SPECIAL GUESTS**

PAY TRIBUTE TO BOB WOOLER, RORY and CASS

PLAQUE UNVEILING AT 7.30 pm Cavern Club by
ALLAN WILLIAMS and BILLY BUTLER

MERSEY BEAT SHOW BEGINS 8.00 pm - Midnight
All profits will be donated to 3 Merseyside Charities

TUESDAY 25th MAY, THE CAVERN CLUB
TICKETS £10,00 FROM THE CAVERN PUB 0151 236 4041
or RING 0151 260 5910 (WIRRAL) 0151 639 8245
or see web purpledays.myby.co.uk

" Be there or be square!

A Splendid Time is Guaranteed For All"

tory as he said that all the "No votes" (35,194) were his followers.

Thursday 23 April 1992

Donovan came to Liverpool's Neptune Theatre on 22 April. Bill Heckle spoke to him in the bar and suggested that he did the Cavern sometime. Donovan replied that he could do it the following night as the next gig had been cancelled. A fee of £1,700 was agreed and he told the 400-strong audience at the Neptune that they could see him tomorrow as well, and the surprise gig was also promoted in the *Liverpool Echo* and on local radio. Over 200 customers saw Donovan at the Cavern and he gave a masterly performance.

Monday 6 July 1992

Pete Best makes his first appearance at the Cavern since July 1966.

Thursday 13/ Sunday 16 August 1992

An eight-strong Sicilian dance troupe stage their Beatles ballet, which is accompanied by Mario Pollicita's exhibition of Beatle-inspired drawings.

Sunday 13 September 1992

George Guinness[842] was in the Cavern dealing with the takings from the previous night, when he got a call from Ringo Starr's stepfather. "I had a call from Harry Graves and he said he had Ringo with him and wanted to come down. Ringo was making a documentary for the Disney channel. He was delivering a running commentary as he was going down the stairs. It was curious as he was talking about how well he remembered it, although he must have known it was not the original Cavern. He went to the front of the Cavern and it seemed to him that it was the place he had played in. He wasn't there that long, but he was very buoyant. He signed the wall, but I was annoyed with myself as we hadn't a camera on the premises at the time. I did ask him when he was going to play the Cavern again and he said, 'You never know', so he hadn't dismissed the thought."

Six months later, Bill Heckle's wife was in America and saw Ringo's documentary, *Going Home*, on TV, which, directed by Stanley Dorfman, is exceptionally good. During the film, he winks to the camera and says, "This'll be a nice surprise for the lads" and autographs the squares for the Beatles and Rory Storm and the Hurricanes. Bill rushed round to the Cavern and sure enough,

Ringo's signature was on the wall twice. Dave told the cleaner that extra care must be taken with the signatures and that no mould must get on them. Unfortunately, the cleaner went on holiday and told the relief cleaner, "They want those bits pristine" and as a result they were wiped off. The signatures had been there for six months without anybody knowing about them, and two weeks later they were gone. The documentary, which was directed by Stanley Dorfman for the Disney Channel, is exceptionally good and includes Ringo's interchanges with the figures in the mural as he walks down the steps.

September 1993

Cilla Black returned to the Cavern for an ITV special on her 30 years in show business. She met Freddie Garrity, the Fourmost and the Swinging Blue Jeans at the Cavern and went on a ferry cross the Mersey with Gerry Marsden.

October 1994

Nigel Clark[843] of Dodgy: "We had recorded all our first album and half our second one in Liverpool with Ian Broudie producing. We launched *Homegrown* at the Cavern and did an acoustic set. We gave out loads of merchandise like a Dodgy nine bob note. It's cool to have a brick on the wall and so be mentioned in the same place as the Beatles as a band who played the Cavern."

Tuesday 14 February 1995

The Chester MP Gyles Brandreth was behind legislation to enable secular premises to be licensed for weddings, which came into force on April 1. The Cavern, naturally, was intrigued by the process as a Beatle-based wedding could be as popular as a Las Vegas one with a counterfeit Elvis. Although not yet licensed for a wedding, Michael Plunkett, the Rector of Speke, blessed the marriage of Cavern DJ Steve Panter and his bride Sharon at a Valentine's Day service there. They were allowed to write their names alongside the musicians on the wall at the back of the stage.

Dave Jones[844]: "We did get registered for weddings, but we haven't renewed the licence. People tend to only get married at peak times, weekends in particular, and so the weddings are getting in the way of existing business. We would confuse people as this is a rock'n'roll and music venue, and you have to draw the line. The Hard Days Night

Hotel will be a great place for weddings and you can do something in the Cavern afterwards. In the end, we have only had one civic ceremony in the Cavern which was when one of our cooks, Sheena, got married."

Monday 8 May 1995

"Take cover on VE Day in the world's most famous air-raid shelter." Well, it's one way to publicise a gig.

In 1995 the club announced its new facility, Upstairs At The Cavern, which offered conference facilities and could cater for business meetings, seminars and press launches. Roy Adams had taken the giant Beatle heads, a sculpture by Dave Webster, home when the Cavern/ Revolution closed and he sold them to the new owners for the upstairs bar.

Bill Heckle staked £500 with William Hill that the Beatles would have the Number One ay Christmas. He placed his bet before he had even heard the single: "Free As A Bird" peaked at Number Two. The Christmas chart-topper was Michael Jackson's "Earth Song".

By making Cavern quarter traffic free, a new improved environment is envisaged with street cafés and bars.

Lord Lichfield was employed by the British Tourist Authority to take photographs around the UK and when he came to Liverpool, he took photographs in the Cavern and of the Magical Mystery Tour bus.

Bill Heckle[845]: "It was difficult with live music. Splash Promotions were on Monday, Tuesday and Wednesday nights when we were less busy. Roag Best pulled out after a couple of years as it wasn't going that well and we wanted a fresh direction. Up And Running were hugely popular in the city and every time we would put them on, we would pack the place. That gave us the confidence: we had been picking the wrong bands. Alex McKechnie from Up and Running took over the management of the live music and he took it onto another level. What we said we would do in 1991 wasn't fully achieved until 1996 and it was certainly down to Alex's impetus."

Alex McKechnie was placed in charge of bookings in 1997 and from then on there was plenty of live music. A £40,000 sound system was installed, which put it on a par with other music venues.

Alex McKechnie[846]: "I held the diary for Up and Running and Bill Heckle said that Judith Chalmers and her *Holiday* show were coming to Liverpool for a weekend break and they wanted live music on the Cavern. They wanted us to play there on Saturday afternoon and we did that. People turned up and we filled the place. The BBC showed us on TV and the takings on the bar were great, so we started playing on Saturday afternoons. I then signed a support band to open the show for us. They were the Bitter Pills. They had younger fans than us. It was good for both of us. I went to LIPA and asked them for a stage manager for Saturday afternoon and they produced a student called Liam, and I said, 'Your job is to make the show run smoothly, and when you deal with Up And Running, you deal with us the same as you would deal with any other band. You make sure that we are on and off on time and you make sure that the next band is ready.' The first day the stage manager came up to us and said, 'You're going on ten minutes late, so you are only doing 35 minutes.' Phil said, 'Well, I'm not playing here anymore. 'I'm not having a young kid ordering me around.' So the next week I replaced Up and Running with two other bands and that was the start of me booking bands in the Cavern. The Saturday afternoon sessions led to many sessions during the week."

16 January 1997—40th Birthday Celebrations

It was appropriate that those Beatle copyists, Oasis, should have recorded "Wonderwall" as the Wall of Fame was the latest attraction in Mathew Street. The wall, opposite the Cavern Club and alongside the new Cavern Pub, was unveiled in the 40th anniversary celebrations. It was unveiled by Gerry Marsden and each of the 1,801 bricks bore the name of an act which played the Cavern—about 150 bricks have been added since, and now there is only space to add significant acts. The wall was accompanied by a lifesize statue of John Lennon in his *Rock'n'Roll* album cover pose, which was unveiled by Billy J. Kramer.

Ken Gilmore[847] of the Dark Ages: "We looked and looked for our brick in the Cavern wall and we eventually found it. It is inside the door, right up on the left hand side behind the fire alarm and all you can see is 'The D…' Couldn't someone put that brick somewhere else?" Some people, you see, are never satisfied, and it also demonstrates that the wall merits close scrutiny: every brick tells a story.

Almost 1,000 guests were invited into the Cavern with its upstairs area and hence, the club now had three stages. Liverpool performers from the sixties included Johnny Guitar from Rory Storm and the Hurricanes, Karl Terry and the Cruisers, the Klubs, the Hideaways, the Undertakers and Persuader, which was made up of sixties musicians. Familiar songs were provided by Lennon clone Gary Gibson, Dark Horses, and Status Quid, while Up and Running performed their own, excellent material.

It would have been easy for the organisers to ignore the fact that the Cavern had started as a jazz club, but not a bit of it. Three bands from the opening night in 1957 were there forty years later—the Merseysippi Jazz Band (with guest vocalist George Melly), the Wall City Jazz Band and the Ralph Watmough Band. Lee Curtis was on television complaining that he could not get into the VIP Lounge. The VIPs included football stars and Crispian Mills from Kula Shaker. The most significant event of the day was the reunited Quarry Men (albeit with no Beatles) for a short set.

Wednesday 23 April 1997

The drummer from Widnes band, Route 7, was presented with a drum kit at the Cavern by Mel Gaynor from Simple Minds.

Saturday 10 May 1997

Bob Young had come to Liverpool for the year to organise the 40th birthday celebrations. He had only been there a few days when the Hillsborough support group visited the Cavern's management. They needed funding and hoped that the Cavern could provide it through some form of benefit. Bob was able to secure Anfield from David Moores and within a few days, he had arranged the bill, the sound, the lighting and the merchandise.

The Hillsborough Justice Concert featured the Lightning Seeds, Holly Johnson, the Beautiful South and the London Community Gospel Choir, the Manic Street Preachers, Space, Dodgy, Smaller, the Stereophonics, Frank Skinner, Terry Hall and the Bootleg Beatles. The concert was both a popular and a commercial success and it

was followed with work on the album, the TV rights and royalties. By the time, it was put to bed, the Beatles week was upon the Cavern and the year was almost over. However, the benefit concert, which was under the banner of 'The Cavern Presents…' was seen as a highly relevant contribution.

Tuesday 3 June 1997

Australian cricket captain, Allan Border visited the Cavern and De Coubertin's Sports Bar, also owned by Cavern City Tours.

Saturday 15 November 1997

BBC Radio 2 presented *The Judi Spiers Show* live from the Cavern. The two hour live show featured the Bootleg Beatles, Allan Williams and Bob Wooler. Spiers had to work hard to keep the show suitable for broadcasting as Williams and Wooler bickered continually through their interview.

Alex McKechnie[848]: "The first time I saw the Coral I recognised that they had slightly irreverent attitudes like the Beatles. I featured them a lot at the Cavern. The Zanzibar also had them but I made them resident for six weeks. The first year was called *Beat 97* and then the Coral came the next year and I stopped playing myself in 2000. I had been playing in Up and Running for 20 years and that marked the break-up point."

Thursday 19 August 1999

Sheer glorious madness. A crowd of around 300, mostly ex-hippies, had gathered to see Ken Kesey's Magic Bus meet the Magical Mystery Tour Bus. Kesey's gaily-painted bus had a band on the roof. They sounded like they were banging on dustbin lids. The Merry Pranksters lived on this music and the Grateful Dead, and the sign on the bus said, "Further". The bus had its psychedelic intercourse with the Magical Mystery Tour bus outside the Cavern, and the peace and love vibes were coming through. One of the Pranksters put down white card in the street and day-glo'd people's hands. They got a very friendly reception but they must have had a hard time visiting redneck areas in 1964. Ken Kesey only had thirteen Pranksters (plus himself) at any one time. Thirteen was Ken's lucky number, or so I was told. I said to one of them, "Are you an original Prankster?", and giving me two peace signs, he replied, "We're all

Mathew Street From The Top

MATHEW STREET   Home Of Liverpool's Cavern

MATHEW STREET MUSIC FESTIVAL

8th Magical Musical Mathew Street Experience

LET IT BE LIVERPOOL

Saturday August 26th, Sunday August 27th & Bank Holiday Monday August 28th

Welcome to Liverpool's 8th Mathew Street Festival where hundreds of bands will be making music. Come along! Its a free show and a great weekend for all

...RE INSIDE PLUS GIG & OUT & ABOU...

Mathew Street From The Bottom

John Firminger With The Beatles

Beatle rock is bronze

The world-famous Beatles statue has been returned to Cavern Designer Shopping Centre, Mathew Street, Liverpool - by popular demand.

The statue has been in a secure vault in the Cunard Buildings while the shopping centre underwent a £2 million refurbishment.

The sculpture is part of the Beatles tour but was taken out of the centre a year ago for the refurbishment and, now the work is complete, the statue returns to its home on the lower level of the shopping centre.

Designed by artist John Doubleday, the statue is a 200kg hollow bronze cast. It has been an impressive focal point and tourist attraction at Cavern Designer Shopping Centre since it opened in 1984.

The statue was placed on a new concrete plinth with a crane.

www.cavernshopping.com

original Pranksters, man: it's just that some of us joined later than the others."

Ken Kesey sat at a table in the Cavern and signed anything that was put in front of him including bare flesh. Some people asked him to sign packets of Rizla cigarette papers. He said, "It was harder to get the papers than the drugs in Oregon in 1962." I asked him if he objected to the *Magical Mystery Tour* film, if he felt that the Beatles had ripped him off. He said, "The Beatles gave us so much that I'd be proud if they had taken something from me, so no, I don't mind at all." His daughter Sunshine told me that her dad had never seen the film of *One Flew Over The Cuckoo's Nest* and never would. It was a point of honour.

Tuesday 19 October 1999

A Liverpool edition of *Monopoly* was launched at the Cavern. The Cavern was featured on the board.

December 1999

The fibreglass statue, coated with bronze powder, of John Lennon by Dave Webster in Mathew Street had to be repaired as vandals had taken a hammer to it, damaging John's eyes. Instead of a straight fix, it is given a facelift. The body is still Hamburg, 1961 but the head is now Beatle 1963. A few yards away, Ron Doyle added new bricks in gold lettering for Paul McCartney and his musicians.

Tuesday 14 December 1999

Get back to where you once belonged. Paul McCartney announced his show at the Cavern on ITV's *Parkinson* on December 3. "I am going back for just one night as a nod to the music that has always and will ever thrill me. I can't think of a better way to rock out the end of the century than with a rock'n'roll party at the Cavern." Soon it was being touted as the gig of the century.

Bill Heckle[849]: "Paul McCartney was looking for a promotional opportunity with *Run Devil Run* in 1999 and we had just done the Yellow Submarine day which impressed everybody at Apple. Paul's PR, Geoff Baker asked us to go round to Gambier Terrace, where John used to live with Stu, and negotiate a fee for filming. They didn't want to do it themselves as fees would quadruple if they knew McCartney was involved. They

thought of Gambier Terrace for a promo video because at the time the Beatles would have been listening to the music on *Run Devil Run*. We bandied a few figures around and then Geoff said, 'How would you feel if we did it at the Cavern instead?' Paul had some reservations as he thought the Cavern was on the wrong side of the road. He was told that it was 50% on the same site and had the same address, albeit it is eight foot deeper than the original Cavern. The plans of the back stage were within twelve feet of where they used to play, so it was more relevant to play the back stage than the front. There was also talk of Paul playing a theatre in London. Geoff knew that if he put Paul together with the Cavern, it would be an explosive news story. Stick him in Gambier Terrace; it's a cute angle. Stick him in a theatre in London; it's just another gig. They only agreed to the Cavern three weeks before it happened. We were told not to tell anybody and Paul would announce in on *Parkinson*."

Half of the tickets, that is 150, were raffled and even the raffle forms at HMV were limited. **Bill Heckle**[850]: "There was a lottery for tickets with EMI and there were problems for every Beatle related business including EMI, MPL, Apple, Abbey Road Studios, the Beatles Shop and the Beatles Story as they were being inundated with requests for tickets. Geoff put out that there had been over a million enquiries which could have been true. We were on the phones from seven in the morning right the way through until midnight. There was worldwide attention for these tickets."

Sexual favours were even offered to the Cavern's directors for tickets. Or were they? **Bill Heckle**[851]: "Oh, that caused fun and games at home with my wife. Geoff Baker rang me up and said that he had a real good scam. He said, 'I've just told the press that you as the owner have been offered sex for tickets.' He knew how to tickle the press and manipulate them."

The rehearsals in the afternoon were in front of about ten people. There was Bill Heckle, David Moores and Neil Aspinall. David and Neil thought that they did not know each other, but they did as David Moores ran the sixth form entertainment when he was at Stowe, and had persuaded his father to book the Beatles in April 1963.

Bill Heckle[852]: "We told Paul that Bob Wooler was over the road and he said, 'Bring him over', as he would love to see him again. He was in the Grapes with Ray McFall, and they came over and they met up. Paul gave Bob this huge bear hug. I respectfully moved about ten feet away as it was their own special moment. There was a lot of bonhomie. Paul called me over and said, 'Bob is going to bring me on one more time and that will be great.' Bob was delighted but also very daunted. He made the mistake, which is very Boblike, of going back to the Grapes. Unfortunately he drank too much and the word came over at seven o'clock that he just wasn't up to it. Paul was genuinely disappointed as he could see it would have been really fitting." Paul did give him a name check early in the concert.

McCartney played a storming set, backed by the band from his album of rock'n'roll covers, *Run Devil Run:* that is, Pink Floyd's Dave Gilmour and Deep Purple's Ian Paice plus Mick Green and Pete Wingfield. They performed thirteen songs in 40 minutes and only one song from the Beatles repertoire, "I Saw Her Standing There". His version of Ricky Nelson's "Lonesome Town" was prefaced with the words, "This is dedicated to loved ones: past, present and future", the sole reference to Linda.

As well as the audience in the Cavern itself, thousands of fans gathered on Chevasse Park in the city centre to watch it on a huge screen: brave people as it was a bitterly cold night. The concert had the world's largest netcast up to that point and it was also broadcast on BBC Radio One and, the following night, on television. The concert was a huge success and was subsequently issued on DVD as *Paul McCartney Live At The Cavern Club*.

The best comment on the night came from Neil Aspinall who muttered on the way out, "I've seen better." Of course he had: he'd seen the Beatles live at the Cavern. **Dave Jones**[853]: "I was living on my nerves that day and hoping that everything was working right. The greatest moment for me was at the end when I knew it had all gone well. Because I own the place, I know all the things that can go wrong: the drains could cause a flood: the fire alarm could go off: the power could pack up: somebody could collapse, and it was all live

on TV. There were scores of potential problems; things that don't even happen on a yearly basis but it could have happened that night. I was very relieved that it went off well and it was a huge success. The show itself was sensational."

After the show, there was a party in the adjoining De Coubertin's Sports Bar. **Bill Heckle**[854]: "Paul walked up the ramp to Harrington Street and into the Sports Bar. Five hundred people were there and he spent half an hour posing for photographs. He was in a great mood and very upbeat and he put on a policeman's hat and was conducting everybody with his truncheon. He was singing wartime songs, typically Liverpool working class Irish environment."

The event marked a turning point in McCartney's relationship with the city. Perhaps because of LIPA, perhaps because of his family connections, perhaps because of the Cavern, McCartney has become more and more interested in the city. He includes Liverpool in whatever he is doing: performances at King's Dock, Liverpool Cathedral for his Liverpool Oratorio, the Everyman for his poetry, the Philharmonic Hall for his tribute to Linda, and the Walker Art Gallery for his art. McCartney has become more at ease with his back catalogue and since the mid-eighties, has increasingly included more Beatle songs in his sets: now the repertoire for his live concerts can be as high as two-thirds Beatles.

Thursday 9 March 2000

Leading country-rock guitarist, Albert Lee with his band, Hogan's Heroes

Tuesday 18 April 2000

A festival of live music, sponsored by Dawsons Music, features a bit of everything. Good new local music from Up and Running, tribute bands Led Zed and the Maximum Who, and on 18 April, Wishbone Ash.

Saturday 20 May 2000

Extraordinary—a very limited release of a vinyl-only album of the complete 60s recordings by the Klubs has acquired a cult status, following an appearance on Frankie Connor's BBC Radio Merseyside show and a feature in *Record Collector* as well as being called the magazine's *Record of the Year*. The 50-something Klubs reform for a Cavern show and five songs from the performance are included on their 2001 compilation, *Midnight Love Cycle*.

Thursday 8 June 2000

Paul Rodgers was delighted to be at the Cavern and he incorporated Beatle songs into Bad Company's "Rock And Roll Fantasy". The opening act was his son and daughter, Steve and Jasmine. This was the Cavern's first non-smoking gig as Rodgers felt his voice would be affected. **Raphael Callaghan**[855]: "It was great to see Paul Rodgers in such a small, intimate setting. I had seen him in the past with Free in the Marquee and at the Country Club in Camden, but now he normally only plays large theatres or stadiums."

Dave Jones[856]: "This has been my favourite show at the Cavern. He was so pleasant and his voice hadn't changed at all with the years. You were back listening to Free and Bad Company again. He said it had been his favourite club gig, but everybody loves playing the place."

Bill Heckle[857]: "You can't set fees for these people based on 300 people. Instead of doing a door split, we set a price and that becomes what we pay them and they accept that, so they are getting 100% from us." In other words, these people only play the Cavern because they really want to.

Ray Johnson[858]: "I went to Manchester Airport to meet Paul Rodgers and bring him to Liverpool and get him into the hotel. Apart from the actual show, which was fantastic, he stayed a few days in Liverpool and I had the privilege of taking him round, doing a Beatles tour and showing him the city. He never forgot the hospitality he received. About eighteen months later, he came back with the band to the Royal Court and he invited us all down to the Royal Court. The following day we did another tour on his tour bus and then we went to the Apollo in Manchester with him."

Thursday 24 May 2001

"I've got a brick there," said **Lonnie Donegan**[859], who had visited the club the previous evening, "but they're wrong because I haven't played it yet. I was at the Liverpool Empire in 1958 and I rented it for my skiffle club one Saturday morning. Nobody in Britain knew very much about American folk music, more specifically Afro-American folk music, and so I thought it would be a good idea if I could enlighten the public. I formed the Lonnie Donegan Skiffle Club and we issued a monthly magazine in which I highlighted a different American blues singer each month like Big Bill Broonzy, Josh White and Burl Ives and gave instructions on how to play their better known songs. We gave news of what we were doing and where we were playing. We played everywhere for a week in those days and when we were at the Liverpool Empire, which seats 3,000, we would do two shows a night six days a week. That's over 30,000 people a week, a football stadium a week if you like, and we never stopped working. It's 100,000 a month and a million people a year. I did that for six years and that's a bloody great lot of people."

The Cavern which opened in 1957 was too small for a star of Donegan's magnitude. **Lonnie Donegan**[860]: "Even when I was in a semi-pro jazz band, the Ken Colyer Jazzmen, we were too big to play the Cavern. We played the Picton Hall and that is where we always played in Liverpool."

"What about a live album from the Cavern?"

"No way, the sound would be dreadful."

"It was good enough for Paul McCartney in 1999."

"But he had so many people working for him, scores of people getting it right. I can't afford that. We would have to re-do parts in the studio and it could go for a long time."

"It'd be like the Eagles' live album where, allegedly, the only thing left was the applause."

"That'd be the first thing to go. They want a lot of people in the Cavern and so they will be standing up. No matter how much you like an act, you can't applaud with a glass in your hand. The applause won't be that hot."

Lonnie was wrong: it was a wonderful event and the audience loved him—and showed it. **Stephen Bailey**[861]: "I was applauding quite briskly, but I don't know how as I was holding a drink. It was great hearing 'Rock Island Line' down there as it is the very essence of what I am listening to now. There were a lot of old people there that night."

Bill Heckle[862]: "It is as hot and sweaty as the old days. When I was at Lonnie Donegan's show, I went for a pee and stood next to this big giant of a man of about 65 in a suit and tie. He said, 'These toilets are filthy: it is far too hot and there are too many people, and the music is too loud, but you know what, this is the best night out I have had in 30 years. This takes me back to when I was 21. He laughed his head off and walked out. I was worried that night, seeing people walking in with overcoats but we never got any complains. They were rolling back the years that night."

Carl Jones[863]: "On the way back, I was tired as my normal bedtime is 11pm and there was Lonnie, still full of himself. The first request when he got back was for a cup of tea. I put the kettle on, made a cup of tea and gave it to him. He poured it down the sink, and he said, 'I don't call that a cup of tea.' He got hold of the tea and he put three large spoonfuls of tea in the pot, left it for five minutes and let it stew and poured himself an inky black cup and he said, 'That's what you call a cup of tea, lad.'"

On 12 July 2000 and down at the King's Dock, Chuck Berry played the Summer Pops. **Dave Jones**[864]: "I have seen Chuck Berry live about ten times but I didn't go to the Chuck Berry gig at the Summer Pops as I thought I would be disappointed. We got a phone call to say that he wanted to bring some friends down to the Cavern. They came into the club and he stayed in his E-series Mercedes. He asked me to sit in the back and we chatted to each other. He was a gentleman and he autographed an old album for me. He didn't want to autograph a Chess boxed-set at first as he said it would spoil the package. He said he would play the Cavern again some day but I know that he brings a lot of problems with him."

Tuesday 10 October 2000
Wishbone Ash

Wednesday 15 November 2000
Elton John's guitarist and former Hellecaster, John Jorgenson

Sunday 24 March 2001
Elton John Fan Club Convention

Tuesday 19 April 2001
Tim Hingley from Inspiral Carpets

Wednesday 20 April 2001
John Coghlan's Quo

Sunday 22 April 2001
Eric Bell's Thin Lizzy

Thursday 14 June 2001
Ian Hunter with a guest appearance from **Joe Elliott**[865] of Def Leppard: "Ian Hunter is a great

mate of mine so I joined him at the Cavern and we did 'All The Way To Memphis' together. It was great just being in there. It is too small for Def Leppard but I would like to do something there on my own. I also went to the Beatles Shop and bought an inflatable *Yellow Submarine* armchair."

Sunday 24 June 2001
That white boy with a feather, Jason Downs

Sunday 15 July 2001
Blues rock from Austin, Texas with Lightning Red

Saturday 4 August 2001
Tracie Hunter, Ian's daughter.

Thursday 9 August 2001
Christian rock with leading singer/songwriter Larry Norman

Sunday 7 October 2001
Wishbone Ash

Tuesday 6 November 2001
Hundreds came to the Cavern to hear the preview of Paul McCartney's album, *Driving Rain*, but most of them had already heard it on the web and the evening turned into a sing along.

Thursday 8 November 2001
An acoustic evening with Peter Coyle (Lotus Eaters)

Monday 12 November 2001
Despite being 73, Bo Diddley's contract at the Cavern called for two 70 minute sets in one evening. I went to the first house where he more than fulfilled his obligation with 85 minutes on stage. The only time we heard the famed Bo Diddley beat was in the thunderous opening number. As his five piece band played, Bo Diddley ambled on, wearing a rugby shirt and grey trousers and looking bemused. He plugged in and played some fine licks, but the vocals were spoken during this number which was effectively rapped. He showed us how to clap along with the beat by going "clap, clap your hands" and the sound of 300 people pounding out that famous rhythm was very powerful.

Alex McKechnie[866]: "Bo Diddley was offered to me and the only way I could make it pay was to insist on two performances. By the time you had paid for the flight, his hotels and the hiring of the back line, the Hammond organ from York-

CAVERN WALL OF FAME

THE ARCTIC MONKEYS

MIKE McCARTNEY
& RITCHIE HAVENS

(Clockwise)
Rock'n'Roll Legends THE
CRICKETS
Pop Giants ARCTIC MONKEYS
Great British Rock Drummer
KENNEY JONES
X-Factor Star RAY QUINN
US Folk/Rock performer
RICHIE HAVENS

shire and the Leslie speaker to go with it, it would have to be about £50 entrance otherwise. He did a great show on both performances. He sat in the dressing room and 9/11 had just taken place and he said that he was going to pick up his wife and drive her somewhere because she won't travel on planes because there might be a bomb on board."

Ray Johnson[867]: "When I went to London to pick him up, I had to meet him outside their hotel in London. All the band were there but Bo Diddley, who had gone for a little stroll. Then we saw him walking up the street with his big hat on and he stopped to chat to a down-and-out in a hotel doorway. Bo said, 'How long have you been here, Sonny?' He replied, 'I've been here all night.' Bo said, 'Stand up when you speak to me: don't be sitting there.' It was like his grandfather was speaking to him. Bo handed him a £10 note and he told him to get cleaned up, have some breakfast and coffee, and go and find employment. 'Be a man, don't just be sitting in the gutter. I've been in the gutter, I know what it's like. Here's your start.' The guys in the band said that he was like that with everybody, very generous, very humble and a lovely man. Coming down from London to Liverpool, we had to stop at every service station and at everyone, he would buy a little knick knack or a little toy and he would sit in the back of the bus, playing with these gadgets. Great guy. He was fantastic on stage. It was like the McCartney show, you don't speak for the duration of the show: you stand there in awe. You want to listen and watch. I was like that for both sets with Bo Diddley, an amazing man and an amazing musician."

Tim Adams[868]: "I went to see both the Bo Diddley shows and I thought he was fantastic and the way he worked the crowd was marvellous. Somebody was trying to film the gig and he said, 'Man, would you like me to come into your kitchen and eat your chicken without asking you first?' That was excellent."

Bo Diddley didn't do many of the songs associated with him, but there was "Diddley Daddy" and "Who Do You Love", the fastest song of the evening. He only sang part of "Who Do You Love", preferring long instrumental passages. Mostly Bo was playing slow blues with a strong Muddy Waters influence. His ten-minute "I'm A Man" was taken slowly with Bo relishing every word. Best of all was "Bad Seed" in which the seventeen-year-old Bo had a conversation with his mother whilst we were all chanting "Bo Diddley is a bad seed". Bo sang about young girls and his parents as though he couldn't believe what he had written all those years before.

It was an excellent show, not what I expected but none the worse for that. His second set lasted 90 minutes and included "Mona" and "Road Runner" as well as an extended rap, which name-checked Muddy Waters, Jimmy Reed, Elvis Presley, Chuck Berry, Little Anthony and naturally, himself. The opening act, the London-based Fat Cats, sang jump and jive numbers associated with Amos Milburn and Tiny Bradshaw and were very entertaining. They ended with a fine "Train Kept A-Rollin'" and the crowd would have enjoyed more. **Stephen Bailey**[869]: "It was great to see an artist I've idolised and then find out that he is even better than I imagined him to be. I was exhausted after watching the first set and I can't imagine how he found the stamina to do two sets. He was fantastic."

Friday 16 November 2001
Zoot Money

Thursday 29 November 2001
Tom Robinson was playing at the Cavern the day that George Harrison died and he paid special tribute to him.

Thursday 6 December 2001
Fish, former lead singer of Marillion. Fish enjoys the Cavern so much that he has become a regular, having made four appearances.

Saturday 7 December 2001
Kathryn Williams

Thursday 7 February 2002
Haskell, McIntosh & Stuart—that is, Gordon, Robbie & Hamish.

Thursday 14 February 2002
Round off Valentine's Day with Albert Lee and Hogan's Heroes

Sunday 24 February 2002
The Cavern, *Liverpool Echo* and Radio City combined forces for a tribute concert to George Harrison, hosted by Phil Easton and Billy Butler, which was broadcast on the web. I found it a

strange affair as it included a tribute band (Blue Meanies, Hari Georgeson) when George was disdainful of tribute acts and the sixties hitmakers, the Ivy League had no originals in the line-up. The Merseybeats did a one-hour show but Tony Crane said that they had shortened their set to make way for the Blue Meanies. There was hardly a mention of George Harrison in the first half and not one of his songs.

The second half opened with Pete Waterman telling amusing stories about Simon Cowell, but he did say that George had shown him things on the ukulele. Steve Harley sang Elvis Presley's "Love Me" "which is appropriate tonight", but he forgot to tell us why. Ralph McTell, reduced to two songs, performed "Streets Of London" and the delightful "I Bid You Goodnight". The eighties band, Dare, did "While My Guitar Gently Weeps" and Jennifer John sang "Something"—hooray, some George Harrison songs at last. Hari Georgeson performed nifty versions of "Got My Mind Set On You", "Handle With Care" and "What Is Life". They were the only act to allude to this being George Harrison's birthday. Pete Wylie performed "Badge" and then Shali Shankar proved to be both a most gracious man and a master of the sitar. At 11pm, the Hari Krshna Temple joined Hari Georgeson for "My Sweet Lord".

Billy Butler announced that an old drunk was going to stagger on, and making a few movements as an old drunk, Paul McCartney came on. The applause was thunderous and he described how he came to watch Cliff Richard and the Shadows at the Empire and how he would discuss guitars with George on the 82 bus "long before the Beatles." He said how close he had been to George, asked for an F and started an acappella "Yesterday" with the audience singing along. I liked the Bobby McFerrin touches of him slapping his body for percussion and he changed the lyric to "Why he had to go, I don't know." Everyone was hoping that he would pick a guitar and jam a few songs to give the evening a rousing sendoff (and surely he would be tempted to do that) but it was not to be. At the finale, the Blue Meanies got themselves by Paul McCartney, who became the first Beatle to be photographed with a tribute band. The charity concert raised £40,000.

Bill Heckle[870]: "It was a strange bill. Paul was thinking of doing it but we were told that if we announced anything, he wouldn't. This caused a few big names to drop out because they thought that Paul wasn't doing it, which is horrible really. The Blue Meanies only got on the show that morning and to be fair to them, they did really well. Paul arrived at 9pm and I know he enjoyed what he saw. He said that George would approve of Hari Georgeson. He gave me a big hug at the end."

Wednesday 3 April 2002

Talk about a surreal day: try this. The day before Billy Bob Thornton appeared at the Cavern, I was told that my interview would be at 3pm and that he would be going on stage at 8.15pm. Sounded fine to me, but the next morning there was a change of plan. The interview had been moved to 5pm and when I got to the Cavern, Billy Bob said, "Sorry to mess you around. I've been taking a ferry cross the Mersey with Gerry Marsden. He even sang the song for me—and I've got it on video!" I knew Billy Bob was wild, but Gerry and the Pacemakers—wow! "I'm doing some sixties songs tonight and starting off with one of Gerry's. He's going to see Liverpool playing football and he can't get down 'til ten o'clock. We'll start the show then." Was I hearing things right? Showtime was being delayed for nearly two hours because one solitary member of the audience couldn't get here. This is taking audience participation too far and, in any event, if Gerry were to miss the start, surely Billy Bob could repeat the song for an encore. "No, this is a football town," said Billy Bob, who had been totally indoctrinated by Gerry Marsden, "It's better to start late. The audience will like it more." "Not if they've bought tickets saying 8 o'clock, they won't," I argued, but my reasoning was falling on deaf ears and my hopes for an early night faded away.

Just one thing though, Billy Bob, why Liverpool, what did it say to a boy in Arkansas? **Billy Bob Thornton**[871]: "I love Liverpool. Those records got me through my childhood. It was a world I disappeared into. When the Beatles came out, I wanted to rebel and be in a band. My brother and I were fans of the Beatles as well as the Dave Clark Five, Gerry and the Pacemakers, the Animals, the Kinks and all of the British Invasion Groups. I

More Recent Cave Dwellers

PETER TORK

LONNIE DONEGAN

RICHIE HAVENS

THE CAVERN LIVERPOOL

THE CAVERN 50TH

CAVERN CITY TOURS
OFFICIAL INVITATION
to the
CAVERN'S
50TH
BIRTHDAY PARTY
Tuesday 16th January 2007
Kick-off 1pm

RSVP to:
The Cavern Club, 10 Mathew Street, Liverpool L2 6RE

THE CAVERN 50TH

WORLD'S MOST
FAMOUS CLUB
32 LIVE
BANDS
2 STAGES
A Celebration
OPEN BAR
1pm - 2am

NON TRANSFERABLE   ADMIT ONE

CAVERN 50TH

BO DIDDLEY

At the IPO

TEAZERS

am a huge fan of Gerry and the Pacemakers and it's been a fantastic day sailing the ferry cross the Mersey with Gerry himself. It's the dream of my life to be here in Liverpool and playing the Cavern because this music got me through my childhood."

In case there had been a change of plan, I returned to the Cavern at nine o'clock. The door to the room where Billy Bob would appear, was shut and an audience of 250 was watching a talented duo, Feelin' Groovy, working through some folk-rock classics. Not bad, but I felt that the audience would soon be singing out, "Where have you been all the day, Billy Bob, Billy Bob?" Fortunately, the football match didn't go into overtime. Liverpool had won, and once King Gerry had arrived, we were allowed in the back room.

One by one, Billy Bob's band came out at 10pm and established a funky riff. After a couple of minutes, Billy Bob appeared, wearing a head scarf, and singing a minor hit for the Pacemakers, "It's Gonna Be Alright". The new arrangement gave it more depth that Gerry's single, but "Game Of Love" was more predictable and similar to Wayne Fontana's hit single. Several covers followed during the evening—"Green Tambourine" (with Thornton describing the sitar as "an Indian banjo"), "California Dreamin'", a raucous sing along "Hang On Sloopy" and "I Still Miss Someone" (Johnny Cash meets Nick Cave). Come to think of it, Billy Bob, what's all this about the Beatles? You're an Arkansas boy—you've got Johnny Cash.

Needless to say, Billy Bob was full of his love for Liverpool. With the broadest of smiles, he said, "I thought my family came from Ireland but now I've found out that my mom's people come from Cheshire and my dad's from Yorkshire. I'm a hillbilly but I come from here." The audience cheered, not caring that the wannabe Scouser's geography was a little wayward. Still, it was clear from a heckle that he knew Manchester was only 30 miles away. When he began his litany of favourite Liverpool groups (Beatles, Gerry, Searchers), some wag shouted "What about A Flock Of Seagulls?"

As we climbed the stairs out of the Cavern, everyone was saying how good the show had been

and what a wonderful band it was. The other comment was that he did not appear to be a wild man at all. "He could be the guy next door," someone said to me. Well, not quite. My neighbours won't be showing home movies of Gerry Marsden singing *Ferry Cross The Mersey*.

Sunday 5 May 2002
Glen Matlock, formerly of the Sex Pistols

Sunday 23 June 2002
Tony O'Malley (ex- Arrival, 10cc, Kokomo). The fact that it was billed as 'an intimate evening' suggests that no one was expecting a big turnout.

Monday 24/Tuesday 25 June 2002
Fish—a clever idea: pre-1988 music the first night(including all the *Misplaced Childhood* album) and post-1988 the next.

Thursday 29 August 2002
Dave Sharp (The Alarm)

Wednesday 6 November 2002
Nick Harper

Friday 8 November 2002
Hugh Cornwall (Stranglers)

Sunday 17 November 2002
Joe Brown supported by Henry Gross from Sha Na Na.

Thursday 28 November 2002
The Comets and the Crickets, supported by the Jets. The Comets' lead guitarist, Franny Beecher, was 81 years old. The band consisted of five as-near-as-dammit originals with Jacko Buddin on lead vocals. Franny took a guitar solo on 'Steel Guitar Rag': Marshall Lytle climbed on his double-bass, and Dick Richards had a five minute drum solo.

Tim Adams[872]: "The opening act was the Jets, a three piece act with stand-up bass, who were absolutely brilliant in their own right. The Jets had been frantic but the Crickets started slowly and built up to a crescendo. That was a good contrast to what came before and went after. Sonny Curtis was an excellent front man with some very good chat and very informative too. The Comets were on for an hour and a half and the bass player was getting on for 80 but he got hold of his double bass and lifted it above his shoulder. It was just brilliant. The atmosphere was great as we were so appreciative that such a legendary act was playing the Cavern at such advanced ages."

Karl Terry[873]: "I had seen the Comets at the Odeon in 1957 and they were fantastic. The unison of the drums and the bass and of the guitar and the saxophone were marvellous. I was thrilled that they were coming back to Liverpool and it was thrilling to meet them and find that they still loved rock'n'roll as much as I do. They looked immaculate and they had a drive and a cohesive sound. They stole the evening that night and the other two acts were great."

Bill Heckle[874]: "Lots of people were there for the Crickets who have a big local following and so there was a danger that the Comets would lose the crowd by following the Crickets, but it was a really wonderful show. The Comets blew the Crickets off the stage. To see these 70 year old guys running and jumping around was amazing. One of them even jumped on his double bass. It was a fantastic show."

Sunday 8 February 2003
Jackie Leven (Doll By Doll)

March 2003
Gerry Marsden played a fortieth anniversary show for 'How Do You Do It' backed by the Gary Murphy Band and compèred by Billy Butler.

Tuesday 11 March 2003
Music writer Paul Du Noyer was the subject of Granada TV's *My Liverpool*, which included footage of the Cavern.

Friday 14 March 2003
Tony Wright (Terrorvision)

Wednesday 26 March 2003
The *Woodstock* veteran, Richie Havens appeared with bass and electric guitar, but the emphasis was on the very heavy rhythm from Richie himself. The show was all sweat and percussion. Considering he had recorded several Beatle songs, it was suprising that he only did one ("Here Comes The Sun"), but he did three of Dylan's ("Maggie's Farm", "All Along The Watchtower", "Just Like A Woman"). The conversation between the songs was hippie-based but well-intentioned and naturally very anti-war. The fifties, said Richie, was the decade of dumbing down and so is the 2000s, it's come back. He concluded with a long acappella song, "Turning Away", which was particularly poignant. It was a full house with many of the audience really into his songs, but someone did shout "Get on with it" during one of his raps.

Tuesday 6 May 2003
The Prime Minister, Tony Blair is 50. Cherie almost booked the Cavern for his fiftieth birthday party and he would have performed. Fortunately, somebody thought better of it.

Friday 23 May 2003
Fish

Saturday 31 May 2003
Bill Heckle[875]: "Paul McCartney wanted to have his end of World Tour party at the Cavern. On the Friday before, the usual rules apply, if you tell anyone they cancel and they always have a back-up. We had a poster outside to say that it was a private, retirement party for Barclays Bank. All the people came to the door and didn't realise that McCartney was downstairs singing. It was the first time we met Heather. It was done out like Morocco with a vegetarian buffet and a London soul band, Soul Survivor. McCartney got up and sang with them. He got Heather up too and she was very annoyed about that. She told him not to do it again. He sat with Heather and the day before it was announced that she was pregnant. We rang up our suppliers for some babygrows with the Cavern logo on. She had been in there an hour and was a bit sulky. I got the package and walked up to her. She was very suspicious but I gave it to her. She then screamed with delight and stopped being po-faced and became animated. Paul said it was their first baby present and she was clutching them all night. When they left, he said, 'Tell me where the original Cavern was, Bill.' We had told him in 1999 and even now, he doesn't remember. I suppose it's important to us but not to him."

Alex McKechnie[876]: "McCartney was dancing and the band said, 'Do you want to sing with us?' The band played 'We Are Family' and he got up with them. He did a little rap, 'I'm down in the pool and I think it's cool, and I'm here with our kid' and so on. He got Heather to come up and when he returned to the table, she said, 'Don't ever do that to me again.' She was shouting at him: he was being henpecked and it was a glimpse behind the façade."

Dave Jones[877]: "The Cavern was the hottest it has ever been that night. The production team had decked the front part of the Cavern to look like something from the Arabian nights. They put out some big, thick candles, which gave out a considerable amount of heat as this is a brick cellar. One of the designers complained about the heat when it was all his fault."

Wednesday 4 June 2003
An original Mother and "the Indian of the group", Jimmy Carl Black with the Frank Zappa tribute band, the Muffin Men

Tuesday 17/ Wednesday 18 June 2003
Actor James Marsters (*Buffy The Vampire Slayer*) with his rock band, Ghost Of The Robot.

Thursday 17 July 2003
Fish on the menu

Thursday 21 August 2003
Let's do the time warp again. *This Is Merseybeat* was staged by Merseycats with Juke Box Eddie's, Lee Curtis and the All Stars, Kingsize Taylor and the Dominoes, Ian and the Zodiacs, Faron's Flamingos, Karl Terry and the Cruisers, Earl Preston and the TTs and Dale Roberts and the Jaywalkers. The Del-Renas performed with their original line-up and for one reason or another, there weren't many 60s bands that could do that.

Kingsize Taylor had returned to performing after many years away and he now performed at every opportunity. He was to set up the charity, *Sounds Of The Sixties,* and they had their Sundays nights in the front room at the Cavern. **Ray Johnson**[878]: "The old part of the Cavern is notoriously bad for sound and the acoustics are quite poor but we have overcome that by installing some extra speakers. You don't go for volume, you go for clarity. It is still a funny room but once you get used to it, you know how to work it. It must be difficult for people who come in on a one-off thing and they have to spend hours sorting the acoustics out in there. It is quite easy to authenticate the sixties sound. If you run it on a flat EQ, you will get a sixties sound. It is when you try to get a more modern sound that you have to fight the elements."

Also appearing at the Beatlefest at the Cavern was Lawrence Gilmour from Wings.

Tuesday 9/ Wednesday 10 September 2003
Guitar hero Peter Green had returned to performing with concerts with the Splinter Group.

Tuesday 21 October 2003
An evening with Reece, who are about to spend two weeks in South Africa promoting AIDS awareness.

Thursday 30 October 2003
A sequence for Bill Oddie's *History Hunt* is filmed at the Cavern featuring the Cavern Beatles performing "Please Please Me"

Wednesday 12 November 2003
Caravan

Monday 17 November 2003
Kevin Ayers

Saturday 10 January 2004
The Star-Club Connection featuring Liverpool acts who played Hamburg including Kingsize Taylor and the Dominoes, the Undertakers and Lee Curtis.

Tuesday 27 January 2004
Carl Palmer (drummer with Emerson, Lake and Palmer) and his band.

Sunday 7 March 2004
The Zombies with Rod Argent and Colin Blunstone.

Thursday 18 March 2004
Stan Webb's Chicken Shack

Tuesday 23 March 2004
It was expected that both Paul Kantner and Marty Balin would be part of Jefferson Airplane/Jefferson Starship/Starship or whatever they were calling themselves that week, but only Kantner turned up. Their tour manager wondered why the Cavern management was bothered: "What does it matter? We've already done some gigs and nobody's complained?" This was the grumpiest band to arrive at the Cavern and things were little better when the show started. Paul Kantner, wearing a headband though he had little on top, sat down throughout the two hour performance and smoked non-stop—in-between songs, in instrumental breaks and while singing, this was a *tour de force* in itself. He sat down and looked round the Cavern: "So this is where western civilisation got fucked up. It didn't get fucked up in London, man: it didn't get fucked up in San Francisco,

man: it got fucked up in Liverpool. And hey, man, we're by the sea. How far are we from the fucking North Sea?" This was a valid question and I am not sure that I know the answer—probably 100 miles if he did mean the North Sea: three miles if he meant the Irish Sea—but the audience took it to be a reference to the Mersey and someone shouted, "500 fucking yards, mate." Whatever, we then got "Wooden Ships", so at least a little programming was going on.

Thursday 8 April 2004
Connie Lush and Blues Shouter

Sunday 18 April 2004
Wishbone Ash

Friday 23 April 2004
John Otway, possibly the only person to somersault on the cramped Cavern stage.

Tuesday 1 June 2004
TV filming of the Prellies—audience in sixties dress.

Monday 7 June 2004
Jan Akkerman, formerly of Focus

Monday 21 June 2004
Battle Of The Bands with BOA winning.

Friday 9 July 2004
Karl Terry and the Cruisers

Sunday 18 July 2004
Barry Melton (Country Joe and the Fish)

Thursday 29 July 2004
The Crazy World of Arthur Brown

Thursday 26 August 2004
Pete Best Band

Sunday 19 September 2004
Z Rock Festival of melodic rock featuring War & Peace.

Tuesday 28 September 2004
The Gary (US) Bonds show was opened by local band Juke Box Eddies who consisted of former Merseybeat musicians: the double bass player Owen Clayton had a stint in Johnny Duncan's Blue Grass Boys. He was nearly 70 and he has such distinctive features that you end up watching him. The front man and Casio player Mike Byrne was very polished. The rap DJ, James Klass proudly introduced the Supremes—yes, not a tribute to the Supremes, but the Supremes. As if.

It was three girls in red dresses singing to backing tapes with fadeout endings. Roz who played Diana Ross had a good voice but did she graduate from LIPA just to sing karaoke as a support act? She thanked the audience ecstatically (à la Ross, I suppose) and brought James Klass back for a bow.

Gary (US) Bonds reworked "New Orleans" as, "Even England is really cool, Down the Mersey River down to Liverpool". When he introduced the opening track from his new album, *Can't Teach An Old Dog New Tricks*, he began plugging the CD, saying we could have it for a very reasonable £10. He kept repeating this and someone shouted, "We heard you the first time." Gary's tribute to Otis Redding was a stunning "Dreams To Remember" and by dedicating "Out Of Work" to President Bush, he drew a round of applause. His wife and daughter showed how good they were as they sang the backing vocals for "Dedication". He sang what he described as his favourite song, Steve Van Zandt's ballad "Daddy's Come Home". The homage to the Beatles came with "I Saw Her Standing There" and "It's Only Love". He said, "That was close enough, but you need spandex to get those high notes." Rather strangely, he and Laurie sang "Bitch" as a father and daughter duet, but it worked fine. After a brief acappella "Shop Around" came an exciting "This Little Girl". Gary and the swingingest band they had ever heard closed with an extended "Quarter To Three". It ended with the audience shouting back "Holy shit" to him. Don't ask me why. He ended with an energetic rock'n'roll medley and the next morning he was playing golf.

Tuesday 5 October 2004
The first of two BBC Radio 2 concerts presented by Mark Radcliffe—Travis supported by K.T.Tunstall.

Wednesday 6 October 2004
The second: Embrace with the Basement.

Mark Radcliffe[879]: "I know it's not the original Cavern, having been re-built and moved about a bit, but they've done a cracking job and it's very atmospheric. It was a real thrill to play with Travis on the Cavern stage. You couldn't be a music fan and not feel something for the Cavern, could you? I used to go to Eric's as a punk and we were always very conscious of the fact that the Cavern used to be across the street, and that we were, maybe, part of the next generation. I presented my show from the small stage, in front of the facsimile of the Cavern backdrop, and we played records recorded at the original club. It was amazing to see how small it was and I love the thought that this tiny, sweaty room sent reverberations around the world."

Colin Hall[880]: "Embrace and Travis were great evenings and the Cavern was packed. I'm an older man but I have the same stamina and it is a small space and the best place to hear rock music. The energy is incredible and the rapport lifts the crowd. The bands give 100%. It is much better than some huge cavernous chamber where you are 1,000 miles from the band."

Ray Johnson[881]: "Travis was a great night. They were not like stars, but like an ordinary band that had come to play the Cavern and were very friendly: no prima donnas. Another great milestone for the Cavern and we had Embrace the following night. One thing's for sure. Nobody ever goes away from the Cavern and says it was a bad gig. I find that very interesting; everybody who plays here loves the gig, loves the place, loves the audience and loves the staff. It is one of those places; it is just so friendly, isn't it?"

Wednesday 27 October 2004

An electrifying *Sounds Of The Sixties* concert at the Cavern with Linda Gail Lewis, supported by Juke Box Eddie's, Karl Terry and the Cruisers, Kingsize Taylor and the Undertakers. **Mike Byrne**[882]: "When I went down to the original Cavern, I was using a fifteen watt bass cabinet. The guitarist wouldn't have had 30 watts, maybe a Selmer True Voice and fifteen watts. Nowadays they bring in 2,000 rig PAs. Absolutely crazy. We still only use a 500 watt PA system in Juke Box Eddie's and we do rock'n'roll gigs all around the country and it's acceptable as you don't have to be too loud to be exciting."

Friday 19 November 2004

John Jorgenson's Talamine Guitar Clinic

Saturday 7 February 2005

2 Men & Black—a touring celebration of the 2 Tone label.

Saturday 5 March 2005

John Otway

Monday 21 March 2005

Jan Akkerman

Tuesday 5 April 2005

Steel guitarist B.J. Cole

Friday 13/ Saturday 14 May 2005

Nigel Kennedy had wanted to play the Cavern for some time and some earlier dates had had to be cancelled. The jazz-styled shows with the Jarek Smietana Band went well but while in Liverpool, one of his highly-prized violins was stolen. **Bill Heckle**[883]: "He was going to a Sunday game at Anfield. Ray Johnson said that they could leave everything here overnight, but they took it and it was parked in a van. They went to the football and before they returned home, they went to Chinatown for a meal. It was there that the robbery took place and the police had the footage on CCTV. It was reported that the violin was stolen from the Cavern, but that was wrong."

Saturday 6 June 2005

30th anniversary show for Radio City's Great Easton Express.

Monday 4 July to Friday 15 July 2005

Liverpool Comedy Festival events including Silky, Duncan Oakley, Seymour Mace and Die Clatterschenkenfietermaus, one name I've yet to see on a brick.

Thursday 21/ Friday 22 July 2005

Kenny Joney (Small Faces, Faces, Who) saw *A Hard Day's Fight* and offered to play two shows with his band, the Jones Gang—Kenney Jones, Rick Wills (Cochise, Frampton's Camel, Foreigner) and Rob Hart (Bad Company). Their keyboard player, Mark Read (A1) was about 25 years younger than the rest. There was a photo session for their bricks on the wall and Kenney gave his drum-skin from *Live Aid* to the Cavern Pub. Kenney Jones really wanted to play the Cavern: how do I know? He came by private jet, which he landed at John Lennon airport. The fuel and the parking fees exceeded his fee for the Cavern.

On stage, the Jones Gang was very good indeed and the front man, Rob Hart, was very personable, encouraging the audience to sing along. In an 80 minute set, they only played four songs from the new album ("Angel"—written by Rob Hart and Russ Ballard—was described as the "Number One added song to American radio this week"

RHYTHM REVIEWS
MERSEYBEAT ON DISC

THE BEATLES
Love Me Do; P.S. I Love You
(Parlophone R 4949)**

THE BEATLES sound rather like the Everlys or the Brooks according to "whose side you're on. But in Love Me Do they have got a deceptively simple beater which could grow on you.

Harmonica backing.

P.S. I Love You weaves a little Latin into itself as the boys sing a letter ballad of everyday sentiments.

Sonny Webb and the Cascades
You've Got Everything; Border Of The Blues
(Oriole CB 1873)**

A COUNTRY and western number chanted steadily by Sonny Webb. You've Got Everything is accompanied by plenty of twang and other male voices too. Border Of The Blues is another of those wistful western numbers—includes some attractive guitar.

THE SEARCHERS
Sweet Nothin's; What'd I Say
(Philips BF 1274)

DUG up from the archives of Philips comes this well-timed effort that was recorded at the Star Club in Hamburg, years before the boys had their Pye recording contract. It's an average recording of the Brenda Lee classic, but with nothing outstanding about it. Loud and violent without the class they have since achieved. Will get a lot of sales too—but it wouldn't have meant a thing without "Sweets."

I'm surprised the flip isn't the top side. It's more danceable and is the usual beat group adaptation of the Ray Charles R & B great. Good stuff despite the poor recording etc.

THE MOJOS — They Say; Forever (Decca F 11732)** A Boy group The Mojos shout out a gritty beat number They Say to the usual rhythm spiced but the attacking spirit of the production may get it somewhere. Forever, like the top deck, has plenty of rough edges which I'd rather were rubbed off, but the performance is likeable.

The Remo Four
I Wish I Could Shimmy Like My Sister Kate; Peter Gunn
(Piccadilly N 35175)**

THIS group, until recently the backing unit for Johnny Sandon, are now recording on their own and they've chosen to jump on the Shimmy revival. Whether this attempt to update the old craze of the 20s will mean anything, I'm not sure . . . but the Four's performance is worth sales. Good chant and slick guitar work, too.

Peter Gunn, the old television theme by Henry Mancini, starts off heavily, but generates some interest without really becoming exciting.

JOHNNY SANDON AND THE REMO FOUR
Yes; Magic Potion (Pye 15559)

JOHNNY sings lead on this excellent rendering of the Ben E. King number which is very well performed indeed. There's some good backing sounds and the lead voice of Johnny backed with excellent vocal work from the boys sounds very good. Also the medium-paced plaintive beat ballad is very commercial and could easily give this talented Liverpool group their big hit.

Flip is another beaty sort of thing with a good lyric and some fair old backing work thrown in by the boys, who get out of the Liverpool rut. Good flip.

CY TUCKER: Let Me Call You Sweetheart; I Apologise (Fontana TF 470). Good singer, good song, and an unusual treatment, but the backing tends to overpower on this item.

GERRY AND PACEMAKERS
How Do You Do It?; Away From You
(Columbia DB 4987)

STRAIGHT in the footsteps of the Beatles, this Liverpool group have a first-time stab at fame. Gerry, lead voice, zips into a rather catchy little melody. The beat is not so solidly laid down, but there's plenty happening, including some forceful piano. Gerry's voice is high-pitched and biting. It's risky to tip this for the top but there's no doubt at all that it will sell very well indeed. He strains a wee bit for effect on the flip but there's some unusual sounding harmonic work going on. At least this group has ideas. They deserve success.

BILLY J. KRAMER AND THE DAKOTAS
You Want To Know a Secret; I'll Be On My Way (Parlophone R 5023)

PAUL McCARTNEY and John Lennon of the Beatles wrote this song for the group. It's a fair-old song, and the boys sing it in a very Beatle-ish way. Teen beat rock stuff that must sell well — it seems the disc companies can't sign up these groups quick enough. Good backing from the Dakotas on the plaintive number that moves along at a medium tempo pace. Should be a big hit.

More of the group vocalising from the boys on the flip. They sing well although the Beatles' sound is still there. But it's all pleasant enough.

THREE

THE SWINGING BLUE JEANS
Promise You'll Tell Her; It's So Right (HMV POP 1327).

AFTER a string of three hits comes this merry teen-beat effort penned by the boys themselves. It's maybe not quite as strong as "You're No Good" but nevertheless it's a beaty tuneful affair with plenty of danceable sounds. Loud and commercial with very good backing work. Flip is an interesting beater with a clean sound.

Tommy Quickly and the Remo Four
Kiss Me Now; No Other Love (Will Ever Be The Same)
(Piccadilly N 35151)***

TOMMY QUICKLY should do well with his second release on the Piccadilly label. He has been given a bright up-tempo love song Kiss Me Now and a backing by the Remo Four. This is the group usually heard alongside Johnny Sandon; and chosen for the session I understand because they've worked with Tommy on tour.

No Other Love (Will Ever Be The Same) has a melody which everyone will know at once even if they can't recall its original title. To put you out of your misery . . . it's Dvorak's Humoureske.

CHICK GRAHAM AND THE COASTERS—I Know; Education (Decca F 11859)**—Slight spectre of Phil in the backing as Chick Graham and The Coasters vocal-beat heavily through I Know? Bouncier 'B' side but Education doesn't rate pass marks.

DENNY SEYTON: Short Fat Fannie; Give Me Back My Heart (Mercury MF 814) A bit dated, this old rock sound on the Larry Williams' song. But its persistent and with a good dance beat.

THE MERSEYBEATS —It's Love That Really Counts; The Fortune Teller (Fontana TF 412)**—The name of this team ought to tell you what to expect—boys chanting to guitars and drums for the Bacharach-David song It's Love That Really Counts. I found this rather tedious and unappealing, I'm afraid. There's not a great deal of inspiration or inventiveness to recommend it. The Fortune Teller lifts the spirit a trifle but not enough to make me rush out and buy.

EARL PRESTON
I Know Something; Watch Your Step (TF 406)

PRETTY teen ballad from Earl who handles the medium tempo number well. Soft kind of vocal with a goodly tone and some efficient backing from the group. It's rather plaintive and better than the average number of this type. Should sell very well—could even find a place in the charts.

The Bobby Parker R & B classic is given a beaty going over on the flip. It's an efficient number that the boys perform very well.

FOUR

The Pete Best Four
I'm Gonna Knock On Your Door; Why Did I Fall In Love With You
(Decca F 11929)***

PETE BEST (who actually reached the Hit Parade as the drummer on John Lennon's Ain't She Sweet) gets a chance to try for disc sales with his own group. The ex-Beatle has a hard driving effort in I'm Gonna Knock On Your Door. Big vocal and rhythm noise, but the knock's not exactly a knock-out. On the turnover there's steady twang 'n' chant.

THE FOURMOST
Hello Little Girl; Just In Case
(Parlophone R 5056)

LATEST from the Nems stable is this vocal group which doesn't particularly deviate from the usual Liverpool sound. They're a good harmonising team with a good sound and some fair old noises that all concerned on the Beatles penned number. Fast-ish, insistent with a good beat and perhaps a little muzzyness in the harmonising sometimes. Should do pretty well.

Flip has a strong compelling beat, and it sounds very much like an Everly Brothers thing—mainly because they have actually recorded their one too. A Boudleaux Bryant composition, this one is as good as side one.

THREE

THE ESCORTS — Dizzy Miss Lizzie; All I Want Is You (Fontana TF 453)***—First disc by Messrs. Pete Clarke, Terry Sylvester, John Kinrade and Mike Gregory. I'm a little disappointed to find them out with Dizzy Miss Lizzie but their version is crisp and beaty enough to attract attention. Spin also their lighter filter All I Want Is You and you'll agree this outfit will do well.

LEE CURTIS
Let's Stomp; Poor Unlucky Me
(Decca F 11690)

THE eminently beat-happy Mr. Curtis makes a really good stab at chart status with this one. It's wild, rockingly wild. The All-Stars keep him going full pelt through a real fast number, which was recently a hit in the States for Bobby Comstock. Lee makes a first-class job of it and deserves to sell very well indeed. Much quieter for the flip and Lee shows that he can switch mood with the best of them. There is a distinct bit of the Presley about him in parts. A commendable one — and one to watch.

FOUR

FARON'S FLAMINGOS
See If She Cares; Do You Love Me? (Oriole CB 1834)

FROM one of the better Liverpool groups comes this new effort, with a good tune and lyric. The boys perform well, and the beaty, fast-ish song has a lot of appeal and some fair group vocalising from the boys. One of those discs that, if it does go, will go very well.

The oldie that sold a million for the Contours in the States gets the treatment from the boys. It takes very well to the boys' Liverpool-type harmonising. It's a powerful rock number with a lot of appeal and probably more commercial appeal than side one. Remember that, someone.

IAN AND THE ZODIACS—Beechwood; You Can Think Again (Oriole CB 1849)** — The Miracles did very well in the States with Beechwood, now the British group Ian and the Zodiacs try their luck. The insistent cha-cha beat should please dancers and give the record a lift in consequence. Some of the harmony work is good.

Rapid shuffle beat for You Can Think Again which Ian leads huskily.

King-size Taylor and the Dominoes
Memphis Tennesee; Money
(Polydor NH 66990)***

FOR more than a year King-Size Taylor and The Dominoes have been as good as "regulars" at the Star Club in Hamburg. They are a Liverpool group in origin, but they don't come across as typical Mersey men.

Taylor sings the Chuck Berry hit Memphis Tennesee and should attract new fans. Pity is that the cream's already gone so far as the Parade's concerned.

Money is also too well known, I think, for these beat boys to make the sort of disc impression they may have created with a pair of new numbers.

THE UNDERTAKERS
Everybody Loves A Lover; Mashed Potato (Pye 7N 15543)

RAUCOUS sax leads on this version of the oldie. Very similar in arrangement to a Shirelles version of this song that was a U.S. hit for them, in the States some months back. It's a jerky sort of thing with quite a bit of commercial appeal, but maybe not enough to get it into the charts.

Flip is yet another version of the Danielle disc "Hot Pastrami". It's not particularly good or inspiring but fair to dance to. Rather raucous like side one—and with vocal work that doesn't come off.

THREE

MARK PETERS—Cindy's Gonna Cry; Show Her (Oriole CB 1909)***—One of the most interesting things about Mark Peters is the fact that his manager actually lives in Coronation Street! Should be something of a success omen for Mark, who sends out a Liverpool sound that is gentle and balladic for a change.

whatever that might mean, and "Six To Midnight" is a very entertaining song about losing your sense of time when you are with Ronnie Wood.) Much of the set were covers of songs associated with Kenney Jones even if he didn't always play on the hit recordings—the Who's "Substitute" and "Won't Get Fooled Again", Rod Stewart's "Maggie May", the Faces' "Stay With Me" and the Small Faces' "All Or Nothing" and "Lazy Sunday". There were some Bad Company songs and they closed with two rock'n'rollers—"I Saw Her Standing There" and "Sweet Little Rock'n'Roller".

Thursday 11 August 2005
Dean Howard (T'Pau, Gillan, Bad Company)

Thursday 28 August 2005
Neil Innes

Wednesday 7 September 2005
Preview of Paul McCartney's *Chaos And Creation In The Backyard*, plus Jade Gallagher

Saturday 10 September 2005
Jordan Knight (New Kids On The Block)

Sunday 2 October 2005
For £8, you can see Sheffield band, Arctic Monkeys supported by the Little Flames. **Bill Heckle**[884]: "When the industry spends a lot of money on an act, we know that there has to be a return. Two months before the single came out, we were told that the Arctic Monkeys would be huge. Steve Marsh, the manager at the Cavern, had just left and he was a keen musician who now has his own production company, As he went, he said that he wanted to put the Arctic Monkeys on at the Cavern. We gave them it free of charge, one Sunday night. Tickets went on sale at midday and by 12.45pm it was sold out just through the website. I came down with Shannon who was over for her deal with the Hard Day's Night Hotel and I saw the whole hour and was unimpressed, but the audience was sixteen to twenty year old males and they were singing every word to every song. We couldn't see what the fuss was about but the atmosphere was electric. Then the single came out and my wife got the album and as soon as I started listening, I really got into it. They were very loud and raucous and you had to know the songs. We gave them Cavern T-shirts and we presented them with the brick but it said 'The Arctic Monkeys' and there is no 'The'. They said

that they would be coming back in three months and would do it then. They had the Number One album by then. They put the brick in the wall, and that was the only time a brick has been stolen. It was stolen within 24 hours and we had to replace it."

Shannon[885]: "I was invited to the Cavern on a bitterly cold night. As I cut my way through the thick of body humidity and smoke, ever eager to make it to the far back of the room, the Arctic Monkeys were already in gear and ruling the night as the new Kings of English Rock. It was a heavy drinking, chain smoking, dancing, sweating, head banging crowd. A high percentage of screaming, swearing, young, adolescent males seemed to know every word of every song, even though the Arctic Monkeys hadn't released a record yet. You had to shout at the top of your voice to get a word in to your mate. It simply made me jealous that I wasn't as young as the rest. As an American, it was an alien environment that I enjoyed totally. As a frequent visitor to Liverpool…this was Liverpool!"

Saturday 22 October 2005
Tabby played his first gig since being voted off *The X Factor*. The singer performed in his bare feet but it was not a good idea to take off his boots as they were stolen from the stage.

John Gorman[886]: "A German friend of mine who had gone to Liverpool University in the fifties wanted to come back and see his old haunts. I said okay and we went down to Cavern Walks. I was living in Shropshire then and I hadn't been back for a long time. We saw some American girls there and these lads came out and said, 'Hey girls, d'you wanna do something, know what I mean?' My friend was a professor by now and I was so ashamed of the city and there was litter everywhere. When they applied for the European City of Culture, the whole place changed. When I came back, it was much tidier. They have realised the potential for tourism and the Beatles take all the credit, but remember that they were just one of hundreds of groups. If the city fathers have any sort of inkling, they should be pushing that too. Of course, there's the ferry cross the Mersey, but there is no real celebration of any one else. Okay, there's the Wall of Hits, but look at our record and it's damaged. The Beatles would never have come out of it if they hadn't had all that competition and opportunity. Scouseology helps a bit but the city could do a lot more. Tourism could be even bigger."

Wednesday 11 January 2006

The American singer/songwriter Kevin Montgomery had a band to die for: Al Perkins (steel player with the Flying Burrito Brothers), Mike McAdam (Steve Earle's band) and two Mavericks. Paul Deakin played the drums so energetically (his elbows raised as he battered the kit) that it was hard to believe that he had had heart surgery a couple of years ago. During the final "Bo Diddley" medley (which incorporated "Magic Bus" and "Not Fade Away"), he banged his drumsticks on the ceiling. Robert Reynolds (Mavericks) was a very quirky guy: almost everything he said came out funny, a musical Robin Williams. He was a staunch Beatle fan and he and Kevin did "One After 909". During a rambling but very entertaining middle section, he and Mike did "Ferry Cross The Mersey" and "She's Not There". Al Perkins had his chance to shine with "Ooh Las Vegas" and a five minute workout on "Sleepwalk". Kevin sang "Tennessee Girl", "Red-Blooded American Girl" and several more of his own songs and a couple of his father's, "Flower Of My Heart" and "Heartbeat" ("I've just seen the TV show. It sucks.") The opening act was a gorgeous, model-slim girl called Jill Jackson, who had had a couple of hits as the lead singer of Speedway. She had a very entertaining stage manner, good songs and a fine cover of the Pussycat Girls' "Don't Ya".

Thursday 17 November 2005

The Billy Nayer Show including a showing of their film, *The American Astronaut*.

Friday 25 November 2005

Charity event for breast cancer appeal with Dean Howard and Susan Hedges

Thursday 22 December 2005

Phil Jones and the Ringtones

Sunday 1 January 2006

From the Mersey To The Mississippi—charity event for Hurricane Katrina.

Wednesday 11 January 2006

Americana evening with Kevin Montgomery and the Roadtrippers

Thursday 26 January 2006

Chas and Dave

Friday 10 February 2006

Steve Adler (Guns N'Roses) with Adler's Appetite

Wednesday 1 March 2006

Steve Hogarth (lead singer, Marillion)

Friday 3 March 2006

Glen Matlock and the Philistines

Sunday 5 March 2006

Albert Lee and Hogan's Heroes

Friday 10 March 2006

Connie Lush and Blues Shouter recorded a live CD. Connie has been rightly acclaimed as one of the UK's best British blues singers, but she is far more than that. She has a remarkable stage presence, knowing how to talk to an audience—and answer back. Most of all, she can sing all manner of material, which means that the time flew by during her two hour set at the Cavern. The show was excellently paced and the highlight of the evening was a sensational version of Nina Simone's "Feeling Good", a show tune written by Anthony Newley and Leslie Bricusse. It incorporated snatches of "Hit The Road Jack" and "Mockingbird" and lasted ten minutes. It topped the Nina Simone version and you can't do better than that.

Monday 10 April 2006

Canadian Glam Rock with Robin Black and the Intergalatic Rockstars

Wednesday 3 May 2006

Did anybody know who George Tomsco was? This gig should have been promoted as the Fireballs as he was the lead guitarist of that early sixties instrumental group, and it might then have stood a chance. However, George is still part of the Fireballs in America and he didn't want to confuse things: particularly as he was backed here by an Austin band, 3 Balls Of Fire

George Tomsco was a trim 65 year old and he demonstrated that he could be both a pensioner and a Fireball, especially when he did a Chuck Berry duckwalk. He opened with his first record, "Fireball", and then the Fireballs' first hit, "Torquay", both of which were heavier than the originals, but still true to the records. George had been circulating during the first acts and so he dedicated "Panic Button" by naming half the audience. The drummer came to the fore in "Quite A Party!", and we also had "Vaquero", "Foot Patter", "Bulldog" and "Rik-A-Tik" with its amusing stop/start endings. No complaints there. The 3 Balls Of Fire had their own, very heavy instrumental set but the best received set of the night came from local bluesman, Joey Shields with the Wheels. The highlight was a blistering version of Howlin' Wolf's "Little Red Rooster", given a local twist: "If you see my little red rooster drinking in some Liverpool bar, send him home."

Saturday 3 June 2006

Twelve hour sixties tribute with the Merseybeats, the Kounterfeit Kinks and the Green and compèred by Radio City's Pete Price.

Wednesday 5 July 2006

Tony (T.S) McPhee from the Groundhogs

Tuesday 18 July 2006

American golfer and Open champion, John Daly, told of getting drunk, trashing homes and hotel rooms, and gambling away millions of dollars in his autobiography, *My Life In And Out Of The Rough*. Its UK publication was marked by a party at the Cavern in which he performed with local musicians. Daly amended the lyrics of Bob Dylan's "Knockin' On Heaven's Door": "Haven't made a cut in weeks, My career looks so bleak." In 'Lost Soul', he sang of the death of his mother, his father wanting to shoot him and his wife going to jail. I guess that's why they call it the blues. Possibly because Tiger Woods et al had retired early to prepare for their gruelling day at Hoylake, the sports writers had found something to write about and the event received more column inches than Paul's return to the Cavern in 1999.

Friday 21 July 2006

Swansea band, the Storys, make their Cavern debut. They then tour as support for Elton John.

Saturday 22 July 2006

Kiss Convention with bass player Bob Kulick

Sunday 27/ Monday 28 August 2006

A musical play, *The Cavern Club* by Mark D. Yates was at Liverpool's Royal Court Theatre. It was written independently of Cavern City Tours, and it was an unlikely work, telling the audience next to nothing about the club and featuring lots

of dancing à la Pan's People. As the live band played tribute to name bands which had played at the Cavern, the so-called Bob Wooler and his associates picked up cardboard boxes displaying their names and inserted them at the back of the stage. By the end of the show, they had a wall of names: this was a plot?

Tuesday 29 August 2006

Afternoon and evening double-bills with the Spencer Davis Group and Joey Molland. **Spencer Davis**[887]: "It was as hot and sweaty as like the old days. It was good fun. There is a club like that in Germany, attached to the back of a brewery so the Cavern is not the only one." **Colin Hodgkinson**[888]: "It is not unbearably hot, but it is very, very sticky. It is hard on a long night and it definitely saps your energy if you are not as young as you were."

Thursday 7 September 2006

Chas and Dave

Thursday 28 September 2006

The Gift (a Jam tribute band with Rick Buckler of the Jam)

Tuesday 3 October 2006

Return of Kevin Montgomery

Sunday 15 October 2006

The original of "Do You Love Me?" is heard at the Cavern from the Tamla-Motown group, the Contours.

Monday 23 October 2006

Laurence Juber, a guitarist for three years with Wings, demonstrated Martin Guitars at Dawsons Music during the day and played the Cavern in the evening.

Friday 27 October 2006

That lovable eccentric, John Otway, had coerced his more passionate fans into forking out for a two week trip to hear him play in famous venues around the world. In typical fashion, he had made a mess of chartering the plane, and their proposed increase in fees made the flight impracticable. Everything was cancelled, except for the opening night at the Cavern. Otway fans came to get their refunds and nobody seemed to mind very much. He was joined on stage by Rainbow George, a noted contributor to late night phone-ins, and the songwriter/ producer Barry Upton, who wrote "5, 6. 7, 8" for Steps.

Sunday 12 November 2006
First anniversary of Sounds Of The Sixties shows with a benefit concert for Billy Fury's brother, Albie Wycherley (Jason Eddie)

Saturday 18 November 2006
Catfish Keith

Saturday 2 December 2006
Albie Donnelly's Supercharge

Thursday 28 December 2006
A strong bill featuring two of the most exciting talents on Merseyside, 10 Reasons To Live and Jade Gallagher.

Tuesday 16 January 2007—50th Birthday Celebration
The party for the fiftieth anniversary of the Cavern was a very social event. Richie Havens' surprise guest appearance was wildly applauded; Beryl Marsden promoted her new single, "Baby It's You", and the Merseysippi Jazz Band did some of the tunes from their first set list at the Cavern.

Tuesday 30 January 2007
Hendrix-styled guitarist, Carvin Jones

Thursday 8 February 2007
Appalling weather but a very good and bluesy set from Peter Tork of the Monkees and his band, Shoe Suede Blues.

Friday 16 February 2007
"Knock knock." "Who's there?" "Pete Bennett." "Pete Bennett who?" "You see, you've forgotten him already." *Big Brother* winner has his fifteen minutes of fame.

Thursday 22 February 2007
Eric Faulkner from the Bay City Rollers

Friday 9 March 2007
Local blues band, Last Train, which features Steve Wright (writer of *Brookside* and *Hollyoaks* themes) and drummer Terry McCusker from the Roadrunners.

Sunday 18 March 2007
A mother's day special with eighteen-year-old Ray Quinn, the runner-up from *The X Factor,* who was strongly influenced by Frank Sinatra and Bobby Darin. The event was arranged with Simon Cowell's company, tellingly called Syco. Ray placed his Wall of Fame brick just below Little Stevie Wonder's and he informed the invited audience that his album had just gone to Number One.

Friday 20 April 2007
The Isle of Man Post Office issues a set of six stamps to commemorate Liverpool's 800th anniversary, so King John wasn't all bad. The £1 stamp shows the Wall of Fame in Mathew Street.

Tuesday 29 May 2007
If you have £4,000 to spare, maybe the Rock and Roll Fantasy Camp is for you. It has caught on in America and the first UK one offered a week in London (including Abbey Road) and a night at the Cavern. 51 musicians and campers turned up for the show at the Cavern. I expected the campers to be company executives in their fifties but it was a very mixed bunch. It never crossed my mind than any of them would be female. Indeed, one was a stunning blonde in her thirties. Neil Murray (Whitesnake and Black Sabbath) was the MC and he had a Beatles set list and called out the numbers. Whoever wanted to get up and sing or play could do so. His band included Simon Kirke (Free and Bad Company) on drums and Jamie Moses (Pretenders) on guitar. Any of them would step aside if a camper wanted to have a go. In essence, the evening demonstrated the importance of each member in a band. A female who took over from Simon Kirke just played the same pattern on the drums and the vocals were a real mixed bag: well, no, they were mostly shambolic. The songs included "A Hard Day's Night", "Come Together", "Back In The USSR", "Things We Said Today", "Paperback Writer" and "Taxman" (naturally) and Spencer Davis took the lead for "Keep On Running". Neil said, "We should have had a class on harmony singing." Exactly.

Thursday 31 May/ Friday 1 June 2007
It was 60 years ago today that Sgt. Pepper taught the band to play. Karl Lornie and his band play the entire set live, which is more than the Beatles ever did.

Monday 4 June 2007
Paul McCartney alludes to the sweat in the Cavern and riverboat shuffles on the Royal Iris on his new album, *Memory Almost Full.*

Tuesday 5 June 2007

In essence, the revised licensing laws permit children to come into licensed premises, provided they are accompanied by an adult. The Beatles are part of the national curriculum and so a party of 90 ten-year-olds from Pitmaston Primary School in Worcester came to Liverpool for two nights and spent an evening at the Cavern. Jay from the Merseybeatles played a solo set and the children were given the Beatles map of Liverpool and replica membership cards and had a wonderful time. **Dave Jones**[889]: "If we had spent the last 20 years trying to make money we wouldn't be in business, but we have done a lot of things because it was the right thing to do. We were educating a new generation. The Cavern now is more than a venue: it is a place of culture. No club has ever educated a new generation in its heritage."

Saturday 9 June 2007

The return of Bo Diddley was cancelled, following his stroke.

Sunday 1 July 2007

Stan Boardman described the Germans bombing Liverpool in 1942—"and what do Mr and Mrs Marsden do? They name their son, 'Gerry'."

Friday 6 July 2007

As part of the celebrations for the 50th anniversary of John Lennon meeting Paul McCartney, the Cavern staged an evening with Bob Barty, Jon Keats and John Lennon's original Quarrymen.

Thursday 9 August 2007

Chas and Dave. Despite rumours to the contrary, this was the real Dave. "His wife can confirm that," said Chas, "Mine wishes it was a different Chas."

Sunday 19 August 2007

Magna Carta's fans celebrated the 65th birthday of lead singer/ songwriter Colin Simpson with a surprise party at the Cavern.

Monday 20 August 2007

On the face of it, you might think that putting together a compilation album was easy. You select the tracks you want and the owner licenses them in return for a certain royalty, and effectively earns money for nothing. However, compiling a 3CD set to celebrate the Cavern's fiftieth anniversary was difficult, very difficult. EMI wanted to do it but felt that without the Beatles, it would be like staging Hamlet without the Prince, and Apple very rarely allow the Beatles' material to appear on compilations.

Bob Young proved invaluable as he obtained Ringo Starr's support and following that, Apple agreed. In another unusual move, it was decided to release the album as a joint venture through EMI and Universal. The 3CD set featured several acts rarely seen on compilations including Queen, the Who, Oasis and the Rolling Stones. It became a logistical nightmare as some acts even stipulated their place in the running order! Also, as will be obvious from reading this book, there were scores of candidates for appearances on the album.

The Arctic Monkeys were seen as crucial to the project. They had played the Cavern two months prior to their first single and their inclusion would demonstrate that the Cavern was still a vehicle for young up-and-coming bands. Their record label said the group had nixed appearances on compilations, but their manager thought it sounded right and they came on board. It demonstrated how much goodwill there is towards the Cavern. To fall in with the Cavern's policy of promoting new music, a local band, 10 Reasons To Live, was featured on a hidden track.

The Cavern: The Most Famous Club In The World was TV-advertised and shot into the best-selling chart. At the time of writing (February 2008), sales are approaching 100,000.

Tuesday 28 August 2007

The annual Mathew Street Festival was surrounded by political controversy as the outdoor stages were cancelled for health and safety considerations. The club events were very successful, particularly two sets by Denny Laine in the Cavern. Backed by the Scottish band, Ringer, he performed Wings' greatest hits and naturally, 'Go Now', with strong support from the Mad Dogs from Brazil who reinterpreted Beatle songs in salsa and samba.

Friday 26 October 2007

Echo and the Bunnymen

Wednesday 27 February 2008

The TV documentary, *A Hard Day's Fight*, had shown the problems with the Hard Days Night Hotel project. The finance was reportedly resolved but following 9/11, the financial pack-

CAVERN STOMP

age was cancelled. In December 2002, the project was taken over by two local businessmen, the property developers, Allen Davies and Tony Criss. The Cavern owns 30% of the merchandising rights of the Hard Days Night Hotel (no apostrophe: not a typo!) and both Bill Heckle and Dave Jones supply their expertise on that tricky subject of copyright and the Beatles. Cavern City Tours also operates the Beatles Information Centre in the hotel's gallery. Although Bill and Dave do not own the hotel, they are delighted that their project had come to fruition. There was a soft opening on February 1 and then it was officially opened on February 27.

What is the world's first, Beatles-themed hotel has been beautifully designed and the stunning frontage—an ideal photo-opportunity—includes new sculptures of the Beatles by Dave Webster. Blake's Restaurant pays tribute to all the faces on the *Sgt Pepper* cover. The city's musicians have already decided that Hari's Bar will be a regular watering-hole. The press made much of the John Lennon suite costing £650 a night, but it includes the use of a white piano! There are photographs of the Beatles everywhere, going in roughly chronological order from the basement to the rooftop.

There is an exclusive mural in each of the 110 rooms, all the work of the American artist, **Shannon**[890]. "I wasn't there to take it all in but I know I must be historically accurate. I take every bit of information that has been given to me, and then create. I've had to decide how the events coincide with particular styles of music, hair, guitars, influences, touring, break ups and make ups, motorbike accidents, dental work and character flaws. That coincides with each minute, day, month, and year that they lived and breathed. It also helps to have a few art lessons and I've ended up knowing them better than I know myself."

CONTRIBUTORS

All the quotes from my interviews in *The Cavern: The Most Famous Club In The World* have been numbered and this is a guide to the speakers and where you can find their contributions.

Beryl Adams [573] was Brian Epstein's secretary. Then she worked at the Cavern, managed a few groups, and, for a few uncomfortable years, was married to Bob Wooler. She was a Merseybeat history in herself and she died in great pain from CJD in 2003. A biography, *My Beatles Hell* by Lew Baxter, was published by Barge Pole Press in 2004.

Bodybuilder **Roy Adams** [775 778 782 783 784 789 793] told his stories of owning Merseyside clubs, including the Cavern, in his autobiography, *Hard Nights* (Cavernman, 2003).

Tim Adams [868 872] succinctly reviews gigs for BBC Radio Merseyside.

In 1964, Londoner **Frank Allen** [571] left Cliff Bennett and the Rebel Rousers to join the Searchers. He's still there and is currently writing a biography of the band.

Mose Allison [647] is best known for his compositions 'Parchman Farm' and 'Young Man Blues'. Catch him playing at Pizza Express in London on one of his annual visits.

Don Andrew [339] played bass with the Remo Four and founded the Merseycats charity.

Jon Anderson [503 672] was with the Accrington band, the Warriors, but is known for his time in Yes.

Joe Ankrah [467] was a member of the Chants and is now a university lecturer.

Colin Areethy [692 708] was one of Merseyside's top club singers. Great voice!

Brian Auger [665] fronted the Trinity and made "This Wheel's On Fire" with Julie Driscoll.

Bob Azurdia [21] wrote for *Mersey Beat* and was the first journalist to write about the Beatles in the national press. He joined BBC Radio Merseyside when it opened in 1967 and became its most incisive interviewer.

David Backhouse [278 318 320 393 803 805 806 807 808 809 810 811 813] is the architect who designed Cavern Walks and the reconstituted Cavern Club.

Stephen Bailey [861 869] manages The Beatles Shop in Mathew Street and is often found taking photos from a front row seat.

Julia Baird [828] is John Lennon's half-sister, the author of *Imagine This* (Hodder and Stoughton, 2007) and a director of Cavern City Tours.

Known as Nob, **Ken Baldwin** [83 92 102 185] was a founding member of the Merseysippi Jazz Band in 1949 and played guitar and banjo with them until his death in 2006.

Kenny Ball [289] ran the most commercially successful band of the Trad era and they are still playing today. Biggest single: 'Midnight In Moscow' (1961).

Chris Barber [345] has led one of the UK's top jazz bands for over 50 years. Biggest single; 'Petite Fleur' (1959).

From 1954, **Tony Barrow** [342] wrote Disker's record reviews in *Liverpool Echo* and he worked as a publicist for NEMS Enterprises from 1963 to 1968. He wrote his memoir, *John, Paul, George, Ringo And Me* for André Deutsch in 2005.

David Bash [839] is the founder and organizer of the International Pop Overthrow.

Roger Baskerfield [27] was part of the Coney Island Skiffle Group.

Sheffield's **Dave Berry** [589] is best known for 'The Crying Game' (1964).

Mike Berry [400] [401] is best known for 'Don't You Think It's Time' (1963) and 'The Sunshine Of Your Smile' (1980).

Pete Best [299] [435] played drums for the Beatles when they went to Hamburg in August 1960 and was sacked in mysterious circumstances two years later. He joined Lee Curtis and the All Stars and then formed the Pete Best Four. In recent years, he has reactivated both his playing career and his mother's Casbah Club.

Acker Bilk [298] led his Paramount Jazz Band and recorded 'Stranger On The Shore' in 1961.

UK skiffler **Dickie Bishop** [59] was delighted when Paul McCartney revived his song, 'No Other Baby' in 1999.

Paul Blake [24] has played clarinet with the Wall City Jazzmen for over 50 years.

John Booker [193] [228] [230] [255] [317] was a lunchtime regular at the Cavern.

Joey Bower [239] [566] was in the Four Jays from 1959 to 1962, but at the time did not want to go professional. The Four Jays became the Fourmost and he rejoined his friends after Mike Millward's early death in 1966.

Dave Boyce [358] [445] [470] [489] [499] [561] played drums with the Roadrunners.

Mike Brocken [219] [250] [291] [569] [770] [777] [780] lectures on popular music at Liverpool universities.

In the sixties, **Faith Brown** [490] [730] was part of the Carrolls and she became a fine impressionist and entertainer.

Joe Brown [429] had his biggest hit, 'A Picture Of You', with the Bruvvers in 1962 and married a Liverpool girl, Vicki Haseman from the Vernons Girls. He is perpetually touring, often with Marty Wilde.

Beat poet **Pete Brown** [668] [676] wrote lyrics for Cream and led his band, the Battered Ornaments.

Bill Buck [202] [286] played drums for Dale Roberts and the Jaywalkers and is now with the Wall City Jazzmen.

Eric Burdon [570] was lead singer with the Animals.

And here at the Cavern, the King of Rock'n'Soul, **Solomon Burke** [734].

Billy Butler [392] [408] [415] [481] [517] [634] [640] [644] [657] [690] [697] [700] [716] [724] [727] [735] [742] [751] [761] was part of the *Spin A Disc* panel on *Thank Your Lucky Stars*, a DJ at the Cavern and the lead singer of the Tuxedos. He presents the afternoon show on BBC Radio Merseyside and has had national acclaim for his hilarious *Hold Your Plums* quiz show.

Mike Byrne [141] [319] [373] [458] [631] [821] [882] founded *The Beatles Story* at the Albert Dock and fronts the rock'n'roll band, Juke Box Eddie's.

Blues musician **Raphael Callaghan** [597] [604] [649] [781] [855] recorded as part of Jim and Raphael in the 60s and now has a duo, Blue C, with his partner, Christine Purnell.

The songwriter **Jimmy Campbell** [273] was part of the Kirkbys and 23rd Turnoff.

Paul Carrack [769] was in Warm Dust long before his hits with Ace, Squeeze and Mike and the Mechanics and as a solo artist.

Jean Catharell [328] [552] [643] [836] runs the fan site, Liverpool Beatlescene.

Bruce Channel [412] had his moment of glory with 'Hey! Baby' in 1962, but is writing and playing to this day.

Nigel Clark [843] is the lead singer with Dodgy.

Allan Clarke [492] was the lead singer of the Hollies from 1962 to 1999.

Owen Clayton [52] [208] [244] [271] [272] was Merseybeat's first pensioner. In the 50s, he had a stint with Johnny Duncan and the Blue Grass Boys. Now plays double bass with Juke Box Eddie's.

Con Cluskey [507] was a third of the Bachelors as was brother, Dec.

Dec Clusky [506] was in the Bachelors, who found a niche with new recordings of standards ('Charmaine', 'Diane' and 'I Believe').

John Cochrane [72 159 162 164 195 242 243 259 337 351 391 501 576] was the drummer with Wump and his Werbles and then Freddie Starr and the Midnighters. He drummed for Mr X and never fully established whether or not he was Josef Locke.

Living in Liverpool 8, **Maurice Cockrill** [756] painted and taught on Merseyside for many years. I've just seen his paintings in the Royal Academy's Summer Exhibition: £18,000 each.

Frank O'Connor, now known as **Frankie Connor** [427 497 547 603 615 618 620 641 645 651 675 688 764], presents oldies programmes for BBC Radio Merseyside. Frankie, Alan Crowley (Tuxedos) and Billy Kinsley write and produce contemporary records for Merseybeat performers, known collectively as Class Of '64.

Dennis Conroy [454 462 632 741] now runs a guitar club in Formby with some excellent guests.

Trumpeter **John Cook** [12 48 51 153 279 340 385] led the White Eagle Jazz Band from Leeds.

John Cornelius [763] is a Liverpool singer-songwriter and artist from the late 60s who wrote the witty memoir, *Liverpool 8.*

After being in the Mavericks and the Pacifics, **Tony Crane** [378 486 536 586] formed the Merseybeats in 1962 and has been singing lead and playing guitar with them ever since.

The promoter **David Crosby** [476 484 485 539 626 639 664 689] was a member of the Tabs and he owned the Rox record stores in the Wirral. He is planning a fiftieth anniversary concert with Merseyside performers to commemorate Buddy Holly's appearance at the Philharmonic Hall in 1958.

Liverpool born Tory MP, **Edwina Currie** [268 428 729] was a regular at the Cavern and when she went to Oxford University, she studied politics with fellow student, Bill Clinton.

Lee Curtis [213 384 398 456 457] was managed by his brother, Joe Flannery, and fronted the All Stars. Now living in Southport, he is seen belting out 'Jezebel' at Merseybeat events.

John Dankworth [225 305] is one of the UK's top jazz musicians and arrangers.

Geoff Davies [170 181 247 270 290 297 307 308 323 327 333 362 404 449 500 583 666 733 787] runs the Probe Plus record label, whose key act is Half Man Half Biscuit.

Spencer Davis [638 887] runs, would you believe, the Spencer Davis Group.

Tony Davis [5 6 17 44 55 61 107 152 155 156 731] was the tall one with the penny whistle in the Spinners and he is also a noted singer with north-west jazz bands.

After a long period as a Liverpool solicitor, **David Deacon** [110 150 160 411 585] studied for a degree from the Institute of Popular Music.

Sugar Deen [437 710] was with the Harlems and the Valentinos.

Paddy Delaney [130 322 532 720] was the doorman at the Cavern. He has started his memoirs but not yet found a publisher.

Allan Devon [686 714] was a member of Solomon's Mines.

Valerie Dicks [113 266] was a regular at the Cavern.

Lonnie Donegan [859 860] was to skiffle what Elvis was to rock'n'roll. Many musicians in this list started playing because of Lonnie. He died on tour in November 2002 and an all-star tribute concert took place at the Royal Albert Hall in June 2004.

Like many people in this book, **Dave Donnelly** [685] is a music fan who went down the Cavern.

Dave Dover [375 442 452 636] played with the Cordes and Colonel Bagshot.

Chris Dreja [580] is a member of the Yardbirds.

Tom Earley [204] was a member of the Valkyries.

Norris Easterbrook [755 762] was one of the Klubs, sometimes known as the Wild, Wild Klubs or the Klubbs.

Ian Edwards [196 249 258 262 277 296 306 313 350 356 441 562 588 609] fronted Ian and the Zodiacs. After years as a buyer for Littlewood's, he returned to singing but died of a heart attack in 2007.

Joe Elliott [865] is the vocalist with Def Leppard.

Guitarist **Ralph Ellis** [73 118 211 238] was a founder member of the Swinging Blue Jeans. He became a very successful insurance salesman and was able to indulge his passion for guitars. In 2001 he recorded with the Canadian tribute band, the Beat Makers.

Sue Ellison [582 630 661] is another Cavernite.

Ray Ennis [38 74 91 103 123 125 133 143 158 180 182 187 192 205 237 254 301 321 336 355 390 403 448 463 464 478 587] was, and still is, the lead singer with the Swinging Blue Jeans and is as witty as any comedian. When somebody at the Liverpool Empire shouted out, "I'm from Venezuela", he looked at his watch and said, "You've missed your last bus."

Clive Epstein [642] was Brian's brother and an astute businessman.

Saxophonist **Mike Evans** [498 646 654 659 660 662 667 674 758] was a member of the Clayton Squares and Liverpool Scene as well as being a founding member of Deaf School. In 2002 his book *Elvis—A Celebration* made the best-sellers.

With enough ideas for ten men, **Brian Farrell** [531 773] is the lead singer with Colonel Bagshot.

One of the great Liverpool personalities, **Faron** [533] was the extrovert lead singer of Faron's Flamingos. He has had many physical and personal setbacks in recent years, but keeps on singing.

Betty Fegan [138 367 369 419 426 557 622 633] handed out Cavern membership cards and worked on the snack bar.

Joe Flannery [432] managed Beryl Marsden and his brother, Lee Curtis.

Mick Fleetwood [554] played drums and founded Fleetwood Mac.

Tommy Flude [600 601 746] was part of the Deans and Solomon's Mines.

Wayne Fontana [529] and the Mindbenders had several hits including a US No.1 with 'Game Of Love'.

Dennis Fontenot [446] was a regular at the Cavern.

Salford born **Clinton Ford** [84 116] has sung with the Merseysippi Jazz Band on and off since 1957 and made his mark on numerous radio shows in the 60s. Clint's currently off the road with a bad back: the pain's bad but not as bad as being away from his audiences.

Neil Foster [251] used to edit the rock'n'roll magazine, *Not Fade Away* (which did). His memories of playing sax for the Delacardoes in the early 60s have fuelled his novel, *Cradle Of Rock* (Top F, 2004).

Pete Frame [613] is known for his meticulous Rock Family Trees. He has published a book of Merseybeat ones and he works as a consultant for many Radio 2 programmes, currently the Suzi Quatro series.

John Frankland [229 256 261 264 388 468 487] was part of Kingsize Taylor and the Dominoes.

German paratrooper, **Bob Frettlohr** [49 341] played in the White Eagle Jazz Band. His life story deserves a book of its own.

Irish musician **Rory Gallagher** [541] was one of the world's great rock guitarists.

Ritchie Galvin [416 480 528] who was born Richard Hughes, was the drummer with Earl Preston and the TTs and several Merseyside country bands. Very cheerful and outgoing, he was a public service worker and immensely good company. He died from MRSA in 2001.

Freddie Garrity [439] led the hit-making Manchester group, Freddie and the Dreamers and then moved into panto and cabaret. He died in 2006.

Len Garry [76 78] was in John Lennon's Quarry Men and is their lead singer today.

Brian Gilmore [738] was in the Dark Ages, and so was his brother, **Ken Gilmore** [680 722 728 847].

John Gorman [89 663 815 886] was with Scaffold and then TISWAS. He recently returned to Merseyside and is involved in cultural events on the Wirral.

Bromborough-born **Michael Gray** [178 540 553] is the UK's leading authority on Bob Dylan and the author of *Song And Dance Man* and *The Bob Dylan Encyclopedia*.

Mick Green [386 387 394] played lead guitar for Johnny Kidd and the Pirates and also for Paul McCartney at the Cavern in 1999. Often, they sounded more like the Pirates than Paul McCartney's band.

Mike Gregory [572] was bass player and vocalist for the Escorts before moving to the Swinging Blue Jeans. He led the good-time Rock'n'Roll Circus for many years and is working on a solo album.

Brian Griffiths [625] was a member of the Big Three. He manages a *Mr Music* store in Calgary. When he was in Liverpool in 2002, he brought me some demos of new songs including a poignant 'Waltz For Paddy' to remember Paddy Chambers.

Mick Groves [37 95 655] was a member of the Spinners who became a Labour councillor on the

Wirral. Now living in Devon, he performs his one-man tribute to Ewan MacColl.

George Guinness [786] [829] [842] is a director of Cavern City Tours.

Johnny Guitar [117] [146] whose real name was Johnny Byrne, played for Rory Storm and the Hurricanes. He died of motor neurone disease in 1999 and with typical stoicism, I saw him apologising for a wrist injury and not playing as well as he should.

Paul McCartney has said that **John Gustafson** [542] [549] of the Big Three was the best bass player on Merseyside. A dyed-in-the-wool rock'n'roller but a very versatile player as his list of sessions demonstrates. I saw him perform a rock'n'roll set backed by the Merseybeats at the Locarno a couple of years ago and he was excellent.

Steve Hale [560] [590] [602] [605] [750] [788] is a Merseyside photographer, at home in both beat clubs and football stadiums.

Colin Hall [752] [833] [880] writes for *Folk Roots* and *Mojo* and is the custodian at John Lennon's childhood home, 'Mendips'.

Johnny Hamp [447] was a TV producer for Granada TV.

Colin Hanton [77] played drums with John Lennon's Quarry Men. He upholsters furniture but also plays with the reformed Quarry Men.

Mike Haralambos [698] played with the Almost Blues and wrote *Right On: From Blues To Soul In Black America* (new edition, Causeway Press, 1994).

The rock'n'roll pianist **Sam Hardie** [203] [257] [260] [344] [389] [420] [488] played piano for Kingsize Taylor and the Dominoes and, following retirement, he has returned to playing with Liverpool bands.

A youthful **Sandra Hargrove** [365] helped her mum in the Cavern snack bar.

Thelma Hargrove [136] [137] [139] [265] [366] [368] [371] [715] [719] ran the snack bar at the Cavern.

The joiner **Ian Harris** [11] [67] is Paul McCartney's cousin and a man who built the Cavern and indeed, the Pyramid and the She clubs as well.

Jet Harris [200] played bass with the Shadows.

Bill Harry [269] is the former editor and publisher of the *Mersey Beat* newspaper. Easily the most prolific author on the Beatles, he prefers compiling encyclopedias to writing biographies.

He is determined to establish a lasting tribute to Liverpool music in the 60s somewhere in the city.

Billy Hatton [221] [275] [288] [359] [381] [471] [472] [495] was one of the Fourmost. The Fourmost returned to music by providing the backing in the 2005 Billy Fury musical, *Like I've Never Been Gone,* which was written by Joey Bower's brother, Alan.

Val Hausner [578] was a member of the Liver Birds.

Maureen Hayden [97] was the anti-smooch girl at the Cavern: now lives in Manchester and is called Mollie Shanti.

Bass player **Eric Haydock** [493] [519] was a founder member of the Hollies.

A director of Cavern City Tours, **Bill Heckle** [36] [293] [295] [785] [816] [822] [823] [824] [825] [826] [827] [830] [834] [840] [845] [849] [850] [851] [852] [854] [857] [862] [870] [874] [875] [883] [884] has been one of the owners of the Cavern since 1991.

Keith Hemmings [9] [35] was a young architect involved in the initial stages of the Cavern. His son, Paul, played in the La's and the Lightning Seeds and runs the Viper record label.

A GP by day, **Sid Hoddes** [1] [3] [4] was also one of the Liverpool poets. He has performed in pubs throughout Merseyside and one of his most loved poems is 'My Curry Is Going Through A Dangerous Stage'.

Chas Hodges [399] is the piano-playing half of Chas and Dave.

Colin Hodgkinson [888] plays in the Spencer Davis Group.

Singer/songwriter **Dave Howard** [511] [699] played in Liverpool country bands for over 30 years.

Tommy Hughes [124] [147] played banjo with the Swinging Blue Jeans, and is a fine rock'n'roll pianist. Bursting with enthusiasm and currently playing in the Mojos, he is a model for pensioners everywhere.

Johnny Hutchinson, known as **Johnny Hutch** [544] was the drummer and vocalist with the Big Three. Went into property and was out of the business for years. He presented an award to Sam Leach at Fort Perch Rock in New Brighton in 2007.

Liverpool folk singer, **Brian Jacques** [40] [818] is best known for his series of *Redwall* books.

Dave Jamieson [79] [140] [276] was a friend and road manager to several Merseybeat groups including Rory Storm and the Hurricanes.

Arthur Johnson [64][335] worked for the *Liverpool Echo* for many years and now has his own PR company.

Kenny Johnson [581] led the country-rock band, Sonny Webb and the Cascades, and then became one of the Hillsiders. A popular club act, he presents *Sounds Country* on BBC Radio Merseyside.

Ray Johnson [858][867][878][881] stage manages events at the Cavern and was with the tribute band Dark Horse for many years.

Brian Jones [466] played saxophone with the Undertakers. Mashed potato, yeh!

Carl Jones [863] worked as an agent (unpaid) for his hero, Lonnie Donegan, for many years.

A director of Cavern City Tours, **Dave Jones** [294] [598][599][832][838][841][844][853][856][864][877][889] has been one of the owners of the Cavern since 1991.

Hughie Jones [151] was a member of the Spinners and sings at the many maritime events on Merseyside.

Raymond Jones [314] went into NEMS and asked Brian Epstein for a copy of 'My Bonnie'. Now lives in Spain.

In the 1970s, **Ron Jones** [119][352][798] was the tourism officer for Liverpool and the County of Merseyside and he introduced guided Beatle tours and weekend packages. He is still heavily involved in tourism and his book, *The Beatles' Liverpool*, has been reprinted and updated many times.

In 1952, **Tom Jones** [23][25][126][619] was a founder member of the Wall City Jazzmen

Ain't That Funny, but I'm sure **Jimmy Justice** [425] was an early sixties pop star.

Frieda Kelly [227][233][248][252][791] worked for NEMS Enterprises as Brian Epstein's secretary and ran the official Beatles Fan Club. She could write a wonderful book but, with commendable integrity, she does not want to betray confidences. For many years, she was married to Brian Norris from the Bumblies, the Cryin' Shames and Earl Preston's Realms.

Norman Killon [459][460][526][681][797][817] was the DJ at both the Sink and Eric's.

Billy Kinsley [376][469][473][521][537][624][687] was a founder member of the Merseybeats and Liverpool Express, and still plays with both bands. For 45 years, he has been an integral part of music in the city. Quite simply, everybody knows—and loves—Billy Kinsley.

Ted Knibbs [423] was Billy J. Kramer's first manager. Died many years ago but spent his later years at Beatle Conventions. To give you an idea of how long all this is, if Ted was alive today, he'd be over 100 years old.

Billy J. Kramer [424] was first backed by a Liverpool band, the Coasters, and then a Manchester one, the Dakotas. Now lives in Oyster Bay, New York but sometimes returns to the UK for oldies tours.

Now a leading record industry figure, **Judd Lander** [509][610][617][627][792] played harmonica with the Hideaways and is featured on hit records by Culture Club and the Spice Girls.

By a few months, cornet player **John Lawrence** [15][30][41][100][346] is not quite a founder member of the Merseysippi Jazz Band but he played with them until 2006.

Sam Leach [69][334] was a key Merseybeat impresario and has written his memoirs in *The Rocking City*.

Derek Leckenby [575] played guitar with Herman's Hermits, both pre- and post- Peter Noone. When I asked him why he had split with Peter, he said, "You can only work with a prat for so long." He died from cancer in 1994.

C.P. Lee [747] is a Manchester academic who played in St. Louis Union and Albertos Y Lost Paranoias. He has written a history of Manchester music, *Shake, Rattle And Rain* (great title!), which was published by Hardinge Simpole in 2002.

Will Lee [835] plays bass on *The Late Show With David Letterman* and leads the Fab Faux.

Alan Lewis [567] is the editor of *Record Collector*.

Terry Lightfoot [144] ran his New Orleans Jazzmen.

Brian Linford [111] was the manager of the Mardi Gras and takes a great interest in the local jazz scene.

Steve Lister [396][637] was in the Cordes.

Carol Loftus [431][739] fronts Carol and the Memories…

…and her husband, **Geoff Loftus** [504], plays bass.

Dave Lovelady [338][477] played drums for the Dominoes and then the Fourmost. When the group split, he, Billy Hatton and Joey Bower formed Clouds—Liverpool's answer to Sky!— and are now back as the Fourmost.

Now based in Bristol, **John Duff Lowe** [414] played piano with the Quarry Men and can be heard with them on occasional gigs.

Rob Luke [772 779] was part of Zelda Plum.

Don Lydiatt [33 186] plays clarinet with the Merseysippi Jazz Band.

Mike McCartney [134 234 418 496 677 812] was part of Scaffold.

Jim McCarty [584] was, and still is, drummer with the Yardbirds.

Delbert McClinton [410 413] played harmonica on Bruce Channel's 'Hey! Baby'.

Brendan McCormack [39 474 670] is one of Merseyside's most versatile and respected guitarists, these days mostly giving classical guitar recitals.

John McCormick [42 43 46 70 86 99 222 224 309] played his double-bass with the Spinners.

Terry McCusker [281 310 372 409 494 648] was the drummer with the Roadrunners and now has his own blues band, Last Night.

Chas McDevitt [157] had an international hit when he recorded 'Freight Train' in 1957.

Robin McDonald [382] was a member of the Dakotas.

Ray McFall [129 135 172 207 236 241 354 380 406 596 608 612 673 721 726] owned the Cavern in those crucial, beat group years. Lives in Surrey but is often seen on Merseyside at Convention time.

Against his better judgment, **Bob McGrae** [440 535 563 694 709 711 712 753 767 776 790] was the Cavern DJ, Robbie Rave.

Ron McKay [16 56 62 80 81 85 114 131] was a Bootle-born drummer who played for Cy Laurie and then worked with Alan Sytner at the Cavern. From there, he became the drummer for Acker Bilk and his Paramount Jazz Band.

Alex McKechnie [189 430 759 820 846 848 866 876] was one-half of Up And Running and acted as promotions manager at the Cavern for several years in the nineties.

Pete Maclaine [360] led the Manchester band, the Dakotas.

John McNally [190 395 450] was a founder member of the Searchers and still plays lead guitar in the band.

Guitarist/vocalist **Tony (T.S.) McPhee** [653] founded the Groundhogs.

Glenn MacRae [682 683 737] came to Liverpool with the Canadian band, the Crescendos.

Colin Manley [194] was lead guitarist with the Remo Four and then played with Georgie Fame, Billy J. Kramer and the Swinging Blue Jeans. He died in 1999 and an all-star tribute, *A Concert For Colin*, at the Philharmonic Hall in Liverpool was a celebration of his life.

Beryl Marsden [370 555 592] was unlucky. She never had the hits and yet was an excellent vocalist. In 1966, she was part of Shotgun Express with Rod Stewart and Peter Green. She looks 20 years younger than she is and she launched a new single, 'Baby It's You', at the Cavern in 2007.

Freddie Marsden [169] was Gerry's brother and the drummer in Gerry and the Pacemakers. He ran the Pacemaker driving school in Formby and he died in 2006.

Gerry Marsden [253 263 280 505 512 559] led Gerry and the Pacemakers, and still does. Performs for numerous charities.

Hank Marvin [199] is the Shadows' lead guitarist and about to embark on a fiftieth anniversary tour with Cliff Richard.

Mike Maxfield [353] was the Dakotas' lead guitarist and now runs a recording studio in the basement of his home.

Billy May [831] was a member of the Valkyries and now entertains in the Cavern pub.

John Mayall [635] has led the Bluesbreakers for over 40 years.

If Liverpool's city of culture could be summed up by one man, it would be **George Melly** [142 443], art critic, jazz singer, writer and raconteur extraordinaire. He was a delight to interview: every sentence is quotable. Just before he died in 2007, he said that being a surrealist, dementia had some appeal for him.

Drummer **Colin Middlebrough** [88 104 166 198 217 223 226 304 361 407 417 518] was with the Jaywalkers and the Kansas City Five.

Who could have predicted that 'My Boy Lollipop' by **Millie** [621] would be the launching pad for reggae in the UK?

Joey Molland [671 693] was in the Masterminds, the Iveys and Badfinger.

Zoot Money [520] ran his Big Roll Band.

Peter Morris [47] played banjo for the Dolphins Jazz Band.

Keith Mulholland [794] played with several Merseyside bands, notably Nutz, who recorded for A&M.

Mitch Murray [502] was the young Tin Pan Alley songwriter who wrote 'How Do You Do It?', 'I Like It', 'You Were Made For Me' and many other 60s hits.

Graham Nash [491] was a fifth of the Hollies and then a third of Crosby, Stills and Nash.

I went to see Spooky Tooth's Luther Grosvenor in rehearsal with his band and found **Paul Nicholls** [743] on drums.

Geoff Nugent [212] played guitar and sang with the Undertakers. Still fronts the band.

Liverpool historian **Ray O'Brien** [231 235 475 514] has written *There Are Places I'll Remember* and is featured on *The Beatles Liverpool* DVD.

Mick O'Toole [45 54 145] is an expert on 50s music and Liverpool clubland.

Bass player **Bob Packham** [246 267 754] was in the Galvinisers and is part of the Merseybeats.

John Parkes [19 109 122] played trombone with the Merseyside Jazz Band from 1957 to 1980

As well as playing trombone with the Merseysippi Jazz Band from 1950 to 1956, **Frank Parr** [105 106] kept wicket for Lancashire.

Eddie Parry [510] fronted the Dennisons and then sold insurance. He died in 1995.

Ubiquitous would be the best word to describe guitarist/vocalist **Kenny Parry** [623 679 704 723 765], who is best known for his work with Liverpool Express.

Al Peters [300 701 706 707 736] has led blues bands on Merseyside for 40 years including the Almost Blues and Lawnmower.

Roger Planche [26], a member of the Coney Island Skiffle Group, became a jazz singer and pianist.

Like Beryl Marsden, **Earl Preston** [324 349 374 461 678 696 713] has aged well. He fronted the TTs and still sings from time to time at charity events.

Alan Price [568] played keyboards for the Animals.

Harry Prytherch [191] was the original drummer with the Remo Four and then played with Group One.

Dark glasses, harmonica and lead guitar, **Derek Quinn** [438] was one of Freddie's Dreamers and he became a publican.

Bolton born, **Mark Radcliffe** [879] started at Manchester's Piccadilly Radio and is currently to be heard on Radio 2.

Mike Ramsden [684] was lead singer with the Silkie.

One of the Wirral's first rock'n'roll bands was **Dale Roberts** [168 171 209 220 284 287] and the Jaywalkers. He was healthy and in good form when I interviewed him in 2006 but he died three weeks later.

Stan Roberts [32] played piano for the Wall City Jazzmen.

Frank Robinson [31] played piano for the Merseysippi Jazz Band.

The most fastidious of authors and researchers, **Johnny Rogan** [292] wrote a great book about pop management, *Starmakers And Svengalis* (Queen Anne Press, 1988) and a biting analysis of John Lennon's solo career, *Lennon—The Albums* (Calidore, 2006).

Willy Russell [303 397 421 527 548 740], a Cavern regular, became one of the UK's top playwrights—*Educating Rita, Shirley Valentine* and *Blood Brothers*, among them.

Christine Ruth [804] was part of BBC Radio Merseyside's news team in the 1980s.

Tony Sanders [422] played drums for the Coasters.

Sylvia Saunders [577] played drums for the Liver Birds. She married one of the Bobby Patrick Big Six and they ran a hotel in Blackpool.

Ronnie Scott [87] was part of the Jazz Couriers and is best known for the London club which bears his name.

Ray Scragg [591] sang and played guitar with the Dennisons. He worked for the Prudential for many years but he maintained his friendship with the group and they did some reunion gigs. He formed a new group called the Dennisons 2001 shortly before he died from throat cancer.

John Seddon [748] is a Liverpool impresario, who has opened boutiques and recorded Kop choirs.

Denny Seyton [161 579 629 650] fronted the Sabres and then worked as a buyer for Littlewoods. He had a club act, Old Gold, with John Boyle from the Sabres and he did reform the band for a few of the Merseycats shows. One of the latter-day Sabres, Paul Stewart, invented the supports that are used to strengthen the handles on plastic bags—he patented the idea and made a small fortune! Denny's passion is collecting sheet music from the 50s and 60s and he has an excellent collection.

The American artist **Shannon** [885 890] has painted the murals for the Hard Day's Night Hotel.

Joey Shields [282 312 363 513 766] is one of the best blues singers on Merseyside. Looks old enough to be Willie Nelson's father.

Liverpool's hard man, **Tommy Smith** [814 819] also owned the Cavern.

John Stokes [508] was one of the Bachelors. In an extraordinary court case in 1984, the other Bachelors accused him of singing "like a drowning rat".

Alan Stratton [68 98 132 167 214 325] played bass with the Kansas City Five and in recent years has been working with Johnny Gentle. "People love hearing a double bass," he says.

Andy Summers [703] was part of Zoot Money's Big Roll Band and then a third of Police.

Lawrence Swerdlow [364 606 628] played organ for the St Louis Checks.

Alan Sytner [7 8 10 14 18 20 28 29 50 53 58 65 75 82 94 96 120 128] was the founder and first owner of the Cavern. You may not agree with all he said but, boy, was he entertaining. He died in 2006.

Dicky Tarrach [565] played drums with the Rattles.

Alistair Taylor [316] worked for Brian Epstein as his personal assistant and became known to the Beatles as Mr Fixit. He became General Manager at Apple but was sacked in Allen Klein's purge, and he never appeared to hold this against the Beatles. He worked in hotel and catering for some years and then came back into the Beatle world by appearing at conventions from the late 80s onwards. An all-round good guy who died in June 2004.

Rogan Taylor [232 465] is the Director of the Football Industry Group at the University of Liverpool and a writer and broadcaster.

Back then, butcher's boy Teddy Taylor, better known as **Kingsize Taylor** [108] was 6 foot 5¾ and 22 stone. He and his German wife, Marga, live in Hamburg and frequently organise reunion shows.

Karl Terry [197 216 274 331 873] is still fronting the Cruisers and still doing the splits. Amazing! He says, "I know I could get £100 a night by going

out with backing tapes but I will never do it. I would never feel comfortable singing to tapes and so long as I'm performing, it will be with a live band."

Ken Testi [614 774 795 796] was the manager of Deaf School and the founder owner of Eric's.

Hollywood superstar plays the Cavern! Check out **Billy Bob Thornton** [871]. Without question, the coolest guy I've ever met, although you could argue that a really cool guy wouldn't be talking to someone from local radio.

Frank Townsend [405 656 658 744 837] still can reach those high, high harmonies. I saw him adding his contributions to Tony Rivers and the Castaways at the Cavern in 2003.

Yianni Tsamplakos [732] was part of the Seftons.

Jimmy Tushingham [718] took Ringo Starr's place in Rory Storm and the Hurricanes. He also played in the Connoisseurs and then worked in import and export.

The Cavernite **Ann Upton** [348 357 436 482 483], married Richard Hughes, better known as Ritchie Galvin.

As well as promoting concerts around Chester, **Gordon Vickers** [13 121 148 433] managed the Wall City Jazzmen.

Steve Voce [34 57 66 90 101 154] has written a controversial column in *Jazz Journal* since 1957. His *Jazz Panorama* programme was broadcast for over 30 years on BBC Radio Merseyside. Hates rock music as fervently as most like it.

Noel Walker [173 538 546 594] led the Noel Walker Stompers around Merseyside clubs and became a record producer for Decca, having success with the Big Three and the Fortunes. He produced the EP, *The Big Three At The Cavern* (1963) and the LP, *At The Cavern* (1964) which included Dave Berry and Beryl Marsden.

The hillbilly docker **Hank Walters** [2 71 127 177 183 283] is a Liverpool institution, spending decades singing and playing accordion in clubs and pubs.

Hank Wangford [564] presents alternative country at its most alternative.

Ralph Watmough [22 112] formed his first jazz band in Crosby in 1948. Ralph is often referred to as Bags Watmough because he worked in Lloyds Bank and would carry around money bags. Often led his band in his white bandleader's coat.

Alan Willey [60] [63] [93] played guitar for several skiffle and beat groups.

Allan Williams [174] ran the Jacaranda coffee bar and the Blue Angel night club. As the Beatles' first manager, he is known as the man who gave the Beatles away.

Dave Williams [115] was a troglodyte in the Cavern's jazz days. Later, the chairman of BBC Radio Merseyside's Listening Panel.

Guitarist **Dave Williams** [149] [163] [165] [179] [201] [210] [245] [285] [383] [451] [551] was a member of Dave Roberts and the Jaywalkers and Group One.

Prem Willis-Pitts [215] is the author of *Liverpool, The Fifth Beatle* (Amozen Press, 2000).

As Merseyside's top DJ, **Bob Wooler** [175] [176] [184] [188] [206] [218] [240] [302] [315] [329] [330] [332] [347] [377] [379] [402] [434] [444] [455] [479] [515] [516] [523] [524] [525] [530] [534] [543] [545] [550] [556] [574] [593] [595] [607] [611] [652] [669] [691] [695] [702] [705] [717] [725] [745] [749] [757] [760] [768] [799] [800] [801] [802] introduced the Beatles over 400 times. He booked and introduced hundreds of bands at the Cavern.

Bill Wyman [558] played bass with the Rolling Stones:

Club singer **Alex Young** [311] [326] [453] [522] is noted for his tribute to Guy Mitchell.

Bob Young [771] played harmonica for Status Quo and was their road manager for many years. A superb organiser, he works on special projects for Cavern City Tours.

Guitarist, vocalist and actor, **Ozzie Yue** [343] [616] was a member of the Hideaways. Saw him in 2006 with Albie Donnelly in Supercharge.

saf publishing

www.safpublishing.co.uk
www.cavernclub.org